# Learn Programming with C

Authored by two standout professors in the field of Computer Science and Technology with extensive experience in instructing, *Learn Programming with C: An Easy Step-by Step Self-Practice Book for Learning C* is a comprehensive and accessible guide to programming with one of the most popular languages.

Meticulously illustrated with figures and examples, this book is a comprehensive guide to writing, editing, and executing C programs on different operating systems and platforms, as well as how to embed C programs into other applications and how to create one's own library. A variety of questions and exercises are included in each chapter to test the readers' knowledge.

Written for the novice C programmer, especially undergraduate and graduate students, this book's line-by-line explanation of code and succinct writing style makes it an excellent companion for classroom teaching, learning, and programming labs.

**Sazzad M.S. Imran, Ph.D.**, is Professor in the Department of Electrical and Electronic Engineering, University of Dhaka, Bangladesh. He completed his B.Sc. and M.S. degrees in Applied Physics, Electronics & Communication Engineering from the University of Dhaka and received his Ph.D. degree from the Optical Communication Lab of the Kanazawa University, Japan. Dr. Imran has vast experience in teaching C/C++, Assembly Language, MATLAB®, PSpice, AutoCAD, etc., at the university level (more at sazzadmsi.webnode. com).

**Md Atiqur Rahman Ahad, Ph.D., SMIEEE, SMOPTICA**, is Associate Professor of Artificial Intelligence and Machine Learning at the University of East London, UK; and Visiting Professor at the Kyushu Institute of Technology, Japan. He worked as Professor at the University of Dhaka and Specially Appointed Associate Professor at Osaka University. He has authored/edited 14+ books and published 200+ peer-reviewed papers (more at http://ahadvisionlab.com).

# Learn Programming with C

## An Easy Step-by-Step Self-Practice Book
## for Learning C

Sazzad M.S. Imran, Ph.D.
Md Atiqur Rahman Ahad, Ph.D.

**CRC Press**
Taylor & Francis Group
Boca Raton London New York

CRC Press is an imprint of the
Taylor & Francis Group, an **informa** business

A CHAPMAN & HALL BOOK

MATLAB® is a trademark of The MathWorks, Inc. and is used with permission. The MathWorks does not warrant the accuracy of the text or exercises in this book. This book's use or discussion of MATLAB® software or related products does not constitute endorsement or sponsorship by The MathWorks of a particular pedagogical approach or particular use of the MATLAB® software.

First edition published 2024
by CRC Press
2385 NW Executive Center Drive, Suite 320, Boca Raton FL 33431

and by CRC Press
4 Park Square, Milton Park, Abingdon, Oxon, OX14 4RN

*CRC Press is an imprint of Taylor & Francis Group, LLC*

© 2024 Prof. Sazzad M.S. Imran, Ph.D. and Prof. Md Atiqur Rahman Ahad, Ph.D.

*Library of Congress Cataloging-in-Publication Data*
Names: Imran, Sazzad, author. | Ahad, Md. Atiqur Rahman, author.
Title: Learn programming with C / Prof. Sazzad Imran, Ph.D, and Prof. Md. Atiqur Rahman Ahad, Ph.D.
Description: First edition. | Boca Raton, FL : CRC Press, 2024. | Includes bibliographical references and index. |
  Summary: "Authored by two standout professors in the fields of Computer Science and Technology with extensive experience in instructing, Learn Programming with C is a comprehensive and accessible guide to programming with one of the most popular languages. Meticulously illustrated with figures and examples, this book is a comprehensive guide to writing, editing and executing C programs on different operating systems and platforms, as well as how to embed C programs into other applications and how to create one's own library. A variety of questions and exercises are included in each chapter to test the readers' knowledge Written for the novice C programmer, especially undergraduate and graduate students, this book's line-by-line explanation of code and succinct writing style makes it an excellent companion for classroom teaching, learning and programming labs"—Provided by publisher.
Identifiers: LCCN 2023033790 (print) | LCCN 2023033791 (ebook) | ISBN 9781032299082 (hbk) |
  ISBN 9781032283555 (pbk) | ISBN 9781003302629 (ebk)
Subjects: LCSH: C (Computer program language). | Computer programming.
Classification: LCC QA76.73.C15 I47 2024 (print) | LCC QA76.73.C15 (ebook) | DDC 005.13/3—dc23/eng/20231026
LC record available at https://lccn.loc.gov/2023033790
LC ebook record available at https://lccn.loc.gov/2023033791

ISBN: 9781032299082 (hbk)
ISBN: 9781032283555 (pbk)
ISBN: 9781003302629 (ebk)

DOI: 10.1201/9781003302629

Typeset in Minion
by Apex CoVantage, LLC

Access the Support Material: www.routledge.com/learn-programming-with-c/ahad/p/book/9781032299082

# Contents

Preface, xi

# Preface

C IS A PROGRAMMING LANGUAGE with which every software developer should become familiar. Though numerous books are available on C programming language, most of the example programs are written without algorithms or any flowchart in those books. As a result, it becomes difficult for a student to comprehend the core of a programming language through a self-learning approach. Our experience in teaching C underscores the importance of presenting C programs by the flowchart solution first, then the pseudocode solution, and finally the actual C code with the line-by-line explanation.

It is written for C programming language courses/modules at the undergraduate and graduate levels – mostly for beginners. However, if one has prior knowledge on programming, one may skip the initial couple of chapters. By going through this book, any student or a beginner can learn and understand C programming by taking only a little or no help from an instructor. For the instructors, this book is an easy guidance. Only going through this book will be sufficient for them to teach C programming – as theory lectures and practical lab. We avoid a broad or overly verbose presentation or information overload, and the book presents a concise and definitive perspective to C.

This book is written as a self-practice book for learning programming by going through all the detailed problem solutions and working through the pseudocode, flowchart, and the actual code. In addition, readers can observe a clearer correlation between the individual steps in the pseudocode and the flowchart itself for a better understanding of the program flow.

One of the specialties of this book is that we introduce a new chapter that illustrates on writing and running C codes under various operating systems and platforms. How to embed C codes into other applications is also presented. Each chapter incorporates a number of relevant inquisitive questions and their corresponding answers. A variety of good exercises are also available in the textbook. Another original incorporation of this book is the last chapter, where a number of large projects are presented for students to explore comprehensiveness in the C programming language.

Source codes for all programs in this book will be available for those who will purchase the book. Though we worked hard to ensure the perfection of this book, it may have issues that require amendments. Therefore, please feel free to share at sazzadmsi@du.ac.bd and mahad@uel.ac.uk.

In conclusion, this book is a *guided self-study* for those interested in learning C by following a detailed, *tutorial-type problem-solving book*. We feel that it is a great book for teachers to cover as a *textbook* for C programming language.

**Prof. Sazzad M.S. Imran, Ph.D.**
**Prof. Md Atiqur Rahman Ahad, Ph.D.**

MATLAB® is a registered trademark of The Math Works, Inc. For product information, please contact:

The Math Works, Inc.
3 Apple Hill Drive
Natick, MA 01760-2098
Tel: 508-647-7000
Fax: 508-647-7001
E-mail: info@mathworks.com
Web: http://www.mathworks.com

# CHAPTER 1

# Introduction

C IS A MACHINE-INDEPENDENT, EFFICIENT, easy-to-use structured programming language used to create various applications, operating systems, and sophisticated programs. C is widely recognized as the foundation of programming language, implying that anyone who understands C can quickly acquire or grasp other structured programming languages. Dennis Ritchie, a computer scientist at the Bell Laboratories in the United States, designed the C programming language in 1972.

## 1.1 HISTORY OF PROGRAMMING LANGUAGE

Ada Lovelace created the first programming language in 1843 for an early computing system. She created the first machine algorithm for the Difference Machine of Charles Babbage. However, Konrad Zuse created the first proper programming language, Plankalkul, often known as plan calculus, sometime between 1944 and 1945. After that, in 1947, Kathleen Booth devised assembly language, a low-level programming language that simplified machine coding. John McCauley proposed the first high-level language, Shortcode or Short-order-code, in 1949. Alick Glennie created the first compiled language, Autocode, for the Mark 1 computer in 1952.

John Backus invented FORmula TRANslation, or FORTRAN, in 1957. It was designed for complex scientific, mathematical, and statistical calculations and is still used today. A group of American and European computer scientists collaborated to create ALGOL, or algorithmic language, in 1958. In the same year, John McCarthy of MIT proposed the LISP (list processing) programming language for artificial intelligence. Dr. Grace Murray Hopper oversaw the development of COBOL (Common Business Oriented Language) in 1959, which was created for credit card processors, ATMs, telephone and mobile phone calls, hospital signals, traffic signal systems, and banking systems.

Beginners All-purpose Symbolic Instruction Code, or BASIC, was created in 1964 by Dartmouth College students and later improved by Microsoft founders Bill Gates and Paul Allen. The PASCAL was created in 1970 by Niklaus Wirth in honor of French mathematician Blaise Pascal. It was the first choice of Apple because of its simplicity of use and power. Alan Kay, Adele Goldberg, and Dan Ingalls of the Xerox Palo Alto Research Centre created

Smalltalk in 1972. Leafly, Logitech, and CrowdStrike were among the companies that used it. In the same year, Dennis Ritchie created C for use with the Unix operating system at Bell Telephone Laboratories. C is the basis for several modern languages, including C#, Java, JavaScript, Perl, PHP, and Python. In 1972, IBM researchers Raymond Boyce and Donald Chamberlain created SQL, which stood for Structured Query Language. It is a program that lets you explore and edit data stored in databases.

After mathematician Ada Lovelace, Ada was created in 1980–1981 by a team directed by Jean Ichbiah of CUU Honeywell Bull. Ada is an organized, statically typed, imperative, wide-spectrum, and object-oriented high-level programming language used for air traffic control systems. Bjarne Stroustrup created C++ after modifying the C language at Bell Labs in 1983. C++ is a high-performance programming language used in Microsoft Office, Adobe Photoshop, game engines, and other high-performance software. Brad Cox and Tom Love created the Objective-C programming language in 1983 to construct software for macOS and iOS. Larry Wall designed Perl in 1987 as a general-purpose, high-level programming language for text editing.

Haskell, a general-purpose programming language, was created in 1990 to deal with complex calculations, records, and number crunching. Guido Van Rossum created the general-purpose, high-level programming language Python in 1991, and it is used by Google, Yahoo, and Spotify. Visual Basic is a programming language created by Microsoft in 1991 that allows programmers to use a graphical user interface and is used in various applications such as Word, Excel, and Access. Yukihiro Matsumoto designed Ruby in 1993 as an interpreted high-level language for web application development. James Gosling designed Java in 1995 as a general-purpose, high-level programming language with cross-platform capabilities. Rasmus Lerdorf created the hypertext preprocessor PHP in 1995 to create and maintain dynamic web pages and server-side applications. Brendan Eich wrote JavaScript in 1995 for desktop widgets, dynamic web development, and PDF documents.

Microsoft created C# in 2000 by combining the computing power of C++ with the simplicity of Visual Basic. Almost every Microsoft product currently uses C#. In 2003, Martin Odersky created Scala, which combines functional mathematical and object-oriented programming. Scala is a Java-compatible programming language that is useful in Android development. In 2003, James Strachan and Bob McWhirter created Groovy, a concise and easy-to-learn language derived from Java. Google created Go in 2009, and it has since gained popularity among Uber, Twitch, and Dropbox. Apple created Swift in 2014 to replace C, C++, and Objective-C for desktop, mobile, and cloud applications.

## 1.2 DIFFERENT TYPES OF PROGRAMMING LANGUAGE

To communicate with computers, programmers utilize a programming language. There are three broad categories of computer languages:

(a) *Machine language*

Referred to as machine code or object code, a set of binary digits 0 and 1. Easily understandable by computer systems but not by users.

(b) *Assembly language*

Considered a low-level language and used to implement the symbolic representation of machine codes.

(c) *High-level language*

Easy to understand and code by users. Not understandable by computer systems, hence needs to be transformed into machine code. Different types of high-level languages are as follows:

  (i) Algorithmic languages – FORTRAN, ALGOL, C

  (ii) Business-oriented languages – COBOL, SQL

  (iii) Education-oriented languages – BASIC, Pascal, Logo, Hypertalk

  (iv) Object-oriented languages – C++, C#, Ada, Java, Visual Basic, Python

  (v) Declarative languages – PROLOG, LISP

  (vi) Scripting languages – Perl

  (vii) Document formatting languages – TeX, PostScript, SGML

  (viii) World Wide Web display languages – HTML, XML

  (ix) Web scripting languages – JavaScript, VB Script

## 1.3 IMPORTANCE OF PROGRAMMING

In recent years, programming has become the most in-demand skill. From smart TVs to kitchen appliances, technological disruption is evident practically everywhere. As a result, many new employments are created, and a large number of current jobs are redefined. Programming skills provide a competitive advantage in a variety of career fields. As a result, it is undoubtedly one of the most crucial talents to learn for both present and future generations.

Programming helps us think more logically and analytically. Students who learn programming languages at an early age will have many career options in the future. It is no longer a choice to learn but rather a necessary talent to master. Apart from software and application development, business analysts, graphic artists, and data scientists are among the occupations that require programming knowledge.

## 1.4 C PROGRAM STRUCTURE

The source code of any C program is written according to the syntax of the computer language. The source code for a C program can be written in any text editor and then saved with the .c extension, for example, filename.c. Any alpha-numeric character, including underscores, can be used in the file name, except we cannot use any keyword as a file name. After then, any standard C compiler, such as Turbo C or CodeBlocks, is used to compile and run the source code file. Let us get started with the first C program.

```c
/*Demo program written by Sazzad and Ahad*/
#include <stdio.h>
int main(){
    int age;
    printf("Enter your age: ");
    scanf("%d", &age);
    if (age<18){
        printf("Sorry, you are not eligible for vaccination.");
    }
    else{
        printf("Congratulation, you are eligible for vaccination.");
    }
    return 0;
}
```

Input and Output:

```
Enter your age: 23
Congratulation, you are eligible for vaccination.
```

```
Enter your age: 16
Sorry, you are not eligible for vaccination.
```

Explanation of the program:

Comment: Any comment in a C program begins with '/*' and ends with '*/'. // can also be used to make a single-line comment. Though it is not required to write comments, it is a good practice to do so in order to improve the readability of the program. There can be any number of comments placed anywhere in the program, as the comments are not executed.

include: Many keywords and library functions, such as printf() and scanf(), may be required in any C program. stdio.h, conio.h, and other header files contain prototypes or declarations of the library functions that must be included in the program. The header file stdio.h is included in this program. It provides declarations for the functions printf() that displays data on the standard output terminal and scanf() that reads data from the standard input terminal.

Display: The built-in library function printf() displays anything written inside double quotation marks on the output console. The values of the variables can also be displayed using the format specifiers.

User input: The C library function scanf() takes input from the input terminal. Following the program's execution, the input console awaits input, and once the age is entered, the remaining statements are executed based on the age input.

main() function: The main() function is used to start executing any C program source code; hence, every C program must have one. The main() function has the following structure. The function name is followed by the return type, which can be either int or void. The return type is required for the compiler to determine if the program was successfully compiled or not. We return 0 at the end of the main() function as 0 is the standard for the "successful execution of the program". Also, the ANSI standard does not allow using void main(); therefore, it is preferred to use 'int main()' over 'void main()'. If there are any arguments or parameters after the function name, they are enclosed in parentheses; otherwise, they are left empty. The body of the main() function is comprised of all the statements between the opening and closing curly braces.

## 1.5  STEP-BY-STEP TUTORIAL TO RUN A C PROGRAM

We use Code::Blocks for windows OS to run all the programs available in this book. It is a free, open-source, cross-platform C IDE built to meet the most demanding needs of its users. How to run the programs using other compilers, platforms, or operating systems is available in Chapter 8.

A step-by-step tutorial to run any C program using Code::Blocks is given below.

Step-1: Visit www.codeblocks.org/downloads/binaries/; download, and install code-blocks-20.03mingw-32bit-setup.exe. We prefer 32-bit with mingw package as that version is compatible with graphics.h header file necessary for C graphics programs.

← → C  ⚠ Not secure | codeblocks.org/downloads/binaries/

codeblocks-20.03-32bit-setup.exe                    FossHUB or Sourceforge.net
codeblocks-20.03-32bit-setup-nonadmin.exe FossHUB or Sourceforge.net
codeblocks-20.03-32bit-nosetup.zip              FossHUB or Sourceforge.net
codeblocks-20.03mingw-32bit-setup.exe        FossHUB or Sourceforge.net
codeblocks-20.03mingw-32bit-nosetup.zip     FossHUB or Sourceforge.net

Step-2: Open Code::Blocks and click on File→New→Project . . ., select 'Empty project' and click on Go and then Next>.

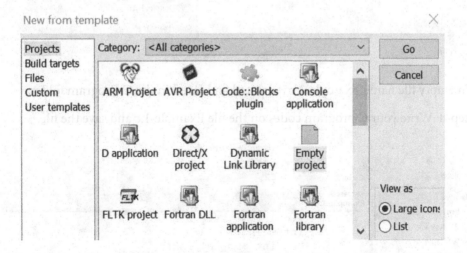

Write C-Program (or any name of your choice) on the 'Project title:' and choose the folder (for example, C:\Users\SazzadImran\Desktop\) where you want to create the project. Click Next>→Finish. A project or folder is created on the desktop.

Please select the folder where you want the new project to be created as well as its title.

Project title:
C-Program

Folder to create project in:
C:\Users\SazzadImran\Desktop\                    ...

Project filename:
C-Program.cbp

Resulting filename:
C:\Users\SazzadImran\Desktop\C-Program\C-Program

Step-3: Double click on C-Program on Workspace to select the project and click File→New→Empty file→Yes. Write a file name of your choice (Example-1, for example) and click Save.

File name: Example-1                                                              ∨

Save as type: C/C++ files                                                        ∨

Hide Folders                                                    Save        Cancel

Check Debug and Release and then press OK.

Multiple selection                                      □     ✕

Select the targets this file should belong to:
✔ Debug                              Wildcard select
✔ Release
                                     Toggle selection

                                     Select All

                                     Deselect All

                                     Selected: 2

                     OK          Cancel

An empty file name Example-1.c is created and saved in the C-Program folder.

Step-4: Write your C program codes on the file Example-1.c and save the file.

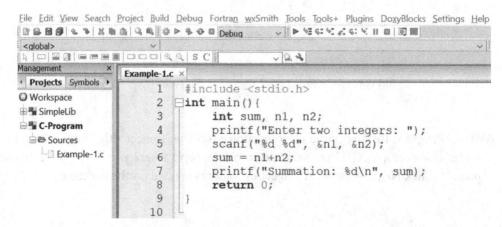

```c
#include <stdio.h>
int main(){
    int sum, n1, n2;
    printf("Enter two integers: ");
    scanf("%d %d", &n1, &n2);
    sum = n1+n2;
    printf("Summation: %d\n", sum);
    return 0;
}
```

Step-5: Click Build→'Compile current file' to compile the program. Correct any error(s) or warning(s) on the codes. Correcting the errors is a must though it is optional to correct the warnings. Recompile the program until we get 0 error(s) and 0 warning(s).

```
Logs & others
◄  🗎 Code::Blocks   ×  🔍 Search results   ×  🗎 Cccc  ×  ◐ Build log  ×  ⚑ Build messages   ×
Output file is bin\Debug\C-Program.exe with size 28.65 KB
Process terminated with status 0 (0 minute(s), 0 second(s))
0 error(s), 0 warning(s) (0 minute(s), 0 second(s))
```

Step-6: Click Build→'Build and run' to execute the program. The output screen will look as follows:

```
▣ C:\Users\SazzadImran\Desktop\C-Program\bin\Debug\C-Program.exe

Enter two integers: 45 67
Summation: 112

Process returned 0 (0x0)   execution time : 7.272 s
Press any key to continue.
```

## 1.6 KEYWORDS

In C programming, 32 reserved words have special meaning to compilers and are utilized as a part of the syntax. These terms cannot be used as names or identifiers for variables. The list of reserved C keywords is as follows:

auto, break, case, char, const, continue, default, do, int, long, register, return, short, signed, sizeof, static, struct, switch, typedef, union, unsigned, void, volatile, while, double, else, enum, extern, float, for, goto, if.

## 1.7 IDENTIFIERS

Variables, functions, structures, and other objects in a program are given unique names called identifiers. For example, in the statement of the preceding demo program

```
int age;
```

int is a keyword and age is an identifier assigned to a variable by the compiler to identify the entity uniquely. When naming an identifier, the following guidelines should be observed.

(1) A valid identifier can include uppercase and lowercase letters, numbers, and underscores.

(2) The first character cannot be a digit.

(3) We cannot use any keyword as an identifier.

(4) The length of the identifier is unlimited.

It is a good practice to give the identifier a meaningful name.

## 1.8 OPERATORS

In C, operators are symbols that perform operations on values or variables. There is a rich set of operators used in C programming.

C arithmetic operators are as follows:

+ (addition)

− (subtraction)

* (multiplication)

/ (division) and

% (modulus or remainder of division)

C increment and decrement operators are as follows:

++ (unary increment, ++a = a++ = a+1) and

−− (unary decrement,−−a = a−−= a−1)

C assignment operators are as follows:

= (a = b)

+= (a += b → a = a + b)

− =

*=

/= and

%=

C relational operators are as follows:

== (equal to, a == b)

> (greater than)

< (less than)

!= (not equal to)

>= (greater than or equal to) and

<= (less than or equal to)

C logical operators are as follows:

&& (AND)

|| (OR) and

! (NOT)

C bitwise operators are as follows:

& (AND)

| (OR)

∧ (EX-OR)

<< (shift left) and

>> (shift right)

## 1.9 OPERATOR PRECEDENCE IN C

When more than one operator is included in a mathematical or logical expression, operator precedence in C decides which operator is evaluated first. When more than one operator of the same precedence is present in an expression, associativity in C determines the precedence of the operators.

The precedence of the mathematical operators is as follows:

(1) *, /, %

(2) +, −

All these operators have the associativity of left to right.

For example: 5+2*3/6 is evaluated as 5+{(2*3)/6}=5+{6/6}=5+1=6 in C.

Precedence of the logical operators are as follows:

(1)  &&

(2)  ||

(3)  !

The operators && and || have left-to-right associativity, while ! has right-to-left associativity.

## 1.10 VARIABLES

When a variable is declared in a C program, it refers to a memory storage space where the data is held. The value of a variable can be altered, but its data type cannot be changed once it has been declared, but type conversion is permitted in a mathematical expression. For example, in the statement

```
int age;
```

age is a variable name that holds any integer type data in a fixed position in memory. The same rules apply to naming variables as they do to naming identifiers.

## 1.11 CONSTANTS

If we want to keep the value of a variable constant or fixed, we can use the term const before the variable's data type. As a result, the variable is now a symbolic constant. For example, PI is a symbolic constant whose value cannot be changed in the program in the following statement:

const double PI = 3.14;

## 1.12 ESCAPE SEQUENCES

In some cases, special sequences are used to represent characters that cannot be typed in a C program. Backslash characters are another name for these. In a C program, the following escape sequences are employed:

\b (backspace)

\f (form feed)

\n (newline)

\r (return)

\t (horizontal tab)

\v (vertical tab)

\\ (backslash)

\' (single quotation mark)

\" (double quotation mark)

\? (question mark) and

\0 (null character)

## 1.13 DATA TYPES

In a C program, data types are used to define variables, which determine the type and size of the variable. The size of a particular data type depends on the compiler. Any data type's size can be determined using the sizeof(variable name) operator. Format specifiers specify the type of data that is displayed or accepted by output or input functions. In C programming, the following is a list of data types and their associated format specifiers:

int [%d, %i]

char [%c]

float [%f]

double [%lf]

short int [%hd]

unsigned int [%u]

long int [%ld, %li]

long long int [%lld, %lli]

unsigned long int [%lu]

unsigned long long int [%llu]

signed char [%c]

unsigned char [%c]

long double [%Lf]

int, float, double, char, and void are the basic data types,

short and long can be used as a type specifier, and

signed and unsigned as type modifiers.

void is used as a return type when a function does not return anything; nevertheless, it does not create variables.

## 1.14 TYPE CASTING

The conversion of one data type to another is known as type casting or type conversion. There are two forms of type conversion:

(1) *Implicit:* In this situation, the compiler casts the values of distinct data types in an expression to a common type, which is the highest hierarchy.

int → unsigned int → long → unsigned long → long long → unsigned long long → float → double → long double

Example:

```
int total = 15;
float count = 6, average;
average = total/count;       //this will give average=2.5
```

Here, because float data type is higher in the hierarchy between float and int, the arithmetic expression total/count gives a float value.

(2) *Explicit*: In this situation, the programmer uses the cast operator to explicitly change values of one type to another. The syntax is as follows:

(type_name) expression

Example:

```
int total=15, count=6;
float average;
average = total/count;        //this will give average=2
average = (float) total/count; //this will give average=2.5
```

First, the total is transformed from an int to a float, and then division is performed. Because total has been converted to float and count has been changed to int, the result is a decimal value because float is higher in the hierarchy than int data type.

## 1.15 EXAMPLES

### PROBLEM-01
**Write a program to print the sentence "Hello! Atiqur Rahman! How are you?" on the screen.**

Programming Code of the Solution:

```
#include <stdio.h>
int main(){
    printf("Hello! Atiqur Rahman!\n");
    printf("How are you?");
    return 0;
}
```

Input and Output of the Executed Program:

```
Hello! Atiqur Rahman!
How are you?
```

Explanation of the Programming Code:

**#include <stdio.h>**
/*header file stdio.h contains prototype of the library function printf(); the header file must be included using preprocessor directive #include before the function is called in the program*/
**int main(){**
/*all C program must have a main() function with return type void or int; here there is no parameter of the main() function and

it returns an integer; opening curly brace specifies start of the main() function and no statement before that curly brace is executed by the compiler*/

```
    printf("Hello! Atiqur Rahman!\n");
    /*this displays the text in double quotes as it is on the screen
    except for a newline replaces \n*/
    printf("How are you?");
    /*this displays the text in double quotes as it is on the
    screen*/
    return 0;
    /*0 is returned as it is the standard for the successful
    execution of the program*/
}
```

/*the closing curly brace specifies the end of the main() function's body, as well as the program's end; after that curly brace, no statement is executed*/

## PROBLEM-02

**Write a program to input an integer and then print the integer value.**

Programming Code of the Solution:

```
#include <stdio.h>
int main(){
    int num;
    printf("Please enter an integer value: ");
    scanf("%d", &num);
    printf("You have entered %d.", num);
    return 0;
}
```

Input and Output of the Executed Program:

```
Please enter an integer value: 8
You have entered 8.
```

Explanation of the Programming Code:

**#include <stdio.h>**
/*header file stdio.h contains prototypes of the library functions printf(), and scanf(); the header file must be included using preprocessor directive #include before the functions are called in the program*/
**int main(){**
/*all C program must have a main() function with return type void or int; here there is no parameter of the main() function and it

returns an integer; opening curly brace specifies start of the main() function and no statement before that curly brace is executed by the compiler*/

```
    int num;
    /*an integer type variable is declared; required memory spaces
    are allocated for it*/
    printf("Please enter an integer value: ");
    /*this displays the text as it is in the double quotations on
    the screen*/
    scanf("%d", &num);
    /*scanf() is an input function that reads an integer from the
    input terminal and stores it in the memory location reserved
    for the num; hence, the address operator & is used before the
    variable name*/
    printf("You have entered %d.", num);
    /*the text inside the double quotes is displayed as it is on
    the screen, except for the value of num replaces the format
    specifier %d*/
    return 0;
    /*0 is returned as it is the standard for the successful
    execution of the program*/
}
```
/*the closing curly brace specifies the end of the main() function's body, as well as the program's end; after that curly brace, no statement is executed*/

## PROBLEM-03
**Write a program that enters two integer values and displays the summation on the screen.**

Programming Code of the Solution:

```
#include <stdio.h>
int main(){
    int num1, num2, sum;
    printf("Please enter two integers: ");
    scanf("%d %d", &num1, &num2);
    sum = num1+num2;
    printf("%d+%d = %d", num1, num2, sum);
    return 0;
}
```

Input and Output of the Executed Program:

```
Please enter two integers: 6 10
6+10 = 16
```

## Explanation of the Programming Code:

```c
#include <stdio.h>
/*header file stdio.h contains prototypes of the library functions
printf() and scanf(); the header file must be included using preprocessor
directive #include before the functions are called in the program*/
int main(){
/*all C program must have a main() function with return type void or
int; here there is no parameter of the main() function and it returns
an integer; opening curly brace specifies start of the main() function
and no statement before that curly brace is executed by the compiler*/
    int num1, num2, sum;
    /*three integer type variables are declared; required memory
    spaces are allocated for each of the variables*/
    printf("Please enter two integers: ");
    /*this printf() function displays the text in double quotations
    as it is on the screen*/
    scanf("%d %d", &num1, &num2);
    /*scanf() function reads two integers from input terminal; the
    first format specifier %d relates to the num1 variable, while
    the second %d corresponds to the num2 variable; while input,
    the two numbers may be separated by a space, tab, or newline*/
    sum = num1+num2;
    /*summation is done with this statement, and the result is
    assigned to the sum variable*/
    printf("%d+%d = %d", num1, num2, sum);
    /*this printf() function displays the text in double quotations
    as it is on the screen except for the value of num1 replaces the
    first format specifier %d, value of num2 replaces the second %d,
    and the value of sum replaces the third %d*/
    return 0;
    /*0 is returned as it is the standard for the successful
    execution of the program*/
}
/*the closing curly brace specifies the end of the main() function's
body, as well as the program's end; after that curly brace, no
statement is executed*/
```

## PROBLEM-04
**Write a program that will input two floating-point numbers and then display the product on the screen.**

Programming Code of the Solution:

```c
#include <stdio.h>
int main(){
    double num1, num2, prod;
    printf("Please enter any two numbers: ");
    scanf("%lf %lf", &num1, &num2);
    prod = num1*num2;
    printf("Product of %0.2lf and %0.2lf is: %0.2lf",
            num1, num2, prod);
    return 0;
}
```

Input and Output of the Executed Program:

```
Please enter any two numbers: 1.3 2
Product of 1.30 and 2.00 is: 2.60
```

**Explanation of the Programming Code:**

**#include <stdio.h>**
/*header file stdio.h contains prototypes of the library functions printf() and scanf(); the header file must be included using preprocessor directive #include before the functions are called in the program*/
**int main(){**
/*all C program must have a main() function with return type void or int; here there is no parameter of the main() function and it returns an integer; opening curly brace specifies start of the main() function and no statement before that curly brace is executed by the compiler*/
    **double num1, num2, prod;**
    /*three double type variables are declared that can store any decimal values*/
    **printf("Please enter any two numbers: ");**
    /*this displays the text in the double quotations as it is on the screen*/
    **scanf("%lf %lf", &num1, &num2);**
    /*two decimal values are read for two %lf format specifiers correspond to num1 and num2, respectively; the address operator must be used before the variable name*/

```
prod = num1*num2;
/*numal is multiplied by num2 and the result is assigned to
variable prod*/
printf("Product of %0.2lf and %0.2lf is: %0.2lf", num1, num2,
      prod);
/*printf() function displays the text inside the double
quotations as it is on the screen, with the exception that
the value of num1 replaces the first format specifier %0.2lf,
value of num2 replaces the second %0.2lf, and the value of prod
replaces the third %0.2lf; the format specifier 0.2lf specifies
that the number is displayed with a precision of two decimal
points*/
return 0;
/*0 is returned as it is the standard for the successful
execution of the program*/
}
```

/*the closing curly brace specifies the end of the main() function's
body, as well as the program's end; after that curly brace, no
statement is executed*/

## PROBLEM-05
**Write a program to input two integers and show the result of the division.**

<u>Programming Code of the Solution:</u>

```
#include <stdio.h>
int main(){
    int num1, num2, quot, remn;
    printf("Enter the dividend: ");
    scanf("%d", &num1);
    printf("Enter the divisor: ");
    scanf("%d", &num2);
    quot = num1/num2;
    remn = num1%num2;
    printf("Quotient = %d\nRemainder = %d", quot, remn);
    return 0;
}
```

<u>Input and Output of the Executed Program:</u>

```
Enter the dividend: 15
Enter the divisor: 6
Quotient = 2
Remainder = 3
```

## Explanation of the Programming Code:

```
#include <stdio.h>
```
/*the prototypes of the printf() and scanf() functions are contained in the stdio.h header file, which must be included using the #include preprocessor directive*/
```
int main(){
```
/*all C program must have a main() function with return type void or int; here there is no parameter of the main() function, and it returns an integer; opening curly brace specifies start of the main() function and no statement before that curly brace is executed by the compiler*/

> ```
> int num1, num2, quot, remn;
> ```
> /*four integer type variables are declared: num1 is used to store the dividend, num2 is used to store the divisor, quot is used to assign the quotient, and remn is used to assign the remainder of the division process.*/
> ```
> printf("Enter the dividend: ");
> ```
> /*this displays the text written in the double quotations as it is on the screen*/
> ```
> scanf("%d", &num1);
> ```
> /*this reads an integer from input terminal and stores the value in the memory location allocated for num1, %d is the format specifier for the integer type data*/
> ```
> printf("Enter the divisor: ");
> ```
> //this displays the text written in the double quotations as it is on the screen
> ```
> scanf("%d", &num2);
> ```
> /*this reads an integer from input terminal and stores the value in the memory location assigned for variable num2*/
> ```
> quot = num1/num2;
> ```
> /*num1 is divided by num2 and the quotient is assigned to variable quot*/
> ```
> remn = num1%num2;
> ```
> /*num1 is divided by num2 and the remainder is assigned to the variable remn*/
> ```
> printf("Quotient = %d\nRemainder = %d", quot, remn);
> ```
> /*this displays the text in the double quotes as it is on the screen except for the value of quot replaces the first format specifier %d, the value of remn replaces the second %d and a newline replaces \n*/
> ```
> return 0;
> ```
> /*0 is returned as it is the standard for the successful execution of the program*/
```
}
```
/*the closing curly brace specifies the end of the main() function's body, as well as the program's end; after that curly brace, no statement is executed*/

## PROBLEM-06
**Write a program to calculate the area and circumference of a circle.**

Programming Code of the Solution:

```c
#include <stdio.h>
#define PI 3.14
int main(){
    int rad;
    float area, circum;
    printf("Enter radius of a circle in cm: ");
    scanf("%d", &rad);
    area = PI*rad*rad;
    circum = 2*PI*rad;
    printf("Area of the circle = %0.2f\n", area);
    printf("Circumference of the circle = %0.2f", circum);
    return 0;
}
```

Input and Output of the Executed Program:

```
Enter radius of a circle in cm: 3.4
Area of the circle = 28.26
Circumference of the circle = 18.84
```

Explanation of the Programming Code:

**#include <stdio.h>**
/*stdio.h header file contains the prototypes of printf() and scanf() functions and hence needs to be included using #include preprocessor directive*/
**#define PI 3.14**
/*here PI is defined as 3.14 using #define preprocessor directive. After that anywhere we use PI it will be replaced by 3.14*/
**int main(){**
/*C program starts from main() function which will return an integer and there is no argument for the function; the opening curly brace indicates the start of the body of the main() function and the program execution starts from the first statement just after this brace*/
    **int rad;**
    /*integer type variable rad is declared which will store radius of the circle*/
    **float area, circum;**
    /*two float type variables are declared, area to store area of the circle and circum to store area of the circumference of the circle*/

```
printf("Enter radius of a circle in cm: ");
/*this will display the message inside the double quotation as
it is on screen*/
scanf("%d", &rad);
/*scanf() is an input function that will take an integer as input
against int type variable rad, hence format specifier %d is used
and address operator & is used with the variable name*/
area = PI*rad*rad;
/*result of the multiplication in the right side will be float
as PI is a decimal value hence the result is assigned to float
type variable area*/
circum = 2*PI*rad;
/*circumference is calculated and assigned to float type
variable circum*/
printf("Area of the circle = %0.2f\n", area);
/*output function printf() will display the message inside the
quotation as it is on the screen except format specifier %0.2f
will be replaced by the value of float type variable area with
2 decimal point precision followed by enter due to the newline
character \n*/
printf("Circumference of the circle = %0.2f", circum);
/*output function printf() will display the message inside the
quotation as it is on the screen except format specifier %0.2f
will be replaced by the value of float type variable circum with
2 decimal point precision*/
return 0;
/*0 is returned as it is the standard for the successful
execution of the program*/
}
```

/*the closing curly brace indicates the end of the body of main()
function and the end of the program. No statement will execute after
that curly brace*/

## PROBLEM-07
**Write a program that calculates the power of a given number.**

Programming Code of the Solution:

```
#include <stdio.h>
#include <math.h>
int main(){
    float base, exp;
    printf("Enter a base number: ");
    scanf("%f", &base);
    printf("Enter an exponent: ");
    scanf("%f", &exp);
    printf("%0.1f^%0.1f = %0.2f", base, exp, pow(base, exp));
    return 0;
}
```

Input and Output of the Executed Program:

```
Enter a base number: 5
Enter an exponent: 3
5.0^3.0 = 125.00
```

**Explanation of the Programming Code:**

`#include <stdio.h>`
/\*header file stdio.h contains prototypes of the library functions printf() and scanf(); the header file must be included using preprocessor directive #include before the functions are called in the program\*/
`#include <math.h>`
/\*header file stdio.h contains prototypes of the library function pow(); the header file must be included using preprocessor directive #include before the function is called in the program\*/
`int main(){`
/\*all C program must have a main() function with return type void or int; here there is no parameter of the main() function and it returns an integer; opening curly brace specifies start of the main() function and no statement before that curly brace is executed by the compiler\*/
  `float base, exp;`
  /\*two float type variables are declared that can store any decimal values\*/
  `printf("Enter a base number: ");`
  /\*this displays the text inside the double quotations as it is on the screen\*/
  `scanf("%f", &base);`
  /\*this reads a decimal value from input terminal and it is stored in the memory location allocated for the variable base\*/
  `printf("Enter an exponent: ");`
  /\*this displays the text inside the double quotations as it is on the screen\*/
  `scanf("%f", &exp);`
  /\*this reads a decimal value from input terminal and it is stored in the memory location allocated for the variable exp\*/
  `printf("%0.1f^%0.1f = %0.2f", base, exp, pow(base, exp));`
  /\*pow(base, exp) function returns base$^{exp}$ and the result is displayed in place of the third format specifier %0.2f with two decimal points precision; the value of base is displayed in place of the first format specifier %0.1f with single point precision and the value of exp in place of the second %0.1f; other text in the double quotes is displayed as it is on the screen\*/

```
    return 0;
    /*0 is returned as it is the standard for the successful
    execution of the program*/
}
```
/*the closing curly brace specifies the end of the main() function's
body, as well as the program's end; after that curly brace, no
statement is executed*/


## PROBLEM-08
**Write a program to find the size of the data types int, float, double, and char.**

Programming Code of the Solution:

```
#include <stdio.h>
int main(){
    int type1;
    float type2;
    double type3;
    char type4;
    printf("Size of int data type is: %d byte\n", sizeof(type1));
    printf("Size of float data type is: %d byte\n", sizeof(type2));
    printf("Size of double data type is: %d byte\n", sizeof(type3));
    printf("Size of char data type is: %d byte", sizeof(type4));
    return 0;
}
```

Input and Output of the Executed Program:

```
Size of int data type is: 4 byte
Size of float data type is: 4 byte
Size of double data type is: 8 byte
Size of char data type is: 1 byte
```

Explanation of the Programming Code:

**#include <stdio.h>**
/*header file stdio.h contains prototypes of the library function
printf(); the header file must be included using preprocessor
directive #include before the function is called in the program*/
**int main(){**
/*all C program must have a main() function with return type void
or int; here there is no parameter of the main() function and it
returns an integer; opening curly brace specifies start of the main()
function and no statement before that curly brace is executed by the
compiler*/
    **int type1;**
    /*integer type variable type1 is declared and required memory
    space is allocated for the variable type1*/

```
float type2;
/*float type variable type2 is declared*/
double type3;
/*double type variable type3 is declared*/
char type4;
/*character type variable type4 is declared*/
printf("Size of int data type is: %d byte\n", sizeof(type1));
/*sizeof(type1) returns the size of variable type1 in bytes, that is
displayed on the screen in place of format specifier %d; other text
in the quotes is displayed as it is except for a newline replaces \n*/
printf("Size of float data type is: %d byte\n", sizeof(type2));
/*sizeof(type2) returns the size of variable type2 in bytes,
that is displayed on the screen in place of format specifier
%d; other text in the quotes is displayed as it is except for
a newline replaces \n*/
printf("Size of double data type is: %d byte\n", sizeof(type3));
/*sizeof(type3) returns the size of variable type3 in bytes,
that is displayed on the screen in place of format specifier
%d; other text in the quotes is displayed as it is except for
a newline replaces \n*/
printf("Size of char data type is: %d byte", sizeof(type4));
/*sizeof(type4) returns the size of variable type4 in bytes,
that is displayed on the screen in place of format specifier
%d; other text in the quotes is displayed as it is except for
a newline replaces \n*/
return 0;
/*0 is returned as it is the standard for the successful
execution of the program*/
}
```
/*the closing curly brace specifies the end of the main() function's
body, as well as the program's end; after that curly brace, no
statement is executed*/

## PROBLEM-09
**Write a program that swaps two numbers.**

Programming Code of the Solution:

```
#include <stdio.h>
int main(){
    float num1, num2, temp;
    printf("\n Enter first number: ");
    scanf("%f", &num1);
    printf(" Enter second number: ");
    scanf("%f", &num2);
    temp = num1;
    num1 = num2;
    num2 = temp;
```

```
    printf(" After swapping:\n\t First number = %0.2f\n", num1);
    printf("\t Second number = %0.2f\n", num2);
    return 0;
}
```

Input and Output of the Executed Program:

```
Enter first number: 12.5
Enter second number: 32.46
After swapping:
        First number = 32.46
        Second number = 12.50
```

Explanation of the Programming Code:

```
#include <stdio.h>
```
/*header file stdio.h contains prototypes of the library functions printf() and scanf(); the header file must be included using preprocessor directive #include before the functions are called in the program*/
```
int main(){
```
/*all C program must have a main() function with return type void or int; here there is no parameter of the main() function and it returns an integer; opening curly brace specifies start of the main() function and no statement before that curly brace is executed by the compiler*/
```
    float num1, num2, temp;
```
/*three float type variables are declared; required memory spaces are allocated for each of them*/
```
    printf("Enter first number: ");
```
/*this displays the text inside the double quotes as it is on the screen*/
```
    scanf("%f", &num1);
```
/*this reads a decimal value from input terminal and stores the value in the memory location allocated for num1; %f is format specifier for float type data; address operator & must be used before variable in scanf() function*/
```
    printf("Enter second number: ");
```
/*this displays the text written inside the double quotations as it is on the screen*/
```
    scanf("%f", &num2);
```
/*scanf() function reads a number from input terminal and assigns the value to num2*/
```
    temp = num1;
```
/*value of num1 is assigned to temp variable so that the value of num1 is not lost*/
```
    num1 = num2;
```
/*value of num2 is assigned to num1; num1 is already stored in temp to preserve the value for future use*/

```
    num2 = temp;
    /*the value of temp=num1 is assigned to num2*/
    printf("After swapping:\n\tFirst number = %0.2f\n", num1);
    /*this printf() function displays the text in double quotations
    as it is on the screen except for a tab replaces \t, a newline
    replaces \n, value of num1 replaces format specifier %0.2f with
    two decimal points precision*/
    printf("\tSecond number = %0.2f", num2);
    /*this printf() function displays the text in the double quotes
    as it is on the screen except for a tab replaces \t and the
    value of num2 replaces format specifier %0.2f with two decimal
    points precision*/
    return 0;
    /*0 is returned as it is the standard for the successful
    execution of the program*/
}
```
/*the closing curly brace specifies the end of the main() function's
body, as well as the program's end; after that curly brace, no
statement is executed*/

## PROBLEM-10
Write a program that displays the ASCII number of a character entered by the user.

Programming Code of the Solution:

```c
#include <stdio.h>
int main(){
    char ch;
    printf("Please enter a character: ");
    scanf("%c", &ch);
    printf("ASCII code of %c is %d.", ch, ch);
    return 0;
}
```

Input and Output of the Executed Program:

```
Please enter a character: Q
ASCII code of Q is 81.
```

Explanation of the Programming Code:

#include <stdio.h>
/*header file stdio.h contains prototypes of the library functions
printf() and scanf(); the header file must be included using
preprocessor directive #include before the functions are called in
the program*/

```
int main(){
```
/*all C program must have a main() function with return type void
or int; here there is no parameter of the main() function and it
returns an integer; opening curly brace specifies start of the
main() function and no statement before that curly brace is executed
by the compiler*/
> **char ch;**
> /*char type variable ch is declared that stores only character*/
> **printf("Please enter a character: ");**
> /*this displays the text inside the double quotations as it is
> on the output screen*/
> **scanf("%c", &ch);**
> /*this reads a character from input terminal and assigns the
> character to ch*/
> **printf("ASCII code of %c is %d.", ch, ch);**
> /*this printf() function displays the text in double quotations
> as it is on the screen except for character ch replaces format
> specifier %c and the ASCII code of that character ch replaces
> format specifier %d*/
> **return 0;**
> /*0 is returned as it is the standard for the successful
> execution of the program*/
```
}
```
/*the closing curly brace specifies the end of the main() function's
body, as well as the program's end; after that curly brace, no
statement is executed*/

## EXERCISES

MCQ with Answers

   1) Who invented C language?

     A) Charles Babbage

     B) Graham Bell

     C) Dennis Ritchie

     D) Steve Jobs

   2) In which laboratories was the C language invented?

     A) Uniliver Labs

     B) IBM Labs

     C) AT&T Bell Labs

     D) Verizon Labs

3) In which year was the C language invented?

A) 1999

B) 1978

C) 1972

D) 1990

4) Which type of language C is?

A) Procedural-oriented programming

B) Semi-object-oriented programming

C) Object-oriented programming

D) None of the above

5) Before execution, the compiler converts a high-level program into a machine language program which is called

A) Source program

B) Object program

C) exe program

D) None of this

6) What is an identifier in C language?

A) Name of a function or variable

B) Name of a macros

C) Name of structure or union

D) All of the above

7) An identifier may contain

A) Letters a–z, A–Z

B) Underscore

C) Numbers 0 to 9

D) All of the above

8) An identifier can start with

A) Alphabet

B) Underscore

C) Any possible typed character

D) Options A and B

9) What is the maximum length of an identifier?

A) 32

B) 16

C) 64

D) 12

10) Which of the following is an integer constant?

A) 3.142

B) 43

C) "125"

D) PI

11) Which of the following is a floating-point constant?

A) 29.4E5

B) 34e12

C) 25.857

D) All of the above

12) Which of the following is a character constant?

A) '9'

B) y

C) T

D) "B"

13) Which of the following statements are right?

A) int totnum = 25; int tot_num = 25;

B) int totnum = 25; int tot.num = 25;

C) int totnum = 25; int tot num = 25;

D) All are right

14) How many keywords are present in C language?

A) 32

B) 34

C) 62

D) 64

15) Each statement in a C program should end with a

A) Semicolon (;)

B) Colon (:)

C) Period/dot (.)

D) None of the above

16) Which of the following is not a valid identifier?

A) _atiqahad

B) 2atiqahad

C) atiq_ahad

D) atiqahad2

17) How many bytes are occupied by void in memory?

A) 0

B) 1

C) 2

D) 4

18) What is the range of signed char?

A) −128 to +127

B) 0 to 255

C) −128 to −1

D) 0 to +127

19) What is the range of unsigned char?

A) −128 to +127

B) 0 to 255

C) −128 to −1

D) 0 to +127

20) Leftmost bit 0 in a singed representation indicates

A) A positive number

B) A negative number

C) An unsigned number

D) None of the above

21) What is the range of signed int?

A) 0 to $2^{16}-1$

B) $-2^{15}$ to $+2^{15}-1$

C) $-2^{15}-1$ to $+2^{15}$

D) 0 to $2^{16}$

22) What is the range of unsigned int?

A) 0 to $2^{16}-1$

B) $-2^{15}$ to $+2^{15}-1$

C) $-2^{15}-1$ to $+2^{15}$

D) 0 to $2^{16}$

23) Which is correct with respect to the size of the data types?

A) char > int > float

B) int > char > float

C) char > int > double

D) double > char > int

24) What is the default value of a local variable?

A) 0

B) 1

C) garbage

D) null

25) What is the default value of a static variable?

A) 0

B) 1

C) Garbage

D) Null

26) Variable that are declared but not initialized contains_____.

A) 0

B) Blank space

C) Garbage

D) None of the above

27) What are the sizes of float, double, and long double in bytes?

A) 4, 8, 16

B) 4, 8, 10

C) 2, 4, 6

D) 4, 6, 8

28) What is the range of signed long variables?

A) $-2^{31}-1$ to $+2^{31}$

B) 0 to $+2^{32}$

C) $-2^{31}$ to $+2^{31}-1$

D) 0 to $2^{32}-1$

29) What is the range of unsigned long variables?

A) $-2^{31}-1$ to $+2^{31}$

B) 0 to $+2^{32}$

C) $-2^{31}$ to $+2^{31}-1$

D) 0 to $2^{32}-1$

30) Which of the following does not store a sign?

A) short

B) int

C) long

D) byte

31) Which is the only function all C programs must contain?

A) getch()

B) main()

C) printf()

D) scanf()

32) Which of the following is not a correct variable type?

A) float

B) real

C) char

D) double

33) How would we round off a value of 3.76 to 4.0?

A) ceil(3.76)

B) floor(3.76)

C) roundup(3.76)

D) roundto(3.76)

34) What is the scope of local variable?

A) Entire program

B) Within the block or function

C) Only main() function

D) All of the above

35) Which of the following is not a valid variable name declaration?

A) #define PI 3.14

B) float PI = 3.14;

C) double PI = 3.14;

D) int PI = 3.14;

36) How many keywords are present in the C language?

A) 45

B) 48

C) 32

D) 16

37) Operator % in C language is called

   A)  Percentage operator

   B)  Quotient operator

   C)  Modulus

   D)  Division

38) What is the output of an arithmetic expression with integers and real numbers by default?

   A)  Integer

   B)  Real number

   C)  Depends on the numbers used in the expression

   D)  None of the above

39) What do we get if both numerator and denominator of a division operation in C language are integers?

   A)  The expected algebraic real value

   B)  Unexpected integer value

   C)  Compiler error

   D)  None of the above

40) Can we use operator % with float and int in C language?

   A)  Only int variables

   B)  Only float variables

   C)  int or float combination

   D)  Numerator int variable, denominator any variable

41) Which of the following operator types has the highest precedence in C?

   A)  Relational operators

   B)  Equality operators

   C)  Logical operators

   D)  Arithmetic operators

42) What is the priority among operators *, /, and % in C language?

   A)  * >/> %

B) % > * > /

C) % =/> *

D) % =/= *

43) What is the priority among operators (*, /, %), (+, −), and (=) in C language?

A) (*, /, %) > (+, −) < (=)

B) (*, /, %) < (+, −) < (=)

C) (*, /, %) > (+, −) > (=)

D) (*, /, %) < (+, −) (+, −) = (=)

44) The result of a logical or relational expression in C is

A) True or false

B) 0 or 1

C) 0 if the expression is false and any positive number if the expression is true

D) None of the mentioned

45) Which of the following is not a logical operator?

A) &

B) &&

C) ||

D) !

46) Expand or abbreviate ASCII in C language.

A) Australian Standard Code for Information Interchange

B) American Standard Code for Information Interchange

C) American Symbolic Code for Information Interchange

D) Australian Symbolic Code for Information Interchange

47) Which of the following statement output "hello world."?

A) scanf("hello world.");

B) printf("hello world");

C) scan("hello world.");

D) print("hello world.");

48) What is the correct way of commenting on a single line?

   A) /*this is a single line comment

   B) //this is a single line comment

   C) /this is a single line comment

   D) /*this is a single line comment/*

49) Which one of the following is not a valid C identifier?

   A) _a

   B) a_b

   C) 1a

   D) a1

50) Which of the following group contains the wrong C keywords?

   A) auto, double, int, struct

   B) break, else, long, switch

   C) case, enum, register, typedef

   D) char, extern, intern, return

51) Which of the following group contains the wrong C keywords?

   A) union, const, var, float

   B) short, unsigned, continue, for

   C) signed, void, default, goto

   D) sizeof, volatile, do, if

52) Which of the following is a correct C keyword?

   A) breaker

   B) go to

   C) shorter

   D) default

53) Which of the following is a valid C keyword?

   A) Float

   B) Int

C) Long

D) double

54) Which of the following is an invalid header file in C?

A) math.h

B) mathio.h

C) string.h

D) ctype.h

55) Which of the following operators has the highest precedence?

A) unary

B) shift

C) equality

D) postfix

56) sizeof() is a _____.

A) Function

B) Variable

C) Both A and B

D) Operator

57) Which operator is known as ternary operator?

A) ::

B) ;

C) ?:

D) :

58) What is the value of x in the following C statement?

int x = 7%4*3/2;

A) 4

B) 1

C) 3

D) 0

59) Which of the following is not an arithmetic operation?

A) num %= 5

B) num /=5

C) num *=5

D) num!= 5

[Ans. C, C, C, A, B, D, D, D, A, B, D, A, A, A, A, B, A, A, B, A, B, A, C, C, A, C, B, C, D, D, B, B, A, B, A, A, C, B, B, A, D, D, C, B, A, B, B, B, C, D, A, D, D, B, D, D, C, A, D]

Questions with Short Answers

1) What are the key features of the C programming language?

Ans. The programming language C is widely used. The language's key features or characteristics are listed below.

(a) C offers a structured approach, as well as a rich set of library functions and data types.

(b) C is not platform independent, although it may be run on various devices with little or no modification.

(c) C is a mid-level programming language that may also be used to construct system applications and support features of a high-level language.

(d) Because C is a structured programming language, we can use functions to split the entire program into smaller parts.

(e) C has an extensive library of built-in functions that can be utilized to develop any program.

(f) C provides the dynamic memory allocation functionality.

(g) The compilation and execution times are both short.

(h) In C, we can use pointers to communicate directly with the memory.

(i) We can call a function within a function, allowing for code reuse.

(j) The C software is easily adaptable to new features.

2) Why is C language being considered a middle-level language?

Ans. C is classified as a middle-level language because it bridges the gap between machine and high-level programming. The C programming language is used to develop system programming for operating systems and application programming for menu-driven client billing systems.

3) What is the significance of C program algorithms?

Ans. The algorithm is created first before a program can be written. An algorithm includes step-by-step instructions on how to solve the problem. It also consists of the stages to consider and the necessary computations and operations within the software.

4) Write the importance of program algorithms.

Ans. A problem is solved using an algorithm, which is a step-by-step approach. Algorithms are used to determine the optimum solution to a problem. Program algorithms are used to

(a) improve the software's accuracy and speed, and

(b) ensure that the least amount of memory and computing power is required.

5) What is a program flowchart? How does it help in writing a program?

Ans. A flowchart is a graphical depiction of a program's various logical steps. The steps are represented by various types of boxes, with arrows linking the boxes in a logical order. This diagram aids in visualizing what is going on and understanding the data flow and problem-solving process.

6) Differentiate source codes from object codes.

Ans. Programming statements written in a text editor and saved in a file are known as source code. The compiler translates the source code into object code, which is machine-readable code. Thus, source code is readable by humans, whereas object code is readable by machines.

7) Compare and contrast compilers and interpreters.

Ans. A compiler is a program translator that reads the entire program and translates it to machine code all at once. On the other hand, an interpreter is a program that imitates the execution of a program by executing one statement at a time. The interpreter does not generate any object code, even though the compiler does. Compiling a program takes longer than interpreting it, but the execution time of a compiled program is faster than that of an interpreted program.

8) What is debugging?

Ans. Debugging is the act of finding and fixing existing and potential errors in program codes that could cause the program to behave abnormally or crash.

9) What are the basic data types associated with C?

Ans. There are five basic data types: char, int, float, double, and void.

10) How many types of errors are possible in the C language?

Ans. There are five types of errors possible in C programming: logical error, run-time error, syntax error, linking error, and semantic error.

11) What is a syntax error?

Ans. When any rule of writing program's source code is broken, this is referred to as a syntax error, also called compilation error. A syntax error occurs when parts of the source code do not follow the C programming language's syntax. Misspelled commands, keywords, misplaced symbols, missing semicolon at the end of statement, missing parenthesis after main() function, etc., are just a few examples.

12) What are logical errors, and how does it differ from syntax errors?

Ans. Any programming logic errors made by the programmer cause logical errors. The software builds and runs successfully in this situation. However, it does not produce the expected result. On the other hand, syntax errors arise when any rules are broken while writing statements or commands in a program, resulting in the program failing to compile and run.

13) What are run-time errors?

Ans. Run-time errors, often known as bugs, are errors that occur in a program when it is executing after it has been successfully compiled. Division by zero, input/output device error, undefined object, an encoding error, and other sorts of run-time errors are all common.

14) What are linking errors?

Ans. The errors due to which the program is compiled successfully but failed to link different object files with the main program module are referred to as linking errors. Incorrect function name, incorrect function prototyping, incorrect header files, etc., are some examples of linking errors. Due to linking errors, no executable file (.exe file) is generated.

15) What are semantic errors?

Ans. Semantic errors occur when any C statement is syntactically correct but has no meaning. For example, when any expression is used on the left side of an assignment operator, semantic error occurs.

16) What are reserved words in the C programming language?

Ans. Reserved words are those with predetermined meanings that cannot be used as identifiers. In C, 32 keywords are reserved, including char, int, float, bread, switch, case, for, register, short, else, return, and so on.

17) Describe the header file and its usage in C?

Ans. Function declaration and macro definition are stored in a header file with the extension .h. All of the compiler's built-in functions are declared in several header files. Programmers can also create their header files. Function declarations and macro definitions are shared between several source files via header files.

18) Does a built-in header file contain a built-in function definition?

Ans. Only declarations of the built-in functions are found in the built-in header file. The functions' definitions can be found in the C library, which is linked by the linker.

19) Why is it that not all header files are declared in all C programs?

Ans. Because different functions are declared in different files, the decision of declaring specific header files at the top of a C program is determined by the functions that are utilized in that program. Including all header files in all C programs increases the file size and load of the program.

20) What is the difference between including the header file within angular braces and double quotes?

Ans. When angle brackets (<>) are used, the compiler looks for the file in the built-in include directory path. If we use double quotes (" "), the compiler looks for the file first in the current directory, then in the include directory path if it is not found.

21) Is it possible to create and use a customized header file in C?

Ans. A header file is a file in which built-in or user-defined functions are declared and used in the main program, resulting in a customized header file. When writing a large C program, a custom header file comes in handy.

22) What are the differences among main(), void main(), and int main()?

Ans. The void main() function neither returns any value nor takes any command-line arguments. Both main() and int main() functions indicate that the function returns data of the integer type but does not take any arguments.

23) Can a program be compiled without a main() function?

Ans. A main() function is required in all C programs to serve as the program's starting point. It is still possible to compile the program if there is no main() function, but it is impossible to run it. The program execution usually stops at the end of the main() function.

24) Can the main() function left empty?

Ans. It is possible to leave the main() function blank. In this situation, the program starts execution, and nothing will happen.

25) What are comments, and how do we insert them in a C program?

Ans. In a C program, comments are explanations of the source code. It improves the readability of the program. In a program, there are two ways to insert comments.

a) Single-line comments begin with a double slash (//).

b) Comments beginning with a slash asterisk (/*) and ending with an asterisk slash (*/) can appear anywhere in the code.

26) Are comments included during the compilation stage and placed in the .exe file as well?

Ans. When the compiler encounters comments, they are disregarded during the compilation stage and are not included in the execution file. Other than improving readability, comments do not influence program functionality.

27) What is the use of a semicolon (;) at the end of every program statement?

Ans. The semicolon serves as a delimiter and marks the conclusion of a statement. As a result, the compiler can break down the statement into smaller chunks to check for syntax errors.

28) What is a variable?

Ans. A variable is a unique identifier that points to a specific memory location and stores data. Variables are changeable, and their values can be altered while a program is running.

29) What is the difference between variable declaration and definition?

Ans. A variable's declaration only specifies the variable's name, data type, and initial value, if any, but it does not allocate memory. The definition, on the other hand, assigns a data type to the variable and allocates memory. In C, there is no distinction between defining and declaring a variable, and they are usually done simultaneously.

30) What is variable initialization, and why is it important?

Ans. The term "initialization" refers to the process of assigning a value to a variable before it is used in a program. Without initialization, the variable would have an unknown value from the memory location assigned to it, resulting in unpredictable results when used in other operations.

31) Is it possible to initialize a variable at the time it was declared?

Ans. In C, it is allowed to initialize variables with values at the time they are declared.

32) What is the modulus operator?

Ans. The modulus operator (%) is an arithmetic operator that yields the remainder of an integer division.

33) What is the remainder for 5.0%2?

Ans. Because the modulus operator can only be used for integer division, and one of the operands for the above % operator is a real value, it would be an invalid operation.

34) What is type casting?

Ans. Converting one data type to another is known as typecasting or type conversion. It can be either implicit (done automatically by the compiler) or explicit (done by the user). When an expression has multiple data types, implicit type casting is used. Type conversion is performed to avoid any data loss.

35) What is constant?

Ans. Constants are fixed values that cannot be altered while the program is running. Constants can be int, float, char, or any other basic data type.

36) Define modifier? What are the modifiers available in C?

Ans. Modifiers are C keywords that increase or decrease the amount of memory space assigned to a variable. They are prefixed with basic data types. Short, long, signed, and unsigned are the four modifiers used in C.

37) Is it possible to use curly braces to enclose a single statement?

Ans. There is no error if a single statement is enclosed in curly braces, and the program compiles and runs fine. Curly braces, on the other hand, are most commonly employed to enclose a set of multiple statements or lines of code.

38) Describe the escape sequence with an example.

Ans. In C, an escape sequence is a set of characters that do not represent themselves but are instead transformed into another character or set of characters. It consists of a backslash (\) and one or more letters that represent the escape sequence. The character \n, for example, is an escape sequence that represents a newline character.

39) How do we construct an increment or decrement statement?

Ans. The increment operator ++ and the decrement operator can create an increment or decrement statement. Both can be used as a prefix (++x, −−x) or postfix (x++, x−−) with variables.

40) What are the differences between sum++ and ++sum, where the sum is an integer type variable?

Ans. sum++ is a postfix operator, which means that the expression is evaluated first with the current sum value. Then the sum value is increased by 1. ++sum, on the other hand, is a prefix operator that signifies the sum value is increased by 1 before the expression is evaluated with the new sum value.

41) What are the different categories of C operators in terms of operand numbers?

Ans. Three categories of operators in C language are as follows:

i) *Unary:* Operators operate on a single operand. Example: sizeof(), ++,−−, etc.

ii) *Binary:* Operators operate on two operands. Example: +,−, =, *, /, %, ==, >, <=, etc.

iii) *Ternary:* Operators operate on three operands. ?: is the only C ternary operator.

42) Can we use int data type to store the value 32768? Why?

Ans. Because the int data type can only store values from −32768 to 32767 ($-2^{15}$ to $2^{15}-1$), it cannot be used to store the value 32768. To store the value 32768, we can use unsigned int or long in.

43) What is wrong in the statement- "scanf("%d", num);"?

Ans. scanf() is a built-in library function that reads a value of a specific data type from the standard input terminal and stores it in the memory locations reserved for the corresponding variable. As a result, the variable name num must be preceded by the address operator &. Therefore, the preceding statement results in a run-time error.

44) The % symbol has particular use in printf() statement. How would we output this character on the screen?

Ans The printf() function can be used to display the % symbol by using %%. For example, to have the output appear as 80% on the screen, write printf("80%%");

45) What does the format %5.2 mean when included in printf() statement?

Ans. This format is employed for two purposes. To begin with, place 5 before the decimal point to specify the number of spaces for the output number. The second integer following the decimal point is used to specify how many decimal places the output number should have. Additional space characters are introduced if the number of spaces filled by the output number is less than 5.

46) What is the purpose of the keyword typedef?

Ans. The keyword typedef is used to create a new name to an existing type or simplify a type's complex declaration. It does not result in the creation of a new data type. For instance, after following the type definition

typedef unsigned long int byte;

the identifier byte can be used as an abbreviation for the type unsigned long int, such as

byte x; is equivalent to declaring unsigned long int x;

47) What is the output of the following program?

```
void main(){
    int a=10, b=7;
    printf("%i", a+b);}
```

Ans. In C, %i is a valid format specifier that serves the same purpose as %d. As a result, the program above will display 17 on the screen.

48) What should be the output of the following program?

```
void main(){
    int a=10/3;
    printf("%d", a);}
```

Ans. Instead of 3.33, the program displays 3 on the screen. The decimal part is discarded because the result of integer division (int/int) is simply an int.

49) What should be the output of the following program?

```
void main(){
    int a=40, b=50;
    printf("%d, %d, ", a++, b--);
    printf("%d, %d", ++a,--b);}
```

Ans. 40, 50, 42, 48

Because, for the first printf() values of a and b are displayed and then increment or decrement operation is performed, a=a+1=41, b=b−1=49. For the second printf(), values of a is incremented, and b is decremented, then the values are displayed. Thus, a=a+1=42 and b=b−1=48 are displayed.

50) What are the values of x, y, and z after the following program statements execute?

```
    int x=10, y, z;
y = x++;
z = ++x;
```

Ans. x=12, y=10, z=12

Because in the y=x++ statement, the value of x=10 is first assigned to y, and then it is incremented to x=10+1=11. After that, in the z=++x statement, value of x=11 is first incremented to x=11+1=12, and then 12 is assigned to z.

## Problems to Practice

1) Write a program to print the sentence "Hello! Atiqur Rahman! How are you?" on the screen.

2) Write a program to input an integer and then print the integer value.

3) Write a program that enters two integer values and displays the summation on the screen.

4) Write a program that will input two floating-point numbers and then display the product on the screen.

5) Write a program to input two integers and show the result of the division.

6) Write a program to calculate the area and circumference of a circle.

7) Write a program to calculate the power of a number.

8) Write a program to find the size of the data types int, float, double, and char.

9) Write a program that swaps two numbers.

10) Write a program to display the ASCII code of a character entered by the user.

11) Write a program to display the ASCII codes of consecutive ten characters where the starting character is entered by the user.

12) Write a program to display your name, date of birth, and mobile number.

13) Write a program to print a block F using hash (#), where the F has a height of seven characters and width of five and four characters.

14) Write a program to compute the perimeter and area of a circle with a radius of 6 inches.

15) Write a program that reads no. of days and converts it into years, weeks, and days.

16) Write a program that reads and converts Centigrade to Fahrenheit.

17) Write a program to input an employee's ID, total worked hours in a day, and the amount he received per hour. Print the employee's ID and monthly salary with two decimal places.

18) Write a program to input the coordinates of two points and calculate the distance between them.

19) Write a program to generate a random number.

20) Write a program to calculate perimeter of a rectangle. Take sides a and b from the user.

21) Take a number n from the user and display its cube.

22) Write a program to display the average of any three numbers. Take the numbers from the user.

# CHAPTER 2

# Flow Control

F LOW CONTROL REFERS TO the sequence in which individual function calls, instructions, or statements are executed when a program is running. Based on the output of an expression, a decision is made on which of the several paths to pursue using a control flow statement. Branching and looping are the two types of control flow available in C.

## 2.1 IF STATEMENT

The statements inside the body of the "if" are executed only if the condition is true. If the condition is false, the "if" statement's body is skipped, and normal execution resumes after the body. Structure of if statement is as follows:

```
if (conditions){
        //blocks of valid C statements
        //these statements are executed if the conditions
        //return true or 1
}
//valid C statements
```

Flow diagram of if statement is as follows:

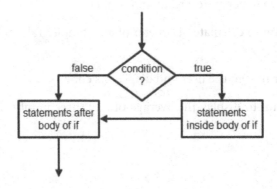

DOI: 10.1201/9781003302629-2

## 2.2 IF..ELSE STATEMENT

If the condition is true, the statements in the body of the "if" statement are executed, skipping the statements in the body of the "else" statement. If the condition is false, the statements in the body of the "else" statement are executed, skipping the statements in the body of the "if" statement. Structure of if..else statement is as follows:

```
if (conditions){
        //blocks of valid C statements
        //these statements are executed if the conditions
        //return true or 1
}
else{
        //blocks of valid C statements
        //these statements are executed if the conditions
        //return false or 0
}
//valid C statements
```

Flow diagram of if..else statement is as follows:

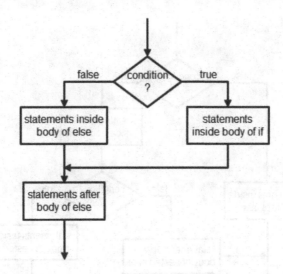

Using opening and closing curly braces is optional if the body of the "if" or "else" includes a single sentence.

## 2.3 NESTED IF..ELSE STATEMENT

If if..else statements are used inside the body of another "if" or "else" statement, it is called nested if..else statement. Structure of nested if..else statements is as follows:

```
if (condition1){
        //blocks of valid C statements
```

```
            /*these statements including following if..else
            statements are executed if condition1 returns 1*/
            if (condition2){
                    //blocks of valid C statements
                    //these statements are executed if
                    //condition2 is true
            }
            else{
                    //blocks of valid C statements
                    //these statements are executed if
                    //condition2 is false
            }
    }
    else{
            //blocks of valid C statements
            //these statements are executed if condition1 is
            //false
    }
```

Flow diagram of nested if..else statement is as follows:

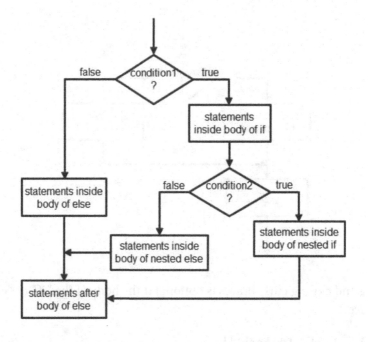

## 2.4 CONDITIONAL OPERATOR

The conditional operator in C is similar to the if..else statement. The if..else statement requires multiple statements to complete a task; the conditional operator can do the same operation in a single statement. It is also known as the ternary operator because it operates on three operands. It helps in the quickest possible writing of the if..else statement.

Syntax of the conditional operator is as follows:

variable = expression1? expression2: expression3

Using if..else statement, the ternary operator (?:) can be visualized as follows:

```
if (expression1)

        variable = expression2;

else

        variable = expression3;
```

Flow diagram of the ternary operator is as follows:

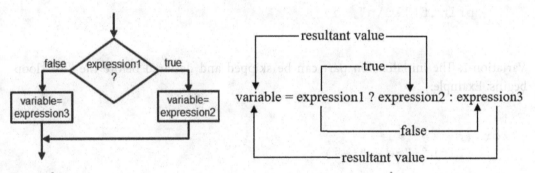

Example:

```
max = (num1>num2) ? num1 : num2;
(num1>=0) ? printf("positive") : printf("negative");
```

## 2.5 FOR LOOP

In C, the "for" loop is used to repeatedly execute a block of statements until certain condition becomes false or returns zero. Syntax of "for" loop is as follows:

```
for (initialization; conditions; increment or decrement){
        //blocks of valid C statements
        //statements are executed repeatedly as long as
        //the conditions are true
}
```

Flow diagram of "for" loop is as follows:

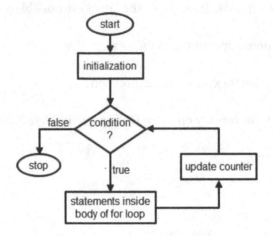

Example:

```
for (i=1; i<=3; i++) {
    printf("%d\n", i);
}
```

Variation-1: The initialization part can be skipped and declared before the "for" loop begins. Example:

```
i=1;
for (; i<=3; i++) {
    printf("%d\n", i);
}
```

Variation-2: The increment or decrement part of the loop can be skipped and done within the body of the "for" loop. Example:

```
for (i=1; i<=3; ) {
    printf("%d\n", i);
    i=i+1;
}
```

Variation-3: In the "for" loop, it is allowed to use multiple initializations, conditions, and/or increments or decrements. Example:

```
for (i=1, j=10; i<=3 && j>=5; i++, j=j-1) {
    printf("%d, %d\n", i, j);
}
```

Nested for loop: Any valid for loop is allowed to use inside another for loop. Example:

```
for (i=1; i<=3; i++){
    printf("%d, ", i);
    for (j=10; i>=5; j=j-1){
        printf("%d\n", j);
    }
}
```

*Note:* If condition in the "for" loop can never be false or always returns 0, it is an infinite loop and using such a condition is a logical error. Example:

```
for (i=10; i>=3; i++){
    printf("%d\n", i);
}
```

## 2.6 WHILE LOOP

In C, a "while" loop is used to repeatedly execute a block of statements until certain condition becomes false or returns zero. Syntax of "while" loop is as follows:

```
initialization;
while (conditions){
        //blocks of valid C statements
        //statements are executed repeatedly as long as
        //the conditions are true
        increment or decrement;
}
```

Flow diagram of "while" loop is as follows:

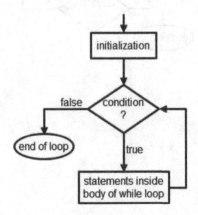

Example:

```
i=1;
while (i<=3){
    printf("%d\n", i);
    i=i+1;
}
```

## 2.7 DO..WHILE LOOP

In C, a do..while loop is used to execute a block of statements until certain condition becomes false or returns 0. Syntax of do..while loop is as follows:

```
initialization;
do{
        //blocks of valid C statements
        //statements are executed repeatedly as long as
        //the conditions are true
        increment or decrement;
}while (conditions);
```

Flow diagram of do..while loop is as follows:

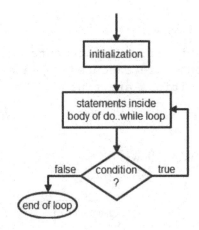

Example:

```
i=1;
do{
    printf("%d\n", i);
    i=i+1;
}
while (i<=3);
```

Differences with "while" loop:

(1) The condition is checked first in a while loop before the statements in the body are executed. Whereas the condition is checked after the loop's body is executed in a do..while loop.

(2) The statements in the body of the do..while loop are executed at least once, even if the condition is false. In contrast, the statements in the body of the while loop are never executed if the condition is false.

(3) A semicolon is used after while (condition) in the do..while loop and no semicolon is used after while (condition) in the while loop.

## 2.8 CONTINUE STATEMENT

When the continue statement appears in a loop, program control moves to the beginning of the loop, skipping the statements following the continue. The flow diagram of the continue statement is as follows:

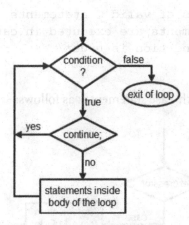

## 2.9 BREAK STATEMENT

When a break statement is found, the program control exits the loop or switch-case instantly. For the practical program of the switch-case, which is discussed later, the break statement should always be used. The flow diagram of the break statement is as follows:

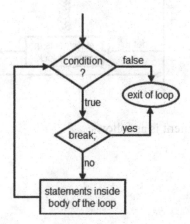

## 2.10 SWITCH..CASE STATEMENT

When there are multiple options to be executed and different tasks must be performed for each option, the switch-case statement is used. The syntax of the switch-case statement is as follows:

```
switch (variable or integer expression) {
    case constant1:
        //blocks of valid C statements
        //statements are executed only if consant1 =
        //variable or integer expression
        break;
    case constant2:
        //blocks of valid C statements
        //statements are executed only if consant2 =
        //variable or integer expression
        break;
    default:
        //blocks of valid C statements
        /*statements are executed in case none of the above
        case condition is true*/
}
```

The flow diagram of the switch-case statement is as follows:

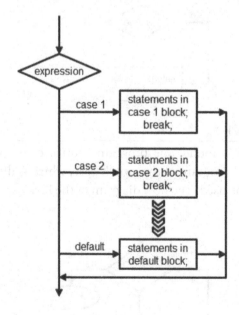

Example of switch-case statement is as follows:

```
int i=2;
switch (i) {
```

```
    case 1:
        printf("case 1");
        break;
    case 2:
        printf("case 2");
        break;
    default:
        printf("default");
}
```

The output of this program is case 2.

If no break statement is used, then the output is case 1 case 2 default.

The break statement causes the program control to exit the switch body. After default, using the break statement is optional and does not affect the program flow or output.

## 2.11 GOTO STATEMENT

When a goto statement is encountered, the program control jumps to the label specified in the goto statement right away. The syntax of the goto statement is as follows:

goto label_name;
    //block-1 of valid C statements
label_name:
    //block-2 of valid C statements
    /*statements are executed as soon as the above goto is encountered, skipping the block-1 statements*/

The flow diagram of the goto statement is as follows:

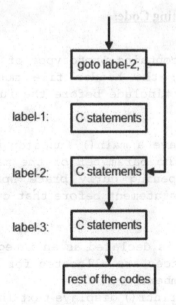

## 2.12 EXAMPLES

### PROBLEM-01
**Write a program to check whether a given number is positive or negative.**

Programming Code of the Solution:

```c
#include <stdio.h>
int main(){
    int num;
    printf("Enter a number: ");
    scanf("%d", &num);
    if (num>=0)
        printf("%d is a positive number.", num);
    else
        printf("%d is a negative number.", num);
    return 0;
}
```

Input and Output of the Executed Program:

```
Enter a number: 45
45 is a positive number.
```

```
Enter a number: -3
-3 is a negative number.
```

### Explanation of the Programming Code:

**#include <stdio.h>**
/*header file stdio.h contains prototypes of the library functions printf(), and scanf(); the header file must be included using preprocessor directive #include before the functions are called in the program*/
**int main(){**
/*all C program must have a main() function with return type void or int; here there is no parameter of the main() function and it returns an integer; opening curly brace specifies start of the main() function and no statement before that curly brace is executed by the compiler*/
    **int num;**
    /*the variable num is declared as an integer type variable, and required memory spaces are allocated for num*/
    **printf("Enter a number: ");**
    /*output function printf() displays text in the double quotations as it is on the screen*/

```
scanf("%d", &num);
```
/*when a value is entered from input terminal, the scanf()
function assigns it to num; the address operator, which must be
used before the variable name since the input value is placed
in the memory location allocated for that variable*/
```
if (num>=0)
```
/*if num is greater than or equal to zero then it is true or 1,
and the following statement is executed*/
```
        printf("%d is a positive number.", num);
```
/*this printf() displays the text inside the quotations
as it is on the screen except for the value of num is
replaces the format specifier %d; as there is only one
statement in the body of if loop no curly brace is
required*/
```
else
```
/*if the above condition is false, then the following statement
is executed*/
```
        printf("%d is a negative number.", num);
```
/*printf() function displays the text inside the quotations
as it is on the screen except for the value of num is
replaces %d; as there is only one statement in the body
of else loop, no curly brace is required*/
```
return 0;
```
/*0 is returned as it is the standard for the successful
execution of the program*/
```
}
```
/*the closing curly brace specifies the end of the main() function's
body, as well as the program's end; after that curly brace, no
statement is executed*/

## PROBLEM-02
**Write a program to check whether a number is even or odd.**

<u>Programming Code of the Solution:</u>

```
#include <stdio.h>
int main(){
    int num;
    printf("Enter an integer to check: ");
    scanf("%d", &num);
    if (num%2)
        printf("%d is odd number.", num);
    else
        printf("%d is even number.", num);
    return 0;
}
```

Input and Output of the Executed Program:

```
Enter an integer to check: 7
7 is odd number.
```

```
Enter an integer to check: 18
18 is even number.
```

## Explanation of the Programming Code:

```
#include <stdio.h>
```
/*header file stdio.h contains prototypes of the library functions printf(), and scanf(); the header file must be included using preprocessor directive #include before the functions are called in the program*/
```
int main(){
```
/*all C program must have a main() function with return type void or int; here there is no parameter of the main() function and it returns an integer; opening curly brace specifies start of the main() function and no statement before that curly brace is executed by the compiler*/
```
    int num;
```
/*integer type variable num is declared that stores only integers*/
```
    printf("Enter an integer to check: ");
```
/*output function printf() displays the text inside the double quotes as it is on standard output screen*/
```
    scanf("%d", &num);
```
/*scanf() reads an integer from the input terminal and assigns the value to num*/
```
    if (num%2)
```
/*num is divided by 2 and returns 0 or 1 depending on value of num; 0 corresponds to false and 1 corresponds to true; if the remainder is 1 following statement is executed*/
```
        printf("%d is odd number.", num);
```
/*printf() function displays the text inside double quotations as it is on screen except for the value of num replaces the format specifier %d*/
```
    else
```
/*if num%2 returns 0, then the condition of 'if' is false and following statement is executed*/
```
        printf("%d is even number.", num);
```
/*printf() function displays the text inside double quotations as it is on the screen except for the value of num replaces the format specifier %d*/
```
    return 0;
```
/*0 is returned as it is the standard for the successful execution of the program*/

}
/*the closing curly brace specifies the end of the main() function's body, as well as the program's end; after that curly brace, no statement is executed*/

## PROBLEM-03
**Write a program to check whether a character is an alphabet or not.**

Programming Code of the Solution:

```c
#include <stdio.h>
int main(){
    char ch;
    printf("Enter a character: ");
    scanf("%c", &ch);
    if ((ch >= 'a' && ch <= 'z') || (ch >= 'A' && ch<= 'Z'))
        printf("%c is an alphabet.", ch);
    else
        printf("%c is not an alphabet.", ch);
    return 0;
}
```

Input and Output of the Executed Program:

```
Enter a character: 9
9 is not an alphabet.
```

```
Enter a character: s
s is an alphabet.
```

Explanation of the Programming Code:

**#include <stdio.h>**
/*header file stdio.h contains prototypes of the library functions printf(), and scanf(); the header file must be included using preprocessor directive #include before the functions are called in the program*/
**int main(){**
/*all C program must have a main() function with return type void or int; here there is no parameter of the main() function and it returns an integer; opening curly brace specifies start of the main() function and no statement before that curly brace is executed by the compiler*/
    **char ch;**
    /*character type variable ch is declare that is used to store the character to check*/
    **printf("Enter a character: ");**
    /*output function printf() displays text in the double quotations as it is on the screen*/

```
    scanf("%c", &ch);
    /*input function scanf() reads a character from the input
    terminal and assigns the character to ch*/
    if ((ch >= 'a' && ch <= 'z') || (ch >= 'A' && ch<= 'Z'))
    /*first two conditions check if the ch is a small letter;
    the last two conditions check whether the ch is a capital
    letter; if ch is either a small letter or a capital letter
    above expression returns true=1 and the following statement is
    executed*/
            printf("%c is an alphabet.", ch);
            /*this printf() function displays %c is an alphabet
            with the value of ch replaces the format specifier %c*/
    else
    /*if ch is neither a small letter nor a capital letter above
    expression of 'if' returns false = 0 and following statement is
    executed*/
            printf("%c is not an alphabet.", ch);
            /*printf() function displays the text inside double
            quotations as it is on the screen except for the
            character ch replaces the format specifier %c*/
    return 0;
    /*0 is returned as it is the standard for the successful
    execution of the program*/
}
/*the closing curly brace specifies the end of the main() function's
body, as well as the program's end; after that curly brace, no
statement is executed*/
```

## PROBLEM-04
**Write a program to count the number of digits in an integer.**

Programming Code of the Solution:

```
#include <stdio.h>
int main(){
    long long num, num1;
    int count = 0;
    printf("Enter an integer: ");
    scanf("%lld", &num);
    num1=num;
    while (num1 != 0){
        num1 = num1/10;
        count++;
    }
    printf("Number of digits in %lld is: %d", num, count);
    return 0;
}
```

Input and Output of the Executed Program:

```
Enter an integer: 4586
Number of digits in 4586 is: 4
```

## Explanation of the Programming Code:

```c
#include <stdio.h>
```
/*header file stdio.h contains prototypes of the library functions printf(), and scanf(); the header file must be included using preprocessor directive #include before the functions are called in the program*/
```c
int main(){
```
/*all C program must have a main() function with return type void or int; here there is no parameter of the main() function and it returns an integer; opening curly brace specifies start of the main() function and no statement before that curly brace is executed by the compiler*/
```c
    long long num, num1;
```
/*two long long integer data type num and num1 are declared to store large values*/
```c
    int count = 0;
```
/*integer type variable count is declared and initialized to 0*/
```c
    printf("Enter an integer: ");
```
/*output function printf() displays text in the double quotations as it is on the screen*/
```c
    scanf("%lld", &num);
```
/*scanf() reads a value from the input terminal and the value is assigned to variable num; %lld is the format specifier for long long int type data*/
```c
    num1=num;
```
/*value of num is assigned to num1; we did this assignment to keep the value of num unchanged as we want to show the value on the screen later; and we use num1 to separate and count the digits in the while loop*/
```c
    while (num1!= 0){
```
/*if num1≠0, the statements enclosed by curly braces are executed; after execution of the body the condition is re-checked; these steps continue until num1=0 at which point the program flow exits the loop*/
```c
        num1 = num1/10;
```
/*in each iteration num is divided by 10, last digit is truncated and new value is assigned to num*/
```c
        count++;
```
/*value of count is incremented by 1 in each iteration for each last digit of the number; if num=238 then

```
After 1st iteration- num=238/10=23, count=0+1=1
After 2nd iteration- num=23/10=2, count=1+1=2
After 3rd iteration- num=2/10=0, count=2+1=3*/
}
/*this closing curly brace specifies the end of the body of the
while loop*/
printf("Number of digits in %lld is: %d", num, count);
/*printf() function displays the text inside the quotations as
it is on the screen, except for the value of num replaces the
format specifier %lld and the value of count replaces %d*/
return 0;
/*0 is returned as it is the standard for the successful
execution of the program*/
}
/*the closing curly brace specifies the end of the main() function's
body, as well as the program's end; after that curly brace, no
statement is executed*/
```

## PROBLEM-05
**Write a program to generate and display multiplication table of a number entered by user.**

Programming Code of the Solution:

```c
#include <stdio.h>
int main(){
    int num, i;
    printf("Enter an integer to display the multiplication table: ");
    scanf("%d", &num);
    for (i=1; i<=10; i++)
        printf("%dx%d = %d\n", num, i, num*i);
    return 0;
}
```

Input and Output of the Executed Program:

```
Enter an integer to display the multiplication table: 6
6x1 = 6
6x2 = 12
6x3 = 18
6x4 = 24
6x5 = 30
6x6 = 36
6x7 = 42
6x8 = 48
6x9 = 54
6x10 = 60
```

**Explanation of the Programming Code:**

```
#include <stdio.h>
```
/*header file stdio.h contains prototypes of the library functions printf(), and scanf(); the header file must be included using preprocessor directive #include before the functions are called in the program*/
```
int main(){
```
/*all C program must have a main() function with return type void or int; here there is no parameter of the main() function and it returns an integer; opening curly brace specifies start of the main() function and no statement before that curly brace is executed by the compiler*/
```
        int num, i;
```
/*two integer type variables are declared*/
```
        printf("Enter an integer to display the multiplication"
               "table:");
```
/*output function printf() displays text in the double quotations as it is on the screen*/
```
        scanf("%d", &num);
```
/*scanf() reads an integer from input terminal and stores the value in the memory locatin assigned for; therefore, format specifier %d is used and address operator & is used with the variable name*/
```
        for (i=1; i<=10; i++)
```
/*i=1 is the initialization, i<=10 is the condition, i++ is the increment; its body contains only one statement, hence no curly brace is required; initialization is done once at the beginning of the loop; the condition is then checked, if it is true, the body is executed;. the condition is re-checked after incrementing the value of i by 1; these steps are repeated until i>0, at which point the program flow exits the loop*/
```
                printf("%dx%d = %d\n", num, i, num*i);
```
/*this printf() displays the text inside the double quotes as it is on the screen except for the value of num replaces the 1st format specifier %d, the value of i replaces the 2nd %d, the result of expression num×i replaces the 3rd %d and a newline replaces \n*/
```
        return 0;
```
/*0 is returned as it is the standard for the successful execution of the program*/
```
}
```
/*the closing curly brace specifies the end of the main() function's body, as well as the program's end; after that curly brace, no statement is executed*/

## PROBLEM-06

**Write a program to determine and display the sum of the following harmonic series for a given value of n.**

$$1 + \frac{1}{2} + \frac{1}{3} + \cdots + \frac{1}{n}$$

The value of n should be given interactively through the terminal.

<u>Flowchart of the Solution:</u>

Figure 2.1 shows the flowchart followed to solve this problem.

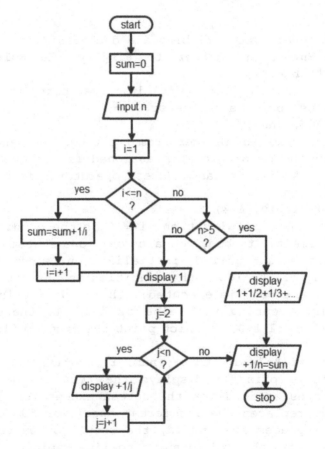

FIGURE 2.1   Flowchart followed to solve the problem.

## <u>Algorithm of the Solution:</u>

Step-1: Start

Step-2: Initialize sum←0

Step-3: Read value of n

Step-4: Initialize i←1

Step-5: If i<=n

    5.1: sum←sum+1/i

    5.2: i←i+1

    5.3: Go to Step-5

Step-6: If n>5

    6.1: Display 1+1/2+1/3+...

    6.2: Go to Step-10

Step-7: Display 1

Step-8: Initialize j←2

Step-9: If j<n

    9.1: Display +1/j

    9.2: j←j+1

    9.3: Go to Step-9

Step-10: Display +1/n=sum

Step-11: Stop

<u>Programming Code of the Solution:</u>

```c
#include <stdio.h>
int main(){
    int n, i, j;
    float sum=0;
    printf("Please enter an integer: ");
    scanf("%d", &n);
    for (i=1; i<=n; i++)
        sum=sum+(1/(float)i);
    if (n>5)
        printf("1 + 1/2 + 1/3 + ...");
    else{
        printf("1");
        for (j=2; j<n; j++)
            printf(" + 1/%d", j);
    }
    printf(" + 1/%d = %0.2f\n", n, sum);
    return 0;
}
```

Input and Output of the Executed Program:

```
Please enter an integer: 11
1 + 1/2 + 1/3 + ... + 1/11 = 3.02
```

## Explanation of the Programming Code:

```
#include <stdio.h>
```
/*header file stdio.h contains prototypes of the library functions printf(), and scanf(); the header file must be included using preprocessor directive #include before the functions are called in the program*/
```
int main(){
```
/*all C program must have a main() function with return type void or int; here there is no parameter of the main() function and it returns an integer; opening curly brace specifies start of the main() function and no statement before that curly brace is executed by the compiler*/
```
    int n, i, j;
```
/*three int type variables are declared; compiler assigns required spaces in memory for these three variables*/
```
    float sum=0;
```
/*the float type variable sum is declared and initialized to 0; this variable is used in the summation operation; thus, it must be initialized to 0; otherwise, some garbage value is added in the first addition, and we get the wrong answer; because when a variable is declared, memory space is allocated for that variable, and the assigned memory space may contain some garbage value*/
```
    printf("Please enter an integer: ");
```
/*output library function printf() displays the text inside the double quotes as it is on the standard output terminal*/
```
    scanf("%d", &n);
```
/*input library function scanf() reads an integer from input terminal and stores the value in the memory location assigned for n*/
```
    for (i=1; i<=n; i++)
```
/*i=1 is initialization, i<=n is condition and i++ is increment; initialization is done once at the beginning of the loop; next the condition is checked, and if it is true, the statement in the body is executed; the value of i is incremented by 1 before the condition is re-checked; this process continues until the condition becomes false at which point the program flow exits the loop*/

```
        sum=sum+(1/(float)i);
        /*in each iteration of the loop, the type of i is converted
        to float from int, so that 1/i gives a decimal value;
        this action sequentially adds 1/1, 1/2, 1/3, . . . to the
        sum*/
if (n>5)
/*if n>5 then the condition is true and following statement is
executed*/
        printf("1 + 1/2 + 1/3 + . . . ");
        /*this printf() function displays the text inside the
        double quotations as it is on the screen*/
else{
/*statements in the body of else, enclosed by curly braces, are
executed if the condition of 'if' is false, that is, n<=5*/
        printf("1");
        /*output function printf() displayes 1 on the screen*/
        for (j=2; j<n; j++)
        /*j=2 is initialization, i<=n is condition and i++ is
        increment; initialization is done once at the beginning
        of the loop; then the condition is checked, and if it is
        true, the statement in the body is executed; the value of
        j is incremented by 1 before the condition is re-checked;
        these procedures are repeated until the condition is no
        longer true at which point the program flow exits the
        loop*/
            printf(" + 1/%d", j);
            /*printf() function displays the text inside the double
            quores as it is on the screen except for the value of j
            replaces the format specifier %d*/
}
/*this closing curly brace specifies the end of else*/
printf(" + 1/%d = %0.2f\n", n, sum);
/*the printf() function displays the text in the double-quotes
as it is on the screen, with the exception that the value of n
replaces the format specifier %d, the value of sum replaces the
format specifier %0.2f with two decimal points precision, and
a newline replaces \n*/
return 0;
/*0 is returned as it is the standard for the successful
execution of the program*/
}
/*the closing curly brace specifies the end of the main() function's
body, as well as the program's end; after that curly brace, no
statement is executed*/
```

**PROBLEM-07**

**Write a program to find the number and sum of all integers greater than 100 and less than 200 divisible by 7.**

Flowchart of the Solution:

Figure 2.2 shows the flowchart followed to solve this problem.

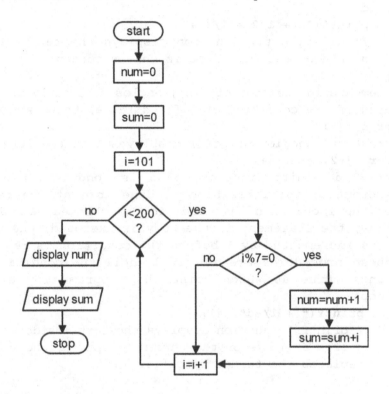

FIGURE 2.2   Flowchart followed to solve the problem.

## Algorithm of the Solution:

Step-1: Start

Step-2: Initialize num←0, sum←0 and i←101

Step-3: If i<200

3.1: If i%7=0

    3.1.1: num←num+1

    3.1.2: sum←sum+i

3.2: i←i+1

3.3: Go to Step-3

Step-4: Display values of num and sum

Step-5: Stop

## Programming Code of the Solution:

```c
#include <stdio.h>
int main(){
    int num=0, sum=0, i;
    for (i=101; i<200; i++)
        if (!(i%7)){
            num++;
            sum+=i;
        }
    printf("Number of required integers is: %d\n", num);
    printf("Sum of all required integers is: %d\n", sum);
    return 0;
}
```

## Input and Output of the Executed Program:

```
Number of required integers is: 14
Sum of all required integers is: 2107
```

## Explanation of the Programming Code:

`#include <stdio.h>`
/*header file stdio.h contains prototypes of the library functions printf(), and scanf(); the header file must be included using preprocessor directive #include before the functions are called in the program*/
`int main(){`
/*all C programs must have a main() function with return type void or int; here, there is no parameter of the main() function, and it returns an integer; opening curly brace specifies the start of the main() function and no statement before that curly brace is executed by the compiler*/

```
int num=0, sum=0, i;
```
/*three integer type variables are declared; variables num and sum are initialized to 0; otherwise, some garbage values are added in the first summation involving num and sum, and we get the wrong answers; this is because memory spaces are allocated for the variables when they are declared, and the assigned memory spaces may contain some garbage values*/

```
for (i=101; i<200; i++)
```
/*i=101 is the initialization, i<200 is the condition, i++ is the increment; the body of this for loop simply comprises the following if statement, thus no curly brace is required; the condition is checked once at the beginning of the loop; if it is true, the next if statement is executed; the value of i is incremented by 1 before the condition is re-checked; these processes continue until i=200, at which point the program flow exits the loop*/

```
    if (!(i%7)){
```
/*i=101 is divided by 7 in the first iteration; if the remainder is 0, the condition is true, then the body of the 'if' is executed; the second iteration starts with i=102 being divided by 7; these processes continue until the value of i reaches 200; hence, all values from 101 to 199 are sequentially checked*/

```
        num++;
```
/*if i is divisible by 7, the value of num is incremented by 1*/

```
        sum+=i;
```
/*if i is divisible by 7, value i is added with sum*/

```
    }
```
/*this closing curly brace specifies the end of the 'if' condition; because this 'if' is the lone statement in the 'for' loop, it also marks the end of the 'for' loop*/

```
printf("Number of required integers is: %d\n", num);
```
/*printf() function displays the text in the double quotes as it is on the screen except for the value of num replaces the format specifier %d and a newline replaces\n*/

```
printf("Sum of all required integers is: %d\n", sum);
```
/*printf() function displays the text in the double quotes as it is on the screen except for the value of sum replaces the format specifier %d and a newline replaces \n*/

```
return 0;
```
/*0 is returned as it is the standard for the successful execution of the program*/

```
}
```
/*the closing curly brace specifies the end of the main() function's body, as well as the program's end; after that curly brace, no statement is executed*/

**PROBLEM-08**

**Write a program to compute the roots of a quadratic equation:**

$$ax^2 + bx + c = 0$$

The program should request the values of the constants a, b, and c and display the values of the roots.

Flowchart of the Solution:

Figure 2.3 shows the flowchart followed to solve this problem.

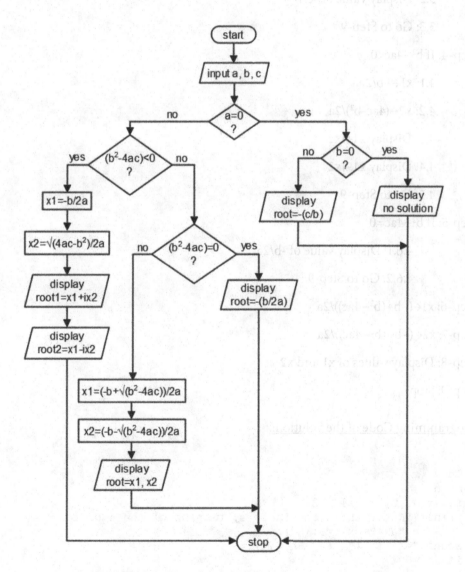

FIGURE 2.3   Flowchart followed to solve the problem.

## Algorithm of the Solution:

Step-1: Start

Step-2: Read values of a, b, and c

Step-3: If a=0

   3.1: If b=0

      3.1.1: Display 'no solution'

      3.1.2: Go to Step-9

   3.2: Display value of -c/b

   3.3: Go to Step-9

Step-4: If $b^2-4ac<0$

   4.1: x1←−b/2a

   4.2: x2←(4ac−b²)/2a

   4.3: Display x1+ix2

   4.4: Display x1−ix2

   4.5: Go to Step-9

Step-5: If $b^2-4ac=0$

      4.6.1: Display value of -b/2a

      4.6.2: Go to Step-9

Step-6: x1←(−b+(b²−4ac))/2a

Step-7: x2←(−b−(b²−4ac))/2a

Step-8: Display values of x1 and x2

Step-9: Stop

Programming Code of the Solution:

```
#include <stdio.h>
#include <math.h>
int main(){
    float a, b, c, x1, x2;
    printf("Enter three constants a, b and c of the equation "
            "ax^2+bx+c=0:\n");
    scanf("%f %f %f", &a, &b, &c);
    if (a==0){
        if (b==0)
            printf("Sorry, there is no solution to the equation.\n");
```

```
        else
            printf("The only root of the equation is: %0.2f\n", -(c/b));
    }
    else if ((b*b-4*a*c)<0){
        x1=-b/(2*a);
        x2=sqrt(4*a*c-b*b)/(2*a);
        printf("Two imaginary roots of the equation are:\n");
        printf("(1) %0.2f+i%0.2f\n(2) %0.2f-i%0.2f\n", x1, x2, x1, x2);
    }
    else if ((b*b-4*a*c)==0)
        printf("The only root of the equation is: %0.2f\n", -b/(2*a));
    else{
        x1=(-b+sqrt(b*b-4*a*c))/(2*a);
        x2=(-b-sqrt(b*b-4*a*c))/(2*a);
        printf("The roots of the equation are: %0.2f and %0.2f\n",
                x1, x2);
    }
    return 0;
}
```

Input and Output of the Executed Program:

```
Enter three constants a, b and c of the equation ax^2+bx+c=0:
0 0 4
Sorry, there is no solution to the equation.
```

```
Enter three constants a, b and c of the equation ax^2+bx+c=0:
0 5 8
The only root of the equation is: -1.60
```

```
Enter three constants a, b and c of the equation ax^2+bx+c=0:
2 4 2
The only root of the equation is: -1.00
```

```
Enter three constants a, b and c of the equation ax^2+bx+c=0:
6 4 2
Two imaginary roots of the equation are:
(1) -0.33+i0.47
(2) -0.33-i0.47
```

```
Enter three constants a, b and c of the equation ax^2+bx+c=0:
2 8 2
The roots of the equation are: -0.27 and -3.73
```

## Explanation of the Programming Code:

```
#include <stdio.h>
```
/*header file stdio.h contains prototypes of the library functions
printf(), and scanf(); the header file must be included using

preprocessor directive #include before the functions are called in the program*/

**#include <math.h>**

/*header file math.h contains prototype of the library function sqrt(); the header file must be included using preprocessor directive #include before the function is called in the program*/

**int main(){**

/*all C program must have a main() function with return type void or int; here there is no parameter of the main() function and it returns an integer; opening curly brace specifies start of the main() function and no statement before that curly brace is executed by the compiler*/

    **float a, b, c, x1, x2;**

    /*five float type variables are declared; required memory spaces are assigned for each variable*/

    **printf("Enter three constants a, b and c of the equation"**
        **"ax^2+bx+c=0:\n");**

    /*output function printf() displays the texts inside double quotations as it is on the screen except for a newline replaces \n, here the long string was broken into two lines using two double quotes ("")*/

    **scanf("%f %f %f", &a, &b, &c);**

    /*scanf() function reads three floating point values separated by space, tab or enter from input terminal; 1st value is assigned to a, 2nd value to b and 3rd value to c*/

    **if (a==0){**

    /*if the a=0 then if..else statement is executed; if a≠0, then the program flow jumps to next 'else if' statement skipping the body of this 'if'*/

        **if (b==0)**

    /*if the b=0, then both a=0 and b=0 and following statement is executed*/

        **printf("Sorry, there is no solution to the"**
            **"equation.\n");**

        /*function printf() displays the texts inside double quotations as it is on the screen except for a newline replaces \n*/

    **else**

    /*if b≠0, then a=0 but b≠0 and in that case following statement is executed*/

        **printf("The only root of the equation is: %0.2f\n",**
            **-(c/b));**

        /*output function printf() displays the texts inside double quotations as it is on the screen except for the value of operation - (c/b) replaces the format specifier %0.2f with two decimal points precision and a newline replaces \n*/

```
}
```
/*this is the end of first if statement with the condition
(a==0)*/
**else if ((b\*b-4\*a\*c)<0){**
/*if a≠0, then this else if condition is checked; if b$^2$-4ac<0,
the statements in the body of 'else if' enclosed with curly
braces are executed*/
    **x1=-b/(2\*a);**
    /*first multiplication operation inside first brackets and
    then the division operation are done, the result is assigned
    to x1*/
    **x2=sqrt(4\*a\*c-b\*b)/(2\*a);**
    /*sqrt() function returns the square root value of its
    argument 4ac-b$^2$, this value is divided by 2a and the result
    is assigned to x2*/
    **printf("Two imaginary roots of the equation are:\n");**
    /*output function printf() displays the text inside the
    double quotations as it is on the screen except for a
    newline \n*/
    **printf("(1) %0.2f+i%0.2f\n(2) %0.2f-i%0.2f\n", x1, x2, x1,**
        **x2);**
    /*this printf() function displays the text inside the
    double quotations as it is on the screen except for a
    newline replaces \n; 1st and 3rd format specifiers %0.2f are
    replaced by the values of x1 two decimal points precision
    while 2nd and 4th %0.2f by the values of x2*/
```
}
```
/*this closing curly brace specifies the end of 'else if' with
condition b$^2$-4ac<0*/
**else if ((b\*b-4\*a\*c)==0)**
/*if a≠0 and b$^2$-4ac≥0 then program flow jumps to this 'else if'
condition; if b$^2$-4ac=0, then the statement in this 'else if'
body is executed*/
    **printf("The only root of the equation is: %0.2f\n",**
        **-b/(2\*a));**
    /*this printf() function displays the text inside double
    quotations as it is on the screen except for the format
    specifier %0.2f is replaced by the value of operation - b/2a
    with two decimal points precision and a newline replaces
    \n*/
**else{**
/*statements in the body of this else are executed only if all
the above conditions a==0, b$^2$-4ac<0 and b$^2$-4ac==0 are false*/
    **x1=(-b+sqrt(b\*b-4\*a\*c))/(2\*a);**
    /*sqrt() returns square root of its argument b$^2$-4ac; result
    of operation (-b+√(b$^2$-4ac))/2a is assigned to x1*/

```
x2=(-b-sqrt(b*b-4*a*c))/(2*a);
/*sqrt() returns square root of its argument b²-4ac; result
of operation (-b-√(b²-4ac))/2a is assigned to x1*/
printf("The roots of the equation are: %0.2f and %0.2f\n",
     x1, x2);
/*this printf() function displays the text inside the double
quotes as it is on the screen except for a newline replaces
\n; 1st format specifier %0.2f is replaced by the value of
x1 with two decimal points precision while the 2nd %0.2f by
the value of x2*/
}
/*this closing curly brace specifies the end of else*/
return 0;
/*0 is returned as it is the standard for the successful
execution of the program*/
}
```
/*the closing curly brace specifies the end of the main() function's
body, as well as the program's end; after that curly brace, no
statement is executed*/

## PROBLEM-09
**Write a program to compute the sum of individual digits of a given positive integer number.**

### Flowchart of the Solution:

Figure 2.4 shows the flowchart followed to solve this problem.

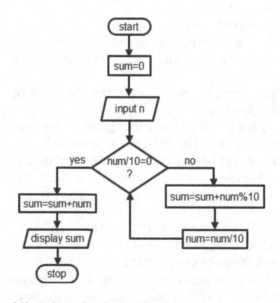

FIGURE 2.4  Flowchart followed to solve the problem.

## Algorithm of the Solution:

Step-1: Start

Step-2: Initialize sum←0

Step-3: Read value of n

Step-4: If (num/10)≠0

      4.1: sum←sum+num%10

      4.2: num←num/10

      4.3: Go to Step-4

Step-5: sum←sum+num

Step-6: Display value of sum

Step-7: Stop

## Programming Code of the Solution:

```
#include <stdio.h>
int main(){
    int sum=0, num;
    printf("Enter any integer: ");
    scanf("%d", &num);
    while (num/10){
        sum+=num%10;
        num=num/10;
    }
    sum+=num;
    printf("The sum of the digits is: %d\n", sum);
    return 0;
}
```

## Input and Output of the Executed Program:

```
Enter any integer: 345
The sum of the digits is: 12
```

## Explanation of the Programming Code:

```
#include <stdio.h>
```
/*header file stdio.h contains prototypes of the library functions
printf(), and scanf(); the header file must be included using

preprocessor directive #include before the functions are called in the program*/
**int main(){**
/*all C program must have a main() function with return type void or int; here there is no parameter of the main() function and it returns an integer; opening curly brace specifies start of the main() function and no statement before that curly brace is executed by the compiler*/

    **int sum=0, num;**
    /*two integer type variables, sum and num, are declared; variable sum is initialized to 0, otherwise some garbage value is added in the first summation involving sum, and we get the wrong answer; this is because when a variable is declared, memory space is allocated for it, and the assigned memory space may contain some garbage value*/
    **printf("Enter any integer: ");**
    /*output function printf() displays text in the double quotations as it is on the screen*/
    **scanf("%d", &num);**
    /*scanf() reads an integer from keyboard and assigns the value to variable num*/
    **while (num/10){**
    /*here num is divided by 10; the statements in the body of while are executed if the quotient is nonzero; for multi-digit numbers, the quotient is nonzero and the condition is true; for single digit numbers, the condition is false since the quotient is zero*/

        **sum+=num%10;**
        /*num contains more than one digit as long as the condition is true; num is divided by 10 and the remainder, which might be the num's last digit, is added with sum in each iteration. */
        **num=num/10;**
        /*num contains more than one digit as long as the condition is true; num is divided by 10 in each iteration, and the quotient, that might be the value with the final digit truncated, is assigned to num; the new assigned value of num is used in the next iteration; if num=386 then
        After 1st iteration-   sum=sum+num%10=0+386%10=0+6=6
                            num=num/10=386/10=38

```
        After 2nd iteration-    sum=sum+num%10=6+38%10=6+8=14
                                num=num/10=38/10=3*/
}
/*this closing curly brace specifies the end of the while
loop*/
sum+=num;
/*when num equals the number's first digit, the program exits
the "while" loop since the condition is false; hence, the first
digit must be added with sum outside the while loop, which is
done in this statement; for above example-
sum=sum+num=14+3=17*/
printf("The sum of the digits is: %d\n", sum);
/*printf() function displays the text in the double quotations
as it is on the screen except for the value of sum replaces the
format specifier %d, and a newline replaces \n*/
return 0;
/*0 is returned as it is the standard for the successful
execution of the program*/
}
/*the closing curly brace specifies the end of the main() function's
body, as well as the program's end; after that curly brace, no
statement is executed*/
```

## PROBLEM-10

**Develop a program to implement a calculator. The program should request the user to input two numbers and display one of the following as per the desire of the user (consider the operators "+", "−", "*", "/", "%" and use "switch" statement):**

(a) Sum of the numbers

(b) Difference of the numbers

(c) Product of the numbers

(d) Division of the numbers

Flowchart of the Solution:

Figure 2.5 shows the flowchart followed to solve this problem.

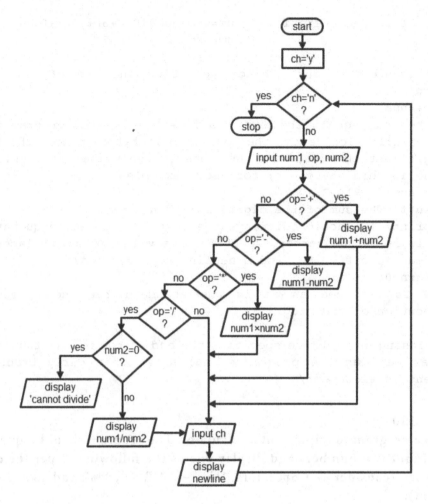

FIGURE 2.5   Flowchart followed to solve the problem.

## Algorithm of the Solution:

Step-1: Start

Step-2: Initialize ch←'y'

Step-3: If ch≠'n'

   3.1: Read values of num1, num2, and op

   3.2: If op='+'

      3.2.1: Display value of num1+num2

      3.2.2: Go to Step-3.6

   3.3: If op='−'

      3.3.1: Display value of num1−num2

      3.3.2: Go to Step-3.6

3.4: If op='*'

    3.4.1: Display value of num1×num2

    3.4.2: Go to Step-3.6

3.5: If op='/'

    3.5.1: If num2≠0

        3.5.1.1: Display value of num1/num2

        3.5.1.2: Go to Step-3.6

    3.5.2: Display 'cannot divide by zero'

3.6: Read value of ch (=y/n)

3.7: Display enter

3.8: Go to Step-3

Step-4: Stop

<u>Programming Code of the Solution:</u>

```c
#include <stdio.h>
#include <conio.h>
int main(){
    char ch='y', op;
    float num1, num2;
    printf("This is a simple calculator...\n");
    while (ch!='n'){
        printf("Enter op1+op2 or op1-op2 or op1*op2 or op1/op2 "
               "followed by enter...\n ");
        scanf("%f %c %f", &num1, &op, &num2);
        switch (op){
            case '+':
                printf("%0.2f + %0.2f = %0.2f\n", num1, num2,
                       num1+num2);
                break;
            case '-':
                printf("%0.2f - %0.2f = %0.2f\n", num1, num2,
                       num1-num2);
                break;
            case '*':
                printf("%0.2f x %0.2f = %0.2f\n", num1, num2,
                       num1*num2);
                break;
            case '/':
                if (num2)
                    printf("%0.2f / %0.2f = %0.2f\n", num1,
                           num2, num1/num2);
                else
                    printf("Cannot divide by zero.\n");
        }
```

```
        printf(" Want to do another operation? (y/n): ");
        ch=getche();
        printf("\n");
    }
    return 0;
}
```

Input and Output of the Executed Program:

```
This is a simple calculator...
Enter op1+op2 or op1-op2 or op1*op2 or op1/op2 followed by enter...
5+3
5.00 + 3.00 = 8.00
Want to do another operation? (y/n): y
Enter op1+op2 or op1-op2 or op1*op2 or op1/op2 followed by enter...
8-12
8.00 - 12.00 = -4.00
Want to do another operation? (y/n): y
Enter op1+op2 or op1-op2 or op1*op2 or op1/op2 followed by enter...
5/0
Cannot divide by zero.
Want to do another operation? (y/n): y
Enter op1+op2 or op1-op2 or op1*op2 or op1/op2 followed by enter...
8.1*3.4
8.10 x 3.40 = 27.54
Want to do another operation? (y/n): n
```

Explanation of the Programming Code:

**#include <stdio.h>**
/*header file stdio.h contains prototypes of the library functions printf(), and scanf(); the header file must be included using preprocessor directive #include before the functions are called in the program*/
**#include <conio.h>**
/*getche() is a non-standard function declared in the conio.h header file; the header file must be included using the preprocessor directive #include before the function is called in the program*/
**int main(){**
/*all C program must have a main() function with return type void or int; here there is no parameter of the main() function and it returns an integer; opening curly brace specifies start of the main() function and no statement before that curly brace is executed by the compiler*/
    **char ch='y', op;**
    /*char type variable op is declared that can hold an operator +, -, * or/as character; another variable ch is declared and initialized to y*/

```
float num1, num2;
```
/*two float type variables are declared to hold the two values
on which operation is performed*/
```
printf("This is a simple calculator . . . \n");
```
/*this displays the text inside the double quotes as it is on
the screen followed by a newline replaces \n*/
```
while (ch!='n'){
```
/*if ch≠'n', the condition is true and statements in the body
of loop, enclosed by curly braces, are executed*/
```
        printf("Enter op1+op2 or op1-op2 or op1*op2 or op1/op2"
            "followed by enter . . . \n");
```
/*printf() function displays the text in the quotations as
it is on the screen except for a newline replaces \n*; here
long string was broken into multiple lines using two double
quotes ("")/
```
    scanf("%f %c %f", &num1, &op, &num2);
```
/*scanf()function reads two decimal values and a character
from input terminal; first format specifier %f corresponds
to num1, second %c corresponds to op and third %f corresponds
to num2*/
```
    switch (op){
```
/*the switch() function moves the program control flow to
one of the following cases, based on the value of op*/
```
        case '+':
```
/*if op=+, then following statements are executed*/
```
            printf("%0.2f + %0.2f = %0.2f\n", num1, num2,
                num1+num2);
```
/*this printf() displays the text as it is on the
screen except for the value of num1 replaces the
first format specifier %0.2f with two decimal points
precision, the value of num2 replaces the second
%0.2f, and the value of the operation num1+num2
replaces the third %0.2f*/
```
            break;
```
/*program control flow immediately comes out of the
switch-case statement*/
```
        case '-':
```
/*if op=-, then following statements are executed*/
```
            printf("%0.2f - %0.2f = %0.2f\n", num1, num2, num1-
                num2);
```
/*this printf() displays the text as it is on the
screen except for the value of num1 replaces the
first format specifier %0.2f with two decimal points
precision, the value of num2 replaces the second
%0.2f, and the value of the operation num1-num2
replaces the third %0.2f*/
```
            break;
```

```
                  /*program control flow immediately comes out of the
                  switch-case*/
            case '*':
            /*if op=*, then following statements are executed*/
                  printf("%0.2f  x  %0.2f  =  %0.2f\n",  num1,  num2,
                        num1*num2);
                  /*this printf() displays the text as it is on the
                  screen except for the value of num1 replaces the
                  first format specifier %0.2f with two decimal points
                  precision, the value of num2 replaces the second
                  %0.2f, and the value of the operation num1xnum2
                  replaces the third %0.2f*/
                  break;
                  /*program control flow immediately comes out of the
                  switch-case statement*/
            case '/':
            /*following if..else is execute if op = /*/
                  if (num2)
                  /*if value of num2 is anything other than 0 then
                  the condition is true and following statement is
                  executed*/
                        printf("%0.2f/%0.2f  =  %0.2f\n",  num1,  num2,
                              num1/num2);
                        /*this printf() displays the text as it is
                        on the screen except for the value of num1
                        replaces the first format specifier %0.2f with
                        two decimal points precision, the value of
                        num2 replaces the second %0.2f, and the value
                        of the operation num1/num2 replaces the third
                        %0.2f*/
                  else
                  /*if num2=0, the condition is false, and the
                  next statement is executed skipping the above
                  printf()*/
                        printf("Cannot divide by zero.\n");
                        /*this printf() function displays the text in
                        the quotations as it is on the screen except
                        for a newline replaces \n*/
            }
            /*this closing curly brace specifies the end of switch-case
            statement*/
            printf("Want to do another operation? (y/n): ");
            /*output function printf() displays the text in the double
            quotations as it is on the screen*/
            ch=getche();
            /*the getche() function waits for character input from the
            keyboard, and when a character is typed, it is echoed on
```

the output screen without waiting for enter to be hit, and
the character is assigned to ch*/
```
printf("\n");
```
/*this printf() function displays a newline on the screen*/
```
}
```
/*this closing curly brace specifies the end of the while loop*/
```
return 0;
```
/*0 is returned as it is the standard for the successful
execution of the program*/
```
}
```
/*the closing curly brace specifies the end of the main() function's
body, as well as the program's end; after that curly brace, no
statement is executed*/

## PROBLEM-11

A person has 10 vori gold, 25 vori silver, and tk 10,000.00 in cash. He also has tk 5,000.00 in debt, and he owes his cousin tk 7,500.00. Calculate the amount of money he has to pay for piety tax this year. Piety tax is payable to the poor, 2.5% of total wealth (gold, silver, cash, or any business items) one person has after one lunar year if his total wealth is more than 7.5 vori gold or 52.5 vori silver or its equivalent money whichever is smaller.

Flowchart of the Solution:

Figure 2.6 shows the flowchart followed to solve this problem.

## Algorithm of the Solution:

Step-1: Start

Step-2: Read values of gold, silver, bank, cash, item, debt, owe, gdprice, and srprice

Step-3: nisab←gdprice×7.5

Step-4: If silver≠0

    4.1: Go to Step-8.1

Step-5: If bank≠0

    5.1: Go to Step-8.1

Step-6: If cash≠0

    6.1: Go to Step-8.1

Step-7: If item≠0

    7.1: Go to Step-8.1

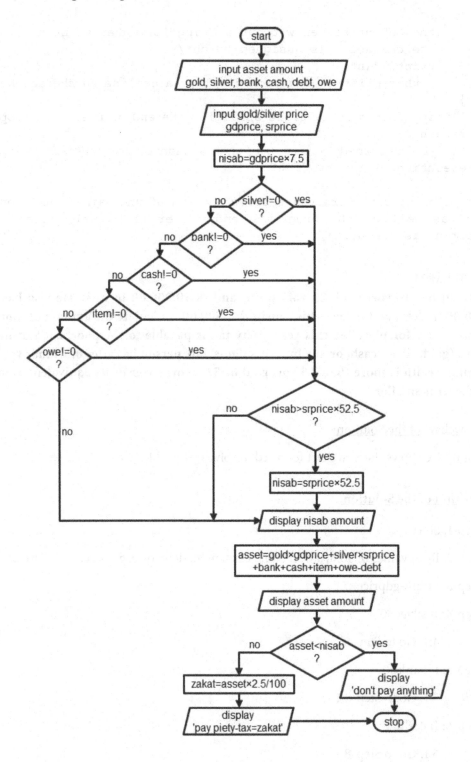

FIGURE 2.6  Flowchart followed to solve the problem.

Step-8: If owe≠0

        8.1: If nisab>srprice×52.5

               8.1.1: nisab←srprice×52.5

Step-9: Display value of nisab

Step-10: asset←gold×gdprice+silver×srprice+bank+cash+item+owe−debt

Step-11: Display value of asset

Step-12: If asset<nisab

        12.1: Display 'no piety-tax'

        12.2: Go to Step-15

Step-13: zakat←asset×2.5/100

Step-14: Display value of zakat

Step-15: Stop

<u>Programming Code of the Solution:</u>

```c
#include <stdio.h>
int main(){
    float gold, silver, bank, cash, item;
    float debt, owe, gdprice, srprice;
    float nisab, asset, pttax, zakat;
    printf("This is a simple piety tax calculator...\n\n");
    printf("How much gold (in vori) do you have? ");
    scanf("%f", &gold);
    printf("How much silver (in vori) do you have: ");
    scanf("%f", &silver);
    printf("What is your bank balance (in taka) today? ");
    scanf("%f", &bank);
    printf("Amount of cash (in taka) in your hand today? ");
    scanf("%f", &cash);
    printf("Enter total market price of your business items, if any\n");
    printf("(or enter 0 if you have no business item)? ");
    scanf("%f", &item);
    printf("Do you have any debt to anyone that you have to pay "
           "recently? ");
    scanf("%f", &debt);
    printf("Do you owe anyone anything that you will get recently? ");
    scanf("%f", &owe);
    printf("Enter the price of gold per vori today? ");
    scanf("%f", &gdprice);
    printf("Enter the price of silver per vori today? ");
    scanf("%f", &srprice);
    nisab=gdprice*7.5;
    if (silver!=0||bank!=0||cash!=0||item!=0||owe!=0)
        if (nisab>srprice*52.5)
            nisab=srprice*52.5;
```

```
    printf("\nYour nisab (threshold amount) is %0.2f taka.\n", nisab);
    asset=gold*gdprice+silver*srprice+bank+cash+item+owe-debt;
    printf("Your asset is %0.2f taka.\n", asset);
    if (asset<nisab)
        printf("You don't have to pay any piety-tax in this lunar "
              "year.\n");
    else{
        zakat=asset*2.5/100;
        printf("Payable piety-tax to poor in this year is %0.2f taka."
              "\n", zakat);
    }
    return 0;
}
```

Input and Output of the Executed Program:

```
This is a simple piety tax calculator...

How much gold (in vori) do you have? 8.5
How much silver (in vori) do you have: 34.5
What is your bank balance (in taka) today? 300000
Amount of cash (in taka) in your hand today? 12000
Enter total market price of your business items, if any
(or enter 0 if you have no business item)? 0
Do you have any debt to anyone that you have to pay recently? 2000
Do you owe anyone anything that you will get recently? 15000
Enter the price of gold per vori today? 78000
Enter the price of silver per vori today? 1200

Your nisab (threshold amount) is 63000.00 taka.
Your asset is 1029400.00 taka.
Payable piety-tax to poor in this year is 25735.00 taka.
```

## Explanation of the Programming Code:

**#include <stdio.h>**
/*header file stdio.h contains prototypes of the library functions
printf(), and scanf(); the header file must be included using preprocessor
directive #include before the functions are called in the program*/
**int main(){**
/*all C program must have a main() function with return type void or
int; here there is no parameter of the main() function and it returns
an integer; opening curly brace specifies start of the main() function
and no statement before that curly brace is executed by the compiler*/
    **float gold, silver, bank, cash, item;**
    /*five float type variables are declared; required memory spaces
    are allocated for each variable*/
    **float debt, owe, gdprice, srprice;**
    /*four float type variables are declared; required memory spaces
    are allocated for each variable*/

```
float nisab, asset, pttax, zakat;
```
/*four float type variables are declared; required memory spaces
are allocated for each variable*/
```
printf("This is a simple piety tax calculator . . . \n\n");
```
/*printf() function displays the text in the quotation as it is
on screen except for a newline replaces \n*/
```
printf("How much gold (in vori) do you have? ");
```
/*output function printf() displays text in the double quotations
as it is on the screen*/
```
scanf("%f", &gold);
```
/*input function scanf() reads a decimal value from input
terminal and stores it in the memory spaces allocated to gold*/
```
printf("How much silver (in vori) do you have: ");
```
/*printf() function displays the text in the quotation as it is
on the screen*/
```
scanf("%f", &silver);
```
/*scanf() function reades a decimal value from input terminal
and stores it in the memory spaces allocated to silver*/
```
printf("What is your bank balance (in taka) today? ");
```
/*output function printf() displays text in the double quotations
as it is on the screen*/
```
scanf("%f", &bank);
```
/*scanf() function takes a decimal value from input terminal
and stores it in the memory spaces allocated to bank*/
```
printf("Amount of cash (in taka) in your hand today? ");
```
/*output function printf() displays text in the double quotations
as it is on the screen*/
```
scanf("%f", &cash);
```
/*scanf() function reads a decimal value from input terminal
and stores it in the memory spaces allocated to cash*/
```
printf("Enter total market price of your business items, if"
        "any\n");
```
/*printf() function displays the text in the quotation as it is
on screen except for a newline replaces \n*/
```
printf("(or enter 0 if you have no business item)? ");
```
/*output function printf() displays text in the double quotations
as it is on the screen*/
```
scanf("%f", &item);
```
/*function scanf() reads a decimal value from input terminal
and stores it in the memory spaces allocated to item*/
```
printf("Do you have any debt to anyone that you have to pay"
        "recently? ");
```
/*printf() function displays the text in the quotation as it is
on the screen, here the long string was broken into two lines
using two double quotes ("")*/
```
scanf("%f", &debt);
```
/*function scanf() reads a decimal value from input terminal
and stores it in the memory spaces allocated to debt*/

```
printf("Do  you  owe  anyone  anything  that  you  will  get"
       "recently?");
```
/*output function printf() displays text in the double quotations as it is on the screen*/
```
scanf("%f", &owe);
```
/*function scanf() reads a decimal value from input terminal and stores it in the memory spaces allocated to owe*/
```
printf("Enter the price of gold per vori today? ");
```
/*printf() function displays the text in the quotations as it is on the screen*/
```
scanf("%f", &gdprice);
```
/*function scanf() reads a decimal value from input terminal and stores it in the memory spaces allocated to gdprice*/
```
printf("Enter the price of silver per vori today? ");
```
/*printf() function displays the text in the quotations as it is on the screen*/
```
scanf("%f", &srprice);
```
/*function scanf() reads a decimal value from input terminal and stores it in the memory spaces allocated to srprice*/
```
nisab=gdprice*7.5;
```
/*value of gdprice is multiplied by 7.5 and the result is assigned to nisab*/
```
if (silver!=0||bank!=0||cash!=0||item!=0||owe!=0)
```
/*this if condition is used to check if the person concerned has any other assets except gold and adjust the nisab accordingly; if other assets are available, the condition is true, and the next 'if' statement is executed*/
```
    if (nisab>srprice*52.5)
```
/*if the nisab calculated from gold price is larger than 52.5 times the silver price, then the following statement is executed to adjust the nisab amount*/
```
        nisab=srprice*52.5;
```
/*value of srprice is multiplied by 52.5 and the result is assigned to nisab*/
```
printf("\nYour nisab (threshold amount) is %0.2f taka.\n",
       nisab);
```
/*printf() function displays the text in the quotations as it is on the screen except for the format specifier %0.2f is replaced by the value of nisab with two decimal points precision and a newline replaces \n*/
```
asset=gold*gdprice+silver*srprice+bank+cash+item+owe-debt;
```
/*total asset of the person concerned is calculated*/
```
printf("Your asset is %0.2f taka.\n", asset);
```
/*printf() function displays the text in the quotations as it is on the screen except for format specifier %0.2f is replaced by the value of asset with two decimal points precision and a newline replaces \n*/

```
if (asset<nisab)
/*if value of asset is less than nisab amount then above condition
is true and following statement is executed*/
        printf("You don't have to pay any piety-tax in this lunar"
                "year.\n");
        /*printf() function displays the text in the quotations as
        it is on the screen except for a newline replaces \n*/
else{
/*if asset>=nisab then above condition is false, and following
statements, enclosed by curly braces, are executed*/
        zakat=asset*2.5/100;
        /*zakat or piety-tax amount of the person concerned is
        calculated*/
        printf("Payable piety-tax to poor in this year is %0.2f"
                "taka.\n", zakat);
        /*printf() function displays the text in the quotations as
        it is on the screen except for the format specifier %0.2f
        is replaced by the value of zakat with two decimal points
        precision and a newline replaces \n*/
}
/*this closing curly brace specifies the end of else*/
return 0;
/*0 is returned as it is the standard for the successful
execution of the program*/
}
/*the closing curly brace specifies the end of the main() function's
body, as well as the program's end; after that curly brace, no
statement is executed*/
```

## PROBLEM-12

A person gets a monthly salary of tk 60,000.00 with two festival allowances of tk 80,000.00. He also gets tk 50,000.00 from monthly house rent. His average monthly expenditure is tk 45,000.00, and he has to pay tk 5,000.00 for provident fund and tk 10,000.00 for life insurance premium. He also has to pay tk 30,000.00 for City Corporation Tax for his apartment. Calculate the amount of income tax he has to pay to the government in this year. The government fixes the tax for this year as follows:

| Income | Tax |
| --- | --- |
| First tk 2,20,000.00 | Nil |
| Next tk 3,00,000.00 | 10% |
| Next tk 4,00,000.00 | 15% |
| Next tk 5,00,000.00 | 20% |
| Rest amount | 25% |
| Minimum payable tax is tk 3,000.00 | |

Provident funds, life insurance, and share investment are considered personal invest-ments, and the taxpayer gets a 15% rebate on his total investment. Festival allowance and other allowances are exempted from the tax.

Flowchart of the Solution:

Figure 2.7 shows the flowcharts followed to solve this problem.

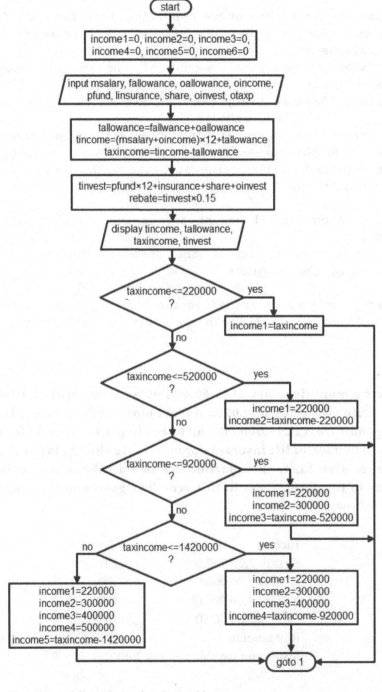

FIGURE 2.7   Flowcharts followed to solve the problem.

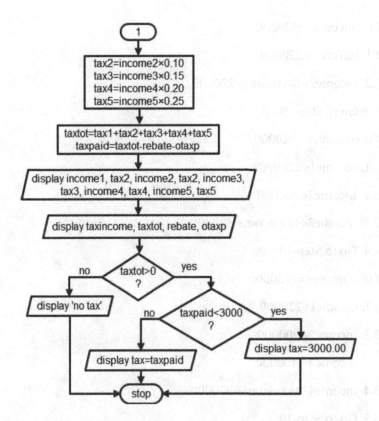

FIGURE 2.7 (Continued)

## **Algorithm of the Solution:**

Step-1: Start

Step-2: Initialize income1←0, income2←0, income3←0, income4←0, and income5←0

Step-3: Read values of msalary, fallowance, oallowance, oincome, pfund, linsurance, share, oinvest, and otaxp

Step-4: tallowance←fallowance+oallowance

Step-5: tincome←(msalary+oincome)×12+tallowance

Step-6: taxincome←tincome-tallowance

Step-7: tinvest←pfund×12+linsurance+share+oinvest

Step-8: rebate←tinvest×15/100

Step-9: Display values of tincome, tallowance, taxincome, and tinvest

Step-10: If taxincome<=220000

      10.1: income1←taxincome

      10.2: Go to Step-19

Step-11: If taxincome<=520000

       11.1: income1←220000

       11.2: income2←taxincome-220000

       11.3: Go to Step-19

Step-12: If taxincome<=920000

       12.1: income1←220000

       12.2: income2←300000

       12.3: income3←taxincome-520000

       12.4: Go to Step-19

Step-13: If taxincome<=1420000

       13.1: income1←220000

       13.2: income2←300000

       13.3: income3←400000

       13.4: income4←taxincome-920000

       13.5: Go to Step-19

Step-14: income1←220000

Step-15: income2←300000

Step-16: income3←400000

Step-17: income4←500000

Step-18: income5←taxincome-1420000

Step-19: tax2←income2×10/100

Step-20: tax3←income3×15/100

Step-21: tax4←income4×20/100

Step-22: tax5←income5×25/100

Step-23: taxtot←tax1+tax2+tax3+tax4+tax5

Step-24: taxpaid←taxtot-rebate-otaxp

Step-25: Display values of income1, income2, tax2, income3, tax3, income4, tax4, income5, tax5, taxincome, taxtot, rebate, and otaxp

Step-26: If taxtot>0

       26.1: If taxpaid<3000

26.1.1: Display 3000.00

26.1.2: Go to Step-28

26.2: Display value of taxpaid

26.3: Go to Step-28

Step-27: Display 'no tax'

Step-28: Stop

Programming Code of the Solution:

```
#include <stdio.h>
int main(){
    float msalary, fallowance, oallowance, oincome;
    float pfund, linsurance, share, oinvest, otaxp;
    float tincome, tallowance, taxincome, tinvest, rebate, taxpaid;
    float income1=0.0, income2=0.0, income3=0.0, income4=0.0;
    float income5=0.0, tax2, tax3, tax4, tax5, taxtot;
    printf("This is a simple income tax calculator...\n");
    printf("What is your monthly basic salary? ");
    scanf("%f", &msalary);
    printf("Amount of festival allowance you have got in this year? ");
    scanf("%f", &fallowance);
    printf("Amount of any other allowance you have got in this year? ");
    scanf("%f", &oallowance);
    printf("Amount of any other income/month (house rent, business"
            " etc.)? ");
    scanf("%f", &oincome);
    printf("Amount of provident fund per month you have to pay? ");
    scanf("%f", &pfund);
    printf("Amount of life insurance premium you have to pay? ");
    scanf("%f", &linsurance);
    printf("Amount of your investment in share market? ");
    scanf("%f", &share);
    printf("Amount of your other investment (DPS, Prizebond etc.)? ");
    scanf("%f", &oinvest);
    printf("Amount of any other tax paid to the government? ");
    scanf("%f", &otaxp);
    tallowance=fallowance+oallowance;
    tincome=(msalary+oincome)*12+tallowance;
    taxincome=tincome-tallowance;
    tinvest=pfund*12+linsurance+share+oinvest;
    rebate=tinvest*15/100;
    printf("\nTotal Income: %0.2f taka", tincome);
    printf("\nTotal Allowances: %0.2f taka", tallowance);
    printf("\nTotal Taxable Income: %0.2f taka", taxincome);
    printf("\nTotal Investment: %0.2f taka", tinvest);
    if (taxincome<=220000)
        income1=taxincome;
    else if (taxincome<=520000){
        income1=220000;
        income2=taxincome-220000;
    }
    else if (taxincome<=920000){
        income1=220000;
```

```
    else if (taxincome<=920000){
        income1=220000;
        income2=300000;
        income3=taxincome-520000;
    }
    else if (taxincome<=1420000){
        income1=220000;
        income2=300000;
        income3=400000;
        income4=taxincome-920000;
    }
    else{
        income1=220000;
        income2=300000;
        income3=400000;
        income4=500000;
        income5=taxincome-1420000;
    }
    tax2=income2*10/100;
    tax3=income3*15/100;
    tax4=income4*20/100;
    tax5=income5*25/100;
    taxtot=tax2+tax3+tax4+tax5;
    taxpaid=taxtot-rebate-otaxp;
    printf("\n\nCalculation of Tax Liabilities");
    printf("\nOn the first Tk220000 @0%% (%0.2f): 0.00", income1);
    printf("\nOn the next Tk300000 @10%% (%0.2f): %0.2f", income2,
            tax2);
    printf("\nOn the next Tk400000 @15%% (%0.2f): %0.2f", income3,
            tax3);
    printf("\nOn the next Tk500000 @20%% (%0.2f): %0.2f", income4,
            tax4);
    printf("\nOn the balance amount @25%% (%0.2f): %0.2f", income5,
            tax5);
    printf("\n\nTotal taxable income= %0.2f", taxincome);
    printf("\nTotal income tax= %0.2f", taxtot);
    printf("\nRebate on investment= %0.2f", rebate);
    printf("\nOther tax paid to the government= %0.2f", otaxp);
    if (taxtot>0){
        if (taxpaid<3000)
            printf("\nNet tax payable= (Minimum) 3000.00\n");
        else
            printf("\nNet tax payable= %0.2f\n", taxpaid);
    }
    else
        printf("\nNet tax payable= (No Tax) 0.00\n");
    return 0;
}
```

Input and Output of the Executed Program:

```
This is a simple income tax calculator...
What is your monthly basic salary? 65000
Amount of festival allowance you have got in this year? 130000
Amount of any other allowance you have got in this year? 23000
Amount of any other income/month (house rent, business etc.)? 0
Amount of provident fund per month you have to pay? 6500
Amount of life insurance premium you have to pay? 5000
Amount of your investment in share market? 0
Amount of your other investment (DPS, Prizebond etc.)? 5000
Amount of any other tax paid to the government? 0

Total Income: 933000.00 taka
Total Allowances: 153000.00 taka
Total Taxable Income: 780000.00 taka
Total Investment: 88000.00 taka

Calculation of Tax Liabilities
On the first Tk220000 @0% (220000.00): 0.00
On the next Tk300000 @10% (300000.00): 30000.00
On the next Tk400000 @15% (260000.00): 39000.00
On the next Tk500000 @20% (0.00): 0.00
On the balance amount @25% (0.00): 0.00

Total taxable income= 780000.00
Total income tax= 69000.00
Rebate on investment= 13200.00
Other tax paid to the government= 0.00
Net tax payable= 55800.00
```

## Explanation of the Programming Code:

```c
#include <stdio.h>
```
/*header file stdio.h contains prototypes of the library functions printf(), and scanf(); the header file must be included using preprocessor directive #include before the functions are called in the program*/
```c
int main(){
```
/*all C program must have a main() function with return type void or int; here there is no parameter of the main() function and it returns an integer; opening curly brace specifies start of the main() function and no statement before that curly brace is executed by the compiler*/
```c
    float msalary, fallowance, oallowance, oincome;
```
/*four float type variables are declared; required memory spaces are assigned for each variable*/
```c
    float pfund, linsurance, share, oinvest, otaxp;
```

```
/*five float type variables are declared that can store only
decimal values; required memory spaces are assigned for each
variable*/
float tincome, tallowance, taxincome, tinvest, rebate, taxpaid;
/*six float type variables are declared; required memory spaces
are assigned for each variable*/
float income1=0.0, income2=0.0, income3=0.0, income4=0.0;
/*four float type variables are declared and initialized to
0.0; required memory spaces are assigned for each variable;
they are used to save income that falls into distinct slabs;
if income is not that high, income in that slab remains at
0.0*/
float income5=0.0, tax2, tax3, tax4, tax5, taxtot;
/*six float type variables are declared; required memory spaces
are assigned for each variable; 1st variable is initialized to
0.0 and used to save income of another slab*/
printf("This is a simple income tax calculator . . . \n");
/*function printf() displays the text inside the double
quotations as it is on the screen except for a newline replaces
\n*/
printf("What is your monthly basic salary? ");
/*output function printf() displays the text in the double
quotes as it is on screen*/
scanf("%f", &msalary);
/*input function scanf() reads a decimal value from input
terminal and it is assigned to msalary*/
printf("Amount of festival allowance you have got in this"
       "year? ");
/*function printf() displays the text in double quotations as
it is on the screen*/
scanf("%f", &fallowance);
/*scanf() reads a decimal value from input terminal and it is
assigned to fallowance*/
printf("Amount of any other allownces you have got in this"
        "year? ");
/*function printf() displays the text in double quotations as
it is on the screen*/
scanf("%f", &oallowance);
/*scanf() reads a decimal value from input terminal and it is
assigned to oallowance*/
printf("Amount of any other income/month (house rent, business,"
        "etc.)? ");
/*printf() displays the text in the double quotations as it is
on the screen; here long string was broken into multiple lines
using two double quotes ("")*/
```

```
scanf("%f", &oincome);
/*scanf() reads a decimal value from input terminal and ite is
assigned to oincome*/
printf("Amount of provident fund per month you have to pay? ");
/*printf() displays the text in double quotations as it is on
the screen*/
scanf("%f", &pfund);
/*scanf() reads a decimal value from input terminal and it is
assigned to pfund*/
printf("Amount of life insurance premium you have to pay? ");
/*function printf() displays the text in the double quotations
as it is on the screen*/
scanf("%f", &linsurance);
/*scanf() takes a decimal value from input terminal and it is
assigned to linsurance*/
printf("Amount of your investment in share market? ");
/*function printf() displays the text in the double quotations
as it is on the screen*/
scanf("%f", &share);
/*scanf() reads a decimal value from input terminal and it is
assigned to share*/
printf("Amount of your other investment (DPS, Prizebond etc.)? ");
/*function printf() displays the text in the double quotations
as it is on the screen*/
scanf("%f", &oinvest);
/*scanf() reads a decimal value from input terminal and it is
assigned to oinvest*/
printf("Amount of any other tax paid to the government? ");
/*function printf() displays the text in the double quotations
as it is on the screen*/
scanf("%f", &otaxp);
/*scanf() reads a decimal value from input terminal and it is
assigned to otaxp*/
tallowance=fallowance+oallowance;
/*total allowance in the year is calculated by summing festival
and other allownces*/
tincome=(msalary+oincome)*12+tallowance;
/*total annual income is computed from monthly salaries and
other sources of income, as well as total allowance*/
taxincome=tincome-tallowance;
/*taxable income is calculated by deducting nontaxable allowance
from total income*/
tinvest=pfund*12+linsurance+share+oinvest;
/*total annual investment is calculated from monthly provident
fund, life insurance premium, share debenture and other
investments, if any*/
```

```
rebate=tinvest*15/100;
/*tax rebate is calculated from total investment*/
printf("\nTotal Income: %0.2f taka", tincome);
/*this printf() function displays the text inside double
quotations as it is on the screen except for a newline replaces
\n and the format specifier %0.2f is replaced by the value of
tincome with two decimal points precision*/
printf("\nTotal Allowances: %0.2f taka", tallowance);
/*this printf() function displays the text inside double
quotations as it is on the screen except for a newline replaces
\n and format specifier %0.2f is replaced by the value of
tallowance with two decimal points precision*/
printf("\nTotal Taxable Income: %0.2f taka", taxincome);
/*this printf() function displays the text inside the double
quotations as it is on the screen except for a newline replaces
\n and the format specifier %0.2f is replaced by the value of
taxincome with two decimal points precision*/
printf("\nTotal Investment: %0.2f taka", tinvest);
/*this printf() function displays the text inside the double
quotations as it is on the screen except for a newline replaces
\n and the format specifier %0.2f is replaced by the value of
tinvest with two decimal points precision*/
if (taxincome<=220000)
/*if the taxable income falls into the lowest income bracket,
the condition is true, and the next statement is executed*/
    income1=taxincome;
    /*total income is assigned to income1; income2 to income5
    remain unchanged at 0.0*/
else if (taxincome<=520000){
/*if the taxable income exceeds the lowest slab but falls within
the second, the else..if condition is true, and the following
statements are executed to divide the taxable income into two
parts*/
    income1=220000;
    /*first 220000 income is assigned to income1*/
    income2=taxincome-220000;
    /*remaining income is allocated to income2; income3 through
    income5 remain unchanged at 0.0*/
}
/*this is the end of else..if with condition (taxincome<=520000)*/
else if (taxincome<=920000){
/*if the taxable income exceeds the 2nd slab but falls within
the 3rd, the else..if condition is true and the following
statements are executed to divide the taxable income into three
parts*/
    income1=220000;
    /*first 220000 income is assigned to income1*/
```

```
income2=300000;
/*next 300000 income is assigned to income2*/
income3=taxincome-520000;
/*remaining income is assigned to income3; income4 and
income5 remain unchanged at 0.0*/
}
```
/*this is the end of else..if with condition (taxincome<=920000)*/
```
else if (taxincome<=1420000){
```
/*if the taxable income exceeds the 3rd slab but falls within
the 4th, the else..if condition is true and the following
statements are executed to divide the taxable income into four
parts*/
```
income1=220000;
/*first 220000 income is assigned to income1*/
income2=300000;
/*next 300000 income is assigned to income2*/
income3=400000;
/*next 400000 income is assigned to income3*/
income4=taxincome-920000;
/*remaining is assigned to income4; income5 remains unchanged
at 0.0*/
}
```
/*this is the end of else..if with condition (taxincome<=1420000)*/
```
else{
```
/*if taxable income exceeds the 4th slab, the condition of
else..if is true and following statements are executed to divide
the taxable income into five parts*/
```
income1=220000;
/*first 220000 income is assigned to income1*/
income2=300000;
/*next 300000 income is assigned to income2*/
income3=400000;
/*next 400000 income is assigned to income3*/
income4=500000;
/*next 500000 income is assigned to income4*/
income5=taxincome-1420000;
/*remaining income is assigned to income5*/
}
```
/*this is the end of body of the above else*/
```
tax2=income2*10/100;
```
/*the tax amount for the 2nd income level is computed; if the
taxable income falls within the 1st slab, the tax amount is 0.00
(income2=0.0)*/
```
tax3=income3*15/100;
```
/*the tax amount for the 3rd income level is computed; it is
0.00 if the taxable income falls inside the 2nd slab, since
income3=0.0*/

```
tax4=income4*20/100;
```
/*the tax amount for the 4th income level is computed; it is
0.00 if the taxable income falls inside the 3rd slab, since
income4=0.0*/
```
tax5=income5*25/100;
```
/*the tax amount for the 5th income level is computed; if the
taxable income falls within the 4th slab, the tax amount is 0.00
(income5=0.0)*/
```
taxtot=tax2+tax3+tax4+tax5;
```
/*the total tax amount is calculated by adding all of the
previous tax amounts together*/
```
taxpaid=taxtot-rebate-otaxp;
```
/*the amount of tax that must be paid is calculated by subtracting
the tax rebate and any other taxes that have been paid from the
total tax amount*/
```
printf("\n\nCalculation of Tax Liabilities");
```
/*this printf() function displays the text inside the double
quotations as it is on the screen except for a newline replaces
\n*/
```
printf("\nOn the first Tk220000 @0%% (%0.2f): 0.00", income1);
```
/*this printf() function displays the text inside the double
quotations as it is on the screen except for a newline replaces
\n and the format specifier %0.2f is replaced by value of
income1 with two decimal points precision*/
```
printf("\nOn the next Tk300000 @10%% (%0.2f): %0.2f", income2,
       tax2);
```
/*printf() function displays the text inside the double quotes
as it is on the screen except for a newline replaces \n; 1st
format specifier %0.2f is replaced by the value of income2 with
two decimal points precision while 2nd %0.2f by the value of
tax2*/
```
printf("\nOn the next Tk400000 @15%% (%0.2f): %0.2f", income3,
       tax3);
```
/*printf() function displays the text inside the double quotes
as it is on the screen except for a newline replaces \n; 1st
format specifier %0.2f is replaced by the value of income3 with
two decimal points precision while 2nd %0.2f by value of tax3*/
```
printf("\nOn the next Tk500000 @20%% (%0.2f): %0.2f", income4,
       tax4);
```
/*printf() function displays the text inside the double quotes
as it is on the screen except for a newline replaces \n; 1st
format specifier %0.2f is replaced by the value of income4 with
two decimal points precision while 2nd %0.2f by value of tax4*/
```
printf("\nOn the balance amount @25%% (%0.2f): %0.2f", income5,
       tax5);
```
/*printf() function displays the text inside the double quotes
as it is on the screen except for a newline replaces \n; 1st

format specifier %0.2f is replaced by the value of income5 with
two decimal points precision while 2nd %0.2f by value of tax5*/
**printf("\n\nTotal taxable income= %0.2f", taxincome);**
/*printf() function displays the text inside the double quotes
as it is on the screen except for a newline replaces \n; format
specifier %0.2f is replaced by the value of taxincome with two
decimal points precision*/
**printf("\nTotal income tax= %0.2f", taxtot);**
/*printf() function displays the text inside the double quotes
as it is on the screen except for a newline replaces \n; the
format specifier %0.2f is replaced by the value of taxtot with
two decimal points precision*/
**printf("\nRebate on investment= %0.2f", rebate);**
/*printf() function displays the text inside the double quotes
as it is on the screen except for a newline replaces \n; format
specifier %0.2f is replaced by the value of rebate with two
decimal points precision*/
**printf("\nOther tax paid to the government= %0.2f", otaxp);**
/*printf() function displays the text inside the double quotes
as it is on the screen except for a newline replaces \n; format
specifier %0.2f is replaced by the value of otaxp with two
decimal points precision*/
**if (taxtot>0){**
/*if there is a tax to be paid, the above condition is true, and
the if..else statement is executed*/
    **if (taxpaid<3000)**
    /*if the amount of tax to be paid is less than tk. 3000, the
    preceding condition is true, and the following statement is
    executed*/
        **printf("\nNet tax payable= (Minimum) 3000.00\n");**
        /*printf() function displays the text inside the double
        quotes as it is on the screen except for a newline
        replaces \n*/
    **else**
    /*if the computed tax to be paid is equal to or greater
    than tk. 3000, the previous condition is false, and the
    following statement is executed*/
        **printf("\nNet tax payable= %0.2f\n", taxpaid);**
        /*printf() function displays the text inside the double
        quotes as it is on the screen except for a newline
        replaces \n; format specifier %0.2f is replaced by the
        value of taxpaid with two decimal points precision*/
**}**
/*this is the end of above if with condition (taxtot>0)*/
**else**
/*if there is no tax to pay (the calculated tax amount is 0),
the if condition is false, and the statement below is executed*/

```
    printf("\nNet tax payable= (No Tax) 0.00\n");
    /*printf() function displays the text inside the double
    quotes as it is on the screen except for a newline replaces
    \n*/
return 0;
    /*0 is returned as it is the standard for the successful
    execution of the program*/
}
/*the closing curly brace specifies the end of the main() function's
body, as well as the program's end; after that curly brace, no
statement is executed*/
```

## PROBLEM-13

**Write a program to generate random numbers between a given range. The minimum and maximum ranges and number of random numbers to be generated are input interactively.**

Flowchart of the Solution:

Figure 2.8 shows the flowchart followed to solve this problem.

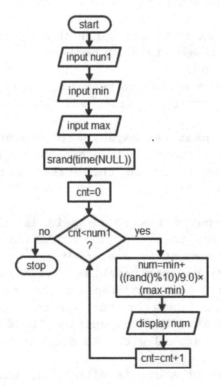

FIGURE 2.8 Flowchart followed to solve the problem.

## Algorithm of the Solution:

Step-1: Start

Step-2: Read values of num1, min, and max

Step-3: srand(time(NULL))

Step-4: Initialize cnt←0

Step-5: If (cnt<num1)

    5.1: num←min+((rand()%10)/9.0)×(max−min)

    5.2: Display value of num

    5.3: cnt←cnt+1

    5.4: Go to Step-5

Step-6: Stop

## Programming Code of the Solution:

```
#include <stdio.h>
#include <stdlib.h>
#include <time.h>
int main(){
    int cnt, num1, min, max;
    float num;
    printf("Enter no. of random numbers you want? ");
    scanf("%d", &num1);
    printf("Enter minimum value of random number? ");
    scanf("%d", &min);
    printf("Enter maximum value of random number? ");
    scanf("%d", &max);
    printf("%d random numbers between %d and %d:\n",
            num1, min, max);
    srand(time(NULL));
    for (cnt=0; cnt<num1; cnt++){
        num=min+((rand()%10)/9.0)*(max-min);
        printf("%0.2f, ", num);
    }
    return 0;
}
```

Input and Output of the Executed Program:

```
Enter no. of random numbers you want? 10
Enter minimum value of random number? 12
Enter maximum value of random number? 88
10 random numbers between 12 and 88:
45.78,  45.78,  12.00,  20.44,  88.00,  12.00,  71.11,  62.67,  71.11,  20.44,
```

```
Enter no. of random numbers you want? 8
Enter minimum value of random number? 0
Enter maximum value of random number? 1
8 random numbers between 0 and 1:
0.00,   1.00,   0.11,   0.67,   0.33,   0.22,   0.33,   0.11,
```

## Explanation of the Programming Code:

**#include <stdio.h>**
/*header file stdio.h contains prototypes of the library functions printf(), and scanf(); the header file must be included using preprocessor directive #include before the functions are called in the program*/
**#include <stdlib.h>**
/*header file stdlib.h includes prototypes for the standard library functions rand() and srand(); the header file must be included using the #include preprocessor directive before the functions are called in the program*/
**#include <time.h>**
/*standard library function time() is declared in the header file time.h; the header file must be included using the preprocessor directive #include before the function is called in the program*/
**int main(){**
/*all C program must have a main() function with return type void or int; here there is no parameter of the main() function and it returns an integer; opening curly brace specifies start of the main() function and no statement before that curly brace is executed by the compiler*/
　　**int cnt, num1, min, max;**
　　/*four integer type variables are declared; compiler assigns required spaces in memory for these variables*/
　　**float num;**
　　/*float type variable num is declared; compiler assigns required spaces in memory for the variable*/
　　**printf("Enter no. of random numbers you want? ");**
　　/*output library function printf() displays text inside the double quotations as it is on the screen*/
　　**scanf("%d", &num1);**
　　/*input library function scanf() reads an integer from input terminal and stores the value in the memory space assigned for

num1; hence %d is used as format specifier and address operator & is used with the variable name*/
**printf("Enter minimum value of random number? ");**
/*function printf() displays text inside the double quotations as it is on the screen*/
**scanf("%d", &min);**
/*function scanf() reads an integer from input terminal and stores the value in the memory space assigned for min*/
**printf("Enter maximum value of random number? ");**
/*function printf() displays text inside the double quotations as it is on the screen*/
**scanf("%d", &max);**
/*scanf() reads an integer from input terminal and stores the value in the memory space assigned for max*/
**printf("%d random numbers between %d and %d:\n", num1, min, max);**
/*printf() displays the text inside the quotation as it is on screen except for the value of num1 replaces the first format specifier %d, the value of min replaces the second %d, the value of max replaces the third %d and a newline replaces \n*/
**srand(time(NULL));**
/*the seed of the random number generator algorithm used by rand() is set by the srand() function; we continuously modify the seed of the function srand()to ensure that the numbers returned by rand() are truly random; the library function time() returns the current computer time in seconds, which varies in each program run*/
**for (cnt=0; cnt<num1; cnt++){**
/*this for loop is used to generate num1 random numbers, one number in each iteration; cnt=0 is the initialization; cnt<num1 is the condition; and cnt++ is the increment; the initialization is done once at the beginning of the loop; if cnt is smaller than num1, the body of the loop is executed; now the value of cnt is incremented by 1 before the condition is re-checked; these steps continue until the condition becomes false at which point the program flow exits the loop*/
    **num=min+((rand()%10)/9.0)*(max-min);**
    /*the rand() function generates a random number in each iteration; rand()%10 returns a random value between 0 and 9, so (rand()%10)/9.0 returns a random decimal value between 0 and 1; ((rand()%10)/9.0)×(max-min) returns a random number ranging from 0 to (max-min), and finally min+((rand()%10)/9.0)×(max-min) returns a random number ranging from min to max; the final random value is assigned to variable num*/
    **printf("%0.2f, ", num);**
    /*printf() displays the value of num in place of the format specifier %0.2f with two decimal points precision on the screen followed by a comma and a space*/

```
    }
    /*this closing curly brace specifies the end of the for loop*/
    return 0;
    /*0 is returned as it is the standard for the successful
    execution of the program*/
}
/*the closing curly brace specifies the end of the main() function's
body, as well as the program's end; after that curly brace, no
statement is executed*/
```

## PROBLEM-14
**Write a program to compute the value of PI using the Monte Carlo method.**

Flowchart of the Solution:

Figure 2.9 shows the flowchart followed to solve this problem.

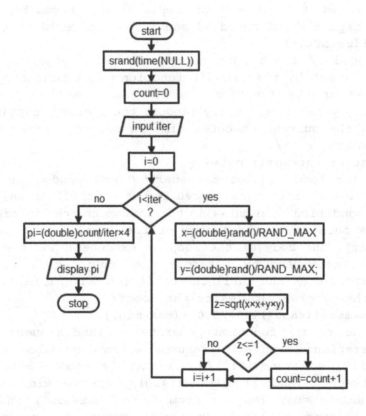

FIGURE 2.9 Flowchart followed to solve the problem.

## Algorithm of the Solution:

Step-1: Start.

Step-2: Define SEED←time(NULL)

Step-3: srand(SEED).

Step-4: Initialize count←0

Step-5: Read value of iter.

Step-6: Initialize i←0

Step-7: If i<iter

    7.1: x←(double)rand()/RAND_MAX

    7.2: y←(double)rand()/RAND_MAX

    7.3: z←sqrt($x^2+y^2$)

    7.4: If z<=1

        7.4.1: count←count+1

    7.5: pi←(double)count/iter×4

    7.6: Go to Step-7

Step-8: Display value of pi.

Step-9: Stop.

Programming Code of the Solution:

```c
#include <stdio.h>
#include <stdlib.h>
#include <math.h>
#include <time.h>
#define SEED time(NULL)
int main(){
    srand(SEED);
    int i, iter, count=0;
    double x, y, z, pi;
    printf("Enter no. of iteration: ");
    scanf("%d", &iter);
    for (i=0; i<iter; i++){
        x = (double)rand()/RAND_MAX;
        y = (double)rand()/RAND_MAX;
        z = sqrt(x*x+y*y);
        if (z<=1)
            count++;
    }
    pi = (double)count/iter*4;
    printf("Approximate value of PI is %0.4lf", pi);
    return 0;
}
```

Input and Output of the Executed Program:

```
Enter no. of iteration: 90000
Approximate value of PI is 3.1404
```

## Explanation of the Programming Code:

```
#include <stdio.h>
```
/*header file stdio.h contains prototypes of the library functions printf(), and scanf(); the header file must be included using preprocessor directive #include before the functions are called in the program*/
```
#include <stdlib.h>
```
/*header file stdlib.h includes prototypes for the standard library functions rand() and srand(); the header file must be included using the #include preprocessor directive before the functions are called in the program*/
```
#include <math.h>
```
/*header file math.h contains prototype of the library function sqrt(); the header file must be included using the preprocessor directive #include before the function is called in the program*/
```
#include <time.h>
```
/*library function time() is declared in the time.h header file; time.h must be included using the preprocessor directive #include before the function is called in the program*/
```
#define SEED time(NULL)
```
/*#define is a preprocessor directive that defines a constant variable; in this case, SEED is the constant variable that takes the value returned by the function time(); the library function time() returns the current computer time in seconds, therefore the value of SEED varies with each program run*/
```
int main(){
```
/*here main() function returns an integer and parameters/ arguments of the main() function also remain void; execution of the program starts with main() function; no statement before opening curly brace of the main() function is executed by the compiler*/
```
    srand(SEED);
```
/*srand() function sets the seed of the random number generator algorithm used by rand(); to truly randomize the numbers generated by rand(), we change the seed of the function srand() in each program run*/
```
    int i, iter, count=0;
```
/*two integer type variables i and iter are declared; another integer type variable count is declared and initialized to 0*/
```
    double x, y, z, pi;
```
/*four double type variables are declared; required memory spaces are allocated for each of the variables*/

```
printf("Enter no. of iteration: ");
```
/*output function printf() displays text in the double quotations
as it is on the screen*/
```
scanf("%d", &iter);
```
/*input function scanf() reads an integer value from keyboard
and stores the value in the memory spaces assigned for iter*/
```
for (i=0; i<iter; i++){
```
/*i=0 is the initialization, i<iter is the condition and i++ is
the increment; the initialization is done once at the beginning
of the loop; after that, the condition is checked, if it is
true, the statement in the body is executed, and the value of
i is incremented by 1 before the condition is re-checked; these
procedures are repeated until the condition is no longer true at
which point the program flow exits the loop*/

 ```x = (double)rand()/RAND_MAX;```
 /*library function rand() returns a random integer number
 in the range 0 to RAND_MAX; the value is converted to
 double type using the type conversion so that the division
 operation rand()/RAND_MAX returns a decimal random number
 between 0 and 1; the value is assigned to variable x; here
 we generate the x coordinate of a random number*/

 ```y = (double)rand()/RAND_MAX;```
 /*another decimal random number in the range 0 to 1 is
 generated and assigned to y; here we generate y cooridante
 of the random number*/

 ```z = sqrt(x*x+y*y);```
 /*the distance of the randomly generated point (x, y) from
 the origin is computed; sqrt() function gives square root
 value of its parameter*/

 ```if (z<=1)```
 /*if the generated point is inside the 1st quadrant then
 the distance z is within 1, above condition is true and
 following statement is executed*/

  ```count++;```
  /*when the value of z is within 1, the value of 'count'
  is incremented by 1 to count how many randomly generated
  points are within the first quadrant*/

}
```
/*this closing curly brace specifies the end of the for loop*/
```
pi = (double)count/iter*4;
```
/*the value of pi is determined by multiplying the ratio of
inside-count and total-sample-count by 4; type conversion is
done so that the ratio produces a decimal result; otherwise,
we would only obtain an integer result (which is incorrect)
because count and iter are both integers*/
```
printf("Approximate value of PI is %0.4lf", pi);
```
/*printf() function displays the text in double quotations as
it is on the screen except for the value of pi replaces the
format specifier %0.4lf with four decimal points precision*/

```
    return 0;
    /*0 is returned as it is the standard for the successful
    execution of the program*/
}
```
/*the closing curly brace specifies the end of the main() function's
body, as well as the program's end; after that curly brace, no
statement is executed*/

## PROBLEM-15
**Write a program to find the root of a nonlinear equation using the Newton–Raphson method.**

Flowchart of the Solution:

Figure 2.10 shows the flowchart followed to solve this problem.

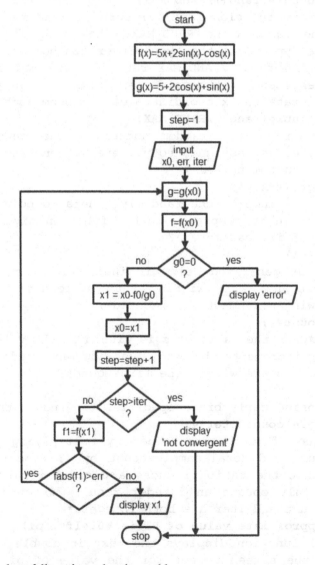

FIGURE 2.10 Flowchart followed to solve the problem.

## Algorithm of the Solution:

Step-1: Start.

Step-2: Define f(x)←5x+2sin(x)−cos(x)

Step-3: Define g(x)←5+2cos(x)+sin(x)

Step-4: Initialize step←1

Step-5: Read value of x0, err, and iter

Step-6: g0←g(x0)

Step-7: f0←f(x0)

Step-8: If (g0=0.0)

      8.1: Display 'error'

      8.2: Go to Step-17

Step-9: x1←x0-f0/g0

Step-10: Display values of step, x0, f0, x1, and f1

Step-11: x0←x1

Step-12: step←step+1

Step-13: If (step>iter)

      13.1: Display 'not convergent'

      13.2: Go to Step-17

Step-14: f1←f(x1)

Step-15: If (fabs(f1)>err)

      15.1: Go to Step-6

Step-16: Display value of x1

Step-17: Stop.

## Programming Code of the Solution:

```
#include<stdio.h>
#include<math.h>
#include<stdlib.h>
#define f(x) 5*x+2*sin(x)-cos(x)
#define g(x) 5+2*cos(x)+sin(x)
int main(){
    float x0, x1, f0, f1, g0, err;
    int step=1, iter;
```

```
    printf("Enter initial guess: ");
    scanf("%f", &x0);
    printf("Enter tolerable error: ");
    scanf("%f", &err);
    printf("Enter maximum iteration: ");
    scanf("%d", &iter);
    printf("\nStep\tx0\t\tf(x0)\t\tx1\t\tf(x1)\n");
    do{
        g0 = g(x0);
        f0 = f(x0);
        if (g0==0.0){
            printf("Error, exiting...");
            exit(0);
        }
        x1 = x0-f0/g0;
        printf("%d\t%f\t%f\t%f\t%f\n", step, x0, f0, x1, f1);
        x0 = x1;
        step = step+1;
        if (step>iter){
            printf("Not convergent, exiting...");
            exit(0);
        }
        f1 = f(x1);
    }while (fabs(f1)>err);
    printf("\nRoot is: %0.3f", x1);
    return 0;
}
```

<u>Input and Output of the Executed Program:</u>

```
Enter initial guess: 2.7
Enter tolerable error: 0.0001
Enter maximum iteration: 20

Step    x0              f(x0)           x1              f(x1)
1       2.700000        15.258832       -1.516037       0.000000
2       -1.516037       -9.631920       0.826947        -9.631920
3       0.826947        4.929344        0.131706        4.929344
4       0.131706        -0.070162       0.141568        -0.070162

Root is: 0.142
```

<u>Explanation of the Programming Code:</u>

**#include <stdio.h>**
/*header file stdio.h contains prototypes of the library functions printf(), and scanf(); the header file must be included using preprocessor directive #include before the functions are called in the program*/

```
#include <math.h>
```
/*header file math.h contains prototypes of the library functions
fabs(), sin() and cos(); the header file must be included using
preprocessor directive #include before the functions are called in
the program*/
```
#include<stdlib.h>
```
/*header file stdlib.h contains prototype of the library function
exit(); the header file must be included using preprocessor directive
#include before the function is called in the program*/
```
#define f(x) 5*x+2*sin(x)-cos(x)
```
/*#define is a preprocessor directive that defines a constant
variable; in this case, f(x) is the constant variable that holds
the value of the expression 5x+2sinx-cosx at x=x1*/
```
#define g(x) 5+2*cos(x)+sin(x)
```
/*the #define preprocessor directive is used to define another
constant variable, g(x), which takes the value of the expression
f'(x)=5+2cosx+sinx at x=x1*/
```
int main(){
```
/*here main() function returns an integer and parameters/
arguments of the main() function also remain void; execution of
the program starts with main() function; no statement before
opening curly brace of the main() function is executed by the
compiler*/
```
    float x0, x1, f0, f1, g0, err;
```
/*six float type variables are declared; required memory spaces
are allocated for each of the variables*/
```
    int step=1, iter;
```
/*integer type variables step and iter are declared; required
memory spaces are allocated for each of the variables; variable
step is initialized to 1*/
```
    printf("Enter initial guess: ");
```
/*output function printf() displays text in the double quotations
as it is on the screen*/
```
    scanf("%f", &x0);
```
/*input function scanf() reads a decimal value from the keyboard
and stores it in the memory spaces assigned for x0*/
```
    printf("Enter tolerable error: ");
```
/*output function printf() displays text in double quotations
as it is on the screen*/
```
    scanf("%f", &err);
```
/*function scanf() reads a decimal value from the keyboard and
assigns it to err*/
```
    printf("Enter maximum iteration: ");
```
/*function printf() displays text in the double quotations as
it is on the screen*/
```
    scanf("%d", &iter);
```
/*input function scanf() reads an integer from the keyboard and
stores the value in the memory spaces assigned for iter*/

```
printf("\nStep\tx0\t\tf(x0)\t\tx1\t\tf(x1)\n");
/*printf() function displays text in the double quotations as
it is on the screen except for a newline replaces \n and a tab
replaces \t*/
do{
/*following statements, enclosed within the curly braces,
repeatedly execute as long as the condition in the following
while remains true*/
    g0 = g(x0);
    /*value of the derivative of the equation at x=x0 is computed
    and assigned to g0*/
    f0 = f(x0);
    /*value of the equation at x=x0 is calculated and assigned
    to f0*/
    if (g0==0.0){
    /*if the function's derivative at x=x0 is 0, then above
    condition is true and following statements execute*/
        printf("Error, exiting . . . ");
        /*printf() displays text in the double quotations as it
        is on the screen*/
        exit(0);
        /*if g0=0, we can't divide the value f0 by g0 in the
        next statement, which is required to calculate a new
        approximate root using the Newton-Raphson method,
        therefore exit() is used to terminate the program
        early*/
    }
    /*this closing curly brace specifies the end of 'if' with
    condition (g0==0.0)*/
    x1 = x0-f0/g0;
    /*from the previous guess x0 and the values of the function
    and its derivative at x=x0, we compute a better approximation
    of the root x1*/
    printf("%d\t%f\t%f\t%f\t%f\n", step, x0, f0, x1, f1);
    /*printf() displays the results of this step on the screen;
    value of step is displayed in place of the first format
    specifier %d, x0 in place of first %f, f0 in place of second
    %f, x1 in place of third %f, f1 in place of fourth %f, a
    newline in place of \n and a tab in place of \t*/
    x0 = x1;
    /*calculated better estimate value x1 is assigned to x0
    so that in the following iteration of the loop, a better
    approximation than x1 can be computed*/
    step = step+1;
    /*the number of steps required to obtain the approximate
    root of the function is counted by incrementing the value
    of step by 1*/
```

```
    if (step>iter){
    /*if the number of steps exceeds the maximum number of
    iteration, the above condition is true, and the next two
    statements are executed*/
        printf("Not convergent, exiting . . . ");
        /*printf() displays text in the double quotations as it
        is on screen*/
        exit(0);
        /*if step>iter and we still don't get a root within
        our limit of error, the function isn't converging fast
        enough, so we terminate the program early with exit();
        exit(0) specifies an error-free program termination;
        we may need more iterations to achieve the desired
        outcome*/
    }
    /*this closing curly brace specifies the end of 'if' with
    condition (step>iter)*/
    f1 = f(x1);
    /*value of the function is calculated at a new approximate
    root x=x1 and assigned to f1*/
}while (fabs(f1)>err);
/*absolute value of f(x) at x=x1 is compared with our limit
of tolerable error; if the approximate root does not give us
function value within our limit of tolerable error, the above
condition of while is true, and the statements in the body of
do..while are executed again; these steps continue until we
get the root that gives us function value within our limit of
tolerable error*/
printf("\nRoot is: %0.3f", x1);
/*printf() function displays the text in the double-quotes as
it is on the screen, with the exception that the value of x1
replaces the format specifier %0.3f with three decimal points
precision and a newline replaces \n*/
return 0;
/*0 is returned as it is the standard for the successful
execution of the program*/
}
/*the closing curly brace specifies the end of the main() function's
body, as well as the program's end; after that curly brace, no
statement is executed*/
```

## PROBLEM-16
**Write a program to find the roots of a nonlinear equation using the Secant method.**

Flowchart of the Solution:

Figure 2.11 shows the flowchart followed to solve this problem.

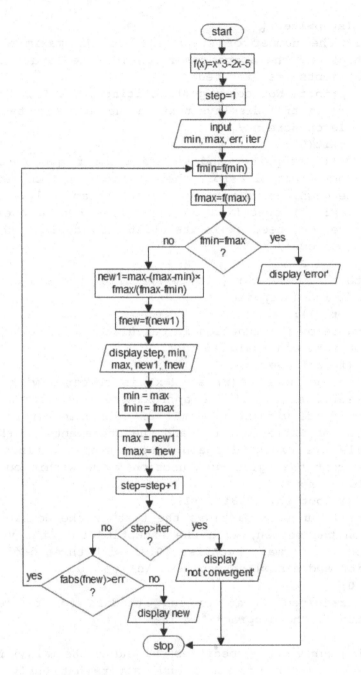

FIGURE 2.11  Flowchart followed to solve the problem.

## Algorithm of the Solution:

Step-1: Start.

Step-2: Define f(x)←x³–2x–5

Step-3: Initialize step←1

Step-4: Read values of min, max, err, and iter.

Step-5: fmin←f(min)

Step-6: fmax←f(max)

Step-7: If (fmin=fmax)

      7.1: Display 'error'

      7.2: Go to Step-19

Step-8: new1←max−(max−min)×fmax/(fmax−fmin)

Step-9: fnew←f(new1)

Step-10: Display values of step, min, max, new1, and fnew.

Step-11: min←max

Step-12: fmin←fmax

Step-13: max←new1

Step-14: fmax←fnew

Step-15: step←step+1

Step-16: If (step>iter)

      16.1: Display 'not convergent'

      16.2: Go to Step-19

Step-17: If (fabs(fnew)>err)

      17.1: Go to Step-5

Step-18: Display value of new1

Step-19: Stop

Programming Code of the Solution:

```c
#include<stdio.h>
#include<math.h>
#include<stdlib.h>
#define f(x) x*x*x-2*x-5
int main(){
    float min, max, new1, fmin, fmax, fnew, err;
    int step=1, iter;
    printf("Enter minimum initial guess: ");
    scanf("%f", &min);
    printf("Enter maximum initial guess: ");
    scanf("%f", &max);
    printf("Enter tolerable error: ");
    scanf("%f", &err);
    printf("Enter maximum iteration: ");
```

```
        scanf("%d", &iter);
        printf("\nStep\tmin\t\tmax\t\tnew\t\tf(new)\n");
        do{
            fmin = f(min);
            fmax = f(max);
            if (fmin==fmax){
                printf("Mathematical error, exiting...");
                exit(0);
            }
            new1 = max-(max-min)*fmax/(fmax-fmin);
            fnew = f(new1);
            printf("%d\t%f\t%f\t%f\t%f\n", step, min, max,
                    new1, fnew);
            min = max;
            fmin = fmax;
            max = new1;
            fmax = fnew;
            step = step+1;
            if (step>iter){
                printf("Not convergent, exiting...");
                exit(0);
            }
        }while (fabs(fnew)>err);
        printf("\nRoot is: %0.3f", new1);
        return 0;
}
```

Input and Output of the Executed Program:

```
Enter minimum initial guess: 1.2
Enter maximum initial guess: 9.3
Enter tolerable error: 0.0002
Enter maximum iteration: 20

Step   min           max           new           f(new)
1      1.200000      9.300000      1.258420      -5.523980
2      9.300000      1.258420      1.314916      -5.356337
3      1.258420      1.314916      3.120009      19.131571
4      1.314916      3.120009      1.709751      -3.421475
5      3.120009      1.709751      1.923698      -1.728529
6      1.709751      1.923698      2.142143      0.545524
7      1.923698      2.142143      2.089740      -0.053560
8      2.142143      2.089740      2.094425      -0.001415
9      2.089740      2.094425      2.094552      0.000004

Root is: 2.095
```

## Explanation of the Programming Code:

**#include<stdio.h>**
/*header file stdio.h contains prototypes of the library functions printf(), and scanf(); the header file must be included using preprocessor directive #include before the functions are called in the program*/
**#include<math.h>**
/*header file math.h contains prototype of the standard library function fabs(); the header file must be included using the preprocessor directive #include before the function is called in the program*/
**#include<stdlib.h>**
/*header file stdlib.h contains prototype of the standard library function exit(); the header file must be included using the #include preprocessor directive before the function is called in the program*/
**#define f(x) x*x*x-2*x-5**
/*#define is a preprocessor directive that defines a constant variable; in this case, f(x) is the constant variable that holds the value of the expression $x^3-2x-5$ at x=x1*/
**int main(){**
/*here main() function returns an integer and parameters/arguments of the main() function also remain void; execution of the program starts with main() function; no statement before opening curly brace of the main() function is executed by the compiler*/
    **float min, max, new1, fmin, fmax, fnew, err;**
    /*seven float type variables are declared; required memory spaces are allocated for each of the variables*/
    **int step=1, iter;**
    /*integer type variables step and iter are declared; required memory spaces are allocated for each of the variables; variable step is initialized to 1*/
    **printf("Enter minimum initial guess: ");**
    /*output function printf() displays text in the double quotations as it is on the screen*/
    **scanf("%f", &min);**
    /*input function scanf() reads a decimal value from keyboard and stores the value in the memory spaces assigned for min*/
    **printf("Enter maximum initial guess: ");**
    /*output function printf() displays text in the double quotations as it is on the screen*/
    **scanf("%f", &max);**
    /*input function scanf() reads a decimal value from keyboard and stores the value in the memory spaces assigned for max*/
    **printf("Enter tolerable error: ");**
    /*output function printf() displays text in the double quotations as it is on the screen*/

```
scanf("%f", &err);
/*scanf() takes a decimal value from keyboard and assigns the
value to err*/
printf("Enter maximum iteration: ");
/*output function printf() displays text in the double quotations
as it is on the screen*/
scanf("%d", &iter);
/*input function scanf() reads an integer from keyboard and
stores the value in the memory spaces assigned for iter*/
printf("\nStep\tmin\t\tmax\t\tnew\t\tf(new)\n");
/*printf() function displays text in the double quotations as
it is on the screen except for a newline replaces \n and a tab
replaces \t*/
do{
/*following statements enclosed in curly braces are executed
repeatedly as long as the condition in the while loop remains
true*/
    fmin = f(min);
    /*value of the function f(x) at x=min is calculated and
    assigned to fmin*/
    fmax = f(max);
    /*value of the function f(x) at x=max is calculated and
    assigned to fmax*/
    if (fmin==fmax){
    /*if the values of f(x) at x=min and x=max are the same,
    the condition above is true, and the following statements
    are executed*/
        printf("Mathematical error, exiting . . . ");
        /*printf() displays text in the double quotations as it
        is on the screen*/
        exit(0);
        /*if fmin=fmax, we can't divide fmax by (fmax-fmin) in
        the next statement, which is required to compute a new
        approximate root using the Secant method, therefore we
        call the built-in library function exit() to terminate
        the program prematurely*/
    }
    /*this closing curly brace specifies the end of 'if' with
    condition (fmin==fmax)*/
    new1 = max-(max-min)*fmax/(fmax-fmin);
    /*we derive a new approximate root from prior minimum and
    maximum guesses, as well as values of f(x) at x=min and
    x=max*/
    fnew = f(new1);
    /*the value of f(x) at a new approximation, x=new1, is
    computed and assigned to fnew*/
```

```
printf("%d\t%f\t%f\t%f\t%f\n", step, min, max, new1, fnew);
```
/*results of this step are displayed on the screen using
output function printf(); value of step is displayed in
place of the first format specifier %d, value of min in
place of the first %f, value of max in place of the second
%f, value of new1 in place of the third %f, value of fnew
in place of the fourth %f, a newline in place of \n, and a
tab in place of \t*/

```
min = max;
```
/*value of the minimum approximation min has been changed
to the value of the maximum approximation max*/

```
fmin = fmax;
```
/*value of f(x) at x=min is changed to the value at
x=max*/

```
max = new1;
```
/*the maximum approximation value max has been changed to
the newly calculated approximation value new1*/

```
fmax = fnew;
```
/*value of f(x) at x=max is changed to the value at
x=new1

thus, in this iteration, we change the minimum and maximum
approximations min and max, as well as calculate the values
of function at these two approximations, in order to
calculate a better approximation in the next iteration of
the loop*/

```
step = step+1;
```
/*the number of steps required to obtain the approximate
root of the function is counted by incrementing the value
of step by one*/

```
if (step>iter){
```
/*if the number of steps exceeds the maximum number of
iteration, the above condition is true, and the next two
statements are executed*/

```
    printf("Not convergent, exiting . . . ");
```
/*printf() displays text in the double quotations as it
is on the screen*/

```
    exit(0);
```
/*if step>iter and we still don't get a root within
our limit of error, the function isn't converging fast
enough, so we terminate the program early with exit();
exit(0) specifies an error-free program termination;
we may need more iterations to achieve the desired
outcome*/

```
}
```
/*this closing curly brace specifies the end of 'if' with
condition (step>iter)*/

```
    }while (fabs(fnew)>err);
    /*absolute value of f(x) at x=new is compared with our limit of
    tolerable error; if the approximate root does not give us function
    value within our limit of tolerable error, the above condition of
    while is true, and the statements in the body of do..while are
    executed again; these steps continue until we get root that gives
    us function value within our limit of tolerable error*/
    printf("\nRoot is: %0.3f", new1);
    /*printf() function displays the text in the double quotations
    as it is on the screen except for the value of new replaces the
    format specifier %0.3f with three decimal points precision, and
    a newline replaces \n*/
    return 0;
    /*0 is returned as it is the standard for the successful
    execution of the program*/
}
/*the closing curly brace specifies the end of the main() function's
body, as well as the program's end; after that curly brace, no
statement is executed*/
```

## PROBLEM-17

**Write a program to find the value of an unknown function from a discrete set of known data points using the Lagrange interpolation formula.**
**[note: please address this problem after completing Chapter 3, as its solution relies on the use of arrays]**

Flowchart of the Solution:

Figure 2.12 shows the flowchart followed to solve this problem.

**Algorithm of the Solution:**

Step-1: Start.

Step-2: Initialize dum←'y'

Step-3: Read value of num.

Step-4: Initialize i←0

Step-5: If i<num

      5.1: Input x[i] and y[i]

      5.2: i←i+1

      5.3: Go to Step-5

Step-6: Initialize i←0

Step-7: If i<num

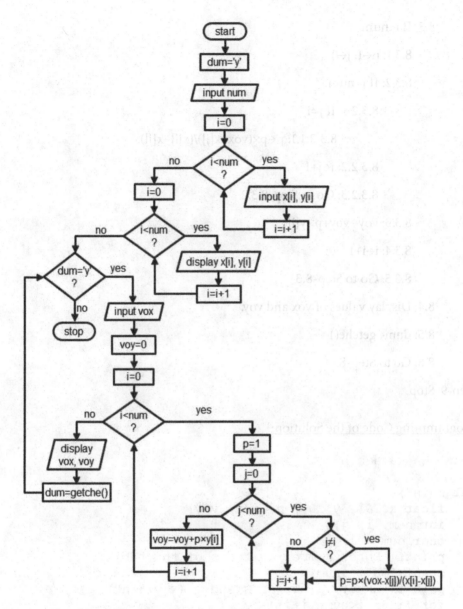

FIGURE 2.12 Flowchart followed to solve the problem.

7.1: Display values of x[i] and y[i]

7.2: i←i+1

7.3: Go to Step-7

Step-8: If dum='y'

8.1: Input vox

8.2: Initialize voy←0, i←0

8.3: If i<num

8.3.1: p←1, j←0

8.3.2: If j<num

8.3.2.1: If j≠i

8.3.2.1.1: p←p×(vox−x[j])/(x[i]−x[j])

8.3.2.2: j←j+1

8.3.2.3: Go to Step-8.3.2

8.3.3: voy←voy+p×y[i]

8.3.4: i←i+1

8.3.5: Go to Step-8.3

8.4: Display values of vox and voy.

8.5: dum←getche()

8.6: Go to Step-8

Step-9: Stop.

<u>Programming Code of the Solution:</u>

```c
#include <stdio.h>
#include <conio.h>
int main(){
    float x[20], y[20], p, vox, voy;
    int num, i, j;
    char dum='y';
    printf("Enter number of terms of the table: ");
    scanf("%d", &num);
    printf("Enter values of x and y (x y):\n");
    for (i=0; i<num; i++){
        printf("x[%d] y[%d]: ", i+1, i+1);
        scanf("%f %f", &x[i], &y[i]);
    }
    printf("\nThe table you entered is:\n");
    printf("x\t\ty\n");
    for (i=0; i<num; i++)
        printf("%0.2f\t\t%0.2f\n", x[i], y[i]);
    while (dum=='y'){
        printf("\nEnter value of x to find the respective value"
                " of y: ");
```

```
        scanf("%f", &vox);
        voy=0;
        for (i=0; i<num; i++){
            p=1;
            for (j=0; j<num; j++)
                if (j!=i)
                    p = p*(vox-x[j])/(x[i]-x[j]);
            voy = voy+p*y[i];
        }
        printf("Value of y at x=%0.3f is: %0.3f\n", vox, voy);
        printf("\nPress y to continue, n to exit: ");
        dum=getche();
    }
    return 0;
}
```

## Input and Output of the Executed Program:

```
Enter number of terms of the table: 8
Enter values of x and y (x y):
x[1] y[1]: 1.23 5.68
x[2] y[2]: 45.67 98.32
x[3] y[3]: 98 198
x[4] y[4]: 189 34
x[5] y[5]: 34.87 76.98
x[6] y[6]: 171 876
x[7] y[7]: 78 257
x[8] y[8]: 57.8 175

The table you entered is:
x                  y
1.23               5.68
45.67              98.32
98.00              198.00
189.00             34.00
34.87              76.98
171.00             876.00
78.00              257.00
57.80              175.00

Enter value of x to find the respective value of y: 50
Value of y at x=50.000 is: 122.562

Press y to continue, n to exit: y
Enter value of x to find the respective value of y: 34
Value of y at x=34.000 is: 78.426

Press y to continue, n to exit: n
```

## Explanation of the Programming Code:

```
#include <stdio.h>
```
/*header file stdio.h contains prototypes of the library functions printf(), and scanf(); the header file must be included using preprocessor directive #include before the functions are called in the program*/
```
#include <conio.h>
```
/*non-standard function getche() is declared in the conio.h header file; the header file must be included using the preprocessor directive #include before the function is called in the program*/
```
int main(){
```
/*all C program must have a main() function with return type void or int; here there is no parameter of the main() function and it returns an integer; opening curly brace specifies start of the main() function and no statement before that curly brace is executed by the compiler*/
```
    float x[20], y[20], p, vox, voy;
```
/*two float type arrays x[] and y[] of size 20 and three float type variables p, vox and voy are declared*/
```
    int num, i, j;
```
/*three integer type variables are declared*/
```
    char dum='y';
```
/*character type variable dum is declared and initialized to 'y'*/
```
    printf("Enter number of terms of the table: ");
```
/*output function printf() displays text in double quotations as it is on the screen*/
```
    scanf("%d", &num);
```
/*input function scanf() reads an integer from keyboard and stores the value in the memory spaces assigned for num*/
```
    printf("Enter values of x and y (x y):\n");
```
/*output function printf() displays text in double quotations as it is on the screen followed by a newline in place of \n*/
```
    for (i=0; i<num; i++){
```
/*this for loop is used to input set of tabulated data $(x_i, y_i)$, one pair per iteration; here i=0 is initialization, i<num is condition and i++ is increment; the initialization is done once at the beginning of the loop; after that, the condition is checked, if it is true, the statement in the body is executed, and the value of i is incremented by 1 before the condition is re-checked; these steps are repeated until the condition is no longer true at which point the program flow exits the loop*/
```
        printf("x[%d] y[%d]: ", i+1, i+1);
```
/*output function printf() displays text in the double quotations as it is on the screen except for the value of i+1 replaces both format specifiers %d*/

```
    scanf("%f %f", &x[i], &y[i]);
    /*scanf() reads two decimal values from the keyboard
    separated by a space, tab, or newline; the first value
    corresponds to array element x[i], and the second value
    corresponds to array element y[i]; in the first iteration,
    input values correspond to x[0] and y[0]; in the second
    iteration, input values correspond to x[1] and y[1], and
    so on*/
}
/*this closing curly brace specifies the end of the for loop*/
printf("\nThe table you entered is:\n");
/*output function printf() displays text in double quotations
as it is on the screen except for a newline replaces \n*/
printf("x\t\ty\n");
/*printf() displays text in the double quotations as it is on
the screen except for a newline replaces \n and a tab replaces
\t*/
for (i=0; i<num; i++)
/*this for loop is used to display the set of input data,
one pair per iteration; here i=0 is initialization, i<num is
condition and i++ is increment; the initialization is done
once at the beginning of the loop; after that, the condition
is checked, if it is true, the statement in the body is
executed, and the value of i is incremented by 1 before the
condition is re-checked; these steps are repeated until the
condition is no longer true at which point the program flow
exits the loop*/
    printf("%0.2f\t\t%0.2f\n", x[i], y[i]);
    /*printf() function displays value of x[i] in place of first
    format specifier %0.2f with two decimal points precision on
    the screen, value of y[i] in place of second %0.2f, a tab
    in place of \t and a newline in place of \n*/
while (dum=='y'){
/*if dum='y' then above condition is true and following
statements, enclosed by curly braces, are executed as long as
the condition remains true*/
    printf("\nEnter value of x to find the respective value"
        " of y: ");
    /*output function printf() displays text in the double
    quotations as it is on the screen except for a newline
    replaces \n*/
    scanf("%f", &vox);
    /*input function scanf() reads a decimal value from input
    terminal and stores the value in the memory spaces assigned
    for vox*/
    voy=0;
    /*0 is assigned to the variable voy; otherwise, the summation
    operation involving voy in the next 'for' loop may yield
```

an incorrect result because, when we declare a variable, memory space is allocated for that variable, and the memory space may contain some garbage value; also, voy stores the result of the previous iteration in the second and third iterations of the 'while' loop; when we sequentially add data with voy and the result is accumulated in the voy variable, the garbage value or result from the previous iteration may be added in the first summation*/

```
for (i=0; i<num; i++){
```
/*i=0 is initialization, i<num is condition and i++ is increment; initialization is done once at the beginning of the loop; then the condition is checked, if it is true, statements in the body are executed and value of i is incremented by 1 before the condition is re-checked; these steps continue until the condition becomes false at which point the program flow exits the loop*/

```
    p=1;
```
/*1 is assigned to the variable p; otherwise, the multiplication operation involving p in the following 'for' loop may yield an incorrect result because, when we declare a variable, memory space is allocated for that variable, and the memory space may contain some garbage value; also, in the second and third iterations of the above 'for' loop, p stores the result of the previous iteration; when we multiply data with p in a sequential manner, the garbage value or result from the previous iteration may be multiplied in the first operation*/

```
for (j=0; j<num; j++)
```
/*j=0 is initialization, j<num is condition and j++ is increment; initialization is done once at the beginning of the loop; then condition is checked, if it is true, statements in the body are executed and value of j is incremented by 1 before the condition is re-checked; these steps continue until the condition becomes false at which point the program flow exits the loop; for each value of i, following if statement is executed num times*/

```
    if (j!=i)
```
/*if j≠i, the condition is true and following statement is executed*/

```
        p = p*(vox-x[j])/(x[i]-x[j]);
```
/*for i=0, at 1st iteration j=i, so no statement executes
At 2nd iteration, p=1×(vox-x[1])/(x[0]-x[1])
At 3rd iteration, p=p×(vox-x[2])/(x[0]-x[2])

```
            for  i=1,  at  1st  iteration,  p=px(vox-x[0])/
            (x[1]-x[0])
            At 2nd iteration j=i, so no statement executes
            At 3rd iteration, p=px(vox-x[2])/(x[1]-x[2])
            for  i=2,  at  1st  iteration,  p=px(vox-x[0])/
            (x[2]-x[0])
            At 2nd iteration, p=px(vox-x[1])/(x[2]-x[1])
            At 3rd iteration j=i, so no statement executes*/
        voy = voy+p*y[i];
        /*at 1st iteration, voy=0+pxy[0]
        at 2nd iteration, voy=voy+pxy[1]
        at 3rd iteration, voy=voy+pxy[2]*/
    }
    /*this is the end of 'for' loop with condition (i=0;
    i<num; i++)*/
    printf("Value of y at x=%0.3f is: %0.3f\n", vox, voy);
    /*output function printf() displays the text in double
    quotations as it is on the screen except for value of
    vox replaces first format specifier %0.3f with three
    decimal points precision, value of voy replaces second
    %0.3f, and a newline replaces \n*/
    printf("\nPress y to continue, n to exit: ");
    /*output function printf() displays the text in the
    double quotations as it is on the screen except for a
    newline replaces \n*/
    dum=getche();
    /*the getche() function waits for character input from
    the keyboard, and when a character is typed, it is
    echoed on the output screen without waiting for enter
    to be hit, and the character is assigned to dum*/
    }
    /*this is the end of the while loop*/
    return 0;
    /*0 is returned as it is the standard for the successful
    execution of the program*/
}
```
/*the closing curly brace specifies the end of the main() function's
body, as well as the program's end; after that curly brace, no
statement is executed*/

## PROBLEM-18
**Write a program to solve ordinary differential equations using Euler's method.**

Flowchart of the Solution:

Figure 2.13 shows the flowchart followed to solve this problem.

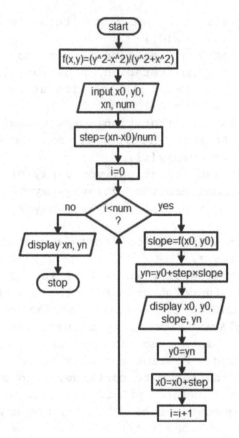

FIGURE 2.13    Flowchart followed to solve the problem.

## Algorithm of the Solution:

Step-1: Start.

Step-2: Define $f(x,y) \leftarrow (y^2-x^2)/(y^2+x^2)$

Step-3: Read values of x0, y0=f(x0), xn, and num.

Step-4: step←(xn−x0)/num

Step-5: Initialize i←0

Step-6: If i<num

      6.1: slope←f(x0, y0)

      6.2: yn←y0+step×slope

      6.3: Display values of x0, y0, slope, and yn

      6.4: y0←yn

      6.5: x0←x0+step

      6.6: i←i+1

6.7: Go to Step-6

Step-7: Display values of xn and yn

Step-8: Stop.

## Programming Code of the Solution:

```c
#include<stdio.h>
#define f(x,y) (y*y-x*x)/(y*y+x*x)
int main(){
    float x0, y0, xn, yn, step, slope;
    int i, num;
    printf("Enter Initial Condition:\n");
    printf("x0: ");
    scanf("%f", &x0);
    printf("y(%0.2f): ", x0);
    scanf("%f", &y0);
    printf("Enter calculation point xn: ");
    scanf("%f", &xn);
    printf("Enter number of steps: ");
    scanf("%d", &num);
    step = (xn-x0)/num;
    printf("\nx0\ty0\tslope\tyn\n");
    for (i=0; i<num; i++){
        slope = f(x0, y0);
        yn = y0+step*slope;
        printf("%0.3f\t%0.3f\t%0.3f\t%0.3f\n", x0, y0, slope, yn);
        y0 = yn;
        x0 = x0+step;
    }
    printf("\nValue of y at x=%0.2f is %0.3f", xn, yn);
    return 0;
}
```

## Input and Output of the Executed Program:

```
Enter Initial Condition:
x0: 0
y(0.00): 1
Enter calculation point xn: 3.2
Enter number of steps: 8

x0      y0      slope    yn
0.000   1.000   1.000    1.400
0.400   1.400   0.849    1.740
0.800   1.740   0.651    2.000
1.200   2.000   0.471    2.188
1.600   2.188   0.303    2.309
2.000   2.309   0.143    2.367
2.400   2.367   -0.014   2.361
2.800   2.361   -0.169   2.294

Value of y at x=3.20 is 2.294
```

## Explanation of the Programming Code:

```
#include<stdio.h>
```
/*header file stdio.h contains prototypes of the library functions printf(), and scanf(); the header file must be included using preprocessor directive #include before the functions are called in the program*/
```
#define f(x,y) (y*y-x*x)/(y*y+x*x)
```
/*#define is a preprocessor directive that defines a constant variable; in this case, f(x) is the constant variable that holds the value of the expression $(y^2-x^2)/(y^2+x^2)$ at x=x1 and y=y1*/
```
int main(){
```
/*here main() function returns an integer and parameters/arguments of the main() function also remain void; execution of the program starts with main() function; no statement before opening curly brace of the main() function is executed by the compiler*/
```
    float x0, y0, xn, yn, step, slope;
```
/*six float type variables are declared; required memory spaces are allocated for each of the variables*/
```
    int i, num;
```
/*two integer type variables i and num are declared; required memory spaces are allocated for each of the variables*/
```
    printf("Enter Initial Condition:\n");
```
/*printf() function displays the text' in double quotations as it is on the screen except for a newline replaces \n*/
```
    printf("x0: ");
```
/*output function printf() displays text in double quotations as it is on the screen*/
```
    scanf("%f", &x0);
```
/*input function scanf() reads a decimal value from keyboard and stores the value in the memory spaces assigned for x0*/
```
    printf("y(%0.2f): ", x0);
```
/*printf() function displays the text in the double quotations as it is on the screen except for the value of x0 replaces format specifier %0.2f with two decimal points precision*/
```
    scanf("%f", &y0);
```
/*input function scanf() reads a decimal value from keyboard and stores the value in the memory spaces assigned for y0*/
```
    printf("Enter calculation point xn: ");
```
/*output function printf() displays text in double quotations as it is on the screen*/
```
    scanf("%f", &xn);
```
/*input function scanf() reads a decimal value from keyboard and stores the value in the memory spaces assigned for xn*/
```
    printf("Enter number of steps: ");
```
/*output function printf() displays text in double quotations as it is on the screen*/

```
scanf("%d", &num);
/*function scanf() reads an integer from input terminal and
stores the value in the memory spaces assigned for num*/
step = (xn-x0)/num;
/*step-size is calculated from calculation point, initial point
and number of steps*/
printf("\nx0\ty0\tslope\tyn\n");
/*printf() function displays the text in double quotations as
it is on the screen except for a newline replaces \n and a tab
replaces \t*/
for (i=0; i<num; i++){
/*this for loop is used to calculate f(xn) from f(x0), with each
iteration takes a small step forward to calculate f(x0+i*step);
i=0 is initialization, i<num is condition and i++ is increment;
the initialization is done once at the beginning of the loop;
after that, the condition is tested, if it is true, the statements
in the body are executed, and the value of i is incremented by
one before the condition is re-checked; these procedures are
repeated until the condition becomes false at which point the
program flow exits the loop*/
    slope = f(x0, y0);
    /*slope to the curve at x0 is computed from the differential
    equation, f(x0, y(x0))=f(x0, y0) [value of f(x, y) at x=x0
    and y=y0=y(x0)]*/
    yn = y0+step*slope;
    /*next slope to the curve at a point small step forward
    from x0 is calculated from y0=y(x0), step size and slope at
    previous point*/
    printf("%0.3f\t%0.3f\t%0.3f\t%0.3f\n", x0, y0, slope, yn);
    /*results of this step are displayed on screen using output
    function printf(); value of x0 is displayed in place of
    first format specifier %0.3f with three decimal points
    precision, y0 in place of second %0.3f, slope in place of
    third %0.3f and yn in place of fourth %0.3f; other text is
    displayed as it is except for a newline replaces \n and a
    tab replaces \t*/
    y0 = yn;
    /*calculated slope value yn is assigned to y0 so that it
    can be used to compute slope at the next point in the next
    iteration of the loop*/
    x0 = x0+step;
    /*next point is calculated by stepping a small step forward;
    this value is used to compute slope at the next point in the
    next iteration of the loop*/
}
/*this closing curly brace specifies the end of for loop*/
```

```
printf("\nValue of y at x=%0.2f is %0.3f", xn, yn);
/*output function printf() displays the text in the double
quotes as it is on the screen except for the value of xn replaces
format specifier %0.2f with two decimal points precision, yn
replaces %0.3f with three decimal points precision and a newline
replaces \n*/
return 0;
/*0 is returned as it is the standard for the successful
execution of the program*/
}
/*the closing curly brace specifies the end of the main() function's
body, as well as the program's end; after that curly brace, no
statement is executed*/
```

## PROBLEM-19
**Write a program to approximate the definite integral of a continuous function using Simpson's 1/3 rule.**

Flowchart of the Solution:

Figure 2.14 shows the flowchart followed to solve this problem.

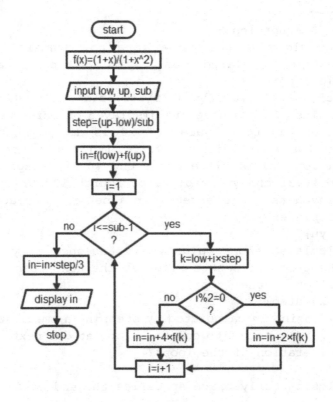

FIGURE 2.14   Flowchart followed to solve the problem.

## Algorithm of the Solution:

Step-1: Start.

Step-2: Define $f(x) \leftarrow (1+x)/(1+x^2)$

Step-3: Read values of low, up, and sub.

Step-4: step←(up-low)/sub

Step-5: in←f(low)+f(up)

Step-6: Initialize i←1

Step-7: If i<=sub−1

    7.1: k←low+i×step

    7.2: If i%2=0

        7.2.1: in←in+2×f(k)

        7.2.2: Go to Step-7.4

    7.3: in←in+4×f(k)

    7.4: i←i+1

    7.5: Go to Step-7

Step-8: in←in×step/3

Step-9: Display value of in

Step-10: Stop.

## Programming Code of the Solution:

```
#include<stdio.h>
#define f(x) (1+x)/(1+x*x)
int main(){
    float low, up, in, step, k;
    int i, sub;
    printf("Enter lower limit of integration: ");
    scanf("%f", &low);
    printf("Enter upper limit of integration: ");
    scanf("%f", &up);
    printf("Enter number of sub-intervals: ");
    scanf("%d", &sub);
    step = (up-low)/sub;
    in = f(low)+f(up);
    for (i=1; i<=sub-1; i++){
        k = low+i*step;
        if (i%2==0)
```

```
            in = in+2*f(k);
        else
            in = in+4*f(k);
    }
    in = in*step/3;
    printf("Required value of integration is: %0.3f", in);
    return 0;
}
```

Input and Output of the Executed Program:

```
Enter lower limit of integration: -1
Enter upper limit of integration: 1
Enter number of sub-intervals: 10
Required value of integration is: 1.571
```

## Explanation of the Programming Code:

**#include<stdio.h>**
/*header file stdio.h contains prototypes of the library functions printf(), and scanf(); the header file must be included using preprocessor directive #include before the functions are called in the program*/
**#define f(x) (1+x)/(1+x*x)**
/*#define is a preprocessor directive that defines a constant variable; in this case, f(x) is the constant variable that holds the value of the expression $(1+x)/(1+x^2)$ at x=x1*/
**int main(){**
/*here main() function returns an integer and parameters/arguments of the main() function also remain void; execution of the program starts with main() function; no statement before opening curly brace of the main() function is executed by the compiler*/
    **float low, up, in, step, k;**
    /*five float type variables are declared; required memory spaces are allocated for each of the variables by the compiler*/
    **int i, sub;**
    /*two integer type variables are declared; required memory spaces are allocated for each variable*/
    **printf("Enter lower limit of integration: ");**
    /*output function printf() displays the text in the quotations as it is on the screen*/
    **scanf("%f", &low);**
    /*scanf() reads a decimal value from the input terminal and stores the value in the memory space allocated for variable low*/
    **printf("Enter upper limit of integration: ");**
    /*output function printf() displays the text in the quotations as it is on the screen*/

```
scanf("%f", &up);
```
/*scanf() reads a decimal value from the input terminal and stores the value in the memory space allocated for variable up*/
```
printf("Enter number of sub-intervals: ");
```
/*output function printf() displays the text in the quotations as it is on the screen*/
```
scanf("%d", &sub);
```
/*scanf() reads an integer from the input terminal and stores the value in the memory space allocated for variable sub*/
```
step = (up-low)/sub;
```
/*step size is calculated from upper limit, lower limit and no. of sub-intervals

Simpson's 1/3 rule-

$$\int_{low}^{up} f(x)dx = \frac{step}{3}\left[f(low) + 2\sum_{i=1}^{sub/2-1} f(x_{2i}) + 4\sum_{i=1}^{sub/2} f(x_{2i-1}) + f(up)\right]*/$$

```
in = f(low)+f(up);
```
/*values of function at x=up and atbx=low are calculated and their summation is assigned to in*/
```
for (i=1; i<=sub-1; i++){
```
/*this for loop is used to compute the two summation terms in the Simpson's 1/3 rule; i=1 is initialization, i<=sub-1 is condition and i++ is increment; the condition is checked once at the beginning of the loop; if it is true, statements in the body are executed and the value of i is incremented by 1 before the condition is re-checked; these steps continue until the condition becomes false at which point the program flow exits the loop; for i=0, k=low and for i=sub, k=up; values of the f(x) at these two points f(low) and f(up) were considered before that loop; hence this loop starts with i=1 and ends at i=sub-1*/
```
    k = low+i*step;
```
/*next point x=k is calculated from the lower limit and step size*/
```
    if (i%2==0)
```
/*if i is an even number, following statement is executed and skipped the next else statement*/
```
        in = in+2*f(k);
```
/*first summation term of the Simpson's 1/3 rule is calculated and added to in*/
```
    else
```
/*if i is an odd number, following statement is executed skipping the previous if statement*/
```
        in = in+4*f(k);
```
/*second summation term of the Simpson's 1/3 rule is calculated and added to in*/

```
}
/*this closing curly brace specifies the end of the for loop*/
in = in*step/3;
/*integral value of the function is calculated by multiplying
the total summation in by 1/3rd of the step size*/
printf("Required value of integration is: %0.3f", in);
/*printf() displays the text in the quotations as it is on the
screen except for the value of in replaces format specifier
%0.3f with three decimal points precision*/
return 0;
/*0 is returned as it is the standard for the successful
execution of the program*/
}
/*the closing curly brace specifies the end of the main() function's
body, as well as the program's end; after that curly brace, no
statement is executed*/
```

## EXERCISES

MCQ with Answers

1) Which loop is faster in C language, for, while, or do..while?

   A) for

   B) while

   C) do..while

   D) All work at the same speed

2) Which loop executes at least once even if the condition is false?

   A) do..while

   B) while

   C) for

   D) None of the above

3) Which type of loop while and for are?

   A) Entry control

   B) Exit control

   C) Both of the above

   D) None of the above

4) What is the way to suddenly come out of or quit any loop?

   A) continue statement

B) break statement

C) leave statement

D) quit statement

5) Choose a correct statement about the break statement.

A) A single break statement can force execution control to come out of only one loop

B) A single break statement can force execution control to come out of a maximum of two nested loops

C) A single break statement can force execution control to come out of a maximum of three nested loops

D) None of the above

6) break statement is used to _____.

A) Quit a program

B) Quit the current iteration

C) Both A and B

D) None of the above

7) Which of the following is a C conditional operator?

A) ?:

B) :?

C) :<

D) <:

8) Which of the following is the correct syntax of the ternary operator?

A) condition? expression1: expression2

B) condition: expression1? expression2

C) condition? expression1 < expression2

D) condition < expression1? expression2

9) Which of the following is a valid statement regarding if..else statement?

A) else..if is compulsory to use with if statement

B) else is compulsory to use with if statement

C) else or else..if is optional with if statement

D) None of the above

10) Choose a correct statement regarding loop for(;;);

    A) for loop works exactly the first time

    B) for loop works an infinite number of times

    C) Syntax error

    D) None of the above

11) Which of the following cannot be checked in a switch..case statement?

    A) character

    B) integer

    C) float

    D) enum

12) What is the value of a, after execution of the following program statement?

    int a = 5<2? 4: 3;

    A) 4

    B) 3

    C) 5

    D) 2

13) What is the value of count after execution of the following program fragment?

    for (i=0, count=0; i<5; i++);

    for (j=0; j<5; j++);

    count++;

    A) 25

    B) 0

    C) 1

    D) 55

14) What is the value of count after execution of the following program fragment?

    for (i=0, count=0; i<5; i++)

    for (j=0; j<5; j++)

    count++;

    A) 25

B) 0

C) 1

D) 55

[Ans. D, A, A, B, A, B, A, A, C, B, C, B, C, A]

## Questions with Short Answers

1) What is the difference between = and == symbols in C?

   Ans. = is an assignment operator that is used in mathematical operations to assign a value to a variable. == is a relational operator that is used to compare two variables or constants.

2) What is || operator, and how does it function in a program?

   Ans. In C, || is called OR logical operator. It is used to assess logical conditions. If any condition of the expression is TRUE, the complete condition statement is TRUE.

3) What are the types of loops available in C?

   Ans. Four types of loops available in C are while, do..while, for, and nested loop.

4) What is a nested loop?

   Ans. A nested loop is when one or more loops are used inside another while, do.. while, or for loop. Example:

   x=1;

   while (x<=10){

       for (y=0; y<10; y++)

           printf("do nothing . . .\n");

       x++;}

5) What is a loop control statement? What are the loop control statements available in C?

   Ans. The loop control statement changes the typical execution sequence. break, continue, and goto are the loop control statements available in C.

6) What are the valid places to have a keyword break?

   Ans. Only within the loop control and switch statements can a break occur. When a break statement is encountered in a loop, the loop is terminated immediately, and program control is passed to the next statement after the loop.

7) Explain the syntax of 'for' loop.

Ans. Syntax of 'for' loop is as follows:

for (initialization; condition; increment/decrement){

    //statements to be executed if condition is true

}

The loop's initialization is done only once, at the beginning, and then the condition is checked. If the condition is true, the statements in the loop's body are executed, and the counter's value is incremented or decremented. Now, the condition is rechecked. These steps (condition→body→counter→condition) repeat until the condition becomes false, at which point the program control exits the loop.

8) What is an infinite loop?

Ans. When a loop has no terminating condition, such as a condition that causes the loop to restart or a condition that is never satisfied, the loop continues indefinitely and is referred to as an infinite loop. Example is as follows:

for (x=10; x<=20; x –);

9) What is the equivalent code of the following statement in 'while' loop format:

for (a=1; a<=9; a++)?

Ans. a=1;

      while (a<=9)

         a++;

10) What are compound statements?

Ans. Compound statements are made up of two or more program statements that are all executed together. These statements are frequently encased in curly braces and used in an if..else condition or loop, where the compound statements are executed based on whether the condition is true or false.

11) When is a 'switch' statement preferable over an 'if' statement?

Ans. When there are more than two conditions on a single variable, the 'switch' statement is preferred. The 'if' statement is preferred in other situations involving multiple variables or complex if..else clauses.

12) What will happen in a 'switch' statement if the break statement is omitted?

Ans. Based on the switch expression, switch-case statements are used to execute just particular case statements. If no break statement is used at the end of each case, the program executes all subsequent case statements until the next break statement is found or the end of the switch case block is reached.

13) What are the differences between 'while' and 'do..while' loops?

Ans. The while loop always tests the condition before executing the while loop's statements, whereas the do..while loop tests the condition after executing the loop's statements. As a result, even if the condition is false, the statements in the do..while loop are executed at least once.

14) What is the output of the following program fragment?

```
if (4>5)
      printf("Atiq...");
      printf("Ahad...");
```

Ans. Ahad...

The first printf() statement is not executed because the 'if' condition is false, and the second printf() statement displays the text Ahad ... on the screen.

15) What is the output of the following program fragment?

```
if (10>9)
      printf("Dhaka...");
else if (6%3==0)
      printf("Karachi...");
      printf("Delhi...");
```

Ans. Dhaka ... Delhi ...

Because the if condition is true, the first printf() is executed, displaying Dhaka ... on the screen, and the else..if condition is not entered, so the second printf() is not executed. The third printf() function displays the text Delhi ... on the screen.

16) What is the output of the following program fragment?

```
while (true){
      printf("Singapore...");
      break;}
```

Ans. Because TRUE or true is not a keyword, the while statement fails and causes a compilation error.

17) What is the output of the following program fragment?

```
int num=5;
while (num=12){
      printf("nothing...");
      break;}
```

Ans. nothing . . .

Because while (num=12) == while (12) == while (non-zero) == true, printf() displays nothing . . . on the screen and the break statement terminates the loop immediately.

18) What is the output of the following program fragment?

int num=40;

do{

printf("%d . . .", num);

num++;} while (num<=30);

Ans. 40 . . .

Because statements in the "do" are executed at least once before the while condition is checked, the result is 40 . . .. The false condition is now checked, and the loop is terminated.

19) What is the output of the following program fragment?

for (i=1, j=10; i<=5; i++)

printf("%d, ", i+j);

Ans. 11, 12, 13, 14, 15,

Initialization is done once at the beginning of the loop, i=1, j=10. Because condition i<=5 is true, printf() displays i+j=1+10=11 on the first iteration, and the value of i is incremented by 1 (i++→i=i+1=1+1=2). Because condition i<=5 is true again in the second iteration, the number 12 is displayed, and so on. The number 15 is displayed, and i becomes i=5+1=6 in the fifth iteration; the condition i<=5 is false, and the loop ends after the fifth iteration.

20) What is the output of the following program fragment?

int num=10;

while (num<15){

num++;

if (num>=12 && num<=14)

continue;

printf("%d, ", num);}

Ans. 11, 15,

Because the "if" condition is true and the continue statement is executed between 12 and 14, the printf() statement in the loop skips during that period.

21) What is the output of the following program fragment?

```
int x=0, y=0;
while (++x<4)
        printf("%d, ", x);
while (y++<4)
        printf("%d, ", y);
```

Ans. 1, 2, 3, 1, 2, 3, 4,

The value of x is incremented first in the first 'while' loop, and then the condition is tested. The second 'while' loop, on the other hand, checks the condition first and then increments the value of y.

22) What is the output of the following program fragment?

```
int num=3;
switch (num){
        case 1: printf("1, ");
        case 3: printf("3, ");
        case 5: printf("5, ");
        default: printf("default, ");}
```

Ans. 3, 5, default,

Because there is no break statement after matching and executing the case 3 statement, program control immediately moves to case 5 and default.

23) What is the output of the following program fragment?

```
int num=0;
switch (num){
        case 1: printf("1, ");
        case 3: printf("3, ");
        case 5: printf("5, ");
        default: printf("default, ");}
```

Ans. default,

Because there is no case match in the switch statement, program control goes to default case automatically.

24) What is the output of the following program fragment?

```
char code='s';
switch (code){
    case 's': printf("sun, "); break;
    case 'a': printf("apple, "); break;
    case 't': printf("tire, "); break;
    default: printf("default, ");}
```

Ans. sun,

Because the switch statement's case 's' matches, the corresponding printf() displays sun on the screen because of the break statement, program control exits the switch, ignoring all other cases.

25) What is the output of the following program fragment?

```
int num=32;
switch (num){
    case 16: printf("16, "); break;
    case 32: printf("32, "); break;
    case 16*2: printf("16×2, "); break;
    default: printf("default, ");}
```

Ans. A compilation error will occur. Because C prohibits the use of duplicate case constants in switch statements.

26) What is the output of the following program fragment?

```
int num=3;
switch (num){
    case 1: printf("1, "); break;
    case 3: printf("3, "); break;
    case 5: printf("5, "); continue;
    default: printf("default, ");}
```

Ans. A compilation error will occur. Because the continue statement is not allowed in a switch..case statement as it is not a loop.

27) What is the output of the following program fragment?

for (;;)

    for (;;)

        printf("good-bye");

Ans. The phrase 'goodbye' appears indefinitely on the screen. Because 'for' loop with no initialization, condition, and increment/decrement is an infinite loop.

## Problems to Practice

1) Write a program to check whether a given number is positive or negative.

2) Write a program to check whether a number is even or odd.

3) Write a program to check whether a character is an alphabet or not.

4) Write a program to count the number of digits in an integer.

5) Write a program to generate and display multiplication table of a number entered by user.

6) Write a program to determine and display the sum of the following harmonic series for a given value of n.

$$1+\frac{1}{2}+\frac{1}{3}+\cdots+\frac{1}{n}$$

The value of n should be given interactively through the terminal.

7) Write a program to find the number and sum of all integers greater than 100 and less than 200 divisible by 7.

8) Write a program to compute the roots of a quadratic equation:

$$ax^2 + bx + c = 0$$

The program should request the values of the constants a, b, and c and display the values of the roots.

9) Write a program to compute the sum of individual digits of a given positive integer number.

10) Develop a program to implement a calculator. The program should request the user to input two numbers and display one of the following as per the desire of the user (consider the operators "+", "−", "*", "/", "%" and use "switch" statement):

(a) Sum of the numbers

(b) Difference of the numbers

(c) Product of the numbers

(d) Division of the numbers

11) A person has 10 vori gold, 25 vori silver, and tk 10,000.00 in cash. He also has tk 5,000.00 in debt, and he owes his cousin tk 7,500.00. Calculate the amount of money he has to pay for piety tax this year. Piety tax is payable to the poor, 2.5% of total wealth (gold, silver, cash, or any business items) one person has after one lunar year if his total wealth is more than 7.5 vori gold or 52.5 vori silver or its equivalent money whichever is smaller.

12) A person gets a monthly salary of tk 60,000.00 with two festival allowances of tk 80,000.00. He also gets tk 50,000.00 from monthly house rent. His average monthly expenditure is tk 45,000.00, and he has to pay tk 5,000.00 for provident fund and tk 10,000.00 for life insurance premium. He also has to pay tk 30,000.00 for City Corporation Tax for his apartment. Calculate the amount of income tax he has to pay to the government in this year. The government fixes the tax for this year as follows:

| Income | Tax |
|---|---|
| First tk 2,20,000.00 | Nil |
| Next tk 3,00,000.00 | 10% |
| Next tk 4,00,000.00 | 15% |
| Next tk 5,00,000.00 | 20% |
| Rest amount | 25% |

Minimum payable tax is tk 3,000.00

Provident funds, life insurance, and share investment are considered personal investments, and the taxpayer gets a 15% rebate on his total investment. Festival allowance and other allowances are exempted from the tax.

13) Write a program to generate random numbers between a given range. The minimum and maximum ranges and number of random numbers to be generated are input interactively.

14) Write a program to compute the value of PI using the Monte Carlo method.

15) Write a program to find the root of a nonlinear equation using the Newton–Raphson method.

16) Write a program to find the roots of a nonlinear equation using the Secant method.

17) Write a program to solve ordinary differential equations using Euler's method.

18) Write a program to approximate the definite integral of a continuous function using Simpson's 1/3 rule.

19) Write a program to find the largest of three numbers.

20) Write a program to check if a given number is palindrome or not.

21) Write a program to check if a given number is an Armstrong number or not.

22) Write a program to check if a given number is a natural number or not.

23) Write a program to find the sum of first n natural numbers using while loop.

24) Write a program to find the sum of first n natural numbers using the for loop.

25) Write a program to check if a given year is a leap year or not.

26) Write a program to find the lowest common multiple of two given integers.

27) Write a program to reverse a number entered by the user.

28) Write a program to display half pyramids of * and numbers.

29) Write a program to display full pyramids of * and numbers.

30) Write a program to display inverted half pyramids of * and numbers.

31) Write a program to display inverted full pyramids of * and numbers.

32) Write a program to check if a given character is digit or not.

33) Write a program to display the smallest number of three. The numbers may be taken from the user.

34) Write a program to check if a given number is prime or not.

35) Write a program to display all the prime numbers in a given range.

# Arrays and Pointers

I N C, AN ARRAY is used to hold multiple values of the same data type. The array could be one-dimensional, two-dimensional, or three-dimensional. On the other hand, pointer variables are used to hold addresses rather than values of variables. In terms of memory access, arrays and pointers are synonymous. The first element of an array is referred to by its name, whereas the value of a pointer points to any memory location.

## 3.1 ARRAYS

An array is a collection of data types that are all of the same kind. A single array variable can store, access, and handle a large amount of data. In the following C code, for example,

```
int num[100];
```

num is an integer type array with a total of 100 elements. Starting at 0 and continuing until n-1, each array element can be retrieved using appropriate indexing. The 4th, 5th, and 6th elements of the above num array, for example, are accessed with num[3], num[4], and num[5].

We initialize the array in the same way that we would for any other data type variable.

(1) While declaration of the array:

```
int num[4] = {5, 10, 9, 19};
```

or,

```
int num[] = {5, 10, 9, 19};
```

(2) After declaration of the array:

```
int num[4];
num[4] = {5, 10, 9, 19};
```

DOI: 10.1201/9781003302629-3

or,

```
num[] = {5, 10, 9, 19};
```

(3) Interactively by the user after running the program. In that case, we usually use any of the C loops to access each element of the array. Example:

```
int i, num[4];
for (i=0; i<4; i++)
        scanf("%d", &num[i]);
```

When any array is declared, the array is organized such that all the array elements occupy contiguous space in memory. If the size of the integer data type is 4 bytes, then the memory organization of the array num[4] is as follows:

| num[0] | num[1] | num[2] | num[3] |
|--------|--------|--------|--------|
| 5 | 10 | 9 | 19 |
| 767624 | 767628 | 767632 | 767636 |

## 3.2 2D ARRAYS

A two-dimensional array is an array of arrays. It is also known as a matrix in C and is defined as a set of rows and columns. The following expression represents an integer type 2D array of matrix 2 × 4.

int num[2][4];

When declaring or initializing a 2D array, we must specify the size of the second dimension or the number of columns. The 2D array items are initialized as follows:

(1) int num[2][4] = {

      {5, 10, 9, 19},

      {6, 3, 12, 23}};

(2) int num[][4] = {{5, 10, 9, 19}, {6, 3, 12, 23}};

(3) int num[][4] = {5, 10, 9, 19, 6, 3, 12, 23};

(4) int i, j, num[2][4];

    for (i=0; i<2; i++)

```
        for (j=0; j<4; j++)

            scanf("%d", &num[i][j]);
```

The conceptual memory organization of the 2D array num[3][4] is as follows:

| num[0][0] | num[0][1] | num[0][2] | num[0][3] |
|-----------|-----------|-----------|-----------|
| num[1][0] | num[1][1] | num[1][2] | num[1][3] |
| num[2][0] | num[2][1] | num[2][2] | num[2][3] |

## 3.3 MULTIDIMENSIONAL ARRAYS

The simplest version of multidimensional arrays used in C is 2D arrays discussed earlier. Similar to 2D arrays, 3D arrays are declared as

```
int multi[2][3][4];
```

where multi is a three-dimensional array with 24 entries. Three-dimensional array is initialized as follows:

```
int multi[2][3][4] = {

        {{1, 2, 3, 4}, {5, 7, 9, 11}, {−3, 13, 23, 31}},

        {{2, 4, 6, 8}, {6, 7, −8, 9}, {4, 12, 23, −3}}};
```

The 24 elements of the 3D array can be entered as follows from a standard input terminal:

```
int i, j, k;
for (i=0; i<2; i++)
        for (j=0; j<3; j++)
                for (k=0; k<4; k++)
                        scanf("%d", &multi[i][j][k]);
```

The 24 elements of the 3D array can be displayed on the screen as follows:

```
int i, j, k;
for (i=0; i<2; i++)
        for (j=0; j<3; j++)
                for (k=0; k<4; k++)
                        printf("multi[%d][%d][%d]=%d\n", i, j,
                                k, multi[i][j][k]);
```

## 3.4 STRING

A string is a series of characters that end with the null terminator '\0'. As an example, a string is declared as follows:

char exam[] = {'A', 't', 'i', 'q', '\0'};

or

char exam[] = "Atiq";

//in that case, the null character '\0' is automatically placed at the end

## 3.5 STRING FUNCTIONS

The header file string.h contains prototypes or declarations for various predefined string-related library functions. The following are some important predefined string functions:

gets() – used to read a string from input terminal; example: gets(name) reads any words as string and stores the string to char type variable name

puts() – used to display a string on output console; for example: puts(name) displays string characters stored in char type variable name

strlen() – returns length of a string; example: strlen(exam) → 4

strlwr() – converts each character of a string to lowercase; example: strlwr(exam) → atiq

strupr() – converts each character of a string to uppercase; example: strupr(exam) → ATIQ

strcat() – appends one string at the end of another; example: strcat(exam, "Ahad") → Atiq Ahad

strncat() – appends first n characters of one string into another; example: strncat(exam, "Ahad Samad", 5) → Atiq Ahad

strcpy() – copies a string into another; example: strcpy(exam, "Ahad") → exam = Ahad

strncpy() – copies first n characters of a string into another; example: strncpy(exam, "Atiq Ahad", 4) → exam = Atiq

strcmp() – returns 0 if the two strings are same, otherwise returns positive or negative numbers; example: strcmp(exam, "Atiq") would return 0

strncmp() – compares first n characters of two strings; example: strcmp(exam, "Atiqur", 4) would return 0

strcmpi()/stricmp() – compares two strings ignoring the case of the characters; example: strcmp(exam, "atiQ") would return 0

strnicmp() – compares first n characters of two strings ignoring the case of the characters; example: strnicmp(exam, "atiQahaD", 4) would return 0

strchr() – finds out first occurrence of a given character in a string; example: strchr("atiqahad", 'a') would return atiqahad

strrchr() – finds out last occurrence of a given character in a string; example: strrchr("atiqahad", 'a') would return ad

strstr() – finds out first occurrence of a given substring in another string; example: strstr("atiqahad", "qah") would return qahad

strrev() – use to reverse a string; example: strrev(exam) would return qitA

## 3.6 POINTERS

In C, when a variable is declared, it is instantly assigned a memory location. Another variable known as the pointer holds the variable's address. A pointer's data type must match the data type of the variable whose address the pointer holds. Integer type pointers, for example, only hold the address of integer type variables, while double type pointers only retain the address of double type variables. Example:

int abc = 10; //abc is an integer type variable initialized to 10

int *pt; //pt is an integer type pointer that can hold address

pt = &abc; /*pt is initialized to the address of the variable abc using address operator &*/

In the above example, the address of the memory region assigned to the abc variable is pt, and the value stored in that memory location is *pt. The value at the address is known as *.

## 3.7 MEMORY ALLOCATION

When an array is defined, its memory is fixed, which in some situations may be insufficient. In some circumstances, we can allocate memory space dynamically during the program's execution. To do so, we need to use the malloc(), calloc(), realloc(), and free() functions from the stdlib.h header file.

malloc() allocates a certain number of bytes in memory and returns a void type pointer that can be cast to any data type pointer. If memory cannot be allocated, NULL is returned. The syntax and an example of malloc() are as follows:

ptr = (cast_type*) malloc(size);

ptr = (float*) malloc(20*sizeof(float));

Like malloc(), calloc() allocates a specific number of bytes in memory, but it also initializes all bits to zero. The syntax and an example of calloc() are as follows:

ptr = (cast_type*) calloc(size);

ptr = (float*) calloc(20*sizeof(float));

If the previous allocation size is not appropriate (either insufficient or more than required), realloc() changes the previously allocated memory space size. Syntax:

ptr = realloc(ptr, new_size);

The free() function is used to manually free the memory space that has been dynamically allocated. Syntax:

free(ptr);

## 3.8 EXAMPLES

**PROBLEM-01**
Write a program to input and print the elements of array using pointer.

Programming Code of the Solution:

```c
#include <stdio.h>
int main(){
    int num[10], i;
    printf("Enter any 5 integers: ");
    for (i=0; i<5; i++)
        scanf("%d", num+i);
    printf("You entered: ");
    for (i=0; i<5; i++)
        printf("%d ", *(num+i));
    return 0;
}
```

Input and Output of the Executed Program:

```
Enter any 5 integers: 4 6 8 9 1
You entered:  4  6  8  9  1
```

Explanation of the Programming Code:

**#include <stdio.h>**
/*header file stdio.h contains prototypes of the library functions printf() and scanf(); the header file must be included using preprocessor directive #include before the functions are called in the program*/
**int main(){**
/*all C program must have a main() function with return type void or int; here there is no parameter of the main() function and it returns an integer; opening curly brace specifies start of the main() function and no statement before that curly brace is executed by the compiler*/
    **int num[10], i;**
    /*integer type array num[] with size 10 is declared that stores the input values, and integer type variable i is declared which is used as an index to access each array element*/
    **printf("Enter any 5 integers: ");**
    /*this displays the text inside the double quotations as it is on screen*/
    **for (i=0; i<5; i++)**

```
/*this for loop is used to sequentially input all of the data;
i=0 is the initialization, i<5 is the condition, and i++ →
i=i+1 is the increment; the initialization is done once at the
beginning of the loop; then the condition is checked, if it
is true, the statement in the body is executed; now, the value
of counter i is incremented by 1 before the condition is re-
checked; this iteration continues until the condition becomes
false, at which point the program exits the loop*/
        scanf("%d", num+i);
        /*each iteration of the input function scanf() reads one
        integer and puts it in the array num[] as an array element;
        here, num = &num[0], num+1 = &num[1], num+2 = &num[2], and
        so on*/
    printf("You entered: ");
    /*this displays the text inside the double quotations as it is
    on screen*/
    for (i=0; i<5; i++)
    /*this for loop is used to display all of the data one by one;
    i=0 is the initialization, i<5 is the condition, and i++ → i=i+1
    is the increment; the condition is checked once at the beginning
    of the loop, if it is true, the body statement is executed;
    after that, the value of the counter i is incremented by 1
    before the condition is re-checked; this iteration continues
    until the condition becomes false, at which point the program
    exits the loop*/
        printf("%d ", *(num+i));
        /*each repetition of the function printf() displays value
        of a single array element on the screen; the array element
        is accessible using pointers as num[0] = *num, num[1] =
        *(num+1), num[2] = *(num+2), and so on.*/
    return 0;
    /*0 is returned as it is the standard for the successful
    execution of the program*/
}
/*the closing curly brace specifies the end of the main() function's
body, as well as the program's end; after that curly brace, no
statement is executed*/
```

## PROBLEM-02
**Write a program to find the number of elements in an array.**

Programming Code of the Solution:

```
#include <stdio.h>
int main(){
```

```
    float array[] = {10, 13, 17, 6, 28, 38};
    int num;
    num = sizeof(array)/sizeof(array[0]);
    printf("Number of elements in the array is: %d", num);
    return 0;
}
```

Input and Output of the Executed Program:

```
Number of elements in the array is: 6
```

## Explanation of the Programming Code:

```
#include <stdio.h>
```
/*header file stdio.h contains prototypes of the library functions printf() and scanf(); the header file must be included using preprocessor directive #include before the functions are called in the program*/
```
int main(){
```
/*all C program must have a main() function with return type void or int; here there is no parameter of the main() function and it returns an integer; opening curly brace specifies start of the main() function and no statement before that curly brace is executed by the compiler*/
```
    float array[] = {10, 13, 17, 6, 28, 38};
```
/*a float type array is declared and initialized to 6 different values; it is not necessary to mention size of a one dimensional array if it is initialized while declaring*/
```
    int num;
```
/*integer type variable num is declare*/
```
    num = sizeof(array)/sizeof(array[0]);
```
/*because sizeof(array) returns the entire size of the array and sizeof(array[0]) returns the size of the array's first element, this formula gives the number of elements in the array*/
```
    printf("Number of elements in the array is: %d", num);
```
/*output function printf() displays the text inside the double quotations as it is on the screen except for the value of num replaces the format specifier %d*/
```
    return 0;
```
/*0 is returned as it is the standard for the successful execution of the program*/
```
}
```
/*the closing curly brace specifies the end of the main() function's body, as well as the program's end; after that curly brace, no statement is executed*/

## PROBLEM-03
**Write a program to calculate the average of array elements.**

Programming Code of the Solution:

```c
#include <stdio.h>
int main(){
    int cnt=5, i;
    float num[10], sum=0;
    for (i=0; i<cnt; i++){
        printf("Enter a number, #%d element: ", i+1);
        scanf("%f", &num[i]);
        sum = sum + num[i];
    }
    printf("Average of the number is: %0.2f", sum/cnt);
    return 0;
}
```

Input and Output of the Executed Program:

```
Enter a number, #1 element: 3.4
Enter a number, #2 element: 4.8
Enter a number, #3 element: 10.6
Enter a number, #4 element: 9.8
Enter a number, #5 element: 19
Average of the number is: 9.52
```

Explanation of the Programming Code:

**#include <stdio.h>**
/*header file stdio.h contains prototypes of the library functions printf() and scanf(); the header file must be included using preprocessor directive #include before the functions are called in the program*/
**int main(){**
/*all C program must have a main() function with return type void or int; here there is no parameter of the main() function and it returns an integer; opening curly brace specifies start of the main() function and no statement before that curly brace is executed by the compiler*/
    **int cnt=5, i;**
    /*an integer type variable i is declared; another variable cnt is declared and initialized to 5*/
    **float num[10], sum=0;**
    /*a float type array num[] of size 10 is declared; the array is used to store the data, and each array element is accessed using indices ranging from 0 to 9; another variable, sum, is

declared and initialized to 0; this variable is used to compute and store the sum of data; because when we declare a variable, memory space is allocated for that variable may contain some garbage value, and the garbage value adds in the first summation operation involving sum, giving us the incorrect result*/

```
for (i=0; i<cnt; i++){
```

/*this for loop is used to read all of the data one by one and sequentially add them all up to the sum variable; i=0 is the initialization; i<cnt is the condition; i++ → i=i+1 is the increment; the initialization is done once at the beginning of the loop; the condition is then checked, and if it is true, all of the statements in the body are executed; the condition is then re-checked after the counter value is incremented by 1; this iteration continues until the condition is no longer true, at which point the program flow exits the loop*/

```
    printf("Enter a number, #%d element: ", i+1);
```

/*output function printf() displays the text inside the quotation as it is on the screen, except for the value of i+1 replaces the format specifier %d*/

```
    scanf("%f", &num[i]);
```

/*scanf() input function reads a decimal number from the standard input terminal and stores it in an array; num[0], num[1], . . . on each iteration*/

```
    sum = sum + num[i];
```

/*this performs the addition; in each iteration, one element is added to the sum variable and accumulated; If num[4] = {2, 3, 4, 1} then

After 1st iteration: sum = 0 + 2 = 2
After 2nd iteration: sum = 2 + 3 = 5
After 3rd iteration: sum = 5 + 4 = 9
After 4th iteration: sum = 9 + 1 = 10*/

```
}
```

/*this curly brace specifies the end of the body of the for loop*/

```
printf("Average of the number is: %0.2f", sum/cnt);
```

/*output function printf() displays the text inside the quotations as it is on the screen except for the result of operation sum/cnt replaces the format specifier %0.2f with two points precision*/

```
return 0;
```

/*0 is returned as it is the standard for the successful execution of the program*/

```
}
```

/*the closing curly brace specifies the end of the main() function's body, as well as the program's end; after that curly brace, no statement is executed*/

## PROBLEM-04
**Write a program to find the length of a string with and without strlen().**

Programming Code of the Solution:

```
#include <stdio.h>
#include <string.h>
int main(){
    int i;
    char str[40];
    printf("Enter a string: ");
    gets(str);
    for (i=0; str[i]!='\0'; ++i);
    printf("String length using library function: %d\n",
            strlen(str));
    printf("String length without using library function: %d", i);
    return 0;
}
```

Input and Output of the Executed Program:

```
Enter a string: Sazzad Muhammad
String length using library function: 15
String length without using library function: 15
```

Explanation of the Programming Code:

**#include <stdio.h>**
/*header file stdio.h contains prototypes of the library functions
printf() and gets(); the header file must be included using
preprocessor directive #include before the functions are called in
the program*/
**#include <string.h>**
/*string.h header file contains the prototype or declaration of
the function strlen(); the header file must be included before the
function is called in the program*/
**int main(){**
/*all C program must have a main() function with return type void
or int; here there is no parameter of the main() function and it
returns an integer; opening curly brace specifies start of the
main() function and no statement before that curly brace is executed
by the compiler*/
    **int i;**
    /*an integer type variable i is declared*/
    **char str[40];**
    /*character type array of size 40 is declared. Each array
    element is accessed using indices ranging from 0 to 39, i.e.
    str[0], str[1], . . ., str[39]*/

```
printf("Enter a string: ");
/*this displays the text inside the double quotations as it is
on screen*/
gets(str);
/*input function gets() reads a string including space, tab
etc. from input terminal and stores the string in the character
array str*/
for (i=0; str[i]!= '\0'; ++i);
/*this for loop ends in a semicolon, meaning that it has no
body; initialization i=0 is done once at the beginning of the
loop; the loop then checks a single character of the string to
see if it is a NULL; if not, the index value i is incremented
by 1 to check the next character in the next iteration; this
process continues until it reaches the end of the string denoted
by '\0', at which point the loop terminates*/
printf("String    length    using    library    function:    %d\n",
       strlen(str));
/*strlen() function returns the string length of the argument
str and the value is displayed in place of the format specifier
%d; other text is displayed as it is on the screen except for
a newline replaces \n*/
printf("String length without using library function: %d", i);
/*output function printf() displays the text inside the
quotations as it is on the screen except for the value of i
replaces the format specifier %d*/
return 0;
/*0 is returned as it is the standard for the successful
execution of the program*/
}
```
/*the closing curly brace specifies the end of the main() function's
body, as well as the program's end; after that curly brace, no
statement is executed*/

## PROBLEM-05
**Write a program to print a string using pointer.**

<u>Programming Code of the Solution:</u>

```
#include <stdio.h>
int main(){
    char str[40], *ptr;
    printf("Enter any string: ");
    gets(str);
    ptr = str;
    printf("The input string is: ");
```

```
    while (*ptr != '\0'){
        printf("%c", *ptr);
        ptr = ptr+1;
    }
    return 0;
}
```

Input and Output of the Executed Program:

```
Enter any string: Samaun Imran
The input string is: Samaun Imran
```

## Explanation of the Programming Code:

**#include <stdio.h>**
/*header file stdio.h contains prototypes of the library functions printf() and scanf(); the header file must be included using preprocessor directive #include before the functions are called in the program*/
**int main(){**
/*all C program must have a main() function with return type void or int; here there is no parameter of the main() function and it returns an integer; opening curly brace specifies start of the main() function and no statement before that curly brace is executed by the compiler*/
    **char str[40], *ptr;**
    /*char type array str[] of size 40 is declared; the elements of str[] can be accessed using indices ranging from 0 to 39, that is- str[0], str[1], . . ., str[39]. A character type pointer ptr is declared*/
    **printf("Enter any string: ");**
    /*this displays the text inside the double quotations as it is on the screen*/
    **gets(str);**
    /*input function gets() reads any string including whitespaces and stores the string to the array str[]*/
    **ptr = str;**
    /*address of the first element of the array is assigned to ptr, that is, ptr = &str[0]*/
    **printf("The input string is: ");**
    /*this displays the text inside the double quotations as it is on screen*/
    **while (*ptr!='\0'){**
    /*the character of the array/string referred by ptr is checked to see if it is a NULL, which specifies an end of the string; if not, statements within the loop's body are executed, and

the condition is re-checked; this process repeats until the condition becomes false, at which point the program flow exits the while loop*/

```
    printf("%c", *ptr);
    /*output function printf() displays the character in the
    string/array referred by the pointer ptr; here, ptr = &str[0]
    and *ptr = str[0] in the first iteration; ptr+1 = &str[1] and
    *(ptr+1) = str[1] in the second iteration, and so on*/
    ptr = ptr+1;
    /*value of ptr is incremented by 1 so that it can point to
    the next character in the array in the next iteration of
    the loop*/
}
/*the while loop comes to an end with this closing curly brace*/
return 0;
/*0 is returned as it is the standard for the successful
execution of the program*/
}
```

/*the closing curly brace specifies the end of the main() function's body, as well as the program's end; after that curly brace, no statement is executed*/

## PROBLEM-06
**Write a program to find the frequency of a character in a string.**

<u>Programming Code of the Solution:</u>

```
#include <stdio.h>
int main(){
    char str[50], ch;
    int count = 0, i;
    printf("Enter a string: ");
    gets(str);
    printf("Enter a character to find the frequency of that "
            "character: ");
    scanf("%c", &ch);
    for (i=0; str[i]!='\0'; i++)
        if (str[i]==ch)
            count++;
    printf("%c is occurred in the string %d times.", ch, count);
    return 0;
}
```

<u>Input and Output of the Executed Program:</u>

```
Enter a string: Sazzad Muhammad
Enter a character to find the frequency of that character: d
d is occurred in the string 2 times.
```

**Explanation of the Programming Code:**

```
#include <stdio.h>
```
/*header file stdio.h contains prototypes of the library functions printf(), scanf() and gets(); the header file must be included using preprocessor directive #include before the functions are called in the program*/
```
int main(){
```
/*all C program must have a main() function with return type void or int; here there is no parameter of the main() function and it returns an integer; opening curly brace specifies start of the main() function and no statement before that curly brace is executed by the compiler*/
```
    char str[50], ch;
```
/* char type array str[] of size 50 is declared; the elements of str[] can be accessed using indices ranging from 0 to 39, that is- str[0], str[1], . . ., str[39]. Also a char type variable ch is declared which can store only a single character*/
```
    int count = 0, i;
```
/*two integer type variables are declared; variable count is initialized to 0*/
```
    printf("Enter a string:");
```
/*this displays the text inside the double quotations on the screen*/
```
    gets(str);
```
/*gets() function reads characters including white spaces from input terminal until a newline is encountered*/
```
    printf("Enter a character to find the frequency of that"
           " character: ");
```
/*this displays the text inside the double quotations on the screen; here long string was broken into multiple lines using two double quotes ("")*/
```
    scanf("%c", &ch);
```
/*scanf() function reads a character from input terminal and stores it in char type variable ch*/
```
    for (i=0; str[i]!='\0'; i++)
```
/*i=0 is the initialization; str[i]!='\0' is the condition and i++ is the increment; i=0 is initialized once at the beginning of the loop; then character of the string str[] is checked whether it is a NULL, if it is not the end of the string, statement in the body of the loop is executed; after that the value of i is incremented by 1 (so that next character can be checked in the next iteration of the loop) and the condition is re-checked; this process continues until the end of the string is reached at which point the condition becomes false and the program flow exits the loop*/

```
        if (str[i]==ch)
        /*In each iteration, the 'if' condition compares the character
        ch with the array element str[]; when any character matches with
        ch the condition is true and following statement is executed*/
            count++;
            /*if ch matches any of the character in the string, the
            value of count is incremented by 1*/
    printf("%c is occurred in the string %d times.", ch, count);
    /*output function printf() displays the text inside the quotations
    as it is on the screen except for the character ch replaces the
    format specifier %c and the value of count replaces %d*/
    return 0;
    /*0 is returned as it is the standard for the successful
    execution of the program*/
}
/*the closing curly brace specifies the end of the main() function's
body, as well as the program's end; after that curly brace, no
statement is executed*/
```

## PROBLEM-07
**Write a program to copy a string with and without using strcpy().**

Programming Code of the Solution:

```
#include <stdio.h>
#include <string.h>
int main(){
    char str1[50], str2[50], str3[50];
    int i;
    printf("Enter a string: ");
    gets(str1);
    for (i=0; str1[i]!='\0'; i++)
        str2[i] = str1[i];
    str2[i] = '\0';
    strcpy(str3, str1);
    printf("Copied string without using library function:\n");
    puts(str2);
    printf("Copied string using library function:\n%s", str3);
    return 0;
}
```

Input and Output of the Executed Program:

```
Enter a string: Atiqur Rahman
Copied string without using library function:
Atiqur Rahman
Copied string using library function:
Atiqur Rahman
```

## Explanation of the Programming Code:

```
#include <stdio.h>
```
/*header file stdio.h contains prototypes of the library functions printf(), scanf() and gets(); the header file must be included using preprocessor directive #include before the functions called in the program*/
```
#include <string.h>
```
/*header file string.h contains prototype of the library function strcpy(); the header file must be included using preprocessor directive #include before the function is called in the program*/
```
int main(){
```
/*all C program must have a main() function with return type void or int; here there is no parameter of the main() function and it returns an integer; opening curly brace specifies start of the main() function and no statement before that curly brace is executed by the compiler*/
```
    char str1[50], str2[50], str3[50];
```
   /*three character type arrays are declared each of size 50. Each element of the string is accessed using indices ranging from 0 to 49, like- str1[0], str1[1], . . ., str1[49]*/
```
    int i;
```
   /*integer type variable i is declared*/
```
    printf("Enter a string: ");
```
   /*this displays the text inside the double quotations as it is on the screen*/
```
    gets(str1);
```
   /*the gets() function reads a string from the input terminal, including white spaces, and stores it in the str1[] array*/
```
    for (i=0; str1[i]!='\0'; i++)
```
   /*this for loop is used to sequentially copy each character of the string str1[] to str2[]. i=0 is the initialization; str1[i]!='\0' is the condition and i++ is the increment; i=0 is initialized once at the beginning of the loop; then character of the string str1[] is checked whether it is a NULL, if it is not the end of the string, statement in the body of the for loop is executed and value of i is incremented by 1 so that we can check next character in the string. Now the condition is re-checked. This process continues until the end of the string is reached*/
```
        str2[i] = str1[i];
```
      /*This copies a single character of str1[] to str2[]. For example, in the 1st iteration- str2[0]=str1[0], in the 2nd iteration- str2[1]=str1[1], and so on*/
```
    str2[i] = '\0';
```
   /*Each string must end with a NULL character, thus after copying each character from str1[], the '\0' is appended to the end of str2[]*/

```
strcpy(str3, str1);
/*strcpy() function is called to copy the string str1[] as it
is in str3[]*/
printf("Copied string without using library function:\n");
/*this displays the text inside the double quotations as it is
on the screen followed by a newline in place of \n*/
puts(str2);
/*puts() function is called to display the string str2[] as it
is on the output screen*/
printf("Copied string using library function:\n%s", str3);
/*printf() function displays the text inside the double quotes
as it is on the screen except for a newline replaces \n and
string str3[] replaces the format specifier %s*/
return 0;
/*0 is returned as it is the standard for the successful
execution of the program*/
}
/*the closing curly brace specifies the end of the main() function's
body, as well as the program's end; after that curly brace, no
statement is executed*/
```

## PROBLEM-08
**Write a program to find both the largest and smallest numbers of an array of integers.**

Flowchart of the Solution:

Figure 3.1 shows the flowchart followed to solve this problem.

## Algorithm of the Solution:

Step-1: Start

Step-2: Initialize SIZE←10

Step-3: Read value of value[0]

Step-4: Initialize large←value[0], small←value[0] and i←1

Step-5: if i<SIZE

     5.1: Read value of value[i]

     5.2: If value[i]>large

          7.2.1: large←value[i]

     5.3: If value[i]<small

          7.3.1: small←value[i]

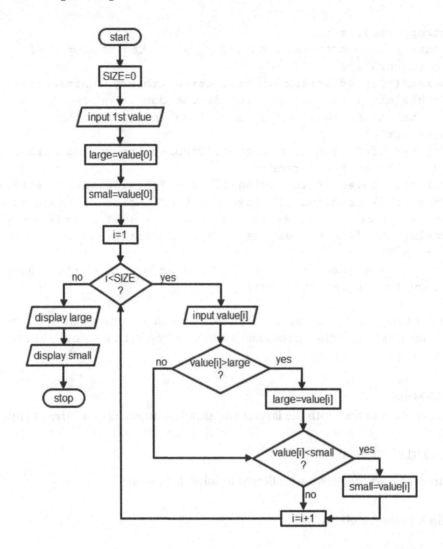

FIGURE 3.1   Flowchart followed to solve the problem.

5.4: i←i+1

5.5: Go to Step-5

Step-6: Display values of large and small

Step-7: Stop

<u>Programming Code of the Solution:</u>

```c
#include <stdio.h>
#define SIZE 10
int main(){
    int value[SIZE], large, small, i;
    printf("Please enter any %d integers (separated by space):\n",
        SIZE);
```

```
    scanf("%d", &value[0]);
    large=value[0];
    small=value[0];
    for (i=1; i<SIZE; i++){
        scanf("%d", &value[i]);
        if (value[i]>large)
            large=value[i];
        if (value[i]<small)
            small=value[i];
    }
    printf("Largest value of the array is: %d\n", large);
    printf("Smallest value of the array is: %d\n", small);
    return 0;
}
```

Input and Output of the Executed Program:

```
Please enter any 10 integers (separated by space):
2 8 4 5 9 7 12 54 3 8
Largest value of the array is: 54
Smallest value of the array is: 2
```

**Explanation of the Programming Code:**

**#include <stdio.h>**
/*header file stdio.h contains prototypes of the library functions printf() and scanf(); the header file must be included using preprocessor directive #include before the functions are called in the program*/
**#define SIZE 10**
/*#define is a preprocessor directive that defines a constant variable; here 10 is assigned to constant variable SIZE; wherever SIZE is used in this program it is replaced by 10*/
**int main(){**
/*all C program must have a main() function with return type void or int; here there is no parameter of the main() function and it returns an integer; opening curly brace specifies start of the main() function and no statement before that curly brace is executed by the compiler*/
    **int value[SIZE], large, small, i;**
    /*an integer type array value[] of size SIZE and three other variables are declared*/
    **printf("Please enter any %d integers (separated by space):"**
        **"\n", SIZE);**
    /*output function printf() displays the text inside the double quotes as it is on screen except for the value of SIZE replaces the format specifier %d and a newline replaces \n*/
    **scanf("%d", &value[0]);**
    /*input function scanf() reads an integer from input terminal and it is assigned to the 1st array element*/

```
large=value[0];
```
/*value of the 1st array element value[0] is assigned to variable large which is used to store the largest number*/
```
small=value[0];
```
/*value of the 1st array element value[0] is assigned to variable small which is used to store the smallest number*/
```
for (i=1; i<SIZE; i++){
```
/*i=1 is the initialization, i<SIZE is the condition and i++ is the increment; initialization is done once at the beginning of the loop; then the condition is checked, if it is true, statements in the body are executed and the value of i is incremented by 1 before the condition is re-checked; these steps continue until the condition becomes false at which point the program flow exits the loop*/
```
    scanf("%d", &value[i]);
```
/*this scanf() function reads an integer from input terminal and stores the value to array value[i]; because this statement is executed in each iteration, value[1] is input in the 1st iteration, value[2] in the 2nd iteration and so on*/
```
if (value[i]>large)
```
/*the input value is compared to the value of large in each iteration; if the input value is greater than large, the condition is true, and the following statement is executed*/
```
        large=value[i];
```
/*if the input value is larger than large, the value of large is updated to the input value, ensuring that large always contains the largest value*/
```
if (value[i]<small)
```
/*the input value is compared to the value of small in each iteration; if the input value is smaller than small, the condition is true, and the following statement is executed*/
```
        small=value[i];
```
/*if the input value is smaller than small, the value of small is updated to the input value, ensuring that small always contains the smallest value*/
```
}
```
/*the for loop comes to an end with this closing curly brace*/
```
printf("Largest value of the array is: %d\n", large);
```
/*output function printf() displays the text inside the double quotations as it is on the screen except for the value of large replaces the format specifier %d and a newline replaces \n*/
```
printf("Smallest value of the array is: %d\n", small);
```
/*output function printf() displays text inside the double quotations as it is on the screen except for the value of

small replaces the format specifier %d and a newline replaces
\n*/
**return 0;**
/*0 is returned as it is the standard for the successful
execution of the program*/
}
/*the closing curly brace specifies the end of the main() function's
body, as well as the program's end; after that curly brace, no
statement is executed*/

## PROBLEM-09

**Write a program to generate the first n terms of a Fibonacci sequence. Also, check whether a given integer is a Fibonacci number or not.**

<u>Flowchart of the Solution:</u>

Figure 3.2 shows the flowcharts followed to solve this problem.

## <u>Algorithm of the Solution:</u>

Step-1: Start

Step-2: Initialize dm←1

Step-3: Read value of n between 3 and 25

Step-4: Initialize fn[0]←0, fn[1]←1 and i←2

Step-5: If i<n

      5.1: fn[i]←fn[i−1]+fn[i−2]

      5.2: i←i+1

      5.3: Go to Step-5

Step-6: Initialize i←0

Step-7: If i<n−1

      7.1: Display value of fn[i]

      7.2: i←i+1

      7.3: Go to Step-7

Step-8: Display value of fn[i]

Step-9: Read value of ck

Step-10: If ck=0

      10.1: Go to Step-11

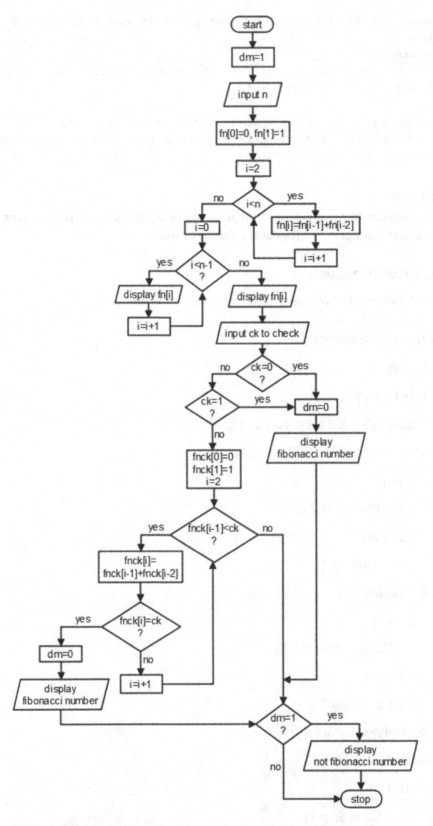

FIGURE 3.2   Flowchart followed to solve the problem.

Step-11: If ck=1

11.1: dm←0

11.2: Display 'Fibonacci number'

11.3: Jump to Step-14

Step-12: Initialize fnck[0]←0, fnck[1]←1 and i←2

Step-13: If fnck[i−1]<ck

13.1: fnck[i]←fnck[i−1]+fnck[i−2]

13.2: If fnck[i]=ck

13.2.1: Display 'Fibonacci number'

13.2.2: dm←0

13.2.3: Go to Step-14

13.3: i←i+1

13.4: Go to Step-13

Step-14: If dm=1

14.1: Display 'not Fibonacci number'

Step-15: Stop

Programming Code of the Solution:

```c
#include<stdio.h>
int main(){
    int fn[25], fnck[25], n, i, ck, dm=1;
    printf("Please enter an integer (3-25): ");
    scanf("%d", &n);
    fn[0]=0;
    fn[1]=1;
    for (i=2; i<n; i++)
        fn[i]=fn[i-1]+fn[i-2];
    printf("First %d Fibonacci sequence:\n", n);
    for (i=0; i<n-1; i++)
        printf("%d, ", fn[i]);
    printf("%d\n", fn[i]);
    printf("Enter an integer to check: ");
    scanf("%d", &ck);
    if (ck==0 || ck==1){
        printf("%d is a Fibonacci number.\n", ck);
        dm=0;
    }
    else{
```

```
        fnck[0]=0;
        fnck[1]=1;
        for (i=2; fnck[i-1]<ck; i++){
            fnck[i]=fnck[i-1]+fnck[i-2];
                if (ck==fnck[i]){
                    printf("%d is a Fibonacci number.\n", ck);
                    dm=0;
                    break;

                }

            }

        }
    if (dm==1)
        printf("%d is not a Fibonacci number.\n", ck);
    return 0;
}
```

Input and Output of the Executed Program:

```
Please enter an integer (3-25): 12
First 12 Fibonacci sequence:
0, 1, 1, 2, 3, 5, 8, 13, 21, 34, 55, 89
Enter an integer to check: 144
144 is a Fibonacci number.
```

```
Please enter an integer (3-25): 14
First 14 Fibonacci sequence:
0, 1, 1, 2, 3, 5, 8, 13, 21, 34, 55, 89, 144, 233
Enter an integer to check: 238
238 is not a Fibonacci number.
```

Explanation of the Programming Code:

**#include<stdio.h>**
/*header file stdio.h contains prototypes of the library functions
printf() and scanf(); the header file must be included using
preprocessor directive #include before the functions are called in
the program*/
**int main(){**
/*all C program must have a main() function with return type void
or int; here there is no parameter of the main() function and it
returns an integer; opening curly brace specifies start of the
main() function and no statement before that curly brace is executed
by the compiler*/
    **int fn[25], fnck[25], n, i, ck, dm=1;**
    /*two integer type arrays fn[] and fnck[] of size 25 each are
    declared; four integer type variables, n, I ck, and dm, are
    declared, with dm initialized to 1*/

```
printf("Please enter an integer (3-25): ");
```
/*output function printf() displays text in double quotations
as it is on the screen*/
```
scanf("%d", &n);
```
/*input function scanf() reads an integer from keyboard and
stores the value in the memory spaces allocated for n*/
```
fn[0]=0;
```
/*1st Fibonacci number is 0 and it is stored in the 1st element
of the array fn[0]*/
```
fn[1]=1;
```
/*2nd Fibonacci number is 1 and it is stored in the 2nd element
of the array fn[1]*/
```
for (i=2; i<n; i++)
```
/*this for loop is used to calculate other Fibonacci numbers in
the sequence; i=2 is the initialization, i<n is the condition
and i++ is the increment; initialization is done once at the
beginning of the loop; then the condition is checked, if it
is true then statement in the body is executed; value of i is
incremented by 1 before the condition is re-checked; these steps
continue until the condition becomes false*/
```
    fn[i]=fn[i-1]+fn[i-2];
```
/*each Fibonacci number is calculated by adding the two
preceding numbers in the sequence; one number is computed
in each loop iteration and placed in the array fn[]; for
n=5, fn[0]=0, fn[1]=1
After 1st iteration- fn[2]=fn[1]+fn[0]=1+0=1
After 2nd iteration- fn[3]=fn[2]+fn[1]=1+1=2
After 3rd iteration- fn[4]=fn[3]+fn[2]=2+1=3
After 4th iteration- fn[5]=fn[4]+fn[3]=3+2=5*/
```
printf("First %d Fibonacci sequence:\n", n);
```
/*printf() function displays the text in double quotes as it is
on the screen, with the exception that the value of n replaces
the format specifier %d and a newline replaces \n*/
```
for (i=0; i<n-1; i++)
```
/*this for loop is used to display Fibonacci sequence stored in
the array; i=0 is the initialization, i<n-1 is the condition
and i++ is the increment; initialization is done once at the
beginning of the loop; then condition is checked, if it is
true then statement in the body is executed; value of i is
now incremented by 1 before the condition is re-checked; these
steps continue until the condition becomes false at which point
the program flow exits the loop*/
```
    printf("%d, ", fn[i]);
```
/*printf() function displays value of single array element
fn[0], fn[1], fn[2], . . . in place of format specifier %d
followed by comma and space in each iteration of the loop*/

```
printf("%d\n", fn[i]);
```
/*this printf() function displays the value of last array element fn[n-1] in place of format specifier %d followed by a newline in place of \n*/
/*following part of the program will check whether a given number is a Fibonacci*/
```
printf("Enter an integer to check: ");
```
/*printf() function displays the text in double quotations as it is on the screen*/
```
scanf("%d", &ck);
```
/*scanf() function reads an integer from input terminal and stores it in the memory spaces location allocated for ck; we want to check if ck is a Fibonacci number*/
```
if (ck==0 || ck==1){
```
/*if the input number ck is either 0 or 1, the condition is true, and the statements, enclosed by curly braces, in the body of the 'if' are executed*/
```
    printf("%d is a Fibonacci number.\n", ck);
```
/*this printf() function displays the text in double quotes as it is on the screen except for the value of ck replaces the format specifier %d and a newline replaces \n*/
```
    dm=0;
```
/*value 0 if assigned to dm*/
```
}
```
/*this is the end of 'if' with condition ck==0||ck==1*/
```
else{
```
/*if ck is neither 0 nor 1, that is, both conditions in the above 'if' are false, statements in the body of this else are executed*/
```
    fnck[0]=0;
```
/*first Fibonacci number, 0, is saved in the 1st element of the array fnck[0]*/
```
    fnck[1]=1;
```
/*second Fibonacci number, 1, is saved in the 2nd element of the array fnck[1]*/
```
    for (i=2; fnck[i-1]<ck; i++){
```
/*this for loop sequentially computes 3rd, 4th, 5th, . . . Fibonacci numbers; i=2 is the initialization, fnck[i-1]<ck is the condition and i++ is the increment; initialization is done once at the beginning of the loop; then the condition is checked, and if it is true, statement in the body is executed; now, the value of i is incremented by 1 before the condition is re-checked; this process continues until the condition becomes false at which point the program flow exits the loop*/
```
        fnck[i]=fnck[i-1]+fnck[i-2];
```
/*by adding two previous Fibonacci numbers, the next Fibonacci number is generated and saved in the array fnck[]*/

```
            if (ck==fnck[i]){
            /*this if compares the Fibonacci number fnck[i],
            generated in previous statement, with the given
            number ck; if they match than the condition is true
            and following statements in the body of 'if' are
            executed*/
                printf("%d is a Fibonacci number.\n", ck);
                /*this printf() function displays the text in the
                double quotes as it is on the screen except for the
                value of ck replaces the format specifier %d and a
                newline replaces \n*/
                dm=0;
                /*this sets the value of dm to 0 */
                break;
                /*we don't need to continue the loop if ck matches
                the generated Fibonacci number in any iteration;
                thus, this break forces the program control flow to
                exit the for loop*/
            }
            /*this is the end of 'if' with condition ck==fnck[i]*/
        }
        /*the 'for' loop ends with this closing curly brace*/
    }
    /*this is the end of 'else' corresponding to 'if' with condition
    ck==0||ck==1*/
    if (dm==1)
    /*if ck does not match any Fibonacci number then dm=1 and the
    condition is true, so following statement is executed*/
        printf("%d is not a Fibonacci number.\n", ck);
        /*this printf() displays the text in double quotations as
        it is on the screen except for the value of ck replaces the
        format specifier %d and a newline replaces \n*/
    return 0;
    /*0 is returned as it is the standard for the successful
    execution of the program*/
}
/*the closing curly brace specifies the end of the main() function's
body, as well as the program's end; after that curly brace, no
statement is executed*/
```

## PROBLEM-10
**Write a program to find the 2's complement of a given binary number.**

Flowchart of the Solution:

Figure 3.3 shows the flowchart followed to solve this problem.

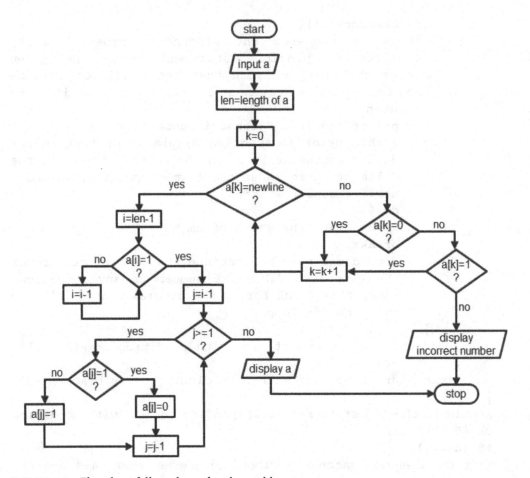

FIGURE 3.3 Flowchart followed to solve the problem.

## Algorithm of the Solution:

Step-1: Start

Step-2: Read value of a

Step-3: len←strlen(a)

Step-4: Initialize k←0

Step-5: If a[k]≠'\0'

    5.1: If a[k]≠'0'

        5.1.1: If a[k]≠'1'

            5.1.1.1: Display 'incorrect number'

            5.1.1.2: Go to Step-11

    5.2: k←k+1

    5.3: Go to Step-5

Step-6: Initialize i←len−1

Step-7: If a[i]≠'1'

    7.1: i←i−1

    7.2: Go to Step-7

Step-8: Initialize j←i−1

Step-9: If j>=0

    9.1: If a[j]=1

        9.1.1: a[j]←0

        9.1.2: Go to Step-9.3

    9.2: a[j]←1

    9.3: j←j−1

    9.4: Go to Step-9

Step-10: Display value of a

Step-11: Stop

## Programming Code of the Solution:

```c
#include<stdio.h>
#include<string.h>
#include<stdlib.h>
int main(){
    char a[20];
    int i, j, k, len;
    printf("Enter any binary string: ");
    gets(a);
    len=strlen(a);
    for (k=0; a[k]!='\0'; k++)
        if (a[k]!='0' && a[k]!='1'){
            printf("Incorrect binary number\nExiting...\n");
            exit(0);
        }
    for (i=len-1; a[i]!='1'; i--);
    for (j=i-1; j>=0; j--)
        if (a[j]=='1')
            a[j]='0';
        else
            a[j]='1';
    printf("2's complement: %s\n", a);
    return 0;
}
```

Input and Output of the Executed Program:

```
Enter any binary string: 1021011
Incorrect binary number
Exiting...
```

```
Enter any binary string: 101101
2's complement: 010011
```

## Explanation of the Programming Code:

**#include<stdio.h>**
/*header file stdio.h contains prototypes of the library functions printf() and scanf(); the header file must be included using preprocessor directive #include using the functions are called in the program*/
**#include<string.h>**
/*header file string.h contains prototype of the library function strlen(); the header file must be included using preprocessor directive #include before the function is called in the program*/
**#include<stdlib.h>**
/*header file stdlib.h contains prototypes of the library functions exit(), abs(), div(), and rand(); the header file must be included using preprocessor directive #include before the functions are called in the program*/
**int main(){**
/*all C program must have a main() function with return type void or int; here there is no parameter of the main() function and it returns an integer; opening curly brace specifies start of the main() function and no statement before that curly brace is executed by the compiler*/
    **char a[20];**
    /*character type array a[] of size 20 is declared; compiler assigns required contiguous spaces in memory for this array; each element of the array is accessed using indices ranging from 0 to 19*/
    **int i, j, k, len;**
    /*four integer type variables are declared; compiler assigns required spaces in memory for these variables*/
    **printf("Enter any binary string: ");**
    /*output library function printf() displays text inside the double quotations as it is on the standard output terminal*/
    **gets(a);**
    /*library function gets() reads string, including whitespace, from input terminal and assigns the string to the array a[];

in this program each bit of the binary number is considered as character '1' or '0'*/
**len=strlen(a);**
/*library function strlen() computes and returns length of string a that is assigned to variable len*/
**for (k=0; a[k]!='\0'; k++)**
/*this loop is used to check each bit of the binary number whether the bit is any value other than 0 or 1; k=0 is the initialization, a[k]!='\0' is the condition and k++ is the increment; initialization is done once at the beginning of the loop; then condition is checked, if it is true, statement in the body is executed; now, value of k is incremented by 1 before the condition is re-checked; these steps continue until the NULL character is reached in the string*/
    **if (a[k]!='0' && a[k]!='1'){**
    /*if any of the bits of the binary number is neither 0 nor 1, then the condition is true and following statements, enclosed by curly braces, are executed*/
        **printf("Incorrect binary number\nExiting . . . \n");**
        /*this printf() function displays the text inside the double quotes as it is on the screen except for a newline replaces \n*/
        **exit(0);**
        /*library function exit() terminates the program immediately without returning any value*/
    **}**
    /*this closing curly brace specifies the end of 'if' condition*/
**for (i=len-1; a[i]!='1'; i--);**
/*this for loop finds the index of the last bit in the binary number that contains 1; i=len-1 is the initialization, a[i]!='1' is the condition, and i - is the decrement; this 'for' loop ends with a semicolon, denoting that it has no body; the index is set to the last character of the string once at the beginning of the loop; then the condition is checked, if it is true, the index value i is decremented by 1 before the condition is re-checked; this process continues until the condition becomes false, at which point the last 1 in the binary number is found and the program flow exits the loop*/
**for (j=i-1; j>=0; j--)**
/*this 'for' loop flips each bit of a binary integer from 1 to 0 and 0 to 1 from the first bit to the bit one bit before the last '1'; the last bit, which contains 1, remains unchanged at 1; j=i-1 is the initialization, j>=0 is the condition, and j - is the decrement; at the beginning of the loop, initialization is done once, which sets index to the character one character

before the last '1' in the string; then the condition is checked, and if true, the statements in the body are executed; before the condition is re-checked, the index value j is decremented by one; these steps are repeated until the first character of the string is reached, at which point the condition becomes false and the program flow exits the loop*/

```
    if (a[j]=='1')
    /*this 'if' checks if the bit a[j] is 1, if it is true,
    following statement is executed*/
        a[j]='0';
        /*this statement flips the bit a[j] from 1 to 0*/
    else
    /*if the checked bit is not '1', then the condition of above
    'if' is false and following statement is executed*/
        a[j]='1';
        /*this statement flips the bit a[j] from 0 to 1*/
printf("2's complement: %s\n", a);
/*this printf() function displays the text inside the double
quotations as it is on the screen except for string a replaces
the format specifier %s, a newline replaces \n*/
return 0;
/*0 is returned as it is the standard for the successful
execution of the program*/
}
```
/*this closing curly brace specifies the end of main() function; no statement is executed after that point*/

## PROBLEM-11
**Write a program to calculate and print transpose of a given matrix.**

Flowchart of the Solution:

Figure 3.4 shows the flowchart followed to solve this problem.

## Algorithm of the Solution:

Step-1: Start

Step-2: Define ROW←4 and COL←4

Step-3: Initialize i←0

Step-4: If i<ROW

    4.1: Initialize j←0

    4.2: If j<COL

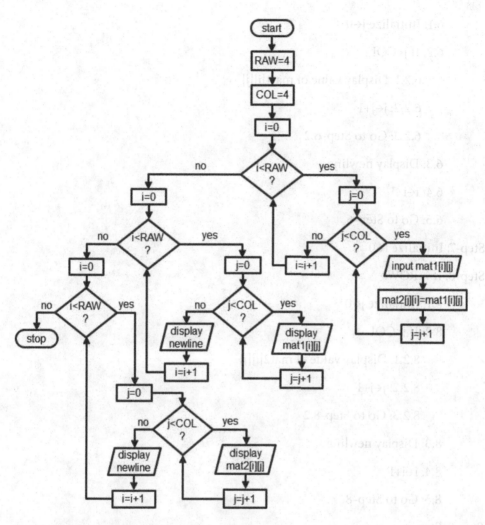

FIGURE 3.4   Flowchart followed to solve the problem.

4.2.1: Read value of mat1[i][j]

4.2.2: mat2[j][i]←mat1[i][j]

4.2.3: j←j+1

4.2.4: Go to Step-4.2

4.3: i←i+1

4.4: Go to Step-4

Step-5: Initialize i←0

Step-6: If i<ROW

6.1: Initialize j←0

6.2: If j<COL

6.2.1: Display value of mat1[i][j]

6.2.2: j←j+1

6.2.3: Go to Step-6.2

6.3: Display newline

6.4: i←i+1

6.5: Go to Step-6

Step-7: Initialize i←0

Step-8: If i<ROW

8.1: Initialize j←0

8.2: If j<COL

8.2.1: Display value of mat2[i][j]

8.2.2: j←j+1

8.2.3: Go to Step-8.2

8.3: Display newline

8.4: i←i+1

8.5: Go to Step-8

Step-9: Stop

<u>Programming Code of the Solution:</u>

```
#include<stdio.h>
#define ROW 4
#define COL 4
int main(){
    int mat1[ROW][COL], mat2[ROW][COL], i, j, m, n;
    printf("Enter Matrix elements:\n");
    for (i=0; i<ROW; i++)
        for (j=0; j<COL; j++){
            printf("Element[%d][%d]: ", i, j);
            scanf("%d", &mat1[i][j]);
            mat2[j][i]=mat1[i][j];
        }
```

```
        printf("\nThe matrix is:\n");
        for (i=0; i<ROW; i++){
            for (j=0; j<COL; j++)
                printf("%d\t", mat1[i][j]);
            printf("\n");
        }
        printf("\nTranspose of the matrix is:\n");
        for (i=0; i<ROW; i++){
            for (j=0; j<COL; j++)
                printf("%d\t", mat2[i][j]);
            printf("\n");
        }
        return 0;
}
```

Input and Output of the Executed Program:

```
Enter Matrix elements:
Element[0][0]: 2
Element[0][1]: 4
Element[0][2]: 6
Element[0][3]: 8
Element[1][0]: 1
Element[1][1]: 3
Element[1][2]: 5
Element[1][3]: 7
Element[2][0]: 3
Element[2][1]: 6
Element[2][2]: 12
Element[2][3]: 9
Element[3][0]: 4
Element[3][1]: 8
Element[3][2]: 16
Element[3][3]: 32

The matrix is:
2       4       6       8
1       3       5       7
3       6       12      9
4       8       16      32

Transpose of the matrix is:
2       1       3       4
4       3       6       8
6       5       12      16
8       7       9       32
```

## Explanation of the Programming Code:

```
#include<stdio.h>
```
/*header file stdio.h contains prototypes of the library functions printf() and scanf(); the header file must be included using preprocessor directive #include before the functions are called in the program*/
```
#define ROW 4
```
/*preprocessor directive #define defines a constant variable ROW that takes the value 4; ROW is substituted by 4 wherever it appears in this program from now on*/
```
#define COL 4
```
/*preprocessor directive #define defines a constant variable ROW that takes the value 4; ROW is substituted by 4 wherever it appears in this program from now on*/
```
int main(){
```
/*all C program must have a main() function with return type void or int; here there is no parameter of the main() function and it returns an integer; opening curly brace specifies start of the main() function and no statement before that curly brace is executed by the compiler*/
```
    int mat1[ROW][COL], mat2[ROW][COL], i, j, m, n;
```
/*four integer type variables i, j, m and n, and two 2-D arrays mat1[][] and mat2[][] of size ROW and COL are declared*/
```
    printf("Enter Matrix elements:\n");.
```
/*output function printf() displays the text in the quotation as it is on the screen except for a newline replaces \n*/
```
    for (i=0; i<ROW; i++)
```
/*this for loop executes following for loop ROW times; i=0 is the initialization, i<ROW is the condition and i++ is the increment; the initialization is done once at the beginning of the loop; then the condition is checked, if it is true, following for loop is executed and value of i is incremented by 1 before the condition is re-checked; these process continues till the condition becomes false at which point the program flow exits the loop; thus, we access all elements of first row in first iteration of this for loop, we access all elements of second row in second iteration, and so on*/
```
        for (j=0; j<COL; j++){
```
/*j=0 is the initialization, j<COL is the condition and j++ is the increment; initialization is done once at the beginning of the loop; then the condition is checked, if it is true statements in the body are executed and value of j is incremented by 1 before the condition is re-checked; these steps continue until the condition becomes false at which point the program flow exits the loop*/
```
            printf("Element[%d][%d]: ", i, j);
```

```
    /*output function printf() displays the text in the
    quotations as it is on the screen except for the value
    of i replaces the first format specifier %d and the
    value of j replaces the second %d*/
    scanf("%d", &mat1[i][j]);
    /*this scanf() function reads an integer from input
    terminal and stores it in the memory spaces allocated
    for the particular array element*/
    mat2[j][i]=mat1[i][j];
    /*transpose of matrix mat1[][] is calculated here
    and stores in mat2[][]; here row of mat1[][] becomes
    column of mat2[][] and column of mat1[][] becomes row
    of mat2[][]; mat2[0][0]=mat1[0]0], mat2[1][0]= mat1[0]
    [1], mat2[2][0]=mat1[0][2], and so on*/
}
    /*this is the end of 'for (j=0; j<COL; j++)' loop*/
printf("\nThe matrix is:\n");
/*output function printf() displays the text in the quotations
as it is on the screen except for a newline replaces \n*/
for (i=0; i<ROW; i++){
/*this for loop executes following for loop ROW times; i=0
is the initialization, i<ROW is the condition and i++ is the
increment; initialization is done once at the beginning of the
loop; then condition is checked, if it is true, following for
loop is executed and value of i is incremented by 1 before
the condition is re-checked; these steps continue until the
condition becomes false at which point the program flow exits
the loop; thus in first iteration all elements of first row are
displayed, in second iteration all elements of second row are
displayed, and so on*/
    for (j=0; j<COL; j++)
    /*j=0 is the initialization, j<COL is the condition and
    j++ is the increment; initialization is done once at the
    beginning of the loop; then the condition is checked, if
    it is true, statements in the body is executed and value of
    j is incremented by 1 before the condition is re-checked;
    these steps continue until the condition becomes false at
    which point the program flow exits the loop*/
        printf("%d\t", mat1[i][j]);
        /*function printf() displays the value of array element
        mat1[i][j] in place of format specifier %d on the screen
        followed by a tab in place of \t*/
printf("\n");
/*this statement is in the body of first for loop; hence, a
newline is displayed on the screen in each iteration of the
first for loop; that is, a newline is displayed after each
row of the 2-D matrix mat1[][] is displayed*/
```

```
}
/*this closing curly brace specifies the end of 'for (i=0;
i<ROW; i++)' loop*/
printf("\nTranspose of the matrix is:\n");
/*output function printf() displays the text in the quotations
as it is on the screen except for a newline replaces \n*/
for (i=0; i<ROW; i++){
/*this for loop executes following for loops ROW times; i=0
is the initialization, i<ROW is the condition and i++ is the
increment; initialization is done once at the beginning of the
loop; then condition is checked, if it is true, following for
loop is executed and value of i is incremented by 1 before
the condition is re-checked; these steps continue till the
condition becomes false at which point the program flow exits
the loop; thus in first iteration all elements of first row are
displayed, in second iteration all elements of second row are
displayed, and so on */
    for (j=0; j<COL; j++)
    /*j=0 is the initialization, j<COL is the condition and
    j++ is the increment; initialization is done once at the
    beginning of the loop; then the condition is checked, if it
    is true, statements in the body are executed and value of
    j is incremented by 1 before the condition is re-checked;
    these steps continue until the condition becomes false at
    which point the program flow exits the loop*/
        printf("%d\t", mat2[i][j]);
        /*function printf() displays the value of array element
        mat2[i][j] in place of format specifier %d on the screen
        followed by a tab in place of \t*/
    printf("\n");
    /*this statement is in the body of first for loop; hence, a
    newline is displayed on the screen in each iteration of the
    first for loop; that is, a newline is displayed after each
    row of the 2-D matrix mat2[][] is displayed*/
}
/*this is the end of 'for (i=0; i<ROW; i++)' loop*/
return 0;
/*0 is returned as it is the standard for the successful
execution of the program*/
}
/*this closing curly brace specifies the end of main() function; no
statement is executed after that point*/
```

## PROBLEM-12
Write a program to search an item from an array of n items. The value of n, n items, and the target item should be given from the keyboard. The program will display the target item and its position in the array.

## Flowchart of the Solution:

Figure 3.5 shows the flowchart followed to solve this problem.

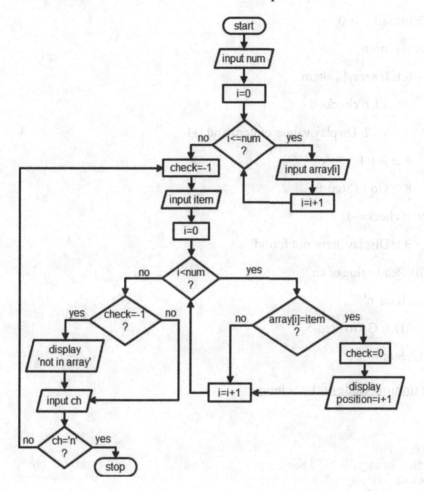

FIGURE 3.5   Flowchart followed to solve the problem.

## Algorithm of the Solution:

Step-1: Start

Step-2: Read value of num

Step-3: Initialize i←0

Step-4: If i<num

        4.1: Read value of array[i]

        4.2: i←i+1

        4.3: Go to Step-4

Step-5: Initialize check←−1

Step-6: Read value of item

Step-7: Initialize i←0

Step-8: If i<num

    8.1: If array[i]=item

        8.1.1: check←0

        8.1.2: Display values of item and i+1

    8.2: i←i+1

    8.3: Go to Step-8

Step-9: If check=−1

    9.1: Display 'item not found'

Step-10: Read value of ch

Step-11: If ch 'n'

    11.1: Go to Step-5

Step-12: Stop

Programming Code of the Solution:

```c
#include <stdio.h>
#include <conio.h>
int main(){
    int array[50], item, num, i, check;
    char ch;
    printf("How many items: ");
    scanf("%d", &num);
    printf("Enter %d items (separated by space):\n", num);
    for (i=0; i<num; i++)
        scanf("%d", &array[i]);
    do{
        check=-1;
        printf("\nEnter the item you want to find: ");
        scanf("%d", &item);
        for (i=0; i<num; i++)
            if (array[i]==item){
                check=0;
                printf("%d is found in position %d of the array.\n",
                    item, i+1);
            }
        if (check==-1)
            printf("%d is not in the array.\n", item);
        printf("Do you want to look for another item? (y/n): ");
        ch=getche();
        printf("\n");
```

```
    }while (ch!='n');
    return 0;
}
```

## Input and Output of the Executed Program:

```
How many items: 10
Enter 10 items (separated by space):
1 3 5 7 9 12 14 16 18 20

Enter the item you want to find: 11
11 is not in the array.
Do you want to look for another item? (y/n): y

Enter the item you want to find: 16
16 is found in position 8 of the array.
Do you want to look for another item? (y/n): n
```

## Explanation of the Programming Code:

```
#include <stdio.h>
```
/*header file stdio.h contains prototypes of the library functions printf() and scanf(); the header file must be included using preprocessor directive #include before the functions are called in the program*/
```
#include <conio.h>
```
/*getche() is a non-standard function that is declared in the conio.h header file; the header file must be included using preprocessor directive #include before the function is called in the program*/
```
int main(){
```
/*all C program must have a main() function with return type void or int; here there is no parameter of the main() function and it returns an integer; opening curly brace specifies start of the main() function and no statement before that curly brace is executed by the compiler*/
```
        int array[50], item, num, i, check;
```
        /*an integer type array of size 50, and four integer type variables are declared; required memory spaces are allocated for the array and each of the variables*/
```
        char ch;
```
        /*a character type variable ch is declared; required memory spaces are allocated for it*/
```
        printf("How many items: ");
```
        /*output function printf() displays the text in the quotation as it is on the screen*/

```
scanf("%d", &num);
```
/*scanf() function reads an integer from input terminal and stores the value in the memory spaces allocated for the num*/
```
printf("Enter %d items (separated by space):\n", num);
```
/*printf() function displays the text in the quotation as it is on the screen except for the value of num replaces the format specifier %d and a newline replaces \n*/
```
for (i=0; i<num; i++)
```
/*i=0 is the initialization, i<num is the condition and i++ is the increment; the initialization is done once at the beginning of the loop; then the condition is checked, if it is true, statement in the body is executed and the value of i is incremented by 1 before the condition is re-checked; these steps continue until the condition becomes false at which point the program flow exits the loop*/
```
    scanf("%d", &array[i]);
```
/*this scanf() function reads an integer from the input terminal and stores the value in the memory spaces allocated for the array[]; array[0] is read in the 1st iteration, array[1] is read in the 2nd iteration, and so on*/
```
do{
```
/*the statements, enclosed by curly braces, in the body are executed; now the condition is checked, if it is true then the body is executed before the condition is re-checked; these steps continue until the condition becomes false at which point the program flow exits the loop*/
```
    check=-1;
```
/*value of the variable check is initialized to -1, means the item has not found yet; value of check is changed only if the item is found in the array*/
```
    printf("\nEnter the item you want to find: ");
```
/*printf() function displays the text in the quotations as it is on screen except for a newline replaces \n*/
```
    scanf("%d", &item);
```
/*function scanf() reads an integer from input terminal and stores the value in the memory spaces allocated for the item*/
```
    for (i=0; i<num; i++)
```
/*i=0 is the initialization, i<num is the condition and i++ is the increment; initialization is done once at the beginning of the loop; then the condition is checked, if it is true, statement in the body is executed and value of i is incremented by 1 before the condition is re-checked; these steps continue until the condition becomes false at which point the program flow exits the loop*/

```
        if (array[i]==item){
        /*if item matches with the array element then the
        condition is true, and the following statements,
        enclosed in the curly braces, are executed; item is
        compared with array[0] at 1st iteration, array[1] at
        2nd iteration and so on*/
            check=0;
            /*if the item is found in the array then the
            condition of 'if' is true and the value of
            check is changed to 0 from -1*/
            printf("%d is found in position %d of the"
                "array.\n", item, i+1);
            /*printf() function displays the text in the
            quotations as it is on the screen except for
            the value i+1 replaces the format specifier %d
            and a newline replaces \n*/
        }
        /*this closing curly brace specifies the end of
        'if' condition*/
    if (check==-1)
    /*if item is not found in the array, then check=-1; so, the
    condition is true and following statement is executed*/
        printf("%d is not in the array.\n", item);
        /*printf() function displays the text in the quotation
        as it is on the screen except for format specifier %d is
        replaced by the value of item and \n by a newline*/
    printf("Do you want to look for another item? (y/n): ");
    /*printf() function displays the text in the quotation as
    it is on the screen*/
    ch=getche();
    /*getche() function reads a character from keyboard, the
    character is echoed on the screen without waiting for enter
    to be pressed and it is assigned to ch*/
    printf("\n");
    /*this printf() function displays a newline on the screen
    in place of \n*/
}while (ch!='n');
/*do..while loop ends here with condition ends with semicolon;
if the condition is true, the body in the loop is executed
before the condition is re-checked*/
return 0;
/*0 is returned as it is the standard for the successful
execution of the program*/
}
/*this closing curly brace specifies the end of main() function; no
statement is executed after that point*/
```

## PROBLEM-13

**Write a program which will read a text and count all occurrences of a particular character.**

Flowchart of the Solution:

Figure 3.6 shows the flowchart followed to solve this problem.

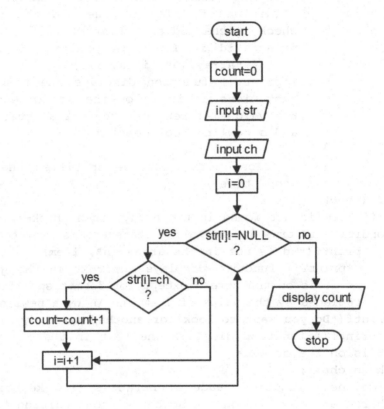

FIGURE 3.6   Flowchart followed to solve the problem.

## Algorithm of the Solution:

Step-1: Start

Step-2: Initialize count←0

Step-3: Read a line of text or character string and save it to array str[]

Step-4: Read a character value of ch

Step-5: Initialize i←0

    5.1: If str[i]≠'\0'

        5.1.1: If str[i]=ch

            5.1.1.1: count←count+1

    5.2: i←i+1

    5.3: Go to Step-5.1

Step-6: Display the value of count

Step-7: Stop

<u>Programming Code of the Solution:</u>

```c
#include <stdio.h>
int main(){
    char str[80], ch;
    int count=0, i;
    printf("Enter a line of text:\n");
    gets(str);
    printf("Enter the character you want to count: ");
    scanf("%c", &ch);
    for (i=0; str[i]!='\0'; i++)
        if(str[i]==ch)
            count++;
    printf("The character %c occurs %d times in the string.\n",
            ch, count);
    return 0;
}
```

<u>Input and Output of the Executed Program:</u>

```
Enter a line of text:
nice to meet you, thank you!
Enter the character you want to count: e
The character e occurs 3 times in the string.
```

<u>Explanation of the Programming Code:</u>

**#include <stdio.h>**
/*header file stdio.h contains prototypes of the library functions printf(), scanf() and gets(); the header file must be included using preprocessor directive #include before the functions are called in the program*/

```
int main(){
```
/*all C program must have a main() function with return type void
or int; here there is no parameter of the main() function and it
returns an integer; opening curly brace specifies start of the
main() function and no statement before that curly brace is executed
by the compiler*/

```
    char str[80], ch;
```
/*character type array str[] of size 80 and a variable ch are
declared; required memory spaces are allocated for them*/

```
    int count=0, i;
```
/*integer type variable count is declared and initialized to 0;
integer type variable i is declared; count is used to calculate
and store total number of a particular character in the text;
if the variable is not initialized to 0 then the memory spaces
allocated for the variable may contain some garbage value
which is added in their first summation and gives an incorrect
result*/

```
    printf("Enter a line of text:\n");
```
/*output function printf() displays the text in the quotations
as it is on the screen except for a newline replaces \n*/

```
    gets(str);
```
/*function gets() reads a character string or any text from
input terminal and assigned it to the array str[]; gets()
function reads any character from the keyboard including
space, tab, etc. and stops reading as soon as enter is
pressed*/

```
    printf("Enter the character you want to count: ");
```
/*output function printf() displays the text in the quotations
as it is on the screen*/

```
    scanf("%c", &ch);
```
/*function scanf() reads a character from input terminal and
stores it in the memory spaces allocated for ch*/

```
    for (i=0; str[i]!='\0'; i++)
```
/*i=0 is the initialization, str[i]!='\0' is the condition
and i++ is the increment; initialization is done once at the
beginning of the loop; then the condition is checked, if it
is true, statement in the body is executed and value of i is
incremented by 1 before the condition is re-checked; these
steps continue until the condition becomes false at which point
the program flow exits the loop; here the condition remains true
till we reach end of the string or text*/

```
        if(str[i]==ch)
```
/*if ch matches with the character of the string or text
then the condition is true, and the following statement is
executed; ch is compared with 1st character str[0] at 1st
iteration, 2nd character str[1] at 2nd iteration and so
on*/

```
        count++;
        /*if character ch is found in the string or text then
        the condition of 'if' is true and the value of count is
        incremented by 1*/
printf("The character %c occurs %d times in the string.\n", ch,
        count);
/*printf() function displays the text in the quotations as it
is on the screen except for character ch replaces the format
specifier %c, value count replaces %d and a newline replaces
\n*/
return 0;
/*0 is returned as it is the standard for the successful
execution of the program*/
}
/*this closing curly brace specifies the end of main() function; no
statement is executed after that point*/
```

## PROBLEM-14
**Write a program to count the number of lines, words, and characters in a given text.**

<u>Flowchart of the Solution:</u>

Figure 3.7 shows the flowchart followed to solve this problem.

## **Algorithm of the Solution:**

Step-1: Start

Step-2: Initialize end←0, chnm←0, word←0, and line←0

Step-3: If end=0

        3.1: Initialize k←0

        3.2: Read value of ch

        3.3: If ch≠'\n'

            3.3.1: str[k]←ch

            3.3.2: Read value of ch

            3.3.3: k←k+1

            3.3.4: Go to Step-3.3

        3.4: str[k]←'\0'

        3.5: If str[0]='\0'

            3.5.1: Go to Step-4

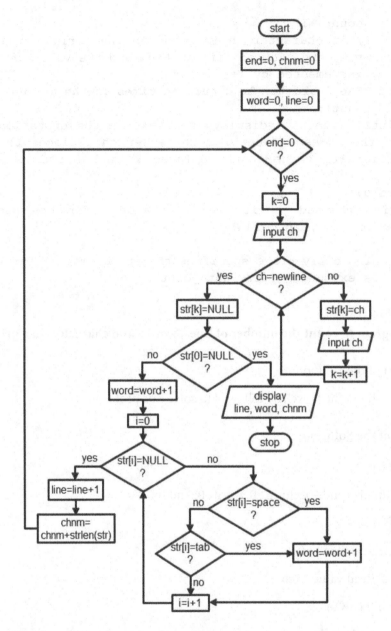

FIGURE 3.7   Flowchart followed to solve the problem.

3.6: word←word+1

3.7: Initialize i←0

3.8: If str[i]≠'\0'

    3.8.1: If str[i]=' '

        3.8.1.1: Go to Step-3.8.2.1

3.8.2: If str[i]='\t'

        3.8.2.1: word←word+1

    3.8.3: i←i+1

    3.8.4: Go to Step-3.8

  3.9: line←line+1

  3.10: chnm←chnm+strlen(str)

Step-4: Display value of line, word, and chnm

Step-5: Stop

<u>Programming Code of the Solution:</u>

```c
#include<stdio.h>
#include<string.h>
int main(){
    char str[80], ch;
    int i, k, end=0, chnm=0, word=0, line=0;
    printf("Enter the text and press ENTER at end.\n");
    while (end==0){
        k=0;
        for (ch=getchar(); ch!='\n'; k++){
            str[k]=ch;
            ch=getchar();
        }
        str[k]='\0';
        if (str[0]=='\0')
            break;
        else{
            word++;
            for (i=0; str[i]!='\0'; i++){
                if (str[i]==' '||str[i]=='\t')
                    word++;
            }
        }
        line=line+1;
        chnm+=strlen(str);
    }
    printf("Number of lines: %d\n", line);
    printf("Number of words: %d\n", word);
    printf("Number of characters: %d\n", chnm);
    return 0;
}
```

Input and Output of the Executed Program:

```
Enter the text and press ENTER at end.
Atiqur Rahman Ahad is a very good person.
Most of us like him very much.
He is very helpful in every aspects.

Number of lines: 3
Number of words: 22
Number of characters: 107
```

## Explanation of the Programming Code:

**#include<stdio.h>**
/*header file stdio.h contains prototypes of the library functions printf(), scanf() and getchar(); the header file must be included using preprocessor directive #include before the functions are called in the program*/
**#include<string.h>**
/*strlen() function is declared in the header file string.h; the header file must be included using preprocessor directive #include before the function is called in the program*/
**int main(){**
/*all C program must have a main() function with return type void or int; here there is no parameter of the main() function and it returns an integer; opening curly brace specifies start of the main() function and no statement before that curly brace is executed by the compiler*/
    **char str[80], ch;**
    /*character type array str[] of size 80 and a variable ch are declared; required memory spaces are allocated for them*/
    **int i, k, end=0, chnm=0, word=0, line=0;**
    /*integer type variables i and k are declared, and end, chnm, word and line are declared and initialized to 0; chnm is used to calculate and store total characters in this program, word is used to calculate and store total words, and line is used to calculate and store total line in the text; if these variables are not initialized to 0 then the memory spaces allocated for the variables may contain some garbage value which is added in their first summation and gives an incorrect result*/
    **printf("Enter the text and press ENTER at end.\n");**
    /*output function printf() displays the text in the quotations as it is on the screen except for a newline replaces \n*/
    **while (end==0){**
    /*if the condition is true, following statements, enclosed by curly braces, are executed, and the condition is re-checked;

this process continues until the condition becomes false at
which point the program flow exits the loop*/
```
    k=0;
    /*variable k is initialized to 0*/
    for (ch=getchar(); ch!='\n'; k++){
```
    /*this for loop is used to input the text, one character in
    each iteration; ch=getchar() is the initialization, ch!='\n'
    is the condition and k++ is the increment; initialization
    is done once at the beginning of the loop, getchar() reads
    a character from keyboard and assigned it to ch; then the
    condition is checked, if enter is not pressed then it is true
    and statements in the body are executed and value of k is
    incremented by 1 before the condition is re-checked; these
    steps continue until the enter is pressed at which point the
    condition becomes false and the program flow exits the loop*/
```
        str[k]=ch;
```
        /*input character ch is stored in the array str[];
        at first iteration ch is saved in str[0], at second
        iteration in str[1], and so on*/
```
        ch=getchar();
```
        /*function getchar() reads a single character from input
        terminal and assigned it to ch; getchar() function
        immediately echoes the input character on the output
        screen and waits to read another character*/
```
    }
```
    /*this closing curly brace specifies the end of for loop*/
```
    str[k]='\0';
```
    /*final character of the array is set to NULL to define it
    as string*/
```
    if (str[0]=='\0')
```
    /*if enter is pressed at the start of any line then this
    condition is true and following statement is executed*/
```
        break;
```
        /*program control flow immediately exits the 'while'
        loop*/
```
    else{
```
    /*if first character of a line is not a newline then the
    condition of 'if' is false, and following statements in the
    body of else are executed*/
```
        word++;
```
        /*this statement counts the first word of a line; if
        first character of a line is not '\0' then there is at
        least one word in that line and word count is incremented
        by 1*/
```
        for (i=0; str[i]!='\0'; i++){
```
        /*this for loop is used to sequentially count each
        word of a line in the text except the first word; i=0

is the initialization, str[i]!='\0' is the condition and i++ is the increment; initialization is done once at the beginning of the loop; then the condition is checked, if we don't reach the end of a line, the condition is true and statements in the body are executed; now, value of i is incremented by 1 before the condition is re-checked; these steps continue until the condition becomes false at which point the program flow exits the loop*/

```
        if (str[i]==' '||str[i]=='\t')
        /*if space or tab is encountered anywhere in the
        line then above condition is true and following
        statement is executed*/
            word++;
            /*word count is incremented by 1*/
    }
    /*this is the end of 'for (i=0; str[i]!='\0'; i++)'
    loop*/
}
/*this is the end of else condition*/
line=line+1;
/*when an enter is encountered after any characters it's a
line; the program flow exits first 'for' loop and skips break
statement in the 'if'; the line count here is incremented
by 1*/
chnm+=strlen(str);
/*function strlen() returns the number of characters in a
line str, the number is added to chnm and the summation is
stored in chnm*/
}
```

/*this is the end of while loop; a single line is entered, its words and characters are counted; now, the condition is checked again, if it is true, the body is executed before the condition is re-checked; this steps continue until enter is pressed at the beginning of a line at which point break statement in the 'if' causes the program to exit the loop*/

```
printf("Number of lines: %d\n", line);
```
/*printf() function displays the text inside the quotations as it is on the screen except for the value of line replaces the format specifier %d and a newline replaces \n*/
```
printf("Number of words: %d\n", word);
```
/*printf() function displays the text inside the quotations as it is on the screen except for the value of word replaces the format specifier %d and a newline replaces \n*/
```
printf("Number of characters: %d\n", chnm);
```
/*printf() displays the text inside the quotations as it is on the screen except for the value of chnm replaces the format specifier %d and a newline replaces \n*/

```
return 0;
/*0 is returned as it is the standard for the successful
execution of the program*/
}
```
/*this closing curly brace specifies the end of main() function; no
statement is executed after that point*/

## EXERCISES

MCQ with Answers

1) An array index in C starts with

   A) –1

   B) 0

   C) 2

   D) 1

2) What is the value of an array element which is not initialized?

   A) 0

   B) 1

   C) It depends on the storage class

   D) None of the above

3) What happens when we try to access an array variable outside its size?

   A) A compiler error is thrown

   B) 0 value is returned

   C) 1 value is returned

   D) Some garbage value is returned

4) What is the size of an array ary[9]?

   A) 8

   B) 9

   C) 10

   D) None of the above

5) What is the maximum index of the array ary[9]?

   A) 8

   B) 9

C) 10

D) None of the above

6) How many bytes are skipped if an integer array pointer is incremented by one to reach the location of the next element?

A) 1

B) 2

C) 8

D) None of the above

7) Which function is used to allocate memory to an array at run time and initialize each array element to 0?

A) calloc()

B) malloc()

C) palloc()

D) kalloc()

8) Which function is used to allocate memory to an array at run time without initializing the array elements?

A) calloc()

B) malloc()

C) palloc()

D) kalloc()

9) What is the size of array float ary[15]?

A) 17

B) 64

C) 16

D) 60

10) What is the dimension of the array ary[5][6]?

A) 5

B) 6

C) 2

D) 30

11) What is the dimension of the array ary[]={1, 2, 3, 4, 5}?

A) 1

B) 2

C) 4

D) 5

12) What is the maximum number of dimensions of an array in C?

A) 2

B) 10

C) 20

D) >20

13) An array of arrays is also called

A) Multi-data array

B) Multi-size array

C) Multidimensional array

D) Multi-byte array

14) Which of the following is the right way to initialize an array?

A) int num[6] = {2, 4, 12, 5, 45, 5};

B) int n{} = {2, 4, 12, 5, 45, 5};

C) int n{6} = {2, 4, 12};

D) int n(6) = {2, 4, 12, 5, 45, 5};

15) int ary[5]={1, 2, 4}; what is the value of ary[4]?

A) 0

B) 3

C) 2

D) 1

16) When the size of the array need not be specified?

A) Initialization is a part of the definition

B) It is a declaration

C) It is a formal parameter

D) All of the above

17) Choose a correct statement about a C multidimensional array.

A) First dimension size is optional when initializing the array at the same time

B) The last dimension size is optional when initializing the array at the same time

C) It is a must to specify all dimensions of a multidimensional array

D) Memory locations of elements of a multidimensional array are not sequential

18) What is a string in C language?

A) A string is a new data type in C

B) A string is an array of characters with a null character as the last element of the array

C) A string is an array of characters with a null character as the first element

D) A string is an array of integers with 0 as the last element of the array

19) Which one is the correct statement about array char ary[]="hello world . . ."?

A) Array ary[] is a string

B) Ary[] has no null character at the end

C) Array size is not mentioned

D) A string cannot contain special characters

20) What is the format specifier used to display string in the C printf() function?

A) %c

B) %C

C) %s

D) %w

21) A char type array is defined as char str[]={'a','t','i','q'}; How do you convert this to string?

A) str[4] = 0;

B) str[4] = '\0'

C) str[]={'a','t','i','q','\0'};

D) All of the above

22) Which of the following function is more appropriate to read multi-word string?

A) scanf()

B) gets()

C) getc()

D) finds()

23) What is the ASCII value of NULL or '\0'?

A) 0

B) 1

C) 10

D) 49

24) A C string elements are always stored in

A) Random memory locations

B) Alternate memory locations

C) Sequential memory locations

D) None of the above

25) What does strcmp() function return if the two strings are identical?

A) 1

B) 0

C) −1

D) True

26) What is actually passed to printf() or scanf() function?

A) Value of string

B) Address of string

C) End address of the string

D) Integer equivalent value of the string

27) What happens if the array size is less than the number of initializers?

A) Generates an error text

B) Extra values are ignored

    C) Size of the array is increased

    D) Size is neglected when values are given

28) Which of the following data types are allowed to create pointers?

    A) Character

    B) Integer

    C) Unsigned integer

    D) All of the above

29) Can we assign null to void pointer?

    A) Yes

    B) No

    C) Error

    D) None

30) Which of the following statement is correct about int **ptr;?

    A) ptr is not a pointer

    B) ptr is a pointer to pointer

    C) Such a statement is not allowed in C

    D) None of these

31) Which operator is used to access value at address stored by a pointer variable?

    A) *

    B) &

    C) #

    D) @

32) What does string concatenation mean?

    A) Combining two strings

    B) Extracting a substring out of a string

    C) Partitioning the string into two strings

    D) Merging two strings

33) Which function is used to append a string to another string?

A) strstr()

B) strnstr()

C) strcat()

D) strapp()

34) Which of the following function is used to find the first occurrence of a given substring in another string?

A) strchr()

B) strrchr()

C) strstr()

D) strnset()

35) Which of the following function is used to find the last occurrence of a given substring in another string?

A) laststr()

B) strstr()

C) strnstr()

D) strrchr()

36) Which of the following function free the allocated memory?

A) remove(var-name);

B) free(var-name);

C) delete(var-name);

D) dalloc(var-name);

[Ans. B, C, D, B, A, B, A, B, D, C, A, D, C, A, A, D, A, B, A, C, D, B, A, C, B, B, A, D, A, B, A, A, C, C, D, B]

## Questions with Short Answers

1) What is a constant pointer in C?

Ans. A constant pointer is a pointer that cannot change the address it is pointing to. This means that once a constant pointer points to a variable, it cannot point to any other variable. A constant pointer is declared as

int *const ptr;

2) What is a pointer to a constant in C?

Ans. A pointer to constant is a pointer that cannot change the value of the variable it points to. However, it is allowed to change the address the pointer points to. A pointer to constant is declared as

const int *ptr;

3) What is a dangling pointer in C?

Ans. A pointer pointing to a memory location that is deleted, freed, or de-allocated is known as a dangling pointer.

4) Describe wild pointer in C?

Ans. A wild pointer is a pointer that is declared but not initialized. It points to some unallocated memory location and may cause a program to crash or behave badly.

5) What is the difference between far and near pointers?

Ans. Near pointer is used to store 16-bit addresses and works within the 64-kb data segment of memory. Far pointer is typically 32 bit and stores both segment and offset addresses. It can access memory outside the current segment. Examples-

char near *nrptr;

int far *frptr;

6) What is a pointer on a pointer in C?

Ans. A pointer on a pointer is known as multiple indirection or chain of pointers. When we define a pointer to a pointer, the first pointer contains the address of the variable, whereas the second pointer contains the address of the first pointer.

7) Is it possible to add pointers to each other?

Ans. Pointers contain addresses. Therefore, though it is possible to add two pointers, it makes no sense to add two addresses, because we do not know what the new address would point to.

8) Distinguish between malloc() and calloc() memory allocation.

Ans. malloc() creates a single block of memory of size specified by the user, and the memory block contains garbage value. calloc(), on the other hand, can assign multiple blocks of memory of a variable, and the memory blocks always initialized to 0.

9) What is a NULL pointer?

Ans. A NULL pointer is a pointer that does not point to a valid memory address. It stores the NULL value and its data type is void. A NULL value or '\0' is assigned to the pointer to define a NULL pointer. Example,

```
char *ptr='\0';

int *ptr=NULL;
```

10) What is the advantage of using a void pointer?

Ans. void pointer is a pointer that has no associated data type with it. It can hold the address of any data type. malloc() and calloc() return void type pointer and can be used to allocate memory of any data type.

11) Define an array?

Ans. An array is a collection of elements of the same data type stored in the con-tiguous memory location. Each element is referenced by index to a unique identi-fier. For example, 20 different values of int type can be stored in a single array rather than using 20 different variables.

12) How can a pointer access an array?

Ans. A pointer to an array points to the 0th element of the array. Now, this pointer can be used to access any element of the array by adding the index value of that element to the pointer. For example, to access the 5th element of the array, the fol-lowing codes are used:

int stud[50];

int *ptr=arr;

printf("%d", ptr+4);

13) How do we access values within an array?

Ans. We can access values within an array by using their index positions. Index position refers to the memory location where the values are saved. For example, the 5th element of an array can be accessed as follows:

int stud[50];

printf("%d", stud[4]);

14) What is the advantage of an array over individual variables?

Ans. An array is used to store multiple values by making use of a single variable. So, it is declared once, and the code can be reused multiple times. Using individual variables to store multiple values is not efficient in terms of coding, reusability, and readability.

15) Can the "if" condition be used in comparing strings?

Ans. In C, it is not allowed to compare two strings using logical operators that may return true or false, so the "if" condition cannot be used in comparing strings.

16) How do we determine the length of a string value that was stored in a variable?

Ans. strlen() function is called with the variable name as its argument to determine the length of a string value that was stored in that variable.

17) What are multidimensional arrays?

Ans. Multidimensional arrays are an array of arrays in which data are stored in tabular form. The total number of elements in a multidimensional array is the multiplication of the sizes of all the dimensions. For example, array[5][6], array[3][4][6], and array [10][4][5][8], etc., are 2D, 3D, and 4D arrays, respectively.

18) What is gets() function? How does it differ from scanf() function?

Ans. Both gets() and scanf() are input library functions that read a string from the input terminal. scanf() reads input until it encounters whitespace, tab, newline, or EOF, whereas gets() reads input until it encounters newline or EOF, it does not stop reading when it encounters whitespace or tab.

Problems to Practice

1) Write a program to input and print the elements of an array using pointer.

2) Write a program to find the number of elements in an array.

3) Write a program to calculate the average of array elements.

4) Write a program to find the length of a string with and without strlen().

5) Write a program to print a string using pointer.

6) Write a program to find the frequency of a character in a string.

7) Write a program to copy a string with and without using strcpy().

8) Write a program to find both the largest and smallest numbers of an array of integers.

9) Write a program to generate the first n terms of a Fibonacci sequence. Also, check whether a given integer is a Fibonacci number or not.

10) Write a program to find the 2's complement of a given binary number.

11) Write a program to calculate and print transpose of a given matrix.

12) Write a program to search an item from an array of n items. The value of n, n items, and the target item should be given from the keyboard. The program will display the target item and its position in the array.

13) Write a program which will read a text and count all occurrences of a particular character.

14) Write a program to count the number of lines, words, and characters in a given text.

15) Write a program to read n number of values in an array and display it in reverse order.

16) Write a program to copy elements of an array into another array.

17) Write a program to count the total number of duplicate elements in an array.

18) Write a program to insert a new value in a sorted list of arrays.

19) Write a program to delete an element at the desired position from an array.

20) Write a program to find the sum of the right diagonals of a matrix.

21) Write a program to find the sum of rows and columns of a matrix.

22) Write a program to calculate the determinant of a square matrix.

23) Write a program to check whether a given matrix is an identity matrix.

24) Write a program to check whether an array is a subset of another array.

25) Write a program to swap two numbers using pointers.

26) Write a program to find the largest of three numbers using pointers.

27) Write a program to store n elements in an array and print the elements using a pointer.

28) Write a program to print a string using pointers.

29) Write a program to convert all lowercase vowels to uppercase in a string.

30) Write a program to convert a string from uppercase and lowercase and vice versa.

31) Write a program to sort a set of strings in ascending alphabetic order.

32) Write a program to count vowels and constants in a string using pointers.

33) Write a program that concatenates two strings without using strcat().

34) Write a program to print individual characters of a string in reverse order.

35) Write a program to count each character in a given string.

36) Write a program to find the maximum between two given numbers using pointers.

37) Write a program to display all the alphabet in English using pointers.

38) Write a program to insert an element at the end of an array.

39) Write a program to display the highest frequency character in a string.

40) Write a program to remove all blank spaces in a string.

41) Write a program that allocates memory for 500 integers using calloc() and then stores first 500 natural numbers in that spaces.

42) Write a program to find the value of an unknown function from a discrete set of known data points using the Lagrange interpolation formula. [see Chapter 2, Problem-17, page 124 for the solution]

# Functions

A FUNCTION IS A SET of statements that performs a specific task. Every C program must have at least one main() function, but any additional functions can be defined and used. This chapter presents and discusses two types of functions: library and user-defined.

## 4.1 FUNCTION TYPES

When we need to execute a block of statements several times, we define a function that contains those statements and call it every time we need it. Functions are used to make the codes more readable and reusable. In C, there are two different types of functions.

(1) *Library functions:* The standard library functions are predefined in the library (.lib) and declared in several header files (.h). We can call these functions anytime we need to do the task that that function defines. printf(), scanf(), gets(), puts(), etc., are some examples. Because functions printf() and scanf() are declared in the stdio.h header file, the header file must be included before they can be called in a C program using the preprocessor directive #include. Example is #include stdio.h>

(2) *User-defined functions:* These functions are defined by the programmer and afterward reused as needed.

## 4.2 FUNCTION STRUCTURE

Syntax of the C functions:

```
return_type function_name(argument_list){
      //blocks of valid C statements
}
```

return_type can be any valid data type like int, char, long int, float, double, etc. It can also be void if the function returns nothing.

Except for any keywords, function name can be any single alphanumeric word, preferably meaningful.

DOI: 10.1201/9781003302629-4

argument_list is a list of variables and their data types that are passed to the function as input. The formal parameter refers to the parameters that appear in the function declaration, whereas the actual parameter refers to the parameters that appear in the function call.

For example, the following function

```
float addition(float a, float b){
    return a+b;
}
```

takes two floating numbers, a and b, as its arguments and returns the total a+b. Here, a and b are the formal parameters, whereas x and y are the real parameters in the addition(x, y) function call.

## 4.3 FUNCTION CALL

When a function is called by reference, the addresses of the actual arguments are passed to the function. Example: addition(&x, &y);

The actual arguments are passed to the function when it is called by value. Example: addition(x, y); or addition(3, 4.5);

## 4.4 ARRAYS AND FUNCTIONS

To pass an entire array to a function, both the name of the array and its size are passed as arguments. Example:

addition(array_name, array_size); or

addition(num, 4);

## 4.5 POINTERS AND FUNCTIONS

When we pass a pointer to a function as an argument, we are passing the variable's address rather than the variable itself. As a result, any change made by the function to the variable affects the value of the actual variable in that address. This is referred to as a function call by reference. Example:

```
int incr (int *ptr){
    return (*ptr)+1;
}
#include <stdio.h>
int main(){
    int val = 5;
    incr(&val);
    printf("%d...", val);      //this shows output as- 6...
    return 0;
}
```

## 4.6 STORAGE CLASS

There are two properties of any C variables:

(1) *Type:* It defines the data type of the variable.

(2) *Storage class:* It determines the lifetime and visibility of a variable. There are four types of storage classes available in C.

(a) *Local variable:* Local variables declared within a block or function are only visible within that block or function.

(b) *Global variable:* Global variables are declared outside of all functions and can be accessed from any function.

(c) *Register variable:* Register variables are declared with the keyword register and are faster than local variables in terms of access.

(d) *Static variable:* The keyword static is used to declare a static variable whose value does not change until the program ends.

Example:

```
int n3 = 8;                //n3 is a global variable
int main(){
      int n1;              //n1 is a local variable to main() function
      register int n5;     //n5 is a register variable
}
void func(){
      int n2;              //n2 is a local variable to func() function
      static int n4;       //n4 is a static variable
}
```

## 4.7 EXAMPLES

### PROBLEM-01
**Write a program to swap two numbers using pointers and function.**

Programming Code of the Solution:

```
#include <stdio.h>
void swap(int *x, int *y);
int main(){
      int num1, num2;
      printf("Enter any two integers: ");
      scanf("%d %d", &num1, &num2);
      swap(&num1, &num2);
      printf("After swapping: %d %d", num1, num2);
      return 0;
}
```

```
void swap(int *x, int *y){
    int temp;
    temp = *x;
    *x = *y;
    *y = temp;
}
```

Input and Output of the Executed Program:

```
Enter any two integers: 8 17
After swapping: 17 8
```

## Explanation of the Programming Code:

**#include <stdio.h>**
/*header file stdio.h contains prototypes of the library functions printf(), and scanf(); the header file must be included using preprocessor directive #include before the functions are called in the program*/
**void swap(int *x, int *y);**
/*this is the prototype (or declaration) of the user-defined function swap() that must end with a semicolon; swap() takes two numbers as parameters, performs some predefined operations, and returns nothing*/
**int main(){**
/*all C program must have a main() function with return type void or int; here there is no parameter of the main() function and it returns an integer; opening curly brace specifies start of the main() function and no statement before that curly brace is executed by the compiler*/
   **int num1, num2;**
   /*two integer type variables are declared; required memory spaces are allocated for the variables*/
   **printf("Enter any two integers: ");**
   /*this displays the text inside the double quotations as it is on the screen*/
   **scanf("%d %d", &num1, &num2);**
   /*function scanf() reads two integers from input terminal and stores values in the memory spaces allocated for num1 and num2; first format specifier %d corresponds to num1 and second %d corresponds to num2*/
   **swap(&num1, &num2);**
   /*user-defined function swap() is called by reference; &num1 and &num2 are the real parameters; the program control flow switches to the function definition*/

```
printf("After swapping: %d %d", num1, num2);
/*output function printf() displays the text inside the
quotations as it is on the screen except for value of num1
replaces the 1st format specifier %d and value of num2 replaces
the 2nd %d*/
return 0;
/*0 is returned as it is the standard for the successful
execution of the program*/
}
```
/\*the closing curly brace specifies the end of the main() function's
body, as well as the program's end; after that curly brace, no
statement is executed\*/
```
void swap(int *x, int *y){
```
/\*this is the header for the user-defined function swap(), which
must be identical to the function prototype except for no semicolon
is used; the function is defined within the curly braces\*/
```
    int temp;
    /*integer type variable temp is declared which is a local
    variable to the function swap()*/
    temp = *x;
    /*x=&num1 and *x=num1, hence temp=*x=num1*/
    *x = *y;
    /*x=&num1 and y=&num2, *x=num1 and *y=num2, hence *x=*y→
    num1=num2*/
    *y = temp;
    /*y=&num2, *y=num2 and temp=num1, hence *y=temp → num2=num1*/
}
```
/\*the closing curly brace specifies the end of the swap() function's
body; the program control flow, at this point, returns to the point
where the function was called\*/

## PROBLEM-02
**Write a program to calculate the power of a number using function.**

Programming Code of the Solution:

```
#include <stdio.h>
int power(int num1, int num2);
int main(){
    int base, exp, res;
    printf("Enter a base number: ");
    scanf("%d", &base);
    printf("Enter power number (must be positive): ");
    scanf("%d", &exp);
    res = power(base, exp);
```

```c
        printf("%d^%d = %d", base, exp, res);
        return 0;
}
int power(int num1, int num2){
    int result = 1;
    while (num2 != 0){
        result = result*num1;
        num2 =  num2 - 1;
    }
    return result;
}
```

Input and Output of the Executed Program:

```
Enter a base number: 4
Enter power number (must be positive): 3
4^3 = 64
```

Explanation of the Programming Code:

**#include <stdio.h>**
/*header file stdio.h contains prototypes of the library functions printf(), and scanf(); the header file must be included using preprocessor directive #include before the functions are called in the program*/
**int power(int num1, int num2);**
/*this is the prototype (or declaration) of the user-defined function power() that must end with a semicolon; power() takes two integers as parameters, performs some predefined operations, and returns an integer*/
**int main(){**
/*all C program must have a main() function with return type void or int; here there is no parameter of the main() function and it returns an integer; opening curly brace specifies start of the main() function and no statement before that curly brace is executed by the compiler*/
    **int base, exp, res;**
    /*three integer type variables are declared; required memory spaces are allocated for each of the variables*/
    **printf("Enter a base number: ");**
    /*this displays the text inside the double quotations as it is on the screen*/
    **scanf("%d", &base);**
    /*function scanf() is reads an integer from input terminal and stores the value in the memory location allocated for base*/

```
printf("Enter power number (must be positive): ");
```
/*this displays the text inside the double quotations as it is
on the screen*/
```
scanf("%d", &exp);
```
/*function scanf() is reads an integer from input terminal and
stores the value in the memory location allocated for exp*/
```
res = power(base, exp);
```
/*user-defined function power() is called by value; here base
and exp are the two real arguments; the program control flow
transfers to the definition of power(); the function returns an
integer base$^{exp}$ which is assigned to res*/
```
printf("%d^%d = %d", base, exp, res);
```
/*this printf() function displays the text in the double quotes
as it is on the screen except for the value of base replaces
the 1st format specifier %d, value of exp replaces the 2nd %d
and res replaces the 3rd %d*/
```
return 0;
```
/*0 is returned as it is the standard for the successful
execution of the program*/
```
}
```
/*the closing curly brace specifies the end of the main() function's
body, as well as the program's end; after that curly brace, no
statement is executed*/
```
int power(int num1, int num2){
```
/*this is the header for the user-defined function power(), which
must be identical to the function prototype except for no semicolon
is used; the function is defined within the curly braces; in this
definition the value of real parameter base replaces the virtual
parameter num1 and the value of exp replaces num2*/
```
int result = 1;
```
/*integer type variable result is declared; the variable is
local to the function power() and is not visible outside the
function; the variable is initialized to 1, otherwise, when
the multiplication operation in the while loop is performed it
gives a wrong answer; because when a variable is declared, a
random memory location is assigned for this variable that may
contain some garbage value present in that location and num1 is
multiplied by that garbage value in the first multiplication
operation*/
```
while (num2!= 0){
```
/*body of the while loop contains the following two statements
which are executed until the condition num2!= 0 becomes false
or returns 0*/
```
    result = result*num1;
```
/*this multiplies the value of result by that of num1 and
the multiplication value is assigned to variable result*/

```
        num2 = num2-1;
        /*if num1=4 and num2=3 then
        after 1st iteration: result=1×4=4, num2=3-1=2
        after 2nd iteration: result=4×4=16, num2=2-1=1
        after 3rd iteration: result=16×4=64, num2=1-1=0*/
    }
    /*this closing curly brace specifies the end of while loop*/
    return result;
    /*this statement returns the final result, which is an integer,
    from the user-defined function power() to the point where the
    function power() was called*/
}
/*the closing curly brace specifies the end of the definition of
the power() function*/
```

## PROBLEM-03
Write a program to calculate the area of an equilateral triangle using function.

Programming Code of the Solution:

```
#include <stdio.h>
#include <math.h>
float area(int x);
int main(){
    int len;
    printf("Enter length of the side of a triangle: ");
    scanf("%d", &len);
    printf("Area of the equilateral triangle is: %0.2f", area(len));
    return 0;
}
float area(int x){
    float ar;
    ar = (sqrt(3)/4)*x*x;
    return ar;
}
```

Input and Output of the Executed Program:

```
Enter length of the side of a triangle: 2
Area of the equilateral triangle is: 1.73
```

Explanation of the Programming Code:

#include <stdio.h>
/*header file stdio.h contains prototypes of the library functions
printf(), and scanf(); the header file must be included using
preprocessor directive #include before the functions are called in
the program*/

```
#include <math.h>
```
/*math.h header file contains the declaration of function sqrt();
the header file must be included using preprocessor directive
#include before the function is called in the program*/
```
float area(int x);
```
/*this is the prototype (or declaration) of the user-defined
function area() that must end with a semicolon; area() takes an
integer argument, performs some predefined operations, and returns
a decimal number*/
```
int main(){
```
/*all C program must have a main() function with return type void
or int; here there is no parameter of the main() function and it
returns an integer; opening curly brace specifies start of the
main() function and no statement before that curly brace is executed
by the compiler*/
```
    int len;
```
/*integer type variable len is declared; required memory spaces
are allocated for the variable*/
```
    printf("Enter length of the side of a triangle: ");
```
/*this displays the text inside the double quotations as it is
on the screen*/
```
    scanf("%d", &len);
```
/*input function scanf() reads an integer from the keyboard and
stores the value in the memory spaces allocated for the variable
len*/
```
    printf("Area of the equilateral triangle is: %0.2f", area(len));
```
/*user-defined function area() is called with real parameter
len; the program control flow shifts to the definition of
area(); the function returns a decimal number which is displayed
in place of the format specifier %0.2f with two decimal points
precision; function printf() displays other text inside the
quotations as it is on the screen*/
```
    return 0;
```
/*0 is returned as it is the standard for the successful
execution of the program*/
```
}
```
/*the closing curly brace specifies the end of the main() function's
body, as well as the program's end; after that curly brace, no
statement is executed*/
```
float area(int x){
```
/*this is the header for the user-defined function area(), which
must be identical to the function prototype except for no semicolon
is used; the function is defined within the curly braces; in this
definition the value of len replaces the virtual parameter x*/

```
float ar;
/*float type variable ar is declared; required memory spaces
are allocated for the variable; variable ar is local to the
function area() and is not visible outside the function*/
ar = (sqrt(3)/4)*x*x;
/*area of the triangle is calculated and assigned to the variable
ar; library function sqrt() returns √3 which is a decimal
number; hence the result in the right side is a decimal number
though x is an integer*/
return ar;
/*this statement returns the value of ar, which is a decimal
number, from the user-defined function area() to the point
where the function area() was called*/
}
/*this closing curly brace specifies the end of the definition of
the area() function*/
```

## PROBLEM-04

**Write a program that displays the prime numbers from 1 to n. The value of n should be given interactively through the terminal.**

Flowchart of the Solution:

Figure 4.1 shows the flowcharts followed to solve this problem.

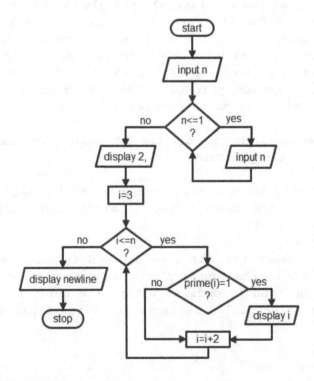

FIGURE 4.1 Flowcharts followed to solve the problem.

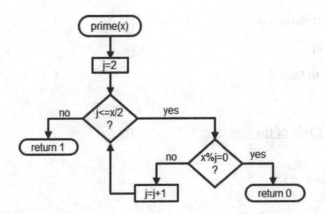

FIGURE 4.1 (Continued)

## Algorithm of the Solution:

Step-1: Start

Step-2: Read value of n

Step-3: If n<=1

       3.1: Display 'invalid entry'

       3.2: Read value of n

       3.3: Go to Step-3

Step-4: Display 2

Step-5: Initialize i←3

Step-6: If i<=n

       6.1: Call function prime(i)

       6.2: If prime(i)=1

           6.2.1: Display value of i

       6.3: i←i+2

       6.4: Go to Step-6

Step-7: Display newline

Step-8: Stop

## Algorithm for the function prime(x):

Step-1: Initialize j←2

Step-2: If j<=x/2

       2.1: If x%j=0

2.1.1: Return 0

2.2: j←j+1

2.3: Go to Step-2

Step-3: Return 1

<u>Programming Code of the Solution:</u>

```c
#include <stdio.h>
int prime(int x);
int main(){
    int n, i;
    printf("Please enter an integer greater than 1: ");
    scanf("%d", &n);
    while (n<=1){
        printf("Invalid entry!\n");
        printf("Please enter an integer greater than 1: ");
        scanf("%d", &n);
    }
    printf("The prime numbers between 1 and %d are: \n", n);
    printf("    2,");
    for (i=3; i<=n; i=i+2)
        if (prime(i)==1)
            printf("%4d,", i);
    printf("\n");
    return 0;
}
int prime(int x){
    int j;
    for (j=2; j<=x/2; j++)
        if ((x%j)==0)
            return 0;
    return 1;
}
```

<u>Input and Output of the Executed Program:</u>

```
Please enter an integer greater than 1: 77
The prime numbers between 1 and 77 are:
    2,  3,  5,  7, 11, 13, 17, 19, 23, 29, 31, 37, 41, 43, 47, 53, 59, 61, 67, 71, 73,
```

**Explanation of the Programming Code:**

**#include <stdio.h>**
/*header file stdio.h contains prototypes of the library functions printf(), and scanf(); the header file must be included using preprocessor directive #include before the functions are called in the program*/
**int prime(int x);**

/*this is the prototype (or declaration) of the user-defined function prime() that must end with a semicolon; prime() takes an integer as parameter, performs some predefined operations, and returns an integer*/

```
int main(){
```
/*all C program must have a main() function with return type void or int; here there is no parameter of the main() function and it returns an integer; opening curly brace specifies start of the main() function and no statement before that curly brace is executed by the compiler*/

```
    int n, i;
```
/*two integer type variables are declared; compiler assigns required spaces in memory for the variables*/

```
    printf("Please enter an integer greater than 1: ");
```
/*output library function printf() displays the text inside the double quotations as it is on the standard output terminal*/

```
    scanf("%d", &n);
```
/*library function scanf() reads an integer from standard input terminal and stores the value in the memory location allocated for n*/

```
    while (n<=1){
```
/*n<=1 is the condition of while loop; first the condition is checked, if it is true then the statements in the body of while loop are executed and the condition is re-checked; these steps continue until the condition becomes false at which point the program flow exits the loop*/

```
        printf("Invalid entry!\n");
```
/*printf() displays the text inside the double quotations as it is on the screen except for a newline replaces \n*/

```
        printf("Please enter an integer greater than 1: ");
```
/*printf() displays the text inside double quotations as it is on the screen*/

```
        scanf("%d", &n);
```
/*scanf() reads an integer from the input terminal and stores the value in the memory location allocated for n*/

```
    }
```
/*this closing curly brace specifies the end of while loop*/

```
    printf("The prime numbers between 1 and %d are: \n", n);
```
/*printf() displays the text inside double quotations as it is on the screen except for the value of n replaces the format specifier %d and a newline replaces \n*/

```
    printf(" 2,");
```
/*printf() displays the text inside the double quotations as it is on the screen*/

```
    for (i=3; i<=n; i=i+2)
```

/\*i=3 is the initialization, i<=n is the condition and i=i+2 is the increment; the initialization is done once at the beginning of the loop; then the condition is checked, if it is true, statement in the body is executed and the value of i is incremented by 2 before the condition is re-checked; these steps continue until the condition becomes false at which point the program flow exits the loop\*/

    **if (prime(i)==1)**

    /\*this is the only statement of the for loop; here prime() function is called with real parameter i and program control flow jumps to the definition of the prime() function; the function do some predefined operation and returns 1 if i is a prime number, otherwise it returns 0; if function prime(i) returns 1 the condition is true and the following statement is executed\*/

        **printf("%4d,", i);**

        /\*this printf() function displays the value of i on the screen occupying 4 spaces, if the number has less than 4 digits then the remaining digits are filled with spaces\*/

**printf("\n");**

/\*this printf() function display a newline on the screen\*/

**return 0;**

/\*0 is returned as it is the standard for the successful execution of the program\*/

**}**

/\*the closing curly brace specifies the end of the main() function's body, as well as the program's end; after that curly brace, no statement is executed\*/

**int prime(int x){**

/\*prime() function is defined here; the function header must be identical to the function prototype except for no semicolon is used and the body is written within the curly braces; here x is the virtual parameter that is replaced by real argument passed during function call\*/

    **int j;**

    /\*an integer type variable j is declared which is a local variable, and is not accessible outside the prime() function\*/

    **for (j=2; j<=x/2; j++)**

    /\*j=2 is the initialization, j<=x/2 is the condition and j++ is the increment; the initialization is done once at the beginning of the loop; then the condition is checked, if it is true, statement in the body is executed, and the value of j is incremented by 1 before the condition is re-checked; these steps continue until the condition becomes false at which point the program flow exits the loop\*/

```
if ((x%j)==0)
/*here, the modulus operator % gives remainder of the
division; number x is divided by the value of j; if remainder
of the division operation is 0, the condition is true and
the following statement is executed*/
    return 0;
    /*if the condition is true then the function
    immediately returns 0 to the point where the function
    was called*/
return 1;
/*here the function prime() returns 1 to the point from where
the function was called; this statement is executed only if
there is no j for which the above if condition is true*/
}
/*this closing curly brace specifies the end of prime() function
definition*/
```

## PROBLEM-05

Write a program to calculate the standard deviation of an array of values. The array elements are read from the terminal. Use functions to calculate the standard deviation and mean.

Flowchart of the Solution:

Figure 4.2 shows the flowcharts followed to solve this problem.

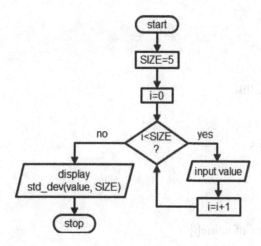

FIGURE 4.2    Flowcharts followed to solve the problem.

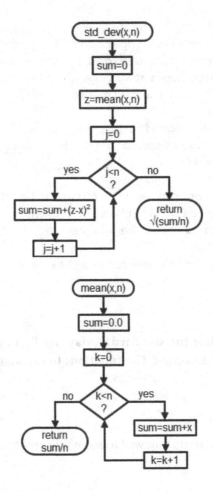

FIGURE 4.2 (Continued)

## Algorithm of the Solution:

Step-1: Start

Step-2: Define SIZE←5

Step-3: Initialize i←0

Step-4: If i<SIZE

      4.1: Read value of value[i]

      4.2: i←i+1

      4.3: Go to Step-4

Step-5: Call function std_dev(value, SIZE)

Step-6: Stop

## Algorithm for the function std_dev(x, n):

Step-1: Initialize sum←0.0

Step-2: z←mean(x, n) [call function mean()]

Step-3: Initialize j←0

Step-4: If j<n

    4.1: sum←sum+(z–x[j])²

    4.2: j←j+1

    4.3: Go to Step-4

Step-5: Return √(sum/n)

## Algorithm for the function mean(x,n):

Step-1: Initialize sum←0.0 and k←0

Step-2: If k<n

    2.1: sum←sum+x[k]

    2.2: k←k+1

    2.3: Go to Step-2

Step-3: Return sum/n

## Programming Code of the Solution:

```c
#include <stdio.h>
#include <math.h>
#define SIZE 5
float std_dev(float x[], int n);
float mean(float x[], int n);
int main(){
    float value[SIZE];
    int i;
    printf("Please enter any %d values (separated by space):\n", SIZE);
    for (i=0; i<SIZE; i++)
        scanf("%f", &value[i]);
    printf("Standard deviation is: %0.2f\n", std_dev(value, SIZE));
    return 0;
}
float std_dev(float x[], int n){
    float z, sum=0.0;
    int j;
    z=mean(x, n);
    for (j=0; j<n; j++)
        sum+=(z-x[j])*(z-x[j]);
    return sqrt(sum/n);
}
```

```
float mean(float x[], int n){
    float sum=0.0;
    int k;
    for (k=0; k<n; k++)
        sum+=x[k];
    return sum/n;
}
```

Input and Output of the Executed Program:

```
Please enter any 5 values (separated by space):
12 32 43 54 65
Standard deviation is: 18.28
```

## Explanation of the Programming Code:

**#include <stdio.h>**
/*header file stdio.h contains prototypes of the library functions printf(), and scanf(); the header file must be included using preprocessor directive #include before the functions are called in the program*/
**#include <math.h>**
/*header file math.h contains prototype of the library functions sqrt(); the header file must be included using preprocessor directive #include before the function is called in the program*/
**#define SIZE 5**
/*preprocessor directive #define defines a constant variable SIZE and assigns 5 to the variable; 5 replaces SIZE if it is used anywhere in this program*/
**float std_dev(float x[], int n);**
/*this is the prototype of the user-defined function std_dev() that must end with a semicolon; std_dev() takes an array and an integer as parameters, performs some predefined operations, and returns a decimal number*/
**float mean(float x[], int n);**
/*this is the declaration of the user-defined function mean() that must end with a semicolon; mean() takes an array and an integer as parameters, performs some predefined operations, and returns a decimal number*/
**int main(){**
/*all C program must have a main() function with return type void or int; here there is no parameter of the main() function and it returns an integer; opening curly brace specifies start of the main() function and no statement before that curly brace is executed by the compiler*/
**float value[SIZE];**
/*a float type array value[] of size SIZE is declared; required contiguous memory spaces are allocated for the array*/

```
int i;
```
/\*an integer type variable is declared and required memory space is allocated for i\*/
```
printf("Please enter any %d values (separated by" "space):\n",
        SIZE);
```
/\*function printf() displays the text in the quotations as it is on the screen except for the value of SIZE replaces the format specifier %d and a newline replaces \n\*/
```
for(i=0; i<SIZE; i++)
```
/\*this for loop reads SIZE number data; here i=0 is the initialization, i<SIZE is the condition and i++ is the increment; initialization is done once at the beginning of the loop; then the condition is checked, if it is true, statement in the body is executed and the value of i is incremented by 1 before the condition is re-checked; these steps continue until the condition becomes false at which point the program flow exits the loop\*/
```
    scanf("%f", &value[i]);
```
/\*scanf() function reads a decimal number from the input terminal and stores the value in the memory spaces allocated for the array; value[0] is read in the 1st iteration, value[1] is read in the 2nd iteration, and so on\*/
```
printf("Standard deviation is: %0.2f\n", std_dev(value,
        SIZE));
```
/\*here std_dev() function takes the array and SIZE as its real parameters and program control flow shifts to the function definition; the function does some predefined operations and returns a floating-point number that is displayed in place of the format specifier %0.2f with two decimal points precision; other text in the quotations is displayed as it is on the screen except for a newline replaces \n\*/
```
return 0;
```
/\*0 is returned as it is the standard for the successful execution of the program\*/
```
}
```
/\*this closing curly brace specifies the end of the main() function's body, as well as the program's end; after that curly brace, no statement is executed\*/
```
float std_dev(float x[], int n){
```
/\*this is the header for the user-defined function std_dev(), which must be identical to the function prototype except for no semicolon is used; the function is defined within the curly braces\*/
```
    float z, sum=0.0;
```
/\*a float type variable z is declared; another float type variable sum is declared and initialized to 0.0; if sum is

not initialized to 0.0 then the memory space allocated for the variable may contain some garbage value which is added in the first summation operation and gives incorrect result*/

```
int j;
```
/*an integer type variable is declared; compiler allocates required spaces in memory for the variable*/

```
z=mean(x, n);
```
/*user-defined function mean() is called with real parameters x and n where x is an array and n is its size; the program control flow shifts to the definition of the mean() function; the function does some predefined operations and returns a decimal number that is assigned to z*/

```
for (j=0; j<n; j++)
```
/*j=0 is the initialization, j<n is the condition and j++ is the increment; initialization is done once at the beginning of the loop; then the condition is checked, if it is true, statement in the body is executed and the value of j is incremented by 1 before the condition is re-checked; these steps continue until the condition becomes false at which point the program flow exits the loop*/

```
    sum+=(z-x[j])*(z-x[j]);
```
/*this operation is equivalent to sum=sum+(z-x[j])2; each iteration considers a single array element x[j], therefore the iteration begins with the first array element x[0] and ends with the last array member x[n-1]*/

```
return sqrt(sum/n);
```
/*at that point, function std_dev() returns square-root of the division sum/n to the point where the function was called*/

```
}
```
/*this closing curly brace specifies the end of the definition of function std_dev()*/

```
float mean(float x[], int n){
```
/*this is the header for the user-defined function mean(), which must be identical to the function prototype except for no semicolon is used; the function is defined within the curly braces*/

```
    float sum=0.0;
```
/*a float type variable sum is declared and initialized to 0.0; if sum is not initialized to 0.0 then the memory space allocated for the variable may contain some garbage value that is added in the first summation operation and gives incorrect result*/

```
    int k;
```
/*an integer type variable is declared; compiler assigns required spaces in memory for the variable*/

```
    for (k=0; k<n; k++)
```
/*this for loop sequentially adds all array elements; k=0 is the initialization, k<n is the condition and k++ is the increment;

initialization is done once at the beginning of the loop; then the condition is checked, if it is true, statement in the body is executed and the value of k is incremented by 1 before the condition is re-checked; these steps continue until the condition becomes false at which point the program flow exits the loop*/

```
    sum+=x[k];
    /*For the array elements x[4] = 2, 5, 9 and 19
    After 1st iteration, sum=sum+x[0]=0+2=2
    After 2nd iteration, sum=sum+s[1]=2+5=7
    After 3rd iteration, sum=sum+s[2]=7+9=16
    After 4th iteration, sum=sum+s[3]=16+19=35*/
    return sum/n;
    /*at this point, the function mean() returns result of the division
    operation sum/n to the point where the function was called*/
}
/*this closing curly brace specifies the end of mean() function
definition*/
```

## PROBLEM-06
**Write a program that computes and displays the factorial for any given number m using a loop and recursive function.**

Flowchart of the Solution:

Figure 4.3 shows the flowcharts followed to solve this problem.

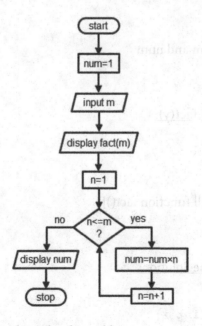

FIGURE 4.3   Flowcharts followed to solve the problem.

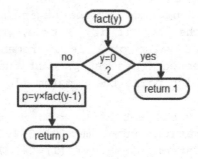

FIGURE 4.3   (Continued)

## Algorithm of the Solution:

Step-1: Start

Step-2: Initialize num←1

Step-3: Read value of m

Step-4: Display value of fact(m)

Step-5: Initialize n←1

Step-6: If n<=m

  6.1: num←num×n

  6.2: n←n+1

  6.3: Go to Step-6

Step-7: Display values of m and num

Step-8: Stop

## Algorithm for the function fact(y):

Step-1: If y=0

  1.1: Return 1

Step-2: p←y×fact(y−1) [call function fact()]

Step-3: Return p

## Programming Code of the Solution:

```c
#include <stdio.h>
unsigned long fact(int x);
int main(){
    int m, n;
```

```
    unsigned long num=1;
    printf("Enter any integer: ");
    scanf("%d", &m);
    printf("%d! = %lu (using recursive function)\n", m, fact(m));
    for (n=1; n<=m; n++)
        num*=n;
    printf("%d! = %lu (using loop)\n", m, num);
    return 0;
}
unsigned long fact(int y){
    unsigned long p;
    if (y==0)
        return 1;
    else
        p=y*fact(y-1);
    return p;
}
```

Input and Output of the Executed Program:

```
Enter any integer: 12
12! = 479001600 (using recursive function)
12! = 479001600 (using loop)
```

Explanation of the Programming Code:

```
#include <stdio.h>
```
/*header file stdio.h contains prototypes of the library functions printf(), and scanf(); the header file must be included using preprocessor directive #include before the functions are called in the program*/
```
unsigned long fact(int x);
```
/*this is the prototype of the user-defined function fact() that must end with a semicolon; fact() takes an integer as parameter, performs some predefined operations, and returns an unsigned long integer with the range $[0, 2 \times 2^{32}+1]$; this data type is used since the factorial value of a larger integer is a very large number*/
```
int main(){
```
/*all C program must have a main() function with return type void or int; here there is no parameter of the main() function and it returns an integer; opening curly brace specifies start of the main() function and no statement before that curly brace is executed by the compiler*/
```
    int m, n;
```
/*two integer type variables are declared; required memory spaces are assigned for that variables*/
```
    unsigned long num=1;
```
/*unsigned long integer type variable num is declared and initialized to 1; if this variable is not initialized to 1,

memory space allocated for that variable may contain some garbage value that is multiplied in the first multiplication operation, resulting in an incorrect answer*/
**printf("Enter any integer: ");**
/*printf() function displays the text in the double quotations as it is on the screen*/
**scanf("%d", &m);**
/*scanf() function reads an integer from input terminal and stores the value to the memory location allocated for m*/
**printf("%d! = %lu (using recursive function)\n", m, fact(m));**
/*here function fact() is called with real parameter m and the program control flow shifts to the function definition; fact() does some predefined operation and returns an unsigned long integer that is displayed in place of the format specifier %lu; printf() function displays the other text in the double quotations as it is on the screen except for the value of m replaces the format specifier %d and a newline replaces \n*/
**for (n=1; n<=m; n++)**
/*this for loop is used to compute m!; here n=1 is the initialization, n<=m is the condition and n++ is the increment; initialization is done once at the beginning of the loop; then the condition is checked, if it is true, statement in the body is executed and the value of n is incremented by 1 before the condition is re-checked; these steps continue until the condition becomes false at which point the program flow exits the loop*/
    **num*=n;**
    /*this multiplies 1, 2, 3, . . . with num in each iteration and the result is stored in num; for m=4
    After 1st iteration- num=num×n=1×1=1
    After 2nd iteration- num=num×n=1×2=2
    After 3rd iteration- num=num×n=2×3=6
    After 4th iteration- num=num×n=6×4=24*/
**printf("%d! = %lu (using loop)\n", m, num);**
/*printf() function displays the text in the double quotations as it is on the screen except for the value of m replaces the format specifier %d and the value of num replaces %lu*/
**return 0;**
/*0 is returned as it is the standard for the successful execution of the program*/
}
/*the closing curly brace specifies the end of the main() function's body, as well as the program's end; after that curly brace, no statement is executed*/

```
unsigned long fact(int x){
```
/*this is the header for the user-defined function fact(), which must be identical to the function prototype except for no semicolon is used; here x is the virtual parameter which is replaced by real argument passed during the function call; the function is defined within the curly braces*/

> `unsigned long p;`
> /*an unsigned long integer type variable is declared; required memory spaces are allocated for that variable to store data*/
> `if (x==0)`
> /*if parameter of the function fact() is 0, following statement is executed*/
>> `return 1;`
>> /*the function fact() returns 1 to the point where the function was called*/
> `else`
> /*if parameter of the function fact() is any number other than 0, following statement is executed*/
>> `p=x*fact(x-1);`
>> /*this is referred to as a recursive function call because function fact() is re-called with parameter x-1 within the definition of fact(); each recursive function returns a value that is multiplied with the previous multiplication result; for x=4
>> After 1st recursion- p=x×fact(x-1)=4×fact(3)
>> After 2nd recursion- p=4×x×fact(x-1)=4×3×fact(2)
>> After 3rd recursion- p=4×3×x×fact(x-1)=4×3×2×fact(1)
>> After 4th recursion- p=4×3×2×x×fact(x-1)=4×3×2×1×fact(0)
>> This gives us- p=4×3×2×1×fact(1)= 4×3×2×1×1=24
>> fact(0) returns 1 as x=0 and the condition of above 'if' satisfies*/
> `return p;`
> /*at this point function fact() returns the value of p to the point where the function was called*/

```
}
```
/*this closing curly brace specifies the end of fact() function definition*/

## PROBLEM-07

**Write a program to find the GCD (greatest common divisor) of two given integers using both recursive function and loop.**

<u>Flowchart of the Solution:</u>

Figure 4.4 shows the flowcharts followed to solve this problem.

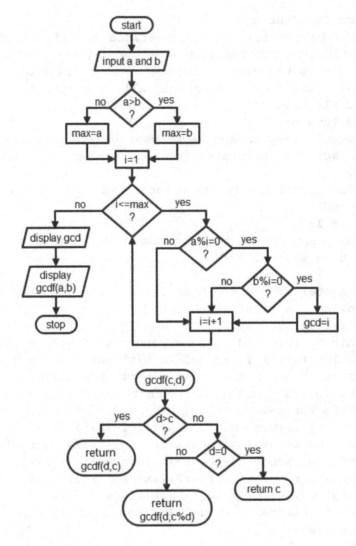

FIGURE 4.4 Flowcharts followed to solve the problem.

## Algorithm of the Solution:

Step-1: Start

Step-2: Read values of a and b

Step-3: If a>b

      3.1: max←b

      3.2: Go to Step-5

Step-4: max←a

Step-5: Initialize i←1

Step-6: If i<=max

    6.1: If a%i=0

        6.1.1: If b%i=0

            6.1.1.1: gcd←i

    6.2: i←i+1

    6.3: Go to Step-6

Step-7: Display value of gcd and gcdf(a, b) [call function gcdf()]

Step-8: Stop

## Algorithm for the function gcdf(c, d):

Step-1: If d>c

    1.1: Return gcdf(d, c)

Step-2: If d=0

    2.1: Return c

Step-3: Return gcdf(d, c%d)

## Programming Code of the Solution:

```c
#include<stdio.h>
int gcdf(int c, int d);
int main(){
    int a, b, gcd, max, i;
    printf("Enter a and b: ");
    scanf("%d %d", &a, &b);
    if (a>b)
        max=b;
    else
        max=a;
    for (i=1; i<=max; i++){
        if (a%i==0 && b%i==0)
            gcd=i;
    }
    printf("\nUsing loop:\nGCD of %d and %d is: %d\n", a, b, gcd);
    printf("\nUsing recursive function:\nGCD of %d and %d is: %d\n\n",
        a, b, gcdf(a,b));
    return 0;
}
int gcdf(int c, int d){
    if (d>c)
        return gcdf(d, c);
    if (d==0)
        return c;
    else
        return gcdf(d, c%d);
}
```

Input and Output of the Executed Program:

```
Enter a and b: 8 12

Using loop:
GCD of 8 and 12 is: 4

Using recursive function:
GCD of 8 and 12 is: 4
```

## Explanation of the Programming Code:

```
#include<stdio.h>
```
/*header file stdio.h contains prototypes of the library functions printf(), and scanf(); the header file must be included using preprocessor directive #include before the functions are called in the program*/
```
int gcdf(int c, int d);
```
/*this is the prototype or declaration of the user-defined function gcdf() that must end with a semicolon; gcdf() takes two integers as parameters, performs some predefined operations, and returns an integer*/
```
int main(){
```
/*all C program must have a main() function with return type void or int; here there is no parameter of the main() function and it returns an integer; opening curly brace specifies start of the main() function and no statement before that curly brace is executed by the compiler*/
```
    int a, b, gcd, max, i;
```
/*five integer type variables are declared; required memory spaces are allocated for each of the variables*/
```
    printf("Enter a and b: ");
```
/*function printf() displays the text in the double quotations as it is on the screen*/
```
    scanf("%d %d", &a, &b);
```
/*function scanf() reads two integers from the input terminal; the first value is placed in memory location a, and the second value is stored in memory location b; the two values must be separated by a space, tab, or enter during input*/
```
    if (a>b)
```
/*this if..else is used to find smaller of the two numbers; if the condition a>b is true, statement in the body of 'if' is executed*/
```
        max=b;
        //this statement assigns the smaller value b to max
    else
```
/*body of this else is executed if the condition a>b of the above 'if' is false*/

```
    max=a;
    /*this statement assigns the smaller value a to max, if a=b
    then also value of a is assigned to max*/
for (i=1; i<=max; i++){
/*this for loop computes the gcd of the two variables; i=1 is
the initialization, i<=max is the condition and i++ is the
increment; initialization is done once at the beginning of the
loop; then condition is checked, if it is true, statement in the
body is executed and the value of i is incremented by 1 before
the condition is re-checked; these steps continue until the
condition becomes false at which point the program flow exits
the loop*/
    if (a%i==0 && b%i==0)
    /*if both a and b are divisible by same number I, the
    statement in the body of 'if' is executed; in 1st iteration
    both a and b is divided by i=1, in 2nd iteration both a and
    b is divided by i=1, and so on*/
        gcd=i;
        /*if both a and b are divisible by same number i then
        the value of i is assigned to gcd*/
}
/*this closing curly brace specifies the end of the 'for'
loop*/
printf("\nUsing non-recursive:\nGCD of %d and %d is: %d\n", a,
    b, gcd);
/*this printf() displays the text in the double quotations as it
is on the screen except for the value of a replaces the first
format specifier %d, the value of b replaces the second %d, the
value of gcd replaces the third %d and a newline replaces the
\n*/
printf("\nUsing recursive function:\nGCD of %d and %d is:"
        "%d\n\n", a, b, gcdf(a, b));
/*user-defined function gcdf() is called with real parameters a
and b, program control flow shifts to the definition of gcdf()
function, gcdf() does some predefined operation, and returns an
integer that is displayed in place of the third format specifier
%d; output function printf() displays the text in the double
quotes as it is on the screen except for the value of a replaces
the first %d, value of b replaces the second %d and a newline
replaces the \n*/
return 0;
/*0 is returned as it is the standard for the successful
execution of the program*/
}
/*the closing curly brace specifies the end of the main() function's
body, as well as the program's end; after that curly brace, no
statement is executed*/
```

```
int gcdf(int c, int d){
```
/*this is the header for the user-defined function gcdf(), which must be identical to the function prototype except for no semicolon is used; the function is defined within the curly braces*/

```
    if (d>c)
```
/*if the value of 2nd argument is greater than that of 1st, the condition is true and the following statement in the body is executed*/

```
        return gcdf(d, c);
```
/*function gcdf() is called to swap the arguments so that the 2nd argument is the smaller of the two between c and d*/

```
    if (d==0)
```
/*if the 2nd argument d equals 0, the condition is true and the following statement in the body is executed; this if is used to check whether the 2nd argument d, which might be the smaller of the two arguments, is 0 or not as we cannot use 0 as divisor*/

```
        return c;
```
/*if the 2nd argument d is 0, d cannot be a divisor and the gcd is the larger number c; hence, this statement returns the value c to the point where the gcdf() function was called*/

```
    else
```
/*if 2nd argument d≠0, following statement in the body of else is executed*/

```
        return gcdf(d, c%d);
```
/*function gcdf() is called with new parameters d and c%d, the program control flow shifts to the function definition, gcdf() does some predefined operations and returns an integer to the point where the function was called; for 6 and 9-
1st function call- gcdf(6, 9) → gcdf(9, 6) [d=9 > c=6, 1st if condition is true]
2nd function call- gcdf(9, 6) → gcdf(6, 9%6) = gcdf(6, 3) [d=6 < c=9, 1st if condition is false; d≠0, 2nd if condition is false]
3rd function call- gcdf(6, 3) → gcdf(3, 6%3) = gcdf(3, 0) [d=3 < c=6, 1st if condition is false; d≠0, 2nd if condition is false]
4th function call- gcdf(3, 0) → return c=3 as gcd [d=0 < c=3, 1st if condition is false; d=0, 2nd if condition is true]*/

```
}
```
/*this closing curly brace specifies the end of gcdf() function definition*/

## PROBLEM-08

Write a program to sort n number of integers in ascending order. The program will display the data before sorting and after sorting.

Flowchart of the Solution:

Figure 4.5 shows the flowcharts followed to solve this problem.

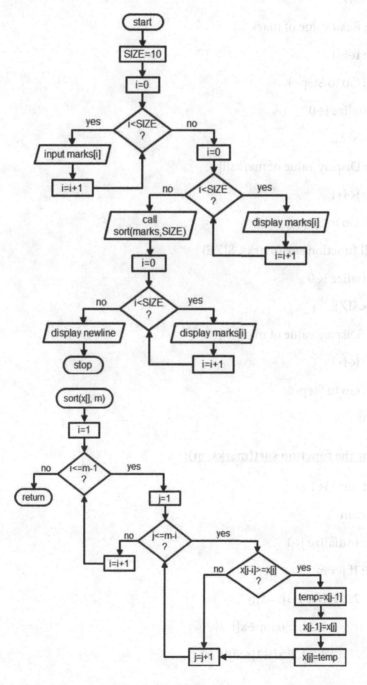

FIGURE 4.5   Flowchart followed to solve the problem.

## Algorithm of the Solution:

Step-1: Start

Step-2: Define SIZE←10

Step-3: Initialize i←0

Step-4: If i<SIZE

      4.1: Read value of marks[i]

      4.2: i←i+1

      4.3: Go to Step-4

Step-5: Initialize i←0

Step-6: If i<SIZE

      6.1: Display value of marks[i]

      6.2: i←i+1

      6.3: Go to Step-6

Step-7: Call function sort(marks, SIZE)

Step-8: Initialize i←0

Step-9: If i<SIZE

      9.1: Display value of marks[i]

      9.2: i←i+1

      9.3: Go to Step-9

Step-10: Stop

## Algorithm for the function sort(marks, m):

Step-1: Initialize i←1

Step-2: If i<=m−1

      2.1: Initialize j←1

      2.2: If j<=m-i

            2.2.1: If x[j−1]>=x[j]

                  2.2.1.1: temp←x[j−1]

                  2.2.1.2: x[j−1]←x[j]

2.2.1.3: x[j]←temp

2.2.2: j←j+1

2.2.3: Go to Step-2.2

2.3: i←i+1

2.4: Go to Step-2

Step-3: Return

<u>Programming Code of the Solution:</u>

```c
#include <stdio.h>
#define SIZE 10
void sort(int x[], int m);
int main(){
    int i, marks[SIZE];
    printf("Enter any %d integers (separated by space):\n", SIZE);
    for (i=0; i<SIZE; i++)
        scanf("%d", &marks[i]);
    printf("Marks before sorting:\n");
    for (i=0; i<SIZE; i++)
        printf("%d, ", marks[i]);
    sort(marks, SIZE);
    printf("\nMarks after sorting:\n");
    for (i=0; i<SIZE; i++)
        printf("%d, ", marks[i]);
    printf("\n");
    return 0;
}
void sort(int x[], int m){
    int i, j, temp;
    for (i=1; i<=m-1; i++)
        for (j=1; j<=m-i; j++)
            if (x[j-1]>=x[j]){
                temp=x[j-1];
                x[j-1]=x[j];
                x[j]=temp;
            }
}
```

<u>Input and Output of the Executed Program:</u>

```
Enter any 10 integers (separated by space):
5 4 2 8 9 13 3 2 78 45
Marks before sorting:
5, 4, 2, 8, 9, 13, 3, 2, 78, 45,
Marks after sorting:
2, 2, 3, 4, 5, 8, 9, 13, 45, 78,
```

## Explanation of the Programming Code:

```
#include <stdio.h>
```
/*header file stdio.h contains prototypes of the library functions printf(), and scanf(); the header file must be included using preprocessor directive #include before the functions are called in the program*/
```
#define SIZE 10
```
/* #define is a preprocessor directive that defines a constant variable SIZE and assigns the value 10 to it; value 10 replaces SIZE if it is used anywhere in this program*/
```
void sort(int x[], int m);
```
/*this is the prototype of the user-defined function sort() that must end with a semicolon; sort() takes an array and a number as parameters, performs some predefined operations, and returns nothing*/
```
int main(){
```
/*all C program must have a main() function with return type void or int; here there is no parameter of the main() function and it returns an integer; opening curly brace specifies start of the main() function and no statement before that curly brace is executed by the compiler*/
```
    int i, marks[SIZE];
```
/*integer type variable i and array marks[] of size are declared; required memory spaces are allocated for them*/
```
    printf("Enter any %d integers (separated by space):\n", SIZE);
```
/*output function printf() displays the text in the quotations as it is on the screen except for the value of SIZE replaces format specifier %d and a newline replaces \n*/
```
    for (i=0; i<SIZE; i++)
```
/*i=0 is the initialization, i<SIZE is the condition and i++ is the increment; initialization is done once at the beginning of the loop; then the condition is checked, if it is true, statement in the body is executed and the value of i is incremented by 1 before the condition is re-checked; these steps continue until the condition becomes false at which point the program flow exits the loop*/
```
        scanf("%d", &marks[i]);
```
/*scanf() function reads an integer from the input terminal and stores the value in the memory spaces allocated for the array; value[0] is read in 1st iteration, value[1] is read in 2nd iteration, and so on*/
```
    printf("Marks before sorting:\n");
```
/*output function printf() displays the text in the quotations as it is on the screen except for a newline replaces \n*/
```
    for (i=0; i<SIZE; i++)
```
/*this for loop displays SIZE number data before sorting; i=0 is the initialization, i<SIZE is the condition and i++ is the

increment; initialization is done once at the beginning of the loop; then the condition is checked, if it is true, statement in the body is executed and the value of i is incremented by 1 before the condition is re-checked; these steps continue until the condition becomes false at which point the program flow exits the loop*/

```
    printf("%d, ", marks[i]);
```
    /*printf() function displays the value of array element followed by a comma and a space on the screen; value[0] is displayed in 1st iteration, value[1] is displayed in 2nd iteration, and so on*/

```
sort(marks, SIZE);
```
/*user-defined function sort() is called with array marks[] and its size SIZE as its real arguments, program control flow shifts to the definition of the function*/

```
printf("\nMarks after sorting:\n");
```
/*output function printf() displays the text in the double quotations as it is on the screen except for a newline replaces \n*/

```
for (i=0; i<SIZE; i++)
```
/*this for loop displays SIZE number data after sorting; i=0 is the initialization, i<SIZE is the condition and i++ is the increment; initialization is done once at the beginning of the loop; then the condition is checked, if it is true, statement in the body is executed and the value of i is incremented by 1 before the condition is re-checked; these steps continue until the condition becomes false at which point the program flow exits the loop*/

```
    printf("%d, ", marks[i]);
```
    /*printf() function displays the value of array element followed by a comma and a space on the screen; value[0] is displayed in 1st iteration, value[1] is displayed in 2nd iteration, and so on*/

```
printf("\n");
```
/*function printf() displays a newline on the screen*/

```
return 0;
```
/*0 is returned as it is the standard for the successful execution of the program*/

```
}
```
/*the closing curly brace specifies the end of the main() function's body, as well as the program's end; after that curly brace, no statement is executed*/

```
void sort(int x[], int m){
```
/*this is the header for the user-defined function sort(), which must be identical to the function prototype except for no semicolon is used; the function is defined within the curly braces*/

```
int i, j, temp;
```
/*three integer type variables are declared; required memory spaces are allocated for these variables; these variables are local to the function sort() and are not accessible outside that function*/
/*bubble sort algorithm is used to sort the data; body of 1st for loop contains the 2nd for loop; 2nd for loop sequentially compares each array element with other elements and saves the largest number in the last array element x[m-1], this is the first iteration of 1st 'for' loop; in the 2nd iteration of 1st 'for' loop, 2nd 'for' loop sequentially compares each array element with others except for the last array element and the 2nd largest element is positioned in x[m-2]; these steps continue until the smallest element is placed in the first array position x[0]*/
```
for (i=1; i<=m-1; i++)
```
/*i=1 is the initialization, i<m-1 is the condition and i++ is the increment; initialization is done once at the beginning of the loop; then the condition is checked, if it is true, statement in the body is executed and the value of i is incremented by 1 before the condition is re-checked; these steps continue until the condition becomes false at which point the program flow exits the loop*/
```
        for (j=1; j<=m-i; j++)
```
/*each iteration of the 1st for loop places a single array element in its proper position; as a result, the number of elements to compare is reduced by 1 after each iteration; here j=1 is the initialization, j<m-i is the condition and j++ is the increment; initialization is done once at the beginning of the loop; then the condition is checked, if it is true, statement in the body is executed and the value of j is incremented by 1 before the condition is re-checked; these steps continue until the condition becomes false at which point the program flow exits the loop*/
```
            if (x[j-1]>=x[j]){
```
/*two contiguous array elements are compared, if the larger number stays above the smaller one, the condition is true and following statements are executed to swap them to keep the smaller number above the larger one*/
```
                temp=x[j-1];
```
/*array element x[j-1] is assigned to the variable temp*/
```
                x[j-1]=x[j];
```
/*array element x[j] is stored in the array element x[j-1]*/

```
        x[j]=temp;
        /*value of temp(=x[j-1]) is stored in the array
        element x[j]*/
    }
        /*this closing curly brace specifies the end of 'if'*/
}
/*the closing curly brace specifies the end of the sort() function's
body; the program control flow, at this point, returns to the point
where the function was called*/
```

## PROBLEM-09

Write a program to produce a matrix that is the sum of two given matrices of same size.
Also produce a matrix that is the product of two given matrices by checking compatibility.

Flowchart of the Solution:

Figure 4.6 shows the flowcharts followed to solve this problem.

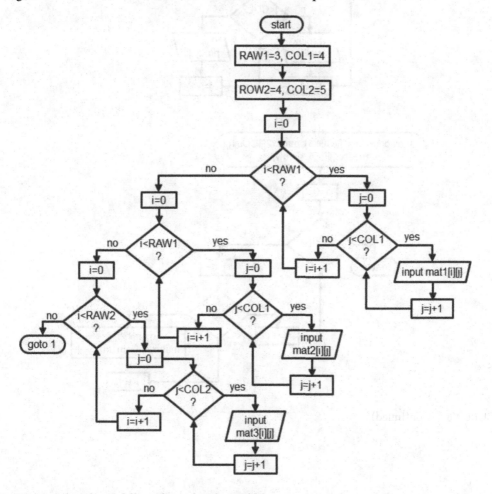

FIGURE 4.6   Flowcharts followed to solve the problem.

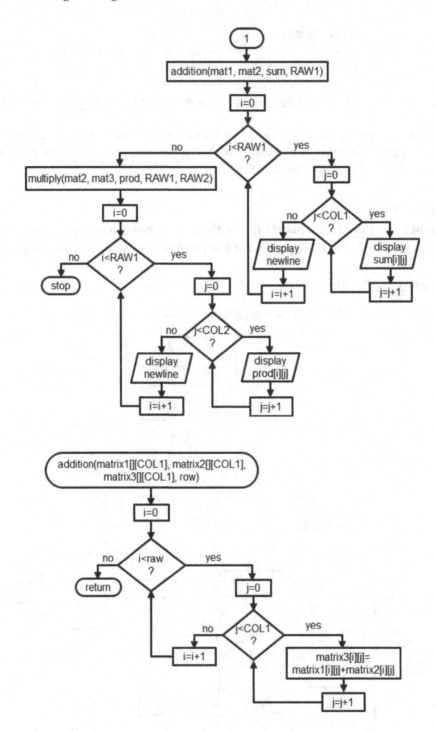

FIGURE 4.6   (Continued)

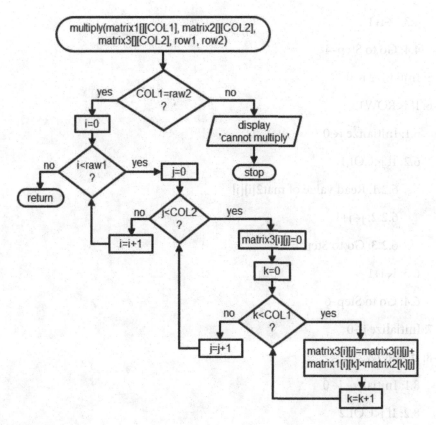

FIGURE 4.6 (Continued)

## Algorithm of the Solution:

Step-1: Start

Step-2: Define ROW1←3, COL1←4, ROW2←4 and COL2←5

Step-3: Initialize i←0

Step-4: If i<ROW1

    4.1: Initialize j←0

    4.2: If j<COL1

        4.2.1: Read value of mat1[i][j]

        4.2.2: j←j+1

        4.2.3: Go to Step-4.2

4.3: i←i+1

4.4: Go to Step-4

Step-5: Initialize i←0

Step-6: If i<ROW1

6.1: Initialize j←0

6.2: If j<COL1

6.2.1: Read value of mat2[i][j]

6.2.2: j←j+1

6.2.3: Go to Step-6.2

6.3: i←i+1

6.4: Go to Step-6

Step-7: Initialize i←0

Step-8: If i<ROW2

8.1: Initialize j←0

8.2: If j<COL2

8.2.1: Read value of mat3[i][j]

8.2.2: j←j+1

8.2.3: Go to Step-8.2

8.3: i←i+1

8.4: Go to Step-8

Step-9: Call function addition(mat1, mat2, sum, ROW1)

Step-10: Initialize i←0

Step-11: If i<ROW1

11.1: Initialize j←0

11.2: If j<COL1

11.2.1: Display value of sum[i][j]

11.2.2: j←j+1

11.2.3: Go to Step-11.2

11.3: Display newline

11.4: i←i+1

11.5: Go to Step-11

Step-12: Call function multiply(mat2, mat3, prod, ROW1, ROW2)

Step-13: Initialize i←0

Step-14: If i<ROW1

14.1: Initialize j←0

14.2: If j<COL2

14.2.1: Display value of prod[i][j]

14.2.2: j←j+1

14.2.3: Go to Step-15.2

14.3: Display newline

14.4: i←i+1

14.5: Go to Step-15

Step-15: Stop

## Algorithm for the Function addition(int matrix1[][COL1], int matrix2[][COL1], int matrix3[][COL1], int row):

Step-1: Initialize i←0.

Step-2: If i<row.

2.1: Initialize j←0

2.2: If j<COL1

2.2.1: matrix3[i][j]←matrix1[i][j]+matrix2[i][j]

2.2.2: j←j+1

2.2.3: Go to Step-2.2

2.4: i←i+1

2.5: Go to Step-2

Step-4: Return.

## Algorithm for the Function multiply(int matrix1[][COL1], int matrix2[][COL2], int matrix3[][COL2], int row1, int row2):

Step-1: If COL1=row2

    1.1: Initialize i←0

    1.2: If i<row1

        1.2.1: Initialize j←0

        1.2.2: If j<COL2.

            1.2.2.1: matrix3[i][j]←0

            1.2.2.2: Initialize k←0.

            1.2.2.3: If k<COL1

                1.2.2.3.1: matrix3[i][j]← matrix3[i][j]+matrix1[i][k]×matrix2[k][j]

                1.2.2.3.2: k←k+1

                1.2.2.3.3: Go to Step-1.2.2.3

            1.2.2.4: j←j+1

            1.2.2.5: Go to Step-1.2.2

        1.2.3: i←i+1

        1.2.4: Go to Step-1.2

    1.3: Go to Step-4

Step-2: Display 'not permissible size'

Step-3: Stop.

Step-4: Return.

Programming Code of the Solution:

```c
#include <stdio.h>
#include <stdlib.h>
#define ROW1 3
#define COL1 4
#define ROW2 4
#define COL2 5
void addition(int matrix1[][COL1], int matrix2[][COL1],
              int matrix3[][COL1], int row);
void multiply(int matrix1[][COL1], int matrix2[][COL2],
              int matrix3[][COL2], int row1, int row2);
```

```c
int main(){
    int mat1[ROW1][COL1], mat2[ROW1][COL1], mat3[ROW2][COL2];
    int sum[ROW1][COL1], prod[ROW1][COL2];
    int i, j;
    printf("Enter the first matrix of size %dx%d:\n", ROW1, COL1);
    for (i=0; i<ROW1; i++)
        for (j=0; j<COL1; j++)
            scanf("%d", &mat1[i][j]);
    printf("Enter the second matrix of size %dx%d:\n", ROW1, COL1);
    for (i=0; i<ROW1; i++)
        for (j=0; j<COL1; j++)
            scanf("%d", &mat2[i][j]);
    printf("Enter the third matrix of size %dx%d:\n", ROW2, COL2);
    for (i=0; i<ROW2; i++)
        for (j=0; j<COL2; j++)
            scanf("%d", &mat3[i][j]);
    addition(mat1, mat2, sum, ROW1);
    printf("\nSum of the first two matrices is:\n");
    for (i=0; i<ROW1; i++){
        for (j=0; j<COL1; j++)
            printf("%4d", sum[i][j]);
        printf("\n");
    }
    multiply(mat2, mat3, prod, ROW1, ROW2);
    printf("\nProduct of the last two matrices is:\n");
    for (i=0; i<ROW1; i++){
        for (j=0; j<COL2; j++)
            printf("%6d", prod[i][j]);
        printf("\n");
    }
    return 0;
}
void addition(int matrix1[][COL1], int matrix2[][COL1],
              int matrix3[][COL1], int row){
    int i, j;
    for (i=0; i<row; i++)
        for (j=0; j<COL1; j++)
            matrix3[i][j]=matrix1[i][j]+matrix2[i][j];
}
void multiply(int matrix1[][COL1], int matrix2[][COL2],
              int matrix3[][COL2], int row1, int row2){
    int i, j, k;
    if (COL1==row2)
        for (i=0; i<row1; i++)
            for (j=0; j<COL2; j++){
                matrix3[i][j]=0;
                for (k=0; k<COL1; k++)
                    matrix3[i][j]+=matrix1[i][k]*matrix2[k][j];
            }
    else{
        printf("Sizes of the matrices do not permit multiplication.\n");
        exit(1);
    }
}
```

Input and Output of the Executed Program:

```
Enter the first matrix of size 3x4:
1 2 3 4 5 6 7 8 9 2 4 6
Enter the second matrix of size 3x4:
2 4 6 8 10 12 14 16 18 20 22 24
Enter the third matrix of size 4x5:
1 3 5 7 9 11 13 15 17 19 21 23 25 27 29 31 33 35 37 39

Sum of the first two matrices is:
   3   6   9  12
  15  18  21  24
  27  22  26  30

Product of the last two matrices is:
   420   460   500   540   580
   932  1036  1140  1244  1348
  1444  1612  1780  1948  2116
```

### Explanation of the Programming Code:

`#include <stdio.h>`

/*header file stdio.h contains prototypes of the library functions printf(), and scanf(); the header file must be included using preprocessor directive #include before the functions are called in the program*/

`#include <stdlib.h>`

/*header file stdlib.h contains prototype of the library functions exit(); the header file must be included using preprocessor directive #include before the function is called in the program*/

`#define ROW1 3`

/*preprocessor directive #define defines a constant variable ROW1 and assigns a value 3 to ROW1; value 3 replaces ROW1 if it is used anywhere in this program*/

`#define COL1 4`

/*preprocessor directive #define defines a constant variable COL1 and assigns a value 4 to COL1; value 4 replaces COL1 if it is used anywhere in this program*/

`#define ROW2 4`

/*preprocessor directive #define defines a constant variable ROW2 and assigns a value 4 to ROW2; value 4 replaces ROW2 if it is used anywhere in this program*/

`#define COL2 5`

/*preprocessor directive #define defines a constant variable COL2 and assigns a value 5 to COL2; value 4 replaces COL2 if it is used anywhere in this program*/

`void addition(int matrix1[][COL1], int matrix2[][COL1], int`
`             matrix3[][COL1], int row);`

```
/*this is the prototype of the user-defined function addition()
that must end with a semicolon; addition() takes three 2-D matrices
and one integer as parameters, performs some predefined operations,
and returns nothing*/
void multiply(int    matrix1[][COL1],    int    matrix2[][COL2],    int
              matrix3[][COL2], int row1, int row2);
/*this is the prototype of the user-defined function multiply()
that must end with a semicolon; multiply() takes three 2-D matrices
and one integer as parameters, performs some predefined operations,
and returns nothing*/
int main(){
/*all C program must have a main() function with return type void
or int; here there is no parameter of the main() function and it
returns an integer; opening curly brace specifies start of the
main() function and no statement before that curly brace is executed
by the compiler*/
    int mat1[ROW1][COL1], mat2[ROW1][COL1], mat3[ROW2][COL2];
    /*integer type 2-D arrays mat1[][] and mat2[][] of size ROW1 and
    COL1, and mat3[][] of size ROW2 and COL2 are declared; required
    memory spaces are allocated for the arrays*/
    int sum[ROW1][COL1], prod[ROW1][COL2];
    /*integer type 2-D arrays sum[][] of size ROW1 and COL1, and
    prod[][] of size ROW1 and COL2 are declared; required memory
    spaces are allocated for the arrays*/
    int i, j;
    /*two integer type variables are declared; required memory
    spaces are allocated for the variables*/
    printf("Enter the first matrix of size %dx%d:\n", ROW1, COL1);
    /*output function printf() displays the text in the quotations
    as it is on the screen except for the value of ROW1 replaces
    the 1st format specifier %d, value of COL1 replaces the 2nd %d,
    and a newline replaces \n*/
    for (i=0; i<ROW1; i++)
    /*i=0 is the initialization, i<ROW1 is the condition and i++ is
    the increment; initialization is done once at the beginning of
    the loop; then the condition is checked, if it is true following
    for loop is executed and the value of i is incremented by 1
    before the condition is re-checked; these steps continue until
    the condition becomes false at which point the program flow
    exits the loop; at 1st iteration we access all elements of the
    1st row, at 2nd iteration we access all elements of the 2nd row,
    and so on*/
        for (j=0; j<COL1; j++)
        /*j=0 is the initialization, j<COL1 is the condition and j++
        is the increment; initialization is done once at the beginning
```

of the loop; then the condition is checked, if it is true,
statements in the body are executed and the value of j is
incremented by 1 before the condition is re-checked; these
steps continue until the condition becomes false at which
point the program flow exits the loop*/

```
    scanf("%d", &mat1[i][j]);
```
/*scanf() function reads an integer from input terminal
and stores the value in the memory spaces allocated for
the array element; in 1st iteration value of 1st row
1st column mat1[0][0] is read, in 2nd iteration value
of 1st row 2nd column mat1[0][1] is read, and so on*/

```
printf("Enter the second matrix of size %dx%d:\n", ROW1, COL1);
```
/*output function printf() displays the text in the quotations
as it is on the screen except for the value of ROW1 replaces
the 1st format specifier %d, value of COL1 replaces 2nd %d, and
a newline replaces \n*/

```
for (i=0; i<ROW1; i++)
```
/*i=0 is the initialization, i<ROW1 is the condition and i++ is
the increment; initialization is done once at the beginning of
the loop; then the condition is checked, if it is true following
for loop is executed and the value of i is incremented by 1
before the condition is re-checked; these steps continue until
the condition becomes false at which point the program flow
exits the loop; at 1st iteration we access all elements of the
1st row, at 2nd iteration we access all elements of the 2nd row,
and so on*/

```
    for (j=0; j<COL1; j++)
```
/*j=0 is the initialization, j<COL1 is the condition and
j++ is the increment; initialization is done once at the
beginning of the loop; then the condition is checked, if it
is true, statements in the body are executed and the value
of j is incremented by 1 before the condition is re-checked;
these steps continue until the condition becomes false at
which point the program flow exits the loop*/

```
        scanf("%d", &mat2[i][j]);
```
/*scanf() function reads an integer from input terminal
and stores the value in the memory spaces allocated for
the array element; in 1st iteration value of 1st row
1st column mat2[0][0] is read, in 2nd iteration value
of 1st row 2nd column mat2[0][1] is read, and so on*/

```
printf("Enter the third matrix of size %dx%d:\n", ROW2, COL2);
```
/*output function printf() displays the text in the quotations
as it is on the screen except for the value of ROW2 replaces
the 1st format specifier %d, value of COL2 replaces 2nd %d, and
a newline replaces \n*/

```
for (i=0; i<ROW2; i++)
```
/*i=0 is the initialization, i<ROW2 is the condition and i++ is
the increment; initialization is done once at the beginning of
the loop; then the condition is checked, if it is true following
for loop is executed and the value of i is incremented by 1
before the condition is re-checked; these steps continue until
the condition becomes false at which point the program flow
exits the loop; at 1st iteration we access all elements of the
1st row, at 2nd iteration we access all elements of the 2nd row,
and so on*/

    ```for (j=0; j<COL2; j++)```
    /*j=0 is the initialization, j<COL2 is the condition and
    j++ is the increment; initialization is done once at the
    beginning of the loop; then the condition is checked, if it
    is true, statements in the body are executed and the value
    of j is incremented by 1 before the condition is re-checked;
    these steps continue until the condition becomes false at
    which point the program flow exits the loop*/

        ```scanf("%d", &mat3[i][j]);```
        /*scanf() function reads an integer from input terminal
        and stores the value in the memory spaces allocated for
        the array element; in 1st iteration value of 1st row
        1st column mat3[0][0] is read, in 2nd iteration value
        of 1st row 2nd column mat3[0][1] is read, and so on*/

```
addition(mat1, mat2, sum, ROW1);
```
/*user-defined function addition() is called with arrays
mat1[][], mat2[][] and sum[][], and row-size ROW1 as its real
arguments; program control flow shifts to the definition of the
function*/

```
printf("\nSum of the first two matrices is:\n");
```
/*output function printf() displays the text in the quotations
as it is on the screen except for a newline replaces \n*/

```
for (i=0; i<ROW1; i++){
```
/*i=0 is the initialization, i<ROW1 is the condition and i++ is
the increment; initialization is done once at the beginning of
the loop; then the condition is checked, if it is true following
for loop is executed and the value of i is incremented by 1
before the condition is re-checked; these steps continue until
the condition becomes false at which point the program flow
exits the loop; at 1st iteration we access all elements of the
1st row, at 2nd iteration we access all elements of the 2nd row,
and so on*/

    ```for (j=0; j<COL1; j++)```
    /*j=0 is the initialization, j<COL1 is the condition and j++
    is the increment; initialization is done once at the beginning
    of the loop; then the condition is checked, if it is true,
    ```

statements in the body are executed and the value of j is incremented by 1 before the condition is re-checked; these steps continue until the condition becomes false at which point the program flow exits the loop*/

```
    printf("%4d", sum[i][j]);
    /*this printf() function displays the value of a single
    array element sum[][] on the screen with at least 4
    characters wide in each iteration; additional blank
    spaces are added as needed to align the output*/
printf("\n");
/*this printf() is in the body of the 1st for loop; hence
a newline is displayed on the screen after each row of the
2-D matrix sum[][] is displayed*/
}
```
/*this closing curly brace specifies the end of 1st for (i=0; i<ROW1; i++) loop*/
```
multiply(mat2, mat3, prod, ROW1, ROW2);
```
/*user-defined function multiply() is called with arrays mat2[] [], mat3[][] and prod[][], and row-size ROW1 and ROW2 as its real arguments, program control flow shifts to the definition of the function*/
```
printf("\nProduct of the last two matrices is:\n");
```
/*output function printf() displays the text in the quotations as it is on the screen except for a newline replaces \n*/
```
for (i=0; i<ROW1; i++){
```
/*i=0 is the initialization, i<ROW1 is the condition and i++ is the increment; initialization is done once at the beginning of the loop; then the condition is checked, if it is true following for loop is executed and the value of i is incremented by 1 before the condition is re-checked; these steps continue until the condition becomes false at which point the program flow exits the loop; at 1st iteration we access all elements of the 1st row, at 2nd iteration we access all elements of the 2nd row, and so on*/
```
    for (j=0; j<COL2; j++)
```
/*j=0 is the initialization, j<COL2 is the condition and j++ is the increment; initialization is done once at the beginning of the loop; then the condition is checked, if it is true, statements in the body are executed and the value of j is incremented by 1 before the condition is re-checked; these steps continue until the condition becomes false at which point the program flow exits the loop*/
```
        printf("%6d", prod[i][j]);
        /*this printf() function displays the value of a single
        array element sum[][] on the screen with at least 6
        characters wide in each iteration; additional blank
        spaces are added as needed to align the output*/
```

```
    printf("\n");
    /*this printf() is in the body of the 1st for loop; hence
    a newline is displayed on the screen after each row of the
    2-D matrix sum[][] is displayed*/
}
/*this closing curly brace specifies the end of the 1st for
(i=0; i<ROW1; i++) loop*/
return 0;
/*0 is returned as it is the standard for the successful
execution of the program*/
}
```
/*the closing curly brace specifies the end of the main() function's body, as well as the program's end; after that curly brace, no statement is executed*/
```
void addition(int  matrix1[][COL1],  int  matrix2[][COL1],  int
           matrix3[][COL1], int row){
```
/*this is the header for the user-defined function addition(), which must be identical to the function prototype except for no semicolon is used; the function is defined within the curly braces*/
```
    int i, j;
```
/*two integer type variables are declared; required memory spaces are allocated for these variables*/
```
    for (i=0; i<row; i++)
```
/*i=0 is the initialization, i<row is the condition and i++ is the increment; initialization is done once at the beginning of the loop; then the condition is checked, if it is true following for loop is executed and the value of i is incremented by 1 before the condition is re-checked; these steps continue until the condition becomes false at which point the program flow exits the loop; at 1st iteration we access all elements of the 1st row, at 2nd iteration we access all elements of the 2nd row, and so on*/
```
        for (j=0; j<COL1; j++)
```
/*j=0 is the initialization, j<COL1 is the condition and j++ is the increment; initialization is done once at the beginning of the loop; then the condition is checked, if it is true, statements in the body are executed and the value of j is incremented by 1 before the condition is re-checked; these steps continue until the condition becomes false at which point the program flow exits the loop*/
```
        matrix3[i][j]=matrix1[i][j]+matrix2[i][j];
```
/*here corresponding elements of matrix1 and matrix2 are added and the sum is placed in the corresponding position of matrix3; for example-
At 1st iteration- matrix3[0][0]=matrix1[0][0]+matrix2[0]
[0]

          At 2nd iteration- matrix3 [0] [1] =matrix1 [0] [1] +matrix2 [0]
          [1]
          At 3rd iteration- matrix3 [0] [2] =matrix1 [0] [2] +matrix2 [0]
          [2]
          At 4th iteration- matrix3 [0] [3] =matrix1 [0] [3] +matrix2 [0]
          [3]
          At 5th iteration- matrix3 [1] [0] =matrix1 [1] [0] +matrix2 [1]
          [0]
          and so on . . . */
}
/*the closing curly brace specifies the end of the addition()
function's body; the program control flow, at this point, returns
to the point where the function was called*/
void multiply(int    matrix1[] [COL1],    int    matrix2 [] [COL2],    int
          matrix3 [] [COL2], int row1, int row2){
/*this is the header for the user-defined function multiply(),
which must be identical to the function prototype except for no
semicolon is used; the function is defined within the curly braces*/
    int i, j, k;
    /*three integer type variables are declared; required memory
    spaces are allocated for these variables*/
    if (COL1==row2)
    /*if no of columns of matrix1[] [] equals the no of rows of
    matrix2 [] [], the condition is true and the following for loop
    is executed*/
        for (i=0; i<row1; i++)
        /*i=0 is the initialization, i<row1 is the condition and
        i++ is the increment; initialization is done once at the
        beginning of the loop; then the condition is checked, if it
        is true following for loop is executed and the value of i is
        incremented by 1 before the condition is re-checked; these
        steps continue until the condition becomes false at which
        point the program flow exits the loop; at 1st iteration we
        access all elements of the 1st row, at 2nd iteration we
        access all elements of the 2nd row, and so on*/
            for (j=0; j<COL2; j++){
        /*j=0 is the initialization, j<COL2 is the condition
        and j++ is the increment; initialization is done once
        at the beginning of the loop; then the condition is
        checked, if it is true, statements in the body are
        executed and the value of j is incremented by 1 before
        the condition is re-checked; these steps continue until
        the condition becomes false at which point the program
        flow exits the loop*/
                matrix3 [i] [j]=0;
          /*at first iteration of above for loops matrix3 [0]
          [0] is initialized to 0, at second iteration
          matrix3 [0] [1] is initialized to 0, and so on*/

/*here each element of matrix3[][] is initialized to 0, otherwise the summation operation may give wrong answer because, when we declare the array memory spaces allocated for each array element may contain some garbage value; the garbage value adds up in the first summing operation involving matrix3[][]*/

**for (k=0; k<COL1; k++)**

/*k=0 is the initialization, k<COL1 is the condition and k++ is the increment; initialization is done once at the beginning of the loop; then the condition is checked, if it is true, following statement is executed and the value of k is incremented by 1 before the condition is re-checked; these steps continue until the condition becomes false at which point the program flow exits the loop*/

**matrix3[i][j]+=matrix1[i][k]*matrix2[k][j];**

/*at 1st iteration- matrix3[0][0]=matrix3[0][0]+matrix1[0][0]*matrix2[0][0]

at 2nd iteration- matrix3[0][0]=matrix3[0][0]+matrix1[0][1]*matrix2[1][0]

thus, after COL1=4 iterations we get 1st element of 1st row of matrix3 and j=1

now, at 1st iteration- matrix3[0][1]=matrix3[0][1]+matrix1[0][0]*matrix2[0][1]

at 2nd iteration- matrix3[0][1]=matrix3[0][1]+matrix1[0][1]*matrix2[1][1]

thus, after another COL1=4 iterations we get 2nd element of 1st row of matrix3 and j=2

after COL1×COL2=4×5=20 iterations, we get all elements of 1st row of matrix3 and i=1, j=0

now, at 1st iteration- matrix3[1][0]=matrix3[1][0]+matrix1[1][0]*matrix2[0][0]

at 2nd iteration- matrix3[1][0]=matrix3[1][0]+matrix1[1][1]*matrix2[1][0]

thus, after another COL1=4 iterations we get 1st element of 2nd row of matrix3 and j=1

these steps continue until value of i becomes row1*/

```
}
```
/*this closing curly brace specifies the end of for (j=0; j<COL2; j++) loop*/

**else{**

/*if no of columns of matrix1[][] is not equal to no of row matrix2[][], the condition of above 'if' is false, and following statements in the body of else, enclosed by curly braces, are executed*/

**printf("Sizes of the matrices do not permit " "multiplication.\n");**

```
            /*output function printf() displays the text in double
            quotations as it is on the screen except for a newline
            replaces \n*/
            exit(1);
            /*exit(1) function causes abnormal termination of the
            program; all buffers, temporary files, streams are
            deleted or cleared before the termination*/
        }
        /*this closing curly brace specifies the end of 'else' condition*/
    }
    /*the closing curly brace specifies the end of the multiply()
    function's body; the program control flow, at this point, returns
    to the point where the function was called*/
```

### PROBLEM-10
**Write a program that uses functions to insert a substring into a given main-string from a given position. Also, define a function to delete n characters from a given position in a given string.**

Flowchart of the Solution:

Figure 4.7 shows the flowcharts followed to solve this problem.

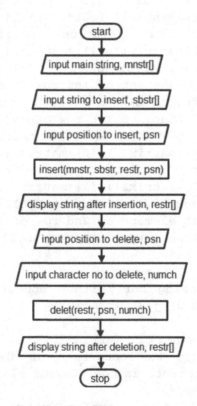

FIGURE 4.7  Flowcharts followed to solve the problem.

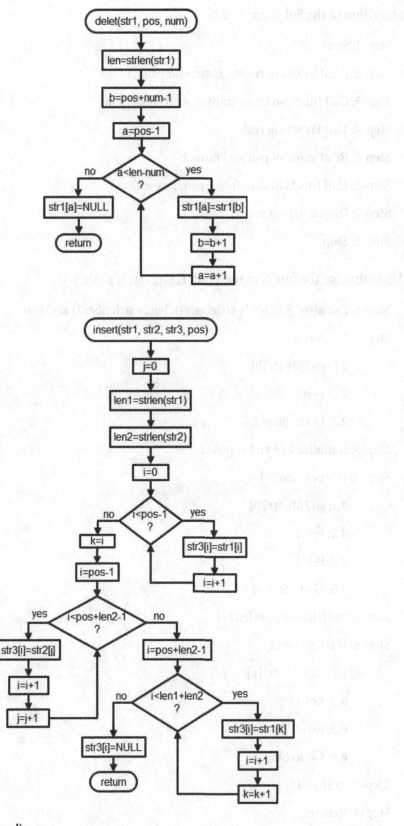

FIGURE 4.7 (Continued)

## Algorithm of the Solution:

Step-1: Start

Step-2: Read values of mnstr, sbstr, and psn

Step-3: Call function insert(mnstr, sbstr, restr, psn)

Step-4: Display string restr

Step-5: Read value of psn and numch

Step-6: Call function delet(restr, psn, numch)

Step-7: Display string restr

Step-8: Stop

## Algorithm for the function insert(str1, str2, str3, pos):

Step-1: Initialize j←0, len1←strlen(str1), len2←strlen(str2) and i←0

Step-2: If i<pos−1

      2.1: str3[i]←str1[i]

      2.2: i←i+1

      2.3: Go to Step-2

Step-3: Initialize k←i and i←pos−1

Step-4: If i<pos+len2−1

      4.1: str3[i]←str2[j]

      4.2: j←j+1

      4.3: i←i+1

      4.5: Go to Step-4

Step-5: Initialize i←pos+len2−1

Step-6: If i<len1+len2

      6.1: str3[i]←str1[k]

      6.2: k←k+1

      6.3: i←i+1

      6.4: Go to Step-6

Step-7: str3[i]←'\0'

Step-8: Return.

## Algorithm for the function delet(str1, pos, num):

Step-1: len←strlen(str1)

Step-2: Initialize b←pos+num−1 and a←pos−1

Step-3: If i<len-num

        3.1: str1[a]←str1[b]

        3.2: b←b+1

        3.3: a←a+1

        3.4: Go to Step-3

Step-4: str1[a]←'\0'

Step-5: Return.

## Programming Code of the Solution:

```c
#include<stdio.h>
#include<string.h>
void insert(char str1[], char str2[], char str3[], int pos);
void delet(char str1[], int pos, int num);
int main(){
    int psn, numch;
    char mnstr[80], sbstr[15], restr[99];
    printf("Enter the main string: ");
    gets(mnstr);
    printf("Enter the string to insert: ");
    gets(sbstr);
    printf("Enter position to insert: ");
    scanf("%d", &psn);
    insert(mnstr, sbstr, restr, psn);
    printf("Resultant string after insertion: %s\n", restr);
    printf("\nEnter position of resultant string to delete: ");
    scanf("%d", &psn);
    printf("Enter Number of characters to delete: ");
    scanf("%d", &numch);
    delet(restr, psn, numch);
    printf("Resultant string after deletion: %s\n", restr);
    return 0;
}
void insert(char str1[], char str2[], char str3[], int pos){
    int len1, len2, i, j=0, k;
    len1=strlen(str1);
    len2=strlen(str2);
    for (i=0; i<pos-1; i++)
        str3[i]=str1[i];
    k=i;
    for (i=pos-1; i<pos+len2-1; i++){
```

```
            str3[i]=str2[j];
            j+=1;
        }
        for (i=pos+len2-1; i<len1+len2; i++){
            str3[i]=str1[k];
            k=k+1;
        }
        str3[i]='\0';
    }
    void delet(char str1[], int pos, int num){
        int len, a, b;
        len=strlen(str1);
        b=pos+num-1;
        for (a=pos-1; a<len-num; a++){
            str1[a]=str1[b];
            b=b+1;
        }
        str1[a]='\0';
    }
```

Input and Output of the Executed Program:

```
Enter the main string: Atiqur Rahman is a good person.
Enter the string to insert: very
Enter position to insert: 20
Resultant string after insertion: Atiqur Rahman is a very good person.

Enter position of resultant string to delete: 20
Enter Number of characters to delete: 5
Resultant string after deletion: Atiqur Rahman is a good person.
```

Explanation of the Programming Code:

**#include<stdio.h>**
/*header file stdio.h contains prototypes of the library functions
printf(), scanf() and gets(); the header file must be included using
preprocessor directive #include before the functions are called in
the program*/
**#include<string.h>**
/*header file string.h contains prototype of the library function
strlen(); the header file must be included using preprocessor
directive #include before the function is called in the program*/
**void insert(char str1[], char str2[], char str3[], int pos);**
/*this is the prototype (or declaration) of the user-defined function
insert() that must end with a semicolon; insert() takes three arrays
and one integer as parameters, performs some predefined operations,
and returns nothing*/
**void delet(char str1[], int pos, int num);**
/*this is the prototype (or declaration) of the user-defined
function delet() that must end with a semicolon; delet() takes

an array and two integers as parameters, performs some predefined operations, and returns nothing*/
```
int main(){
```
/*all C program must have a main() function with return type void or int; here there is no parameter of the main() function and it returns an integer; opening curly brace specifies start of the main() function and no statement before that curly brace is executed by the compiler*/
```
    int psn, numch;
```
/*two integer type variables are declared; required memory spaces are allocated for each of the variables*/
```
    char mnstr[80], sbstr[15], restr[99];
```
/*four character type arrays of different sizes are declared; required contiguous memory spaces are allocated for each of the arrays */
```
    printf("Enter the main string: ");
```
/*output function printf() displays the text in the quotations as it is on the screen*/
```
    gets(mnstr);
```
/*built-in library function gets() reads string, including space, tab etc. until enter is pressed, from input terminal and assigns the string to the character type array mnstr*/
```
    printf("Enter the string to insert: ");
```
/*output function printf() displays the text in the quotations as it is on the screen*/
```
    gets(sbstr);
```
/*built-in library function gets() reads string, including space, tab etc. until enter is pressed, from input terminal and assigns the string to the character type array sbstr*/
```
    printf("Enter position to insert: ");
```
/*output function printf() displays the text in the quotations as it is on the screen*/
```
    scanf("%d", &psn);
```
/*function scanf() reads an integer from input terminal and stores the value in the memory spaces allocated for the psn*/
```
    insert(mnstr, sbstr, restr, psn);
```
/*user-defined function insert() is called with four real parameters mnstr, sbstr, restr and psn; program control flow shifts to the definition of the function*/
```
    printf("Resultant string after insertion: %s\n", restr);
```
/*printf() function displays the text in the quotations as it is on the screen except for the string restr replaces the format specifier %s and a newline replaces \n*/
```
    printf("\nEnter position of resultant string to delete: ");
```
/*printf() function displays the text in the quotations as it is on the screen except for a newline replaces \n*/
```
    scanf("%d", &psn);
```
/*function scanf() reads an integer from input terminal and stores the value in the memory spaces allocated for the psn*/

```
  printf("Enter Number of characters to delete: ");
```
/*printf() function displays the text in the quotations as it
is on the screen*/
```
  scanf("%d", &numch);
```
/*function scanf() reads an integer from input terminal and
stores the value in the memory spaces allocated for the numch*/
```
  delet(restr, psn, numch);
```
/*user-defined function delet() is called with three real
parameters restr, pns and numch; program control flow shifts to
the definition of the function*/
```
  printf("Resultant string after deletion: %s\n", restr);
```
/*printf() function displays the text in the quotations as it is
on the screen except for the string restr replaces the format
specifier %s and a newline replaces \n*/
```
  return 0;
```
/*0 is returned as it is the standard for the successful
execution of the program*/
```
}
```
/*the closing curly brace specifies the end of the main() function's
body, as well as the program's end; after that curly brace, no
statement is executed*/
```
void insert(char str1[], char str2[], char str3[], int pos){
```
/*this is the header for the user-defined function insert(), which
must be identical to the function prototype except for no semicolon
is used; the function is defined within the curly braces*/
```
  int len1, len2, i, j=0, k;
```
/*four integer type variables len1, len2, i and k are declared;
another variable j is declared and initialized to 0; required
memory spaces are allocated for these variables; these variables
are local to the function insert() and are not accessible
outside that function*/
```
  len1=strlen(str1);
```
/*built-in library function strlen() returns length of the
string str1 that is assigned to len1*/
```
  len2=strlen(str2);
```
/*built-in library function strlen() returns length of the
string str2 that is assigned to len2*/
```
  for (i=0; i<pos-1; i++)
```
/*this for loop copies 1st pos number characters of the string
str1[] to the character type array str3[]; here i=0 is the
initialization, i<pos-1 is the condition and i++ is the increment;
initialization is done once at the beginning of the loop; then
the condition is checked, if it is true, following statement
in the body is executed and the value of i is incremented by 1
before the condition is re-checked; these steps continue until
the condition becomes false at which point the program flow
exits the loop*/

```
    str3[i]=str1[i];
```
    /*at 1st iteration str3[0]=str1[0], at 2nd iteration
    str3[1]=str1[1], and so on*/
```
k=i;
```
/*when i=pos-1, the program exits the previous 'for' loop;
i=pos-1 is assigned to k that is used as index of str1[] to
identify rest of the characters in the string to copy*/
```
for (i=pos-1; i<pos+len2-1; i++){
```
/*this for loop copies the sub-string str2[] at the end of
str3[] in which first pos characters of str1[] was copied; here
i=pos-1 is the initialization, i<pos+len2-1 is the condition
and i++ is the increment; initialization is done once at the
beginning of the loop; then the condition is checked, if it is
true, following statement in the body is executed and the value
of i is incremented by 1 before the condition is re-checked;
these steps continue until the condition becomes false at which
point the program flow exits the loop*/
```
    str3[i]=str2[j];
```
    /*at 1st iteration str3[pos-1]=str2[0], at 2nd iteration
    str3[pos]=str2[1], at 3rd iteration str3[pos+1]=str2[2],
    and so on*/
```
    j+=1;
```
    /*index value of str2[] is incremented by 1 in each iteration
    of the loop*/
```
}
```
/*this closing curly brace specifies the end of the for loop
body*/
```
for (i=pos+len2-1; i<len1+len2; i++){
```
/*this for loop copies rest of the string str1[] (pos-1 to end)
at the end of str3[] in which first pos (0 to pos-1) characters
of str1[] was copied and then str2[] was concatenated; here
i=pos+len2-1 is the initialization, i<len1+len2 is the
condition and i++ is the increment; initialization is done
once at the beginning of the loop; then the condition is
checked, if it is true, following statement in the body
is executed and the value of i is incremented by 1 before
the condition is re-checked; these steps continue until the
condition becomes false at which point the program flow exits
the loop*/
```
    str3[i]=str1[k];
```
    /*at 1st iteration str3[pos+len2-1]=str1[pos-1],
    at 2nd iteration str3[pos+len2]=str1[pos],
    at 3rd iteration str3[pos+len2+1]=str2[pos+1], and so on*/
```
    k=k+1;
```
    /*index value of str1[] is incremented by 1 in each iteration
    of the loop*/

```
}
/*this closing curly brace specifies the end of the for loop
body*/
str3[i]='\0';
/*last character of array str3[] is set to NULL to define it
as string*/
}
/*the closing curly brace specifies the end of the insert() function's
body; the program control flow, at this point, returns to the point
where the function was called*/
void delet(char str1[], int pos, int num){
/*this is the header for the user-defined function delet(), which
must be identical to the function prototype except for no semicolon
is used; the function is defined within the curly braces*/
    int len, a, b;
    /*three integer type variables len, a and b are declared;
    required memory spaces are allocated for these variables*/
    len=strlen(str1);
    /*built-in library function strlen() returns length of the
    string str1 that is assigned to len*/
    /*to delete a sub-string of size num that starts at position
    pos-1, we keep the string str1[] unchanged from 0 to pos-2;
    after that we copy characters from position pos-1+num to the end
    (=len-num-1), skipping all characters in the middle*/
    b=pos+num-1;
    /*b is initialized to pos+num-1*/
    for (a=pos-1; a<len-num; a++){
    /*a=pos-1 is the initialization, a<len-num is the condition
    and a++ is the increment; initialization is done once at the
    beginning of the loop; then the condition is checked, if it is
    true, following statement in the body is executed and the value
    of a is incremented by 1 before the condition is re-checked;
    these steps continue until the condition becomes false at which
    point the program flow exits the loop*/
        str1[a]=str1[b];
        /*at 1st iteration str1[pos-1]=str1[pos+num-1],
        at 2nd iteration str1[pos]=str1[pos+num],
        at 3rd iteration str1[pos+1]=str1[pos+num+1], and so on*/
        b=b+1;
        /*index value of source array is incremented by 1 in each
        iteration of the loop*/
    }
    /*this closing curly brace specifies the end of the for loop
    body*/
    str1[a]='\0';
    /*last character of array str1[] is set to NULL to define it
    as string*/
```

```
}
/*the closing curly brace specifies the end of the delet() function's
body; the program control flow, at this point, returns to the point
where the function was called*/
```

**PROBLEM-11**
**Using pointers, write a function that receives a character string and word as arguments and deletes all occurrences of this word in the string.**

Flowchart of the Solution:

Figure 4.8 shows the flowcharts followed to solve this problem.

## Algorithm of the Solution:

Step-1: Start

Step-2: Read values of txt and wrd

Step-3: lnh←strlen(wrd)

Step-4: x←index(txt, wrd) [call function index()]

Step-5: If x≠0

     5.1: Call delet(txt, x–1, lnh)

     5.2: x←index(txt, wrd) [call function index()]

     5.3: Go to Step-5

Step-6: Display string txt

Step-7: Stop

## Algorithm for the function index(text, pat):

Step-1: Initialize k←0

Step-2: len←strlen(pat)

Step-3: Initialize i←0

Step-4: If k≠–1

     4.1: If text[i]=0

          4.1.1: Return 0

     4.2: If text[i]=pat[0]

          4.2.1: k←–1

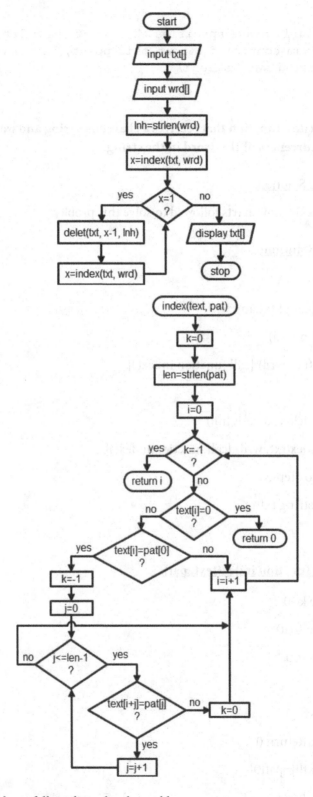

FIGURE 4.8   Flowcharts followed to solve the problem.

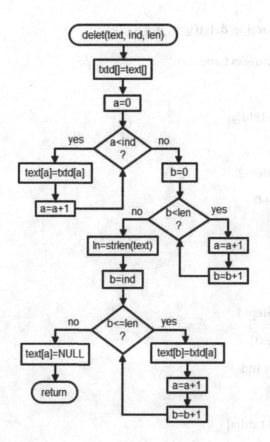

FIGURE 4.8 (Continued)

       4.2.1: Initialize j←0

       4.2.2: If j<=len−1

           4.2.2.1: If text[i+j]≠pat[j]

              4.2.2.1.1: k←0

              4.2.2.1.2: Go to Step-4.3

           4.2.2.2: j←j+1

           4.2.2.3: Go to Step-4.2.2

    4.3: i←i+1

    4.4: Go to Step-4

Step-5: Return value of i

## Algorithm for the function delet(text, ind, len):

Step-1: Initialize txtd←text and a←0

Step-2: If i<ind

      2.1: text[a]←txtd[a]

      2.2: a←a+1

      2.3: Go to Step-2

Step-3: Initialize b←0

Step-4: If b<len

      4.1: a←a+1

      4.2: b←b+1

      4.3: Go to Step-4

Step-5: ln←strlen(text)

Step-6: Initialize b←ind

Step-7: If b<=ln

      7.1: text[b]←txtd[a]

      7.2: a←a+1

      7.3: b←b+1

      7.4: Go to Step-7

Step-8: text[a]←'\0'

Step-9: Return

### Programming Code of the Solution:

```c
#include <stdio.h>
#include <string.h>
int index(char *text, char *pat);
void delet(char *text, int ind, int len);
int main(){
    char txt[80], wrd[10];
    int x, lnh;
    printf("Enter your text: ");
    gets(txt);
    printf("Enter the word you want to delete: ");
```

```
        scanf("%s", wrd);
        lnh=strlen(wrd);
        x=index(txt, wrd);
        while (x){
            delet(txt, x-1, lnh);
            x=index(txt, wrd);
        }
        printf("Resultant text after deletion: %s\n", txt);
        return 0;
}
int index(char *text, char *pat){
        int len, i, j, k=0;
        len=strlen(pat);
        for (i=0; k!=-1; i++){
            if (!text[i])
                return 0;
            if (text[i]==pat[0]){
                k=-1;
                for (j=0; j<=len-1; j++)
                    if (text[i+j]!=pat[j]){
                        k=0;
                        break;
                    }
            }
        }
        return i;
}
void delet(char *text, int ind, int len){
        char *txtd=text;
        int ln, a, b;
        for (a=0; a<ind; a++)
            text[a]=txtd[a];
        for (b=0; b<len; b++)
            a=a+1;
        ln=strlen(text);
        for (b=ind; b<=ln; b++){
            text[b]=txtd[a];
            a=a+1;
        }
        text[a]='\0';
}
```

Input and Output of the Executed Program:

```
Enter your text: Atiqur Rahman is a very good researcher.
Enter the word you want to delete: very
Resultant text after deletion: Atiqur Rahman is a  good researcher.
```

**Explanation of the Programming Code:**

```
#include <stdio.h>
```
/*header file stdio.h contains prototypes of the library functions printf(), scanf() and gets(); the header file must be included using preprocessor directive #include before the functions are called in the program*/

```
#include <string.h>
```
/*header file string.h contains prototype of the library function strlen(); the header file must be included using preprocessor directive #include before the function is called in the program*/

```
int index(char *text, char *pat);
```
/*this is the prototype (or declaration) of the user-defined function index() that must end with a semicolon; index() takes two character type pointers as parameters, performs some predefined operations, and returns an integer*/

```
void delet(char *text, int ind, int len);
```
/*this is the prototype (or declaration) of the user-defined function delet() that must end with a semicolon; delet() takes a character type pointer and two integers as parameters, performs some predefined operations, and returns nothing*/

```
int main(){
```
/*all C program must have a main() function with return type void or int; here there is no parameter of the main() function and it returns an integer; opening curly brace specifies start of the main() function and no statement before that curly brace is executed by the compiler*/

```
    char txt[80], wrd[10];
```
/*two character type arrays of sizes 80 and 10 are declared; required contiguous memory spaces are allocated for each of the arrays*/

```
    int x, lnh;
```
/*two integer type variables are declared; required memory spaces are allocated for each of the variables*/

```
    printf("Enter your text: ");
```
/*output function printf() displays the text in the quotations as it is on the screen*/

```
    gets(txt);
```
/*built-in library function gets() reads a string, including space, tab etc. until enter is pressed, from input terminal and assigns the string to character type array txt[]*/

```
printf("Enter the word you want to delete: ");
```
/*output function printf() displays the text in the quotations as it is on the screen*/
```
scanf("%s", wrd);
```
/*function scanf() reads a string, until space, tab or enter is pressed, from input terminal and stores the string in the memory spaces allocated for the wrd*/
```
lnh=strlen(wrd);
```
/*built-in library function strlen() returns length of the string wrd and assigns the value to lnh*/
```
x=index(txt, wrd);
```
/*user-defined function index() is called with txt and wrd as real arguments; program control flow shifts to the definition of the function; the function returns index value in the string txt[] where the word wrd is found and that index value is assigned to x*/
```
while (x){
```
/*if the word wrd is found in the text txt[], x≠0 and following statements in the body, enclosed by curly braces, are executed until x=0 at which point the program flow exits the loop*/
```
    delet(txt, x-1, lnh);
```
/*user-defined function delet() is called with txt, x-1 and lnh as real arguments; program control flow shifts to the definition of the function*/
```
    x=index(txt, wrd);
```
/*user-defined function index() is called with txt and wrd as real arguments; program control flow shifts to the definition of the function; the function returns index value in the string txt[] where the word wrd is found and that index value is assigned to x*/
/*in each iteration of the loop if wrd is found index() returns the index and delet() deletes the wrd from txt[]; the loop continues until x becomes 0 at which point no wrd is available in txt */
```
}
```
/*this closing curly brace specifies the end of the while loop*/
```
printf("Resultant text after deletion: %s\n", txt);
```
/*printf() function displays the text in the quotations as it is on the screen except for the string txt replaces the format specifier %s and a newline replaces \n*/
```
return 0;
```
/*0 is returned as it is the standard for the successful execution of the program*/
```
}
```
/*the closing curly brace specifies the end of the main() function's body, as well as the program's end; after that curly brace, no statement is executed*/

```
int index(char *text, char *pat){
```
/*this is the header for the user-defined function index(),
which must be identical to the function prototype except for
no semicolon is used; the function is defined within the curly
braces*/

    ```int len, i, j, k=0;```
    /*three integer type variables len, i and j are declared, and
    another variable k is declared and initialized to 0; required
    memory spaces are assigned for these variables; these variables
    are local to the function index() and are not accessible outside
    that function*/
    ```len=strlen(pat);```
    /*built-in library function strlen() returns length of the
    string pat that is assigned to len*/
    ```for (i=0; k!=-1; i++){```
    /*this for loop checks if the word pat[] is present in the
    string text[]; here i=0 is the initialization, k!=-1 is the
    condition and i++ is the increment; initialization is done once
    at the beginning of the loop; then the condition is checked, if
    it is true, following statements in the body are executed and
    the value of i is incremented by 1 before the condition is re-
    checked; these steps continue until the condition becomes false
    at which point the program flow exits the loop*/
        ```if (!text[i])```
        /*if there is no character in text[] at position i then
        there is nothing to check, the condition of 'if' is true
        and following statement is executed*/
            ```return 0;```
            /*function index() immediately returns 0 to the point
            where the function was called*/
        ```if (text[i]==pat[0]){```
        /*if first character of the word pat[] matches with the
        character in any position of the text[] then above condition
        of 'if' is true and following statements, enclosed by curly
        braces, are executed*/
            ```k=-1;```
            /*value of k is assigned to -1*/
            ```for (j=0; j<=len-1; j++)```
            /*this for loop checks if rest of the characters of the
            word pat[] are sequentially available in text[]; here
            j=0 is the initialization, j<=len-1 is the condition
            and j++ is the increment; initialization is done once
            at the beginning of the loop; then the condition is
            checked, if it is true, following statement in the
            body is executed and the value of j is incremented
            by 1 before the condition is re-checked; these steps

```
        continue until the condition becomes false at which
        point the program flow exits the loop*/
        if (text[i+j]!=pat[j]){
            /*in each iteration of the loop, character in pat[]
            is sequentially checked with that in text[], if
            there is any mismatch, above condition becomes true
            and following statements are executed*/
            k=0;
            /*value of k is changed to 0 from -1*/
            break;
            /*program flow exits the for (j=0; j<=len-1;
            j++) loop*/
        }
        /*this is the end of 'if' with condition
        (text[i+j]!=pat[j])*/
    }
    /*this is the end of 'if' with condition (text[i]==pat[0])*/
}
/*this is the end of for (i=0; k!=-1; i++) loop*/
return i;
/*starting index i of the string text[] where the word pat[]
is found is returned to the point where the function was
called*/
}
```

/*the closing curly brace specifies the end of the index() function's
body*/

```
void delet(char *text, int ind, int len){
```

/*this is the header for the user-defined function delet(),
which must be identical to the function prototype except for
no semicolon is used; the function is defined within the curly
braces*/

```
    char *txtd=text;
```

/*character type pointer txtd is declared and initialized to
text; here, txtd[0]=text[0], txtd[1]=text[1], and so on*/

```
    int ln, a, b;
```

/*three integer type variables ln, a and b are declared; required
memory spaces are allocated for these variables; these variables
are local to the function delet() and are not accessible outside
that function*/

/*to delete a word of size len that starts at index ind, we
keep the string text unchanged from 0 to ind-1; after that we
copy characters from index ind+len to the end, skipping all
characters in the middle (from ind to ind+len-1)*/

```
    for (a=0; a<ind; a++)
```

/*a=0 is the initialization, a<ind is the condition and a++ is
the increment; initialization is done once at the beginning

of the loop; then the condition is checked, if it is true, following statement in the body is executed and the value of a is incremented by 1 before the condition is re-checked; these steps continue until the condition becomes false at which point the program flow exits the loop*/

```
    text[a]=txtd[a];
    /*at  1st  iteration  text[0]=txtd[0],  at  2nd  iteration
    text[1]=txtd[1], at 3rd iteration text[2]=txtd[2], and so on*/
for (b=0; b<len; b++)
```

/*this for loop changes index value of source txtd to a=ind+len to delete characters from ind to ind+len-1; here b=0 is the initialization, b<len is the condition and b++ is the increment; initialization is done once at the beginning of the loop; then the condition is checked, if it is true, following statement in the body is executed and the value of b is incremented by 1 before the condition is re-checked; these steps continue until the condition becomes false at which point the program flow exits the loop*/

```
    a=a+1;
    /*value of a is incremented by 1 in each iteration; finally,
    we get a=ind+len*/
ln=strlen(text);
```

/*built-in library function strlen() returns length of the string text that is assigned to ln*/

```
for (b=ind; b<=ln; b++){
```

/*b=ind is the initialization, b<=ln is the condition and b++ is the increment; the initialization is done once at the beginning of the loop; then the condition is checked, if it is true, following statements in the body are executed and the value of b is incremented by 1 before the condition is re-checked; these steps continue until the condition becomes false at which point the program flow exits the loop*/

```
    text[b]=txtd[a];
    /*at 1st iteration text[ind]=txtd[ind+len],
    at 2nd iteration text[ind+1]= txtd[ind+len+1],
    at 3rd iteration text[ind+2]=txtd[ind+len+2], and so on*/
    a=a+1;
    /*index of source array is incremented by 1 in each iteration
    of the loop*/
}
```

/*this closing curly brace specifies the end of for loop */

```
text[a]='\0';
```

/*last character in the text is set to NULL to define it as a string*/

```
}
```

/*the closing curly brace specifies the end of the delet() function's body; the program control flow, at this point, returns to the point where the function was called*/

## PROBLEM-12
**Write a program to solve a polynomial equation and its derivative.**

Flowchart of the Solution:

Figure 4.9 shows the flowcharts followed to solve this problem.

## Algorithm of the Solution:

Step-1: Start.

Step-2: Read value of deg.

Step-3: Initialize i←0

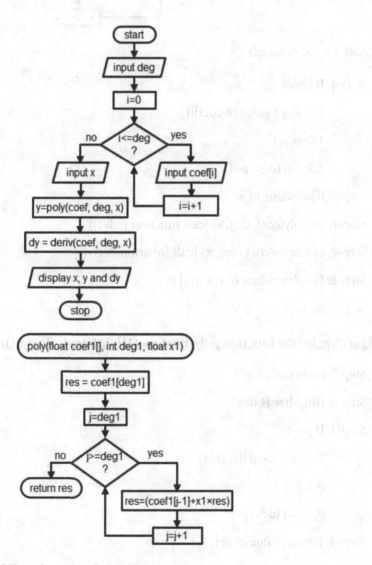

FIGURE 4.9  Flowcharts followed to solve the problem.

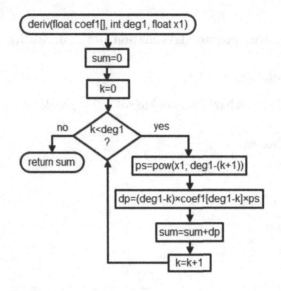

FIGURE 4.9   (Continued)

Step-4: If i<=deg

      4.1: Read value of coef[i]

      4.2: i←i+1

      4.3: Go to Step-4

Step-5: Read value of x

Step-6: y←poly(coef, deg, x) [call function poly()]

Step-7: dy←deriv(coef, deg, x) [call function deriv()]

Step-8: Display values of x, y and dy

Step-9: Stop.

## Algorithm for the function poly(float coef1[], int deg1, float x1):

Step-1: res←coef1[deg1]

Step-2: Initialize j←deg1

Step-3: If j>=1

      3.1: res←(coef1[j−1]+x1*res)

      3.2: j←j−1

      3.3: Go to Step-3

Step-4: Return value of res.

## Algorithm for the function deriv(float coef1[], int deg1, float x1):

Step-1: Initialize sum←0 and k←0

Step-2: If k<deg1

>2.1: ps←pow(x1, deg1–(k+1)) [call function pow()]

>2.2: dp←(deg1–k)×coef1[deg1–k]×ps;

>2.3: sum←sum+dp

>2.4: k←k+1

>2.5: Go to Step-2

Step-3: Return value of sum

## Programming Code of the Solution:

```c
#include <stdio.h>
#include <conio.h>
#include <math.h>
float poly(float coef1[], int deg1, float x1);
float deriv(float coef1[], int deg1, float x1);
int main(){
    float coef[10], x, y, dy;
    int deg, i;
    printf("Enter the degree of polynomial equation: ");
    scanf("%d", &deg);
    for (i=0; i<=deg; i++){
        printf("Enter coefficient of x to the power %d: ", i);
        scanf("%f", &coef[i]);
    }
    printf("Enter value of x for which the equation is to be solved: ");
    scanf("%f", &x);
    y = poly(coef, deg, x);
    dy = deriv(coef, deg, x);
    printf("Solution of polynomial equation at x=%.2f is: %.2f", x, y);
    printf("\nSolution of derivative of the polynomial equation at "
        "x=%.2f is: %.2f", x, dy);
    return 0;
}
float poly(float coef1[], int deg1, float x1){
    float res;
    int j;
    res = coef1[deg1];
    for (j=deg1; j>=1; j--)
        res = (coef1[j-1]+x1*res);
    return res;
}
float deriv(float coef1[], int deg1, float x1){
    float dp, sum=0, ps;
```

```
    int k;
    for (k=0; k<deg1; k++){
        ps = pow(x1, deg1-(k+1));
        dp = (deg1-k)*coef1[deg1-k]*ps;
        sum = sum+dp;
    }
    return sum;
}
```

Input and Output of the Executed Program:

```
Enter the degree of polynomial equation: 3
Enter coefficient of x to the power 0: 4
Enter coefficient of x to the power 1: 3
Enter coefficient of x to the power 2: 1
Enter coefficient of x to the power 3: 2
Enter value of x for which the equation is to be solved: 2
Solution of polynomial equation at x=2.00 is: 30.00
Solution of derivative of the polynomial equation at x=2.00 is: 31.00
```

Explanation of the Programming Code:

**#include <stdio.h>**
/*header file stdio.h contains prototypes of the library functions printf(), scanf() and gets(); the header file must be included using preprocessor directive #include before the functions are called in the program*/
**#include <math.h>**
/*header file math.h contains prototype of the library function pow(); the header file must be included using preprocessor directive #include before the function is called in the program*/
**float poly(float coef1[], int deg1, float x1);**
/*this is the prototype (or declaration) of the user-defined function poly() that must end with a semicolon; poly() takes an array, an integer and a decimal number as parameters, performs some predefined operations, and returns a decimal number*/
**float deriv(float coef1[], int deg1, float x1);**
/*this is the prototype of the user-defined function deriv() that must end with a semicolon; deriv() takes an array, an integer and a decimal number as parameters, performs some predefined operations, and returns a decimal number*/
**int main(){**
/*all C program must have a main() function with return type void or int; here there is no parameter of the main() function and it returns an integer; opening curly brace specifies start of the main() function and no statement before that curly brace is executed by the compiler*/

```
float coef[10], x, y, dy;
```
/*a float type array coef[] of size 10 and three float type variables x, y and dy are declared; required memory spaces are allocated for the array and variables*/

```
int deg, i;
```
/*two integer type variables are declared; required memory spaces are allocated for the variables*/

```
printf("Enter the degree of polynomial equation: ");
```
/*output function printf() displays the text in the quotations as it is on the screen*/

```
scanf("%d", &deg);
```
/*function scanf() reads an integer from input terminal and stores the value in the memory space allocated for the deg*/

```
for (i=0; i<=deg; i++){
```
/*i=0 is the initialization, i<=deg is the condition and i++ is the increment; the initialization is done once at the beginning of the loop; then the condition is checked, if it is true, statements in the body are executed and the value of i is incremented by 1 before the condition is re-checked; these steps continue until the condition becomes false at which point the program flow exits the loop*/

```
    printf("Enter coefficient of x to the power %d: ", i);
```
/*output function printf() displays the text in the quotations as it is on the screen except for the value of i replaces the format specifier %d*/

```
    scanf("%f", &coef[i]);
```
/*function scanf() reads a decimal number from input terminal and stores the value in the array coef[]; for the function $2x^3+3x-1$

At 1st iteration, it reads -1 and saved it in coef[0]
At 2nd iteration, it reads 0 and saved it in coef[1]
At 3rd iteration, it treads 3 and saved it in coef[2]
At 4th iteration, it reads 2 and saved it in coef[3] */

```
}
printf("Enter value of x for which the equation is to be"
        "solved: ");
```
/*output function printf() displays the text in the quotations as it is on the screen*/

```
scanf("%f", &x);
```
/*function scanf() reads a decimal number from the input terminal and stores the value in the memory spaces allocated for the x*/

```
y = poly(coef, deg, x);
```
/*user-defined function poly() is called with three real parameters coef, deg and x; program control flow shifts to the function definition; poly() does some predefined operations on the arguments and returns a decimal number that is assigned to y*/

```
dy = deriv(coef, deg, x);
```
/\*user-defined function deriv() is called with three real parameters coef, deg and x; program control flow shifts to the function definition; deriv() does some predefined operations on the arguments and returns a decimal number that is assigned to dy\*/
```
printf("Solution of polynomial equation at x=%.2f is: %.2f",
       x, y);
```
/\*function printf() displays the text in the quotations as it is on the screen except for the value of x replaces the 1st format specifier %.2f with two decimal points precision and the value of y replaces the 2nd %.2f\*/
```
printf("\nSolution of derivative of the polynomial equation"
       " at x=%.2f is: %.2f", x, dy);
```
/\*function printf() displays the text in the quotations as it is on the screen except for the value of x replaces the 1st format specifier %.2f with two decimal points precision and the value of dy replaces the 2nd %.2f; here long string was broken into multiple lines using two double quotes ("")\*/
```
return 0;
```
/\*0 is returned as it is the standard for the successful execution of the program\*/
```
}
```
/\*the closing curly brace specifies the end of the main() function's body, as well as the program's end; after that curly brace, no statement is executed\*/
```
float poly(float coef1[], int deg1, float x1){
```
/\*this is the header for the user-defined function poly(), which must be identical to the function prototype except for no semicolon is used; the function is defined within the curly braces\*/
```
float res;
```
/\*a float type variable is declared; required memory spaces are allocated for the variable; res is local to the function poly() and is not accessible outside that function\*/
```
int j;
```
/\*an integer type variable is declared; required memory spaces are allocated for the variable; j is local to the function poly() and is not accessible outside that function\*/
```
res = coef1[deg1];
```
/\*coefficient of the highest degree is assigned to variable res; for the function $2x^3+3x-1$, res=coef1[3]=2\*/
```
for (j=deg1; j>=1; j--)
```
/\*this for loop is computes f(x1); j=deg1 is the initialization, j>=1 is the condition and j - is the decrement; the initialization is done once at the beginning of the loop; then the condition is checked, if it is true,

statement in the body is executed and the value of j is decremented by 1 before the condition is re-checked; these steps continue until the condition becomes false at which point the program flow exits the loop*/

    **res = (coef1[j-1]+x1*res);**
    /*for the function $2x^3+3x-1$
    At 1st iteration, res=coef1[2]+x1×res=3+2x1
    At 2nd iteration, res=coef1[1]+x1×res=0+x1×(3+2x1)=3x1+2x1$^2$
    At 3rd iteration, res=coef1[0]+x1×res=-1+x1×(3x1+2x1$^2$)=
    -1+3x1$^2$+2x1$^3$*/

**return res;**
/*value of res is returned to the point where the function was called*/

**}**
/*this closing curly brace specifies the end of poly() function definition*/

**float deriv(float coef1[], int deg1, float x1){**
/*this is the header for the user-defined function deriv(), which must be identical to the function prototype except for no semicolon is used; the function is defined within the curly braces*/

    **float dp, sum=0, ps;**
    /*two float type variables dp and ps are declared; another float type variable sum is declared and initialized to 0; if sum is not initialized to 0 then the memory space allocated for the variable may contain some garbage value which is added in the first summation operation and gives incorrect result*/

    **int k;**
    /*integer type variable k is declared; required memory spaces are allocated for k; k is local to the function deriv() and is not accessible outside that function*/

    **for (k=0; k<deg1; k++){**
    /*this for loop computes $f'(x1)$; k=0 is the initialization, k<deg1 is the condition and k++ is the increment; the initialization is done once at the beginning of the loop; then the condition is checked, if it is true then statements in the body are executed and the value of k is incremented by 1 before the condition is re-checked; these steps continue until the condition becomes false at which point the program flow exits the loop*/

    **ps = pow(x1, deg1-(k+1));**
    /*library function pow() returns x1$^{deg1-(k+1)}$; for $f(x)=2x^3+3x-1$
    At 1st iteration, ps=x1$^{deg1-(k+1)}$=x1$^{3-(0+1)}$=x1$^2$
    At 2nd iteration, ps=x1$^{deg1-(k+1)}$=x1$^{3-(1+1)}$=x1$^1$
    At 3rd iteration, ps=x1$^{deg1-(k+1)}$=x1$^{3-(2+1)}$=x1$^0$*/

```
    dp = (deg1-k)*coef1[deg1-k]*ps;
    /*for the function f(x)=2x³+3x-1
    At 1st iteration, dp=(3-0)×coef1[3-0]×ps=3×2×x1²=6x1²
    At 2nd iteration, dp=(3-1)×coef1[3-1]×ps=2×0×x1=0
    At 3rd iteration, dp=(3-2)×coef1[3-2]×ps=1×3×x1⁰=3*/
    sum = sum+dp;
    /*for the function f(x)=2x³+3x-1
    At 1st iteration, sum=0+6x1²=6x1²
    At 2nd iteration, sum=6x1²+0=6x1²
    At 3rd iteration, sum=6x1²+3 which is the derivative of
    2x³+3x-1 at x1*/
  }
  return sum;
  /*function deriv() returns the value of sum to the point where
  the function was called*/
}
/*this closing curly brace specifies the end of poly() function
definition*/
```

## EXERCISES

MCQ with Answers

1) What is the meaning of the following line:

   ```
   void sum (int, int);
   ```

   A) sum is function which takes int arguments

   B) sum is a function which takes two int arguments and returns void

   C) it will produce compilation error

   D) can't comment

2) The concept of two functions with the same name is known as

   A) Operator overloading

   B) Function overloading

   C) Function overriding

   D) Function renaming

3) What is the storage class of the variable num in the codes given below?

   ```
   void main(){
     int num=10;
     printf("%d", num);}
   ```

A) extern

B) auto

C) register

D) static

4) Which of the following is not a valid storage class?

A) auto

B) extern

C) dynamic

D) register

5) Prototype of a function means _____.

A) Name of function

B) Parameters of function

C) Declaration of function

D) All of the above

6) Which of the following will not return a value?

A) void

B) int

C) null

D) char

7) Which of the following return-type cannot be used for a function in C?

A) char *

B) struct

C) void

D) None of the above

8) Which operator is used to receive the variable number of arguments for a function?

A) Ellipses (…)

B) Backward slash (\)

C) Backward slash and asterisk (\*)

D) Semicolon (;)

9) How many values can a function return to the caller using the return keyword?

A) It cannot return any value

B) Only one

C) Only two

D) Multiple

10) Recursive functions are executed in a _____.

A) FIFO order

B) Load balancing

C) Parallel

D) LIFO order

11) How many functions can be called in a function?

A) Any function can call only a single function

B) A function cannot call any other function

C) Any function can call one or more functions

D) A function cannot call any user-defined function

[Ans. B, B, B, C, D, A, D, A, B, D, C]

Questions with Short Answers

1) What is function overloading in C?

Ans. The C programming language allows us to have two functions with the same name, but the number of arguments and types must be different. This is known as function overloading.

2) What are the available storage classes in C? What is the default value when a local variable is declared?

Ans. In C, there are four different types of storage classes: auto, register, extern, and static. Every storage class has a specific purpose.

Whenever a local variable is declared, it is counted in the auto storage class. Every variable in the storage class has a default value. In the case of auto, garbage is the default value.

3) What is the explanation for the prototype function in C?

Ans. The prototype function is the declaration of the function that must end with a semicolon and contains the following information:

b) Return-type of the function

c) Name of the function

d) Parameters list of the function

Example: `int sum(int x, int y);`

4) What is the general form of function definition in C?

Ans. The function definition in C contains four main sections:

```
return _ type function _ name(parameters list){
body of the function}
```

Example: `int sum(int x, int y){`

```
        int add=x+y;
        return add;}
```

5) What is the keyword auto for?

Ans. By default, every local variable in the function is automatic (auto) and holds a garbage value. An automatic variable cannot be a global variable. Both variables i and j in the following function, for example, are automatic.

```
void func(){
        int i;
        auto int j;}
```

6) What is a static variable?

Ans. A static local variable retains its value between the function call, and its default value is 0. For example, if we call the following function three times, it will display 1, 2, and 3 on the screen.

```
void func(){
        static int num;
        printf("%d, ", ++num);}
```

7) What is the purpose of extern storage specifier?

Ans. The extern storage specifier is used to provide a global variable that is visible in all program files. When extern is used, the variable cannot be initialized; instead, it points the variable name to a previously defined storage location. When a global variable or function is defined that is used in another file, extern is used to provide a reference to the defined variable or function in the other file.

8) When should we use the register storage specifier?

Ans. When a variable is used frequently, it should be declared with the register storage specifier so that the compiler can assign a CPU register to store it. This reduces the time it takes to access the variable.

9) What is a global variable, and how do we declare it?

Ans. The variables that can be accessed from anywhere in the program are known as global variables. The variable is declared just after the preprocessor directives section and before the main() function definition to make it global.

10) What is the difference between formal and actual parameters of a function?

Ans. Actual parameters are the values that are passed into a function when it is called. The called function performs some predefined operations on the values passed as actual parameters. Formal parameters, on the other hand, are the parameters used in the function definition. When a function is called, values of the actual parameters replace the formal parameters.

11) What are the different ways of passing parameters to the functions?

Ans. There are two ways of passing parameters to the functions.

a) *Call by value:* Only values are sent to the function as parameters. We use this option when we do not want the values of the actual parameters to be changed in the function definition. Only their values are used.

b) *Call by reference:* Rather than sending the values, the addresses of the actual arguments are sent. We use this option when we want the values of the actual parameters to be changed by the formal parameters in the function definition.

12) What is a static function?

Ans. By default, functions are global. When a function is declared static, its access is limited to the file where it is declared. The keyword static is used before the function name to declare it as static.

13) Is it possible to have a function as a parameter in another function?

Ans. In C, a function can be used as a parameter in another function. To do that, the entire function prototype is placed in the argument field that will be used.

14) Describe how arrays can be passed to a user-defined function.

Ans. The entire array cannot be passed to a user-defined function. Only a pointer to the first element of the array in memory can be passed. To do so, simply pass the array's name without brackets as an argument.

Problems to Practice

1) Write a program to swap two numbers using pointers and function.

2) Write a program to calculate the power of a number using function.

3) Write a program to calculate the area of an equilateral triangle using function.

4) Write a program that displays the prime numbers from 1 to n. The value of n should be given interactively through the terminal.

5) Write a program to calculate the standard deviation of an array of values. The array elements are read from the terminal. Use functions to calculate the standard deviation and mean.

6) Write a program that computes and displays the factorial for any given number m using a loop and recursive function.

7) Write a program to find the GCD (greatest common divisor) of two given integers using recursive function and loop.

8) Write a program to sort n number of integers in ascending order. The program will display the data before sorting and after sorting.

9) Write a program to produce a matrix that is the sum of two given matrices of the same size. Also, produce a matrix that is the product of two given matrices by checking compatibility.

10) Write a program that uses functions to insert a substring into a given main-string from a given position. Also, define a function to delete n characters from a given position in a given string.

11) Using pointers, write a function that receives a character string and word as arguments and deletes all occurrences of this word in the string.

12) Write a program to solve a polynomial equation and its derivative.

13) Write a program to check whether a given number is even or odd using the function.

14) Write a program to check whether a given number is prime or not using the function.

15) Write a program to display all perfect numbers in a given range using the function.

16) Write a program to check whether two given strings are an anagram.

17) Write a program to find out the maximum and minimum of some values using function.

18) Write a function to find sum of digits of a number.

19) Write a program to calculate the sum of numbers from 1 to n using recursion.

20) Write a program to display Fibonacci Series using recursion.

21) Write a program to find the sum of digits of a number using recursion.

22) Write a program to reverse a string using recursion.

23) Write a program to multiply two matrices using recursion.

24) Write a program to check whether a number can be expressed as the sum of two prime numbers.

25) Write a program that converts a binary number to decimal and vice versa.

26) Write a function to find square root of a number.

27) Write a function to display Hot or Cold depending on the temperature entered by a user.

# CHAPTER 5

# Structure and Union

T HE STRUCTURE IS A collection of variables under a single name that can be of the same type or different types. A union is an object similar to a structure that allows storing different data types, but all its members share the same memory location.

## 5.1 STRUCTURE

Structure is a group of different variables of the same or different data types under a single name. Syntax of creating a struct variable is as follows:

```
struct struct_name{
        data_type member1;
        data_type member2;
        data_type member3;
};
```

struct keyword is short form of structured data type used to create a structure in C.

struct_name is the name of the structure and can be any word other than any keyword.

All the data type inside the curly braces can be of same type or of different types.

Variable of a structure can be declared as follows:

```
struct struct_name var_name1, var_name2;
or
struct struct_name{
        data_type member1;
        data_type member2;
        data_type member3;
} var_name1, var_name2;
```

Members of the structured data type can be accessed through dot (.) operator as follows:

var_name1.member1, var_name2.member3, var_name1.member2

Examples are as follows:

DOI: 10.1201/9781003302629-5

```
struct student_data{
    char name[30];
    int roll;
    float grade;
} stud1, stud2;
stud1.name = "Atiq";
stud1.roll = 2;
stud1.grade = 3.98;
```

Members of the structured data type can also be accessed through arrow (->) operator. To do that, we first have to create pointer to structure. Example:

```
struct student_data *studptr, stud1, stud2;
studptr = &stud1;
```

Now we can access any member using the pointer like

```
studptr->name, studptt->roll, studptr->grade
```

One or more structures can be used inside another structure known as the nested structure. Members of the nested structures are accessed through the chain of dot (.) operator.

## 5.2 UNION

A union is a user-defined data type that may consist of same or different multiple data types. The main difference between structure and union is that structures allocate enough memory space for all of its members, whereas union hold the memory space equal to the size of its largest element and share the same memory for all of its members. Example:

```
union job{
    char name[30];
    int idno;
    float salary;
} empl1, *empl2;
empl2 = &empl1;
```

Like structures, union members can also be accessed using dot (.) or pointer operator. Example:

empl1.name, empl1.idno, empl1.salary or empl2->salary

## 5.3 ENUM

The enum data type consists of integral constants. The element's values are 0, 1, 2, . . ., but the default values can be changed during declaration if needed. Examples are as follows:

```
enum cnst {const1, const2, const3, const4};
```

Here, by default const1 = 0, const2 = 1, const3 = 2, const4 = 3.

```
enum cnst {const1=5, const2=9, const3=19, const4=1};
```

Example of declaring enum variables:

```
enum cnst flags;
enum cnst {const1, const2, const3, const4} flags;
```

## 5.4 DATA STRUCTURE AND ALGORITHM

A data structure is a specified memory region for storing and organizing data. It is a quick and easy approach to get data and update it as needed. There are two sorts of data structures to choose from.

(1) *Linear data structure:* Data are placed in sequential order in a linear data structure. They are simple to implement since the elements are arranged in a specific order. Some famous linear data structures are as follows:

    (a) *Array data structure:* An array's elements are all of the same data type, and they are stored in continuous memory.

    (b) *Stack data structure:* The LIFO (last in, first out) principle governs the storage of elements, which means that the last element in a stack is removed first.

    (c) *Queue data structure:* The FIFO (first in, first out) principle governs the storage of elements; that is, the first element in a queue is removed first.

    (d) *Linked list data structure:* A series of nodes connects data elements, and each node contains data items as well as the addresses of the next and prior nodes.

(2) *Nonlinear data structure:* Data elements in nonlinear data structures are not placed in any particular order. Instead, they are organized in a hierarchical fashion, with one element connected to one or more others. Graph and tree-based data structures are two types of nonlinear data structures.

### ALGORITHM

A set of well-defined instructions for solving a particular problem is known as an algorithm. That is, an algorithm is a step-by-step procedure to get the desired output. A good algorithm may have the following qualities:

(a) Input and output must be well-defined.

(b) Each step of the algorithm should be straightforward.

(c) Among the numerous various ways to solve a problem, algorithms should be the most effective.

(d) Programming code should not be included in an algorithm. Instead, the algorithm should be designed in a way that allows it to be used in a variety of programming languages.

From the data structure point of view, the following are some important categories of algorithms:

(a) Search: to search an item in a data structure.

(b) Sort: to sort items in a particular order.

(c) Insert: to insert an item in a data structure.

(d) Update: to update an existing item in a data structure.

(e) Delete: to delete an existing item from a data structure.

## 5.5 LINKED LIST

A linked list is a data structure that includes a series of connected nodes. Each node of the series consists of two members.

- A data item

- An address of another node

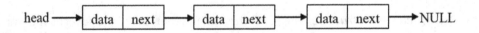

The address of the first node is usually specified as head, and the next portion of the last node always points to NULL. The following example shows how a linked list is created using the structure of a linked list node.

```
/*struct node is defined that has a data item and
a pointer to another struct node*/
struct node{
    int data;
    struct node *next;
};

/*two nodes and a head node, to point to first node, are declared*/
struct node *head, *first, *second;

/*dynamic memory allocation to each node*/
first = malloc(sizeof(struct node));
second = malloc(sizeof(struct node));

/*assigning data values to each node*/
first->data=5;
second->data=12;
```

```
/*connecting first node with second node*/
first->next=second;

/*initializing next portion of the second node as NULL
to set it as last node*/
second->next=NULL;

/*saving address of first node to head to set it as first node*/
head=first;
```

A linked list can break the chain, rejoin it, insert a new node to the chain, delete any node from the chain, etc.

## 5.6 TYPES OF LINKED LIST

There are three types of linked lists commonly available in C and other programming languages:

(a) *Singly linked list:* It is the most common type of linked list. Each node contains data and a pointer to the next node. That type of node is represented as follows:

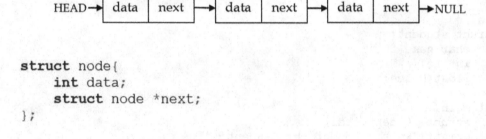

```
struct node{
    int data;
    struct node *next;
};
```

(b) *Doubly linked list:* A doubly linked list can be traversed in both forward and backward directions. Each node of a doubly linked list contains data and two pointers – one to the next node and another to the previous node. That type of node is represented as follows:

```
struct node{
    int data;
    struct node *next;
    struct node *prev;
};
```

(c) *Circular linked list:* Singly linked circular linked list is a variation of a singly linked list in which the next pointer of the last item points to the first item.

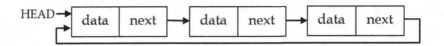

A doubly linked circular linked list is a variation of a doubly linked list in which the next pointer of the last item points to the first item and the previous pointer of the first item points to the last item.

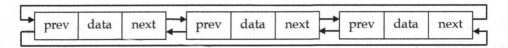

## 5.7 EXAMPLES

**PROBLEM-01**

**Write a program to read and display information of a student using structure.**

Programming Code of the Solution:

```c
#include <stdio.h>
struct student{
    char name[50];
    int roll;
    float grade;
};
int main(){
    struct student std1;
    printf("Enter name of the student: ");
    gets(std1.name);
    printf("Enter roll number of the student: ");
    scanf("%d", &std1.roll);
    printf("Enter grade of the student: ");
    scanf("%f", &std1.grade);
    printf("Displaying information...\n");
    printf("Name: %s\nRoll: %d\nGrade: %.2f", std1.name, std1.roll,
            std1.grade);
    return 0;
}
```

Input and Output of the Executed Program:

```
Enter name of the student: Atiqur Rahman
Enter roll number of the student: 17
Enter grade of the student: 4.98
Displaying information...
Name: Atiqur Rahman
Roll: 17
Grade: 4.98
```

## Explanation of the Programming Code:

```
#include <stdio.h>
```
/*header file stdio.h contains prototypes of the library functions printf(), scanf() and gets(); the header file must be included using preprocessor directive #include before the functions are called in the program*/
```
struct student{
```
/*struct is the keyword used to create structure; student is the name of the structure followed by three members inside the curly braces*/
```
    char name[50];
```
/*character type array of size 50 is declared which is the first member of the structure student*/
```
    int roll;
```
/*integer type variable is declared which is the 2nd member of the structure*/
```
    float grade;
```
/*float type variable is declared which is the 3rd member of the structure*/
```
};
```
/*definition of struct student type data ends with a semicolon; no variable of the defined data type struct student is declared here*/
```
int main(){
```
/*all C program must have a main() function with return type void or int; here there is no parameter of the main() function and it returns an integer; opening curly brace specifies start of the main() function and no statement before that curly brace is executed by the compiler*/
```
    struct student std1;
```
/*struct student type variable std1 is declared that has three members*/
```
    printf("Enter name of the student: ");
```
/*this displays the text inside the double quotations as it is on the screen*/
```
    gets(std1.name);
```
/*gets() function takes a string, including space, tab etc., that end with a NULL character '\0' and stores the string in the first member of the std1 structure which is accessed through dot (.) operator std1.name*/
```
    printf("Enter roll number of the student: ");
```
/*this displays the text inside the double quotations as it is on the screen*/
```
    scanf("%d", &std1.roll);
```
/*scanf() function reads an integer from the input terminal and stores it in the second member of the std1 structure which is accessed through dot (.) operator std1.roll*/

```
printf("Enter grade of the student: ");
/*this displays the text inside the double quotations as it is
on the screen*/
scanf("%f", &std1.grade);
/*scanf() function reads a decimal value from the input terminal
and stores the float value in the third member of the std1
structure which is accessed through dot (.) operator std1.
grade*/
printf("Displaying information . . .\n");
/*this displays the text inside the double quotations on the
screen followed by a newline replaces \n*/
printf("Name: %s\nRoll: %d\nGrade: %.2f", std1.name, std1.roll,
       std1.grade);
/*output function printf() displays the text inside the quotations
as it is on the screen except for the 1st format specifier %s
is replaced by the string std1.name which is the member of the
struct student type variable accessed using dot (.) operator;
this is followed by a newline replaces \n; 2nd format specifier
%d is replaced by the value of std1.roll followed by a newline
and 3rd format specifier %.2f is replaced by the value of std1.
grade with two decimal points precision*/
return 0;
/*0 is returned as it is the standard for the successful
execution of the program*/
}
/*the closing curly brace specifies the end of the main() function's
body, as well as the program's end; after that curly brace, no
statement is executed*/
```

## PROBLEM-02

Write a program to read and display information of n number of students (roll no., name, and marks) using structure and dynamic memory allocation.

Programming Code of the Solution:

```
#include <stdio.h>
#include <stdlib.h>
struct course{
    int roll, marks;
    char name[40];
};
int main(){
    struct course *ptr;
    int i, num;
    printf("Enter number of students: ");
    scanf("%d", &num);
    ptr = (struct course *)malloc(num*sizeof(struct course));
```

```
    for (i=0; i<num; ++i){
        printf("\nInformation of student #%d...\n", i+1);
        printf("Enter roll number: ");
        scanf("%d", &(ptr+i)->roll);
        getchar();
        printf("Enter name: ");
        gets((ptr+i)->name);
        printf("Enter total marks: ");
        scanf("%d", &(ptr+i)->marks);
    }
    printf("\nDisplaying Information...");
    for (i=0; i<num; ++i){
        printf("\nInformation of student #%d...\n", i+1);
        printf("Roll: %d\nName: %s\nMarks: %d\n", (ptr+i)->roll,
                (ptr+i)->name, (ptr+i)->marks);
    }
    free(ptr);
    return 0;
}
```

## Input and Output of the Executed Program:

```
Enter number of students: 2

Information of student #1...
Enter roll number: 201
Enter name: Atiqur Rahman
Enter total marks: 460

Information of student #2...
Enter roll number: 202
Enter name: Samaun Imran
Enter total marks: 390

Displaying Information...
Information of student #1...
Roll: 201
Name: Atiqur Rahman
Marks: 460

Information of student #2...
Roll: 202
Name: Samaun Imran
Marks: 390
```

## Explanation of the Programming Code:

```
#include <stdio.h>
/*header file stdio.h contains prototypes of the library functions
printf(), scanf(), sizeof(), getchar() and gets(); the header file
```

must be included using preprocessor directive #include before the functions are called in the program*/

**#include <stdlib.h>**

/*header file stdlib.h contains prototypes of the library functions malloc() and free(); the header file must be included using preprocessor directive #include before the functions are called in the program*/

**struct course{**

/*keyword struct is used to create a structure; course is the name of the structure followed by three members inside the curly braces*/

    **int roll, marks;**

    /*two integer type variables are declared as the members of the structure course*/

    **char name[40];**

    /*character type array of size 50 is declared which is a member of the structure course*/

**};**

/*definition of structured data type must end with a semicolon; no variable of the defined data type struct course is declared here*/

**int main(){**

/*all C program must have a main() function with return type void or int; here there is no parameter of the main() function and it returns an integer; opening curly brace specifies start of the main() function and no statement before that curly brace is executed by the compiler*/

    **struct course *ptr;**

    /*struct course type pointer ptr is declared; members of the variable pointed by ptr are accessed using arrow (->) operator*/

    **int i, num;**

    /*two integer type variables are declared; required memory spaces are allocated for each of the variables*/

    **printf("Enter number of students: ");**

    /*output function printf() displays the text in the quotations as it is on the screen*/

    **scanf("%d", &num);**

    /*scanf() function reads an integer from the input terminal and stores it in the memory spaces allocated for the variable num*/

    **ptr = (struct course *)malloc(num*sizeof(struct course));**

    /*sizeof() function computes the size of struct course type data, needed to store two integers and a character type array of size 40; num times of that size are dynamically allocated in the memory by malloc(); address of the memory space is assigned to struct course type pointer variable ptr*/

    **for (i=0; i<num; ++i){**

    /*here i=0 is initialization, i<num is condition and ++i is increment; initialization is done once at the beginning of the loop; then the condition is checked, if it is true statements

in the body, enclosed by curly braces, are executed and value of i is incremented by 1 before the condition is re-checked; these steps continue until the condition becomes false in which case the program control flow exits the loop*/

```
        printf("\nInformation of student #%d . . . \n", i+1);
```
        /*output function printf() displays the text in the quotations as it is on the screen except for the value of i+1 replaces the format specifier %d and a newline replaces \n*/
```
        printf("Enter roll number: ");
```
        /*output function printf() displays the text in the quotations as it is on the screen*/
```
        scanf("%d", &(ptr+i)->roll);
```
        /*function scanf() reads an integer from input terminal and stores it in the member roll of struct course type pointer ptr; in each iteration roll number of individual student is read*/
```
        getchar();
```
        /*when we enter roll number of a student and press enter, a \n after the integer stays in the buffer and is accepted as input in following gets() statement; therefore we use this getchar() after entering roll number to solve the problem*/
```
        printf("Enter name: ");
```
        /*output function printf() displays the text in the quotations as it is on the screen*/
```
        gets((ptr+i)->name);
```
        /*gets() function takes a string, including space, tab etc., that end with a NULL character '\0' and stores the string in member name of the struct course type pointer variable ptr which is accessed using arrow (->) operator*/
```
        printf("Enter total marks: ");
```
        /*output function printf() displays the text in the quotations as it is on the screen*/
```
        scanf("%d", &(ptr+i)->marks);
```
        /*function scanf() reads an integer from input terminal and stores it in the member marks of struct course type pointer ptr; in each iteration marks of individual student is read*/
```
}
```
/*this closing curly brace specifies the end of 'for' loop*/
```
printf("\nDisplaying Information . . . ");
```
/*output function printf() displays the text in the quotations as it is on the screen except for a newline replaces \n*/
```
for (i=0; i<num; ++i){
```
/*here i=0 is initialization, i<num is condition and ++i is increment; initialization is done once at the beginning of the loop; then the condition is checked, if it is true statements in the body, enclosed by curly braces, are executed and value

of i is incremented by 1 before the condition is re-checked; these steps continue until the condition becomes false in which case the program control flow exits the loop*/

```
    printf("\nInformation of student #%d . . . \n", i+1);
```
/*output function printf() displays the text in the quotations as it is on the screen except for the value of i+1 replaces the format specifier %d and a newline replaces \n*/

```
    printf("Roll: %d\nName: %s\nMarks: %d\n", (ptr+i)->roll,
        (ptr+i)->name, (ptr+i)->marks);
```
/*output function printf() displays the text in the quotations as it is on the screen except for the value of (ptr+i)->roll replaces the 1st format specifier %d, string value of (ptr+i)->name replaces %s, value of (ptr+i)->marks replaces 2nd %d and a newline replaces \n*/

```
}
```
/*this closing curly brace specifies the end of 'for' loop*/

```
free(ptr);
```
/*memory spaces allocated for struct course type variables are freed*/

```
return 0;
```
/*0 is returned as it is the standard for the successful execution of the program*/

```
}
```
/*the closing curly brace specifies the end of the main() function's body, as well as the program's end; after that curly brace, no statement is executed*/

## PROBLEM-03
**Write a program to add two complex numbers using structure.**

Programming Code of the Solution:

```
#include <stdio.h>
struct complex{
    float real, imag;
};
int main(){
    struct complex num1, num2, sum;
    printf("Enter 1st complex number:\nreal: ");
    scanf("%f", &num1.real);
    printf("imaginary: ");
    scanf("%f", &num1.imag);
    printf("Enter 2nd complex number:\nreal: ");
    scanf("%f", &num2.real);
    printf("imaginary: ");
    scanf("%f", &num2.imag);
    sum.real = num1.real + num2.real;
    sum.imag = num1.imag + num2.imag;
    printf("%.2f+j%.2f + %.2f+j%.2f = %.2f+j%.2f", num1.real,
        num1.imag, num2.real, num2.imag, sum.real, sum.imag);
    return 0;
}
```

Input and Output of the Executed Program:

```
Enter 1st complex number:
real: 2.16
imaginary: 1.33
Enter 2nd complex number:
real: 5.9
imaginary: 6.3
2.16+j1.33 + 5.90+j6.30 = 8.06+j7.63
```

## Explanation of the Programming Code:

```
#include <stdio.h>
```
/*header file stdio.h contains prototypes of the library functions printf(), and scanf(); the header file must be included using preprocessor directive #include before the functions are called in the program*/
```
struct complex{
```
/*struct is the keyword used to create structure; complex is the name of the structure followed by two members of the same data type inside the curly braces*/
```
    float real, imag;
```
/*two float type variables are declared where real is the 1st member and imag is the 2nd member of the structure*/
```
};
```
/*definition of struct complex type data ends with a semicolon; no variable of the defined data type struct complex is declared here*/
```
int main(){
```
/*all C program must have a main() function with return type void or int; here there is no parameter of the main() function and it returns an integer; opening curly brace specifies start of the main() function and no statement before that curly brace is executed by the compiler*/
```
    struct complex num1, num2, sum;
```
/*three struct student type variables are declared, each has three members*/
```
    printf("Enter 1st complex number:\nreal: ");
```
/*this displays the text inside the double quotations as it is on the screen except for a newline replaces \n*/
```
    scanf("%f", &num1.real);
```
/*scanf() function reads a decimal value from the input terminal and stores it in the 1st member of the num1 structure which is accessed through dot (.) operator num1.real*/
```
    printf("imaginary: ");
```
/*this displays the text inside the double quotations as it is on the screen*/

```
scanf("%f", &num1.imag);
```
/*scanf() function reads a decimal value from the input terminal
and stores it in the 2nd member of the num1 structure which is
accessed through dot (.) operator num1.imag*/
```
printf("Enter 2nd complex number:\nreal: ");
```
/*this displays the text inside the double quotations as it is
on the screen except for a newline replaces \n*/
```
scanf("%f", &num2.real);
```
/*function scanf() reads a decimal value from the input terminal
and stores it in the 1st member of the num2 structure which is
accessed through dot (.) operator num2.real*/
```
printf("imaginary: ");
```
/*this displays the text inside the double quotation as it is
on the screen*/
```
scanf("%f", &num2.imag);
```
/*scanf() function reads a decimal value from the input terminal
and stores it in the 2nd member of the num2 structure which is
accessed through dot (.) operator num2.imag*/
```
sum.real = num1.real + num2.real;
```
/*using dot (.) operator we access members of the struct complex
type variables; real parts of both num1 and num2 are added and
the result is stored in member real of the struct complex type
variable sum*/
```
sum.imag = num1.imag + num2.imag;
```
/*imaginary parts of both num1 and num2 are added and the result
is stored in member imag of the struct complex type variable
sum*/
```
printf("%.2f+j%.2f + %.2f+j%.2f = %.2f+j%.2f", num1.real,
        num1.imag, num2.real, num2.imag, sum.real, sum.imag);
```
/*output function printf() displays the text as it is on
the screen except for the value of num1.real replaces the
1st format specifier %.2f with two decimal points precision,
value of num1.imag replaces the 2nd %.2f, value of num2.real
replaces the 3rd %.2f, value of num2.imag replaces the 4th
%.2f, value of sum.real replaces the 5th %.2f, and the value
of sum.imag replaces 6th %.2f; all the variables are members
of the struct complex type variable, and accessed using dot
(.) operator*/
```
return 0;
```
/*0 is returned as it is the standard for the successful
execution of the program*/
```
}
```
/*the closing curly brace specifies the end of the main() function's
body, as well as the program's end; after that curly brace, no
statement is executed*/

## PROBLEM-04
**Write a program to create and display a singly linked list of n nodes.**

Programming Code of the Solution:

```c
#include <stdio.h>
#include <stdlib.h>
struct node{
    int num;
    struct node *next;
} *stnode;
void create(int n);
void display();
int main(){
    int nm;
    printf("Input the number of nodes: ");
    scanf("%d", &nm);
    create(nm);
    printf("\nData entered in the list:\n");
    display();
    return 0;
}
void create(int n){
    struct node *fnNode, *tmp;
    int nm, i;
    stnode = (struct node *)malloc(sizeof(struct node));
    if (stnode == NULL)
        printf("Memory cannot be allocated.");
    else{
        printf("\nInput data for node #1: ");
        scanf("%d", &nm);
        stnode->num = nm;
        stnode->next = NULL;
        tmp = stnode;
        for (i=2; i<=n; i++){
            fnNode = (struct node *)malloc(sizeof(struct node));
            if (fnNode == NULL){
                printf("Memory cannot be allocated.");
                break;
            }
            else{
                printf("Input data for node #%d: ", i);
                scanf("%d", &nm);
                fnNode->num = nm;
                fnNode->next = NULL;
                tmp->next = fnNode;
                tmp = tmp->next;
            }
        }
    }
}
```

```
void display(){
    struct node *tmp;
    if (stnode == NULL)
        printf("List is empty...");
    else{
        tmp = stnode;
        while (tmp != NULL){
            printf("%d, ", tmp->num);
            tmp = tmp->next;
        }
    }
}
```

Input and Output of the Executed Program:

```
Input the number of nodes: 5

Input data for node #1: 12
Input data for node #2: 23
Input data for node #3: 34
Input data for node #4: 45
Input data for node #5: 56

Data entered in the list:
12, 23, 34, 45, 56,
```

Explanation of the Programming Code:

**#include <stdio.h>**
/*header file stdio.h contains prototypes of the library functions printf(), scanf() and sizeof(); the header file must be included using preprocessor directive #include before the functions are called in the program*/
**#include <stdlib.h>**
/*header file stdio.h contains prototype of the library function malloc(); the header file must be included using preprocessor directive #include before the function is called in the program*/
**struct node{**
/*new data type struct node is created using keyword struct; members of struct node are declared in the curly braces*/
    **int num;**
    /*integer type variable num is declared, this is a member of the data type struct node*/
    **struct node *next;**

```
    /*struct node type pointer next is declared as second member
    of the data type struct node; next contains address of another
    node*/                          .
} *stnode;
/*definition of the structured data type must end with a semicolon;
struct node type pointer stnode of the defined data type is declared
here*/
void create(int n);
/*this is the prototype (or declaration) of the user-defined
function create() that must end with a semicolon; create() takes
an integer as parameter, performs some predefined operations, and
returns nothing*/
void display();
/*this is the prototype (or declaration) of the user-defined
function display() that must end with a semicolon; display() takes
no parameter, performs some predefined operations, and returns
nothing*/
int main(){
/*all C program must have a main() function with return type void
or int; here there is no parameter of the main() function and it
returns an integer; opening curly brace specifies start of the
main() function and no statement before that curly brace is executed
by the compiler*/
    int nm;
    /*an integer type variable is declared; required memory space
    is allocated for the variable*/
    printf("Input the number of nodes: ");
    /*printf() function displays the text in the quotations as it
    is on the screen*/
    scanf("%d", &nm);
    /*scanf() function reads an integer from input terminal and
    stores the value in the memory spaces allocated for the nm*/
    create(nm);
    /*user-defined function create() is called with real parameter
    nm that refers to the no. of nodes in the linked list; program
    control flow shifts to the definition of the function*/
    printf("\nData entered in the list:\n");
    /*printf() function displays the text in the quotations as it
    is on the screen except for a newline replaces \n*/
    display();
    /*user-defined function display() is called; program control
    flow shifts to the definition of the function*/
    return 0;
    /*0 is returned as it is the standard for the successful
    execution of the program*/
}
```

```
/*the closing curly brace specifies the end of the main() function's
body, as well as the program's end; after that curly brace, no
statement is executed*/
void create(int n){
/*definition of create() function starts here with function header and
body; function header is same as function prototype without semicolon;
body of the function is enclosed in curly braces; real argument that is
passed during the function call replaces virtual parameter n*/
    struct node *fnNode, *tmp;
    /*two struct node type pointers are declared; fnNode and tmp
    are the addresses of two struct node type variables each has
    two members- num to store an integer and next to store address
    of another struct node type variable*/
    int nm, i;
    /*two integer type variables are declared; required memory spaces
    are allocated for the variables; these variables are local to the
    function create() and is not visible outside that function*/
    stnode = (struct node *)malloc(sizeof(struct node));
    /*sizeof() function computes the size of struct node type data,
    needed to store an integer and address of another node; required
    memory spaces are dynamically allocated by malloc(); address
    of the memory space is assigned to struct node type pointer
    variable stnode*/
    if (stnode == NULL)
    /*if memory cannot be assigned successfully malloc() returns
    a NULL to stnode; if the condition of if is true following
    statement is executed*/
        printf("Memory cannot be allocated.");
        /*printf() function displays the text in the quotations as
        it is on the screen*/
    else{
    /*if the above condition of if is false, following statements,
    enclosed in the curly braces, are executed*/
        printf("\nInput data for node #1: ");
        /*printf() function displays the text in the double
        quotations as it is on the screen except for a newline
        replaces \n*/
        scanf("%d", &nm);
        /*scanf() function reads an integer from input terminal
        and stores the value in the memory spaces allocated for
        the nm*/
        stnode->num = nm;
        /*value of nm is assigned to the member num of the first
        node stnode of the linked list*/
        stnode->next = NULL;
        /*next pointer of the first node is set to NULL; there is
        no more node after that in the linked list*/
```

```
tmp = stnode;
```
/*struct node type pointer tmp refers to the first node of
the linked list stnode*/
```
for (i=2; i<=n; i++){
```
/*this for loop creates other nodes of the linked list
other than the first node; here i=2 is initialization, i<=n
is condition and i++ is increment; initialization is done
once at the beginning of the loop; then the condition is
checked, if it is true statements in the body, enclosed by
curly braces, are executed and value of i is incremented by
1 before the condition is re-checked; these steps continue
until the condition becomes false in which case the program
control flow exits the loop*/
```
    fnNode = (struct node *)malloc(sizeof(struct node));
```
/*sizeof() function computes the size of struct node
type data, needed to store an integer and address of
another node; required memory spaces are dynamically
allocated by malloc(); address of the memory space
is assigned to struct node type pointer variable
fnNode*/
```
if (fnNode == NULL){
```
/*if memory cannot be assigned successfully malloc()
returns a NULL to fnNode; if the condition of if is true
following statements, enclosed in the curly braces, are
executed*/
```
        printf("Memory cannot be allocated.");
```
    /*output function printf() displays the text in the
    quotations as it is on the screen*/
```
        break;
```
    /*as memory cannot be allocated for the node, the
    program control flow immediately exits the loop*/
```
    }
```
/*this closing curly brace specifies the end of 'if'
with condition (fnNode == NULL)*/
```
    else{
```
/*if the above condition of if is false, memory is
successfully allocated for the node and the following
statements, enclosed in the curly braces, are executed*/
```
        printf("Input data for node #%d: ", i);
```
    /*output function printf() displays the text in the
    quotations as it is on the screen except for the
    value of i replaces the format specifier %d*/
```
        scanf("%d", &nm);
```
    /*scanf() function reads an integer from input
    terminal and stores the value in the memory spaces
    allocated for the nm*/
```
        fnNode->num = nm;
```

```
            /*value of nm is assigned to the member num of the
            node fnNode of the linked list*/
            fnNode->next = NULL;
            /*next pointer of the node is set to NULL; there is
            no more node after that in the linked list*/
            tmp->next = fnNode;
            /*newly created node fnNode is linked with the
            previous node tmp by assigning the address of fnNode
            to the next pointer of the node tmp*/
            tmp = tmp->next;
            /*node tmp now refers to the newly created node
            fnNode so that another node can be inserted after
            that tmp (or fnNode) node in the next iteration of
            the loop*/
        }
        /*this closing curly brace specifies the end of 'else'
        with if (fnNode == NULL)*/
    }
    /*this closing curly brace specifies the end of 'for' loop
    }
    /*this closing curly brace specifies the end of 'else' with if
    (stnode == NULL)*/
}
/*this closing curly brace specifies the end of definition of
create() function; program control flow returns to the point where
the function was called*/
void display(){
/*definition of display() function starts here with function header
and body; function header is same as function prototype without
semicolon; body of the function is enclosed in curly braces*/
    struct node *tmp;
    /*struct node type pointer is declared; tmp is the address of
    struct node type variable that has two members- num to store an
    integer and next to store address of another node type variable*/
    if (stnode == NULL)
    /*if starting node stnode is NULL above condition is true and
    following statement is executed*/
        printf("List is empty . . . ");
        /*printf() function displays the text in the quotations as
        it is on the screen*/
    else{
    /*if the linked list is not empty then above condition of 'if'
    is false and the following statements, enclosed in the curly
    braces, are executed*/
        tmp = stnode;
        /*struct node type pointer tmp refers to the first node
        stnode of the linked list*/
```

```
        while (tmp!= NULL){
        /*condition in the while loop checks if tmp refers to the
        last node; the condition is checked, if it is true statements
        in the body, enclosed by curly braces, are executed before
        the condition is re-checked; these steps continue until the
        condition becomes false in which case the program control
        flow exits the loop*/
            printf("%d, ", tmp->num);
            /*printf() function displays the value of num of current
            node tmp on the screen in place of format specifier %d*/
            tmp = tmp->next;
            /*pointer tmp now refers to the next node of the current
            node so that the next node can be checked and displayed
            in the next iteration of the loop*/
        }
        /*this closing curly brace specifies the end of while loop*/
    }
    /*this closing curly brace specifies the end of else*/
}
/*this closing curly brace specifies the end of the definition of
display() function; program control flow returns to the point where
the function was called*/
```

## PROBLEM-05
Write a program to create a doubly linked list of n nodes and display it in reverse order.

Programming Code of the Solution:

```c
#include <stdio.h>
#include <stdlib.h>
struct node{
    int num;
    struct node *prev, *next;
} *stnode, *ednode;
void create(int n);
void display();
int main(){
    int nm;
    stnode = NULL;
    ednode = NULL;
    printf("Input the number of nodes: ");
    scanf("%d", &nm);
    create(nm);
    display();
    return 0;
}
```

```c
void create(int n){
    int i, nm;
    struct node *fnNode;
    stnode = (struct node *)malloc(sizeof(struct node));
    if (stnode != NULL){
        printf("\nInput data for node #1: ");
        scanf("%d", &nm);
        stnode->num = nm;
        stnode->prev = NULL;
        stnode->next = NULL;
        ednode = stnode;
        for (i=2; i<=n; i++){
            fnNode = (struct node *)malloc(sizeof(struct node));
            if (fnNode != NULL){
                printf("Input data for node #%d: ", i);
                scanf("%d", &nm);
                fnNode->num = nm;
                fnNode->prev = ednode;
                fnNode->next = NULL;
                ednode->next = fnNode;
                ednode = fnNode;
            }
            else{
                printf("Memory cannot be allocated.");
                break;
            }
        }
    }
    else
        printf("Memory cannot be allocated.");
}
void display(){
    struct node *tmp;
    if (ednode == NULL)
        printf("No data found in the list yet.");
    else{
        tmp = ednode;
        printf("\nData in reverse order are:\n");
        while (tmp != NULL){
            printf("%d, ", tmp->num);
            tmp = tmp->prev;
        }
    }
}
```

Input and Output of the Executed Program:

```
Input the number of nodes: 5

Input data for node #1: 12
Input data for node #2: 23
Input data for node #3: 34
Input data for node #4: 45
Input data for node #5: 56

Data in reverse order are:
56, 45, 34, 23, 12,
```

## Explanation of the Programming Code:

```
#include <stdio.h>
```
/*header file stdio.h contains prototypes of the library functions printf(), scanf() and sizeof(); the header file must be included using preprocessor directive #include before the functions are called in the program*/
```
#include <stdlib.h>
```
/*header file stdio.h contains prototype of the library function malloc(); the header file must be included using preprocessor directive #include before the function is called in the program*/
```
struct node{
```
/*new data type struct node is created using keyword struct; members of struct node are declared in the curly braces*/
```
    int num;
```
/*integer type variable num is declared, this is a member of the data type struct node*/
```
    struct node *prev, *next;
```
/*two struct node type pointers are declared as members of the data type struct node; prev and next contain addresses of other nodes*/
```
} *stnode, *ednode;
```
/*definition of the structured data type must end with a semicolon; struct node type pointers stnode and ednode of the defined data type are declared here*/
```
void create(int n);
```
/*this is the prototype (or declaration) of the user-defined function create() that must end with a semicolon; create() takes an integer as parameter, performs some predefined operations, and returns nothing*/
```
void display();
```
/*this is the prototype (or declaration) of the user-defined function display() that must end with a semicolon; display() takes

no parameter, performs some predefined operations, and returns nothing*/
```c
int main(){
```
/*all C program must have a main() function with return type void or int; here there is no parameter of the main() function and it returns an integer; opening curly brace specifies start of the main() function and no statement before that curly brace is executed by the compiler*/
```c
    int nm;
```
/*an integer type variable is declared; required memory space is allocated for the variable*/
```c
    stnode = NULL;
```
/*NULL value is assigned to the starting node stnode*/
```c
    ednode = NULL;
```
/*NULL value is assigned to the last node ednode*/
```c
    printf("Input the number of nodes: ");
```
/*printf() function displays the text in the quotations as it is on the screen*/
```c
    scanf("%d", &nm);
```
/*scanf() function reads an integer from input terminal and stores the value in the memory spaces allocated for the nm*/
```c
    create(nm);
```
/*user-defined function create() is called with real parameter nm that refers to the no. of nodes in the linked list; program control flow shifts to the definition of the function*/
```c
    display();
```
/*user-defined function display() is called; program control flow shifts to the definition of the function*/
```c
    return 0;
```
/*0 is returned as it is the standard for the successful execution of the program*/
```c
}
```
/*the closing curly brace specifies the end of the main() function's body, as well as the program's end; after that curly brace, no statement is executed*/
```c
void create(int n){
```
/*definition of create() function starts here with function header and body; function header is same as function prototype without semicolon; body of the function is enclosed in curly braces; real argument that is passed during the function call replaces virtual parameter n*/
```c
    int i, nm;
```
/*two integer type variables are declared; required memory spaces are allocated for the variables; these variables are local to the function create() and is not visible outside that function*/
```c
    struct node *fnNode;
```

/*struct node type pointer is declared; fnNode is the address of a struct node type variable with three members- num to store an integer, and prev and next to store addresses of another node type variables*/

**stnode = (struct node \*)malloc(sizeof(struct node));**

/*sizeof() function computes the size of struct node type data, needed to store an integer and two addresses of other nodes; required memory spaces are dynamically allocated by malloc(); address of the memory space is assigned to struct node type pointer variable stnode*/

**if (stnode!= NULL){**

/*if memory is successfully assigned by malloc() above condition is true and the following statements, enclosed in the curly braces, are executed*/

    **printf("\nInput data for node #1: ");**

    /*printf() function displays the text in the double quotations as it is on the screen except for a newline replaces \n*/

    **scanf("%d", &nm);**

    /*scanf() function reads an integer from input terminal and stores the value in the memory spaces allocated for the nm*/

    **stnode->num = nm;**

    /*value of nm is assigned to the member num of the first node stnode of the linked list*/

    **stnode->prev = NULL;**

    /*prev pointer of the first node is set to NULL; there is no more node before that in the linked list*/

    **stnode->next = NULL;**

    /*next pointer of the first node is set to NULL; there is no more node after that in the linked list*/

    **ednode = stnode;**

    /*both starting node stnode and last node ednode refer to the same node*/

    **for (i=2; i<=n; i++){**

    /*this for loop creates other nodes of the linked list; here i=2 is initialization, i<=n is condition and i++ is increment; initialization is done once at the beginning of the loop; then the condition is checked, if it is true statements in the body, enclosed by curly braces, are executed and value of i is incremented by 1 before the condition is re-checked; these steps continue until the condition becomes false in which case the program control flow exits the loop*/

        **fnNode = (struct node \*)malloc(sizeof(struct node));**

        /*sizeof() function computes the size of struct node type data, needed to store an integer and two addresses of nodes; required memory spaces are dynamically allocated by malloc(); address of the memory space is assigned to struct node type pointer variable fnNode*/

```
if (fnNode!= NULL){
```
/*if memory is assigned successfully by malloc() above condition of if is true and the following statements, enclosed in the curly braces, are executed*/

```
    printf("Input data for node #%d: ", i);
```
/*output function printf() displays the text in the quotations as it is on the screen except for the value of i replaces the format specifier %d*/

```
    scanf("%d", &nm);
```
/*scanf() function reads an integer from input terminal and stores the value in the memory spaces allocated for the nm*/

```
    fnNode->num = nm;
```
/*value of nm is assigned to the member num of the new node fnNode of the linked list*/

```
    fnNode->prev = ednode;
```
/*prev of new node fnNode refers to its previous node ednode*/

```
    fnNode->next = NULL;
```
/*next of new node fnNode refers to NULL; there is no more node after the new node*/

```
    ednode->next = fnNode;
```
/*next of previous node ednode refers to the new node fnNode*/

```
    ednode = fnNode;
```
/*ednode now becomes the new node fnNode so that another node can be inserted after ednode in the next iteration of the loop*/

```
}
```
/*this closing curly brace specifies the end of 'if' with condition (fnNode!= NULL)*/

```
else{
```
/*if memory cannot be assigned successfully malloc() returns a NULL to fnNode; if the condition of above if (fnNode!= NULL) is false following statements, enclosed in the curly braces, are executed*/

```
    printf("Memory cannot be allocated.");
```
/*output function printf() displays the text in the quotations as it is on the screen*/

```
    break;
```
/*as memory cannot be allocated for the node, the program control flow immediately exits the loop*/

```
}
```

```
                /*this closing curly brace specifies the end of 'else'
                with if (fnNode!= NULL)*/
        }
        /*this closing curly brace specifies the end of 'for' loop*/
}
/*this closing curly brace specifies the end of 'if' with
condition (stnode!= NULL)*/
else
/*if memory cannot be assigned successfully malloc() returns a
NULL to stnode; if the condition of above if (stnode!= NULL) is
false following statement is executed*/
        printf("Memory cannot be allocated.");
        /*output function printf() displays the text in the
        quotations as it is on the screen*/
}
/*this closing curly brace specifies the end of definition of
create() function; program control flow returns to the point where
the function was called*/
void display(){
/*definition of display() function starts here with function
header and body; function header is same as function prototype
without semicolon; body of the function is enclosed in curly
braces*/
        struct node *tmp;
        /*struct node type pointer is declared; tmp is the address of
        struct node type variable that has three members- num to store
        an integer, and prev and next to store addresses of another
        struct node type variables*/
        if (ednode == NULL)
        /*if last node ednode is NULL above condition is true and
        following statement is executed*/
                printf("No data found in the list yet.");
                /*printf() function displays the text in the quotations as
                it is on the screen*/
        else{
        /*if the linked list is not empty then above condition of 'if'
        is false and the following statements, enclosed in the curly
        braces, are executed*/
                tmp = ednode;
                /*struct node type pointer tmp refers to the last node
                ednode of the linked list*/
                printf("\nData in reverse order are:\n");
                /*printf() function displays the text in the double quotations
                as it is on the screen except for a newline replaces \n*/
                while (tmp!= NULL){
                /*condition in the while loop checks if tmp refers to the
                first node; the condition is checked, if it is true statements
```

in the body, enclosed by curly braces, are executed before the condition is re-checked; these steps continue until the condition becomes false in which case the program control flow exits the loop*/

```
        printf("%d, ", tmp->num);
        /*printf() function displays the value of num of current
        node tmp on the screen in place of format specifier %d*/
        tmp = tmp->prev;
        /*pointer tmp now refers to the previous node of the
        current node so that the previous node can be checked
        and displayed in the next iteration of the loop*/
    }
    /*this closing curly brace specifies the end of while loop*/
  }
  /*this closing curly brace specifies the end of else*/
}
/*this closing curly brace specifies the end of the definition of
display() function; program control flow returns to the point where
the function was called*/
```

## PROBLEM-06
**Write a program to insert a new node at the beginning of a circular linked list.**

Programming Code of the Solution:

```c
#include <stdio.h>
#include <stdlib.h>
struct node{
    int item;
    struct node *next;
} *stnode;
void create(int n);
void insert(int nm);
void display(int a);
int main(){
    int num1, num2, num3;
    stnode = NULL;
    printf("Input the number of nodes: ");
    scanf("%d", &num1);
    create(num1);
    num2=1;
    display(num2);
    printf("\nInput data to be inserted at the beginning: ");
    scanf("%d", &num3);
    insert(num3);
    num2=2;
    display(num2);
    return 0;
}
```

```c
void create(int n){
    int i, num4;
    struct node *prev, *newn;
    stnode = (struct node *)malloc(sizeof(struct node));
    if (stnode == NULL)
        printf("Memory cannot be allocated.");
    else{
        printf("\nInput data for node #1: ");
        scanf("%d", &num4);
        stnode->item = num4;
        stnode->next = NULL;
        prev = stnode;
        for (i=2; i<=n; i++){
            newn = (struct node *)malloc(sizeof(struct node));
            if (newn == NULL){
                printf("Memory cannot be allocated.");
                break;
            }
            else{
                printf("Input data for node #%d: ", i);
                scanf("%d", &num4);
                newn->item = num4;
                newn->next = NULL;
                prev->next = newn;
                prev = newn;
            }
        }
        prev->next = stnode;
    }
}

void insert(int nm){
    struct node *newn, *curn;
    if (stnode == NULL)
        printf("No data found in the List yet.");
    else{
        newn = (struct node *)malloc(sizeof(struct node));
        if (newn == NULL)
            printf("Memory cannot be allocated.");
        else{
            newn->item = nm;
            newn->next = stnode;
            curn = stnode;
            while (curn->next != stnode)
                curn = curn->next;
            curn->next = newn;
            stnode = newn;
        }
    }
}
```

```
void display(int a){
    struct node *tmp;
    if (stnode == NULL)
        printf("No data found in the List yet.");
    else{
        tmp = stnode;
        if (a==1)
            printf("\nData entered in the list are:\n");
        else
            printf("\nAfter insertion the new list are:\n");
        do{
            printf("%d, ", tmp->item);
            tmp = tmp->next;
        }while (tmp != stnode);
    }
}
```

<u>Input and Output of the Executed Program:</u>

```
Input the number of nodes: 5

Input data for node #1: 12
Input data for node #2: 23
Input data for node #3: 34
Input data for node #4: 45
Input data for node #5: 56

Data entered in the list are:
12, 23, 34, 45, 56,
Input data to be inserted at the beginning: 67

After insertion the new list are:
67, 12, 23, 34, 45, 56,
```

<u>**Explanation of the Programming Code:**</u>

**#include <stdio.h>**
/*header file stdio.h contains prototypes of the library functions printf(), scanf() and sizeof(); the header file must be included using preprocessor directive #include before the functions are called in the program*/
**#include <stdlib.h>**
/*header file stdio.h contains prototype of the library function malloc(); the header file must be included using preprocessor directive #include before the function is called in the program*/
**struct node{**

/*new data type struct node is created using keyword struct; members of struct node are declared in the curly braces*/

    int item;

    /*integer type variable item is declared, this is a member of the data type struct node*/

    struct node *next;

    /*struct node type pointer next is declared as second member of the data type struct node; next contains address of another node*/

} *stnode;

/*definition of the structured data type must end with a semicolon; struct node type pointer stnode of the defined data type is declared here*/

void create(int n);

/*this is the prototype (or declaration) of the user-defined function create() that must end with a semicolon; create() takes an integer as parameter, performs some predefined operations, and returns nothing*/

void insert(int nm);

/*this is the prototype (or declaration) of the user-defined function insert() that must end with a semicolon; insert() takes an integer as parameter, performs some predefined operations, and returns nothing*/

void display(int a);

/*this is the prototype (or declaration) of the user-defined function display() that must end with a semicolon; display() takes an integer as parameter, performs some predefined operations, and returns nothing*/

int main(){

/*all C program must have a main() function with return type void or int; here there is no parameter of the main() function and it returns an integer; opening curly brace specifies start of the main() function and no statement before that curly brace is executed by the compiler*/

    int num1, num2, num3;

    /*three integer type variabls are declared; required memory spaces are allocated for each of the variables*/

    stnode = NULL;

    /*NULL value is assigned to the starting node stnode*/

    printf("Input the number of nodes: ");

    /*printf() function displays the text in the quotations as it is on the screen*/

    scanf("%d", &num1);

    /*scanf() function reads an integer from input terminal and stores the value in the memory spaces allocated for the num1*/

    create(num1);

```
    /*user-defined function create() is called with real parameter
    num1 that refers to the no. of nodes in the linked list; program
    control flow shifts to the definition of the function*/
    num2=1;
    /*value 1 is assigned to the variable num2*/
    display(num2);
    /*user-defined function display() is called with real parameter
    num2; program control flow shifts to the definition of the
    function*/
    printf("\nInput data to be inserted at the beginning: ");
    /*printf() function displays the text in the double quotations
    as it is on the screen except for a newline replaces \n*/
    scanf("%d", &num3);
    /*scanf() function reads an integer from input terminal and
    stores the value in the memory spaces allocated for the
    num3*/
    insert(num3);
    /*user-defined function insert() is called with real parameter
    num3 that refers to the item of node to be inserted in the
    linked list; program control flow shifts to the definition of
    the function*/
    num2=2;
    /*value 2 is assigned to the variable num2*/
    display(num2);
    /*user-defined function display() is called with real parameter
    num2; program control flow shifts to the definition of the
    function*/
    return 0;
    /*0 is returned as it is the standard for the successful
    execution of the program*/
}
/*the closing curly brace specifies the end of the main() function's
body, as well as the program's end; after that curly brace, no
statement is executed*/
void create(int n){
/*definition of create() function starts here with function header
and body; function header is same as function prototype without
semicolon; body of the function is enclosed in curly braces; real
argument that is passed during the function call replaces virtual
parameter n*/
    int i, num4;
    /*two integer type variables are declared; required memory
    spaces are allocated for the variables; these variables are
    local to the function create() and is not visible outside that
    function*/
    struct node *prev, *newn;
```

/*two struct node type pointers are declared; prev and newn are the addresses of two struct node type variables each has two members- item to store an integer and next to store address of another struct node type variable*/
**stnode = (struct node *)malloc(sizeof(struct node));**
/*sizeof() function computes the size of struct node type data, needed to store an integer and address of another node; required memory spaces are dynamically allocated by malloc(); address of the memory space is assigned to struct node type pointer variable stnode*/
**if (stnode == NULL)**
/*if memory cannot be assigned successfully malloc() returns a NULL to stnode; if the condition of if is true following statement is executed*/
 **printf("Memory cannot be allocated.");**
 /*printf() function displays the text in the quotations as it is on the screen*/
**else{**
/*if the above condition of if is false, following statements, enclosed in the curly braces, are executed*/
 **printf("\nInput data for node #1: ");**
 /*printf() function displays the text in the double quotations as it is on the screen except for a newline replaces \n*/
**scanf("%d", &num4);**
/*scanf() function reads an integer from input terminal and stores the value in the memory spaces allocated for the num4*/
**stnode->item = num4;**
/*value of num4 is assigned to the member item of the first node stnode of the linked list*/
**stnode->next = NULL;**
/*next pointer of the first node is set to NULL; there is no more node after that in the linked list*/
**prev = stnode;**
/*struct node type pointer prev refers to the first node of the linked list stnode*/
**for (i=2; i<=n; i++){**
/*this for loop creates other nodes of the linked list other than the first node; here i=2 is initialization, i<=n is condition and i++ is increment; initialization is done once at the beginning of the loop; then the condition is checked, if it is true statements in the body, enclosed by curly braces, are executed and value of i is incremented by 1 before the condition is re-checked; these steps continue until the condition becomes false in which case the program control flow exits the loop*/

```
newn = (struct node *)malloc(sizeof(struct node));
```
/*sizeof() function computes the size of struct node type data, needed to store an integer and address of another node; required memory spaces are dynamically allocated by malloc(); address of the memory space is assigned to struct node type pointer variable newn*/
```
if (newn == NULL){
```
/*if memory cannot be assigned successfully malloc() returns a NULL to newn; if the condition of if is true following statements, enclosed in the curly braces, are executed*/
```
    printf("Memory cannot be allocated.");
```
/*output function printf() displays the text in the quotations as it is on the screen*/
```
    break;
```
/*as memory cannot be allocated for the node, the program control flow immediately exits the loop*/
```
}
```
/*this closing curly brace specifies the end of 'if' with condition (newn == NULL)*/
```
else{
```
/*if the above condition of if is false, memory is successfully allocated for the node and the following statements, enclosed in the curly braces, are executed*/
```
    printf("Input data for node #%d: ", i);
```
/*output function printf() displays the text in the quotations as it is on the screen except for the value of i replaces the format specifier %d*/
```
    scanf("%d", &num4);
```
/*scanf() function reads an integer from input terminal and stores the value in the memory spaces allocated for the num4*/
```
    newn->item = num4;
```
/*value of num4 is assigned to the member item of the node newn of the linked list*/
```
    newn->next = NULL;
```
/*next pointer of the node is set to NULL; there is no more node after that in the linked list*/
```
    prev->next = newn;
```
/*newly created node newn is linked with the previous node prev by assigning the address of newn to the next pointer of the node prev*/
```
    prev = newn;
```
/*node prev now refers to the newly created node newn so that another node can be inserted after that prev (or newn) node in the next iteration of the loop*/
```
}
```

```
            /*this closing curly brace specifies the end of 'else'
            with if (newn == NULL)*/
       }
       /*this closing curly brace specifies the end of 'for' loop*/
       prev->next = stnode;
       /*prev refers to the last node created in the for loop; last
       node prev is linked with the first node stnode by assigning
       the address of stnode to the next pointer of the node prev*/
    }
    /*this closing curly brace specifies the end of 'else' with if
    (stnode == NULL)*/
}
/*this closing curly brace specifies the end of definition of
create() function; program control flow returns to the point where
the function was called*/
void insert(int nm){
/*definition of insert() function starts here with function header
and body; function header is same as function prototype without
semicolon; body of the function is enclosed in curly braces; real
argument that is passed during the function call replaces virtual
parameter nm*/
    struct node *newn, *curn;
    /*two struct node type pointers are declared; newn and curn are
    the addresses of two struct node type variables each has two
    members- item to store an integer and next to store address of
    another struct node type variable*/
    if (stnode == NULL)
    /*if starting node stnode is NULL above condition is true and
    following statement is executed*/
        printf("No data found in the List yet.");
        /*printf() function displays the text in the quotations as
        it is on the screen*/
    else{
    /*if the linked list is not empty then above condition of 'if'
    is false and the following statements, enclosed in the curly
    braces, are executed*/
        newn = (struct node *)malloc(sizeof(struct node));
        /*sizeof() function computes the size of struct node type
        data, needed to store an integer and address of another
        node; required memory spaces are dynamically allocated by
        malloc(); address of the memory space is assigned to struct
        node type pointer variable newn*/
        if (newn == NULL)
        /*if memory cannot be assigned successfully malloc() returns
        a NULL to newn; if the condition of if is true following
        statement is executed*/
            printf("Memory cannot be allocated.");
```

```
            /*printf() function displays the text in the quotations
            as it is on the screen*/
        else{
        /*if the above condition of if is false, following statements,
        enclosed in the curly braces, are executed*/
                newn->item = nm;
                /*value of nm is assigned to the member item of the new
                node newn of the linked list*/
                newn->next = stnode;
                /*next of new node newn refers to the starting or first
                node stnode*/
                curn = stnode;
                /*struct node type pointer curn refers to the starting
                node stnode*/
                while (curn->next!= stnode)
                /*this while loop finds the last node of the linked
                list; if the next of curn does not refer to the first
                node the condition is true and following statement
                is executed before the condition is re-checked; these
                steps continue until the condition becomes false in
                which case the program control flow exits the loop*/
                    curn = curn->next;
                    /*curn refers to the next node of the current node
                    curn so that next node can be checked in the next
                    iteration of the loop*/
                curn->next = newn;
                /*next of last node of the linked list curn refers to
                the new node newn*/
                stnode = newn;
                /*newly inserted node newn becomes the starting or
                first node of the linked list*/
        }
        /*this closing curly brace specifies the end of 'else' with
        if (newn == NULL)*/
    }
    /*this closing curly brace specifies the end of 'else' with if
    (stnode == NULL)*/
}
/*this closing curly brace specifies the end of definition of
insert() function; program control flow returns to the point where
the function was called*/
void display(int a){
/*definition of display() function starts here with function header
and body; function header is same as function prototype without
semicolon; body of the function is enclosed in curly braces; real
argument that is passed during the function call replaces virtual
parameter a*/
```

```
struct node *tmp;
```
/*struct node type pointer is declared; tmp is the address of struct node type variable that has two members- item to store an integer and next to store address of another struct node type variable*/
```
if (stnode == NULL)
```
/*if starting node stnode is NULL above condition is true and following statement is executed*/

   `printf("No data found in the List yet.");`
   /*printf() function displays the text in the quotations as it is on the screen*/
```
else{
```
/*if the linked list is not empty then above condition of 'if' is false and the following statements, enclosed in the curly braces, are executed*/

   `tmp = stnode;`
   /*struct node type pointer tmp refers to the first node stnode of the linked list*/
   `if (a==1)`
   /*if the condition of 'if' is true following statement is executed*/

      `printf("\nData entered in the list are:\n");`
      /*printf() function displays the text in the quotations as it is on the screen except for a newline replaces \n*/

   `else`
   /*if the condition of above 'if' is false following statement is executed*/

      `printf("\nAfter insertion the new list are:\n");`
      /*printf() function displays the text in the quotations as it is on the screen except for a newline replaces \n*/
```
do{
```
/*following statements, enclosed in the curly braces, are executed at the beginning of the loop*/

      `printf("%d, ", tmp->item);`
      /*printf() function displays the value of item of current node tmp on the screen in place of format specifier %d*/
      `tmp = tmp->next;`
      /*pointer tmp now refers to the next node of the current node so that the next node can be checked and displayed in the next iteration of the loop*/
```
}while (tmp!= stnode);
```
/*if the condition in the 'while' is true, the statements in body of 'do' are executed before the condition is re-checked; these steps continue until the condition becomes

> false in which case the program control flow exits the
> loop*/
> }
> /*this closing curly brace specifies the end of 'else' with if
> (stnode == NULL)*/
> }
> /*this closing curly brace specifies the end of the definition of
> display() function; program control flow returns to the point where
> the function was called*/

## PROBLEM-07
**Write a program to display the truth table of three input EX-OR gate.**

Flowchart of the Solution:

Figure 5.1 shows the flowchart followed to solve this problem.

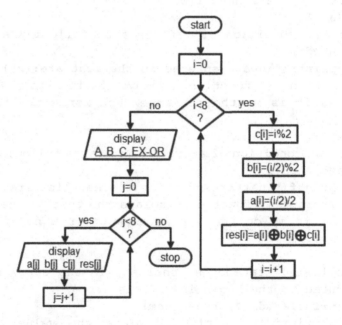

FIGURE 5.1    Flowchart followed to solve the problem.

## Algorithm of the Solution:

Step-1: Start

Step-2: Define struct exor with members a, b, c, and res

Step-3: Initialize i←0

Step-4: If i<8

    4.1: c[i]←i%2

    4.2: b[i]←(i/2)%2

    4.3: a[i]←(i/2)/2

    4.4: res[i]←a[i] ⊕ b[i] ⊕ c[i]

    4.5: i←i+1

    4.6: Go to Step-5

Step-5: Initialize j←0

Step-6: If j<8

    6.1: Display values of a[j], b[j], c[j], res[j]

    6.2: j←j+1

    6.3: Go to Step-6

Step-7: Stop

## Programming Code of the Solution:

```c
#include <stdio.h>
struct exor{
    int a, b, c, res;
};
int main(){
    int i, j;
    struct exor abc[8];
    for (i=0; i<8; i++){
        abc[i].c=i%2;
        abc[i].b=(i/2)%2;
        abc[i].a=(i/2)/2;
        abc[i].res=abc[i].a^abc[i].b^abc[i].c;
    }
    printf(" A\tB\tC\tEX-OR\n");
    printf("-------------------------------\n");
    for (j=0; j<8; j++)
        printf(" %d\t%d\t%d\t  %d\n", abc[j].a, abc[j].b,
                abc[j].c, abc[j].res);
    return 0;
}
```

Input and Output of the Executed Program:

| A | B | C | EX-OR |
|---|---|---|---|
| 0 | 0 | 0 | 0 |
| 0 | 0 | 1 | 1 |
| 0 | 1 | 0 | 1 |
| 0 | 1 | 1 | 0 |
| 1 | 0 | 0 | 1 |
| 1 | 0 | 1 | 0 |
| 1 | 1 | 0 | 0 |
| 1 | 1 | 1 | 1 |

## Explanation of the Programming Code:

```
#include <stdio.h>
```
/*header file stdio.h contains prototypes of the library functions printf() and scanf(); the header file must be included using preprocessor directive #include before the functions are called in the program*/
```
struct exor{
```
/*the keyword struct is used to create the structured data type exor, and its members are declared within the curly braces*/
```
    int a, b, c, res;
```
/*four integer type variables are declared, these are the members of the structured data type exor*/
```
};
```
/*definition of structured data type ends with the semicolon without declaring any variable of the defined data type exor*/
```
int main(){
```
/*all C program must have a main() function with return type void or int; here there is no parameter of the main() function and it returns an integer; opening curly brace specifies start of the main() function and no statement before that curly brace is executed by the compiler*/
```
    int i, j;
```
/*two integer type variables are declared here; required memory spaces are allocated for each variable*/
```
    struct exor abc[8];
```
/*structured exor type array abc of size 8 is declared; each array element abc[0], abc[1], . . . has four integer type members a, b, c and res*/
```
    for (i=0; i<8; i++){
```
/*this for loop is used to generate all 8 combination of 3-digit binary numbers from equivalent decimal numbers (0-7) and ex-or of each combination; i=0 is the initialization, i<8

is the condition and i++ is the increment; initialization is done once at the beginning of the loop; then the condition is checked, if it is true, then statements in the body are executed and value of i is incremented by 1 before the condition is re-checked; these steps continue until the condition becomes false at which point the program flow exits the loop*/

**abc[i].c=i%2;**

/*LSB is calculated from corresponding decimal numbers 0, 1, 2, . . . in each iteration and stored it in the member c of each array element abc[]; hence

After 1st iteration- abc[0].c=abc[0].c=i%2=0%2=0

After 2nd iteration- abc[1].c=abc[1].c=i%2=1%2=1

After 3rd iteration- abc[2].c=abc[2].c=i%2=2%2=0 and so on*/

**abc[i].b=(i/2)%2;**

/*middle-bit is calculated from corresponding decimal number 0, 1, 2, . . . . in each iteration and stored it in the member b of each array element abc[]; hence

After 1st iteration- abc[0].b=abc[0].b=(i/2)%2=(0/2)%2=0%2=0

After 2nd iteration- abc[1].b=abc[1].b=(i/2)%2=(1/2)%2=0%2=0

After 3rd iteration- abc[2].b=abc[2].b=(i/2)%2=(2/2)%2=1%2=1 and so on*/

**abc[i].a=(i/2)/2;**

/*MSB is calculated from corresponding decimal numbers 0, 1, 2, . . . in each iteration and stored it in the member a of each array element abc[]; hence

After 1st iteration- abc[0].a=abc[0].a=(i/2)/2=(0/2)/2=0/2=0

After 2nd iteration- abc[1].a=abc[1].a=(i/2)/2=(1/2)/2=0/2=0

After 3rd iteration- abc[2].a=abc[2].a=(i/2)/2=(2/2)/2=1/2=0 and so on*/

**abc[i].res=abc[i].a^abc[i].b^abc[i].c;**

/*EX-OR of particular combination of 3-digit binary number is calculated in each iteration and stored it in the member res of array element abc[]; hence

After 1st iteration- abc[0].res=abc[0].a^abc[0].b^abc[0].c =0^0^0=0

After 2nd iteration- abc[1].res=abc[1].a^abc[1].b^abc[1].c =0^0^1=1

After 3rd iteration- abc[2].res=abc[2].a^abc[2].b^abc[2].c =0^1^0=0 and so on*/

}

/*this is the end of 'for' loop*/

**printf(" A\tB\tC\tEX-OR\n");**

/*printf() function displays the text inside the double quotations as it is on the screen except for a tab replaces \t and a newline replaces \n*/

**printf("---------------------------\n");**

```
/*output library function printf() displays the text inside
the double quotations as it is on screen except for a newline
replaces \n*/
for (j=0; j<8; j++)
/*this for loop displays all combination of 3-digit binary numbers
and their corresponding ex-or; j=0 is the initialization, j<8 is
the condition and j++ is the increment; initialization is done
once at the beginning of the loop; then the condition is checked,
if it is true then statement in the body is executed and value of
j is incremented by 1 before the condition is re-checked; these
steps continue until the condition becomes false at which point the
program flow exits the loop*/
    printf(" %d\t%d\t%d\t %d\n", abc[j].a, abc[j].b, abc[j].c,
        abc[j].res);
    /*printf() function displays the text inside the double
    quotations as it is on screen except for a tab replaces
    \t and a newline replaces \n; here the value of abc[j].a
    replaces the 1st format specifier %d, the value of abc[j].b
    replaces the 2nd %d, the value of abc[j].c replaces the
    3rd %d and the value of abc[j].res replaces the 4th
    %d; value of j is incremented by 1 from 0 to 7 in each
    iteration*/
return 0;
/*0 is returned as it is the standard for the successful
execution of the program*/
}
/*this closing curly brace specifies the end of main() function; no
statement is executed after that point*/
```

## PROBLEM-08
**Write a program that uses functions to perform the following operations:**

(a) Reading a complex number

(b) Writing a complex number

(c) Addition of two complex numbers

(d) Multiplication of two complex numbers

Flowchart of the Solution:

Figure 5.2 shows the flowcharts followed to solve this problem.

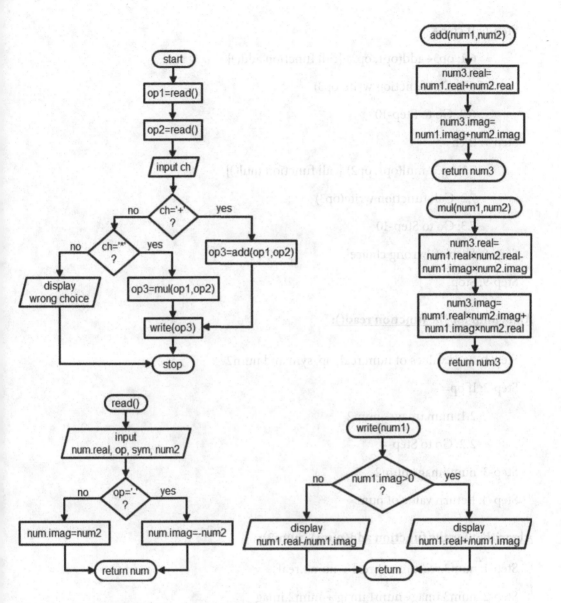

FIGURE 5.2    Flowcharts followed to solve the problem.

## Algorithm of the Solution:

Step-1: Start

Step-2: Define struct complex with members real and imag

Step-3: op1←read() [call function read()]

Step-4: op2←read() [call function read()]

Step-5: Read value of ch

Step-6: If ch='+'

      6.1: op3←add(op1, op2) [call function add()]

      6.2: Call function write(op3)

      6.3: Go to Step-10

Step-7: If ch='*'

      7.1: op3←mul(op1, op2) [call function mul()]

      7.2: Call function write(op3)

      7.3: Go to Step-10

Step-8: Display 'wrong choice'

Step-9: Stop

## Algorithm for the function read():

Step-1: Read values of num.real, op, sym and num2

Step-2: If op='-'

      2.1: num.imag←-num2

      2.2: Go to Step-4

Step-3: num.imag←num2

Step-4: Return value of num

## Algorithm for the function add(num1, num2):

Step-1: num3.real←num1.real + num2.real

Step-2: num3.imag←num1.imag + num2.imag

Step-3: Return value of num3

## Algorithm for the function mul(num1, num2):

Step-1: num3.real←num1.real×num2.real − num1.imag×num2.imag

Step-2: num3.imag← num1.real×num2.imag + num1.imag×num2.real

Step-3: Return value of num3

## Algorithm for the function write(num1):

Step-1: If num1.imag>0

1.1: Display value of num1.real+*i*num1.imag

1.2: Go to Step-2

Step-2: Display value of num1.real-*i*num1.imag

Step-3: Return

<u>Programming Code of the Solution:</u>

```c
#include<stdio.h>
#include<conio.h>
struct complex add(struct complex num1, struct complex num2);
struct complex mul(struct complex num1, struct complex num2);
void write(struct complex num1);
struct complex read();
struct complex{
    float real, imag;
};
int main(){
    struct complex op1, op2, op3;
    char ch;
    printf("Enter 1st complex number ");
    op1=read();
    printf("Enter 2nd complex number ");
    op2=read();
    printf("Enter + for addition, * for multiplication: ");
    ch=getche();

    switch (ch){
        case '+':
            op3=add(op1, op2);
            printf("\n");
            write(op1);
            printf(" + ");
            write(op2);
            printf(" = ");
            write(op3);
            printf("\n");
            break;
        case '*':
            op3=mul(op1, op2);
            printf("\n");
            write(op1);
            printf(" * ");
            write(op2);
            printf(" = ");
            write(op3);
            printf("\n");
```

```c
                break;
            default:
                printf("Entered wrong choice, quitting...");
    }
    return 0;
}
struct complex read(){
    struct complex num;
    char op, sym;
    float num2;
    printf("(num1+inum2 or num1-inum2): ");
    scanf("%f%c%c%f", &num.real, &op, &sym, &num2);
    if (op=='-')
        num.imag=-num2;
    else
        num.imag=num2;
    return num;
}
struct complex add(struct complex num1, struct complex num2){
    struct complex num3;
    num3.real=num1.real+num2.real;
    num3.imag=num1.imag+num2.imag;
    return num3;
}
struct complex mul(struct complex num1, struct complex num2){
    struct complex num3;
    num3.real=num1.real*num2.real-num1.imag*num2.imag;
    num3.imag=num1.real*num2.imag+num1.imag*num2.real;
    return num3;
}
void write(struct complex num1){
    if (num1.imag>=0)
        printf("(%0.2f+i%0.2f)", num1.real, num1.imag);
    else
        printf("(%0.2f-i%0.2f)", num1.real, num1.imag);
}
```

Input and Output of the Executed Program:

```
Enter 1st complex number (num1+inum2 or num1-inum2): 1.2+i1.5
Enter 2nd complex number (num1+inum2 or num1-inum2): 3.7+i8.3
Enter + for addition, * for multiplication: +
(1.20+i1.50) + (3.70+i8.30) = (4.90+i9.80)
```

```
Enter 1st complex number (num1+inum2 or num1-inum2): 3+i1.3
Enter 2nd complex number (num1+inum2 or num1-inum2): 3.4+i4.2
Enter + for addition, * for multiplication: *
(3.00+i1.30) * (3.40+i4.20) = (4.74+i17.02)
```

## Explanation of the Programming Code:

```
#include<stdio.h>
```
/*header file stdio.h contains prototypes of the library functions printf(), and scanf(); the header file must be included using preprocessor directive #include before the functions are called in the program*/
```
#include<conio.h>
```
/*header file conio.h contains prototypes of the nonstandard library function getche(); the header file must be included using preprocessor directive #include before the function is called in the program*/
```
struct complex add(struct complex num1, struct complex num2);
```
/*this is the prototype (or declaration) of the user-defined function add() that must end with a semicolon; add() takes two struct complex type values as parameters, performs some predefined operations, and returns a struct complex type value*/
```
struct complex mul(struct complex num1, struct complex num2);
```
/*another user-defined function mul() is declared that must end with a semicolon; struct complex is the return type, mul is the function name, and num1 and num2 are two struct complex type parameters passed to the function*/
```
void write(struct complex num1);
```
/*this is the declaration of user-defined function write() that must end with a semicolon; this function takes struct complex type variable num1 as argument, displays the complex number num1 in appropriate form and returns nothing*/
```
struct complex read();
```
/*this is the declaration of user-defined function read() that must end with a semicolon; this function has no argument, it reads a complex number from keyboard and returns the number*/
```
struct complex{
```
/*structured data type complex is created using keyword struct; its members are declared within the curly braces*/
```
    float real, imag;
```
/*two float type variables are declared, these are the members of the structured data type complex*/
```
};
```
/*definition of struct complex type data ends with a semicolon; no variable of the defined data type struct complex is declared here*/
```
int main(){
```
/*all C program must have a main() function with return type void or int; here there is no parameter of the main() function and it returns an integer; opening curly brace specifies start of the main() function and no statement before that curly brace is executed by the compiler*/

```
struct complex op1, op2, op3;
/*three structured complex type variables are declared here;
each of the variables has two float type members real and imag
that can be accessed through dot (.) operator*/
char ch;
/*character type variable ch is declared; required memory space
of 1 byte is allocated for the variable*/
printf("Enter 1st complex number: ");
/*printf() function displays the text inside the double
quotations as it is on the screen*/
op1=read();
/*user-defined function read() is called, program control flow
shifts to the definition of the function, function read() reads
a complex number from keyboard and returns the value that is
assigned to variable op1*/
printf("Enter 2nd complex number: ");
/*printf() function displays the text inside the double
quotations as it is on the screen*/
op2=read();
/*user-defined function read() is called, program control flow
shifts to the definition of the function, function read() reads
a complex number from the keyboard and returns the value that
is assigned to variable op2*/
printf("Enter + for addition, * for multiplication: ");
/*printf() function displays the text inside the double
quotations as it is on the screen*/
ch=getche();
/*library function getche() is called that reads a character
from keyboard and assign the value to variable ch; the input
character is echoed on the screen immediately without waiting
for enter to be pressed*/
switch (ch){
/*switch..case is used to choose different sets of statements
to be executed depending on different option; here the value of
char type variable ch is checked and based on the value program
control shifts to any one of the following cases, each case has
single or multiple statements to be executed*/
    case '+':
    /*if ch='+', then all the statements under this case are
    executed*/
        op3=add(op1, op2);
        /*user-defined function add() is called with real
        parameters op1 and op2, program control flow shifts
        to the definition of function add(); add() does some
        defined operation and returns a value that is stored
        in op3*/
        printf("\n");
```

```
/*this printf() function displays a newline on the
screen*/
write(op1);
/*user-defined function write() is called with op1
passed to the function as real parameter; program
control flow shifts to the definition of function
write()*/
printf(" + ");
/*printf() function displays the text inside the double
quotations as it is on the screen*/
write(op2);
/*user-defined function write() is called with op2
passed to the function as real parameter; program
control flow shifts to the definition of function
write()*/
printf(" = ");
/*printf() function displays the text inside the double
quotations as it is on the screen*/
write(op3);
/*user-defined function write() is called with op3
passed to the function as real parameter; program
control flow shifts to the definition of function
write()*/
printf("\n");
/*this printf() function displays a newline on the
screen*/
break;
/*this break statement causes the program control flow
exits the switch..case without executing any of the
following statements inside the switch..case*/
case '*':
/*if ch='*', then all the statements under this case are
executed*/
op3=mul(op1, op2);
/*user-defined function mul() is called with real
parameters op1 and op2, program control flow shifts
to the definition of function mul(); mul() does some
defined operation and returns a value that is stored
in op3*/
printf("\n");
/*this printf() function displays a newline on the
screen*/
write(op1);
/*user-defined function write() is called with op1
passed to the function as real parameter; program
control flow shifts to the definition of function
write()*/
```

```
    printf(" * ");
    /*printf() function displays the text inside the double
    quotations as it is on the screen*/
    write(op2);
    /*user-defined function write() is called with op2 passed
    to the function as real parameter; program control flow
    shifts to the definition of function write()*/
    printf(" = ");
    /*printf() function displays the text inside the double
    quotations as it is on the screen*/
    write(op3);
    /*user-defined function write() is called with op3 passed
    to the function as real parameter; program control flow
    shifts to the definition of function write()*/
    printf("\n");
    /*this printf() function displays a newline on the
    screen*/
    break;
    /*this break statement causes the program control flow
    exits the switch..case without executing any of the
    following statements inside the switch..case*/
default:
/*if ch equals neither '+' nor '*', then any of the above
cases does not match and statement under this default is
executed*/
    printf("Entered wrong choice, quitting . . . ");
    /*printf() function displays text inside the double
    quotations as it is on the screen; as default is
    the last level to be executed, after this statement,
    program control flow immediately exits the switch..
    case*/
}
/*this closing curly brace specifies the end of switch..
case*/
return 0;
/*0 is returned as it is the standard for the successful
execution of the program*/
}
/*the closing curly brace specifies the end of the main() function's
body, as well as the program's end; after that curly brace, no
statement is executed*/
struct complex read(){
/*definition of read() function starts here with function header
and body; function header is same as function prototype without
semicolon; body of the function is enclosed in curly braces*/
    struct complex num;
```

```
/*newly defined struct complex type variable num is declared
here that has two float type members real and imag; both members
can be accessed using dot (.) operator*/
char op, sym;
/*two character type variables are declared; op will be used
to store sign and sym will be used to store symbol i of the
imaginary part of complex number*/
float num2;
/*float type variable num2 is declared that is used to store
value of the imaginary part of complex number*/
printf("(num1+inum2 or num1-inum2) ");
/*printf() function displays text inside the double quotation
as it is on the screen; this printf() gives a text to users
about format of entering complex number and it might be real
part followed by +i/-i followed by imaginary part*/
scanf("%f%c%c%f", &num.real, &op, &sym, &num2);
/*this scanf() function takes four inputs with format displayed
in the above printf(); 1st float number corresponds to first
member real of struct complex type variable num that is accessed
using dot(.) and address operator & as &num.real; 2nd and 3rd
characters correspond to char type variables op and sym; 4th
float number corresponds to variable num2*/
if (op=='-')
/*this if..else initialize second member of the struct complex
type variable num depending on input; if value of op is '-'
then the condition of 'if' is true and following statement
executes*/
    num.imag=-num2;
    /*value of num2 with - ve sign is assigned to num.imag,
    that is, to second member of struct complex type variable
    num*/
else
/*if condition of above 'if' is false, means value of op is '+'
then following statement executes*/
    num.imag=num2;
    /*value of num2 with +ve sign is assigned to num.imag,
    that is, to second member of struct complex type variable
    num*/
return num;
/*here value of num that has two members real and imag is
returned to the point from where the function read() was
called*/
}
/*this closing curly brace specifies the end of read() function
definition*/
struct complex add(struct complex num1, struct complex num2){
```

/*definition of add() function starts here with function header and body; function header is same as function prototype without semicolon; body of the function is enclosed in curly braces; here num1 and num2 are virtual parameters that are replaced with corresponding real parameters used to call the function*/

 **struct complex num3;**

 /*newly defined struct complex type variable num3 is declared here that has two float type members real and imag; both members can be accessed using dot (.) operator*/

 **num3.real=num1.real+num2.real;**

 /*real parts of both the numbers num1 and num2 are added and the summation value is assigned to member real of num3*/

 **num3.imag=num1.imag+num2.imag;**

 /*imaginary parts of both the numbers num1 and num2 are added and the summation value is assigned to member image of num3*/

 **return num3;**

 /*num3 contains the summation of the two complex numbers and the result is returned to the point from where the function add() was called*/

**}**

/*this closing curly brace specifies the end of add() function definition*/

**struct complex mul(struct complex num1, struct complex num2){**

/*this is the header for the user-defined function mul(), which must be identical to the function prototype except for no semicolon is used; the function is defined within the curly braces; in this definition, the value of real parameters replace the virtual parameters num1 and num2*/

 **struct complex num3;**

 /*newly defined struct complex type variable num3 is declared here that has two float type members real and imag; both members can be accessed using dot (.) operator; the variable num3 is local to the function mul() and is not visible outside the function;*/

 **num3.real=num1.real*num2.real-num1.imag*num2.imag;**

 /*imaginary parts of both complex numbers num1 and num2 are multiplied and subtracted from the multiplication of real parts of both complex numbers; the result is assigned to member real of num3*/

 **num3.imag=num1.real*num2.imag+num1.imag*num2.real;**

 /*imaginary part of 1st complex number num1 is multiplied with real part of 2nd complex number num2 and subtracted from the multiplication of real part of num1 and imaginary part of num2; the result is assigned to member real of num3*/

 **return num3;**

```
    /*num3 contains the multiplication of the two complex numbers
    and it is returned to the point where the function mul() was
    called*/
}
void write(struct complex num1){
/*this is the header for the user-defined function write(), which
must be identical to the function prototype except for no semicolon
is used; the function is defined within the curly braces; in this
definition the value of real parameter replaces the virtual parameter
num1*/
    if (num1.imag>=0)
    /*this 'if' checks the sign of imaginary part of the complex
    number; imaginary part is stored in the second member of struct
    complex type variable num1 which is accessed using dot (.)
    operator; if the condition is true, then following statement is
    executed*/
        printf("(%0.2f+i%0.2f)", num1.real, num1.imag);
        /*printf() function displays text inside the double
        quotations as it is on the screen except for value of num1.
        real replaces the first format specifier %0.2f with two
        decimal points precision and value of num1.imag replaces
        the second %0.2f*/
else
/* if the condition of above 'if' is false, means the imaginary
part of the complex number has -ve sign then following statement
is xecuted*/
        printf("(%0.2f-i%0.2f)", num1.real, num1.imag);
        /*printf() function displays text inside the double quotations
        as it is on the screen except for value of num1.real replaces
        1st format specifier %0.2f with two decimal points precision
        and value of num1.imag replaces the 2nd format specifier %0.2f*/
}
/*this closing curly brace specifies the end of write() function
definition*/
```

## PROBLEM-09

The marks distribution for attendance of the Department of EEE, Dhaka University, is given below:

| Attendance | Marks | Attendance | Marks |
|---|---|---|---|
| 90% and above | 5.0 | 70% to <75% | 3.0 |
| 80% to <90% | 4.5 | 65% to <70% | 2.5 |
| 70% to <80% | 4.0 | 60% to <65% | 2.0 |
| 60% to <70% | 3.5 | Less than 60% | 0.0 |

There were 30 classes of EEE-1102 in the current session. Calculate the obtained attendance marks of the following n students:

| Class Roll | No. of Classes | Class Roll | No. of Classes |
| --- | --- | --- | --- |
| 101 | 27 | 106 | 28 |
| 102 | 15 | 107 | 12 |
| 103 | 21 | 108 | 27 |
| 104 | 19 | 109 | 9 |
| 105 | 12 | 110 | 28 |

### Flowchart of the Solution:

Figure 5.3 shows the flowcharts followed to solve this problem.

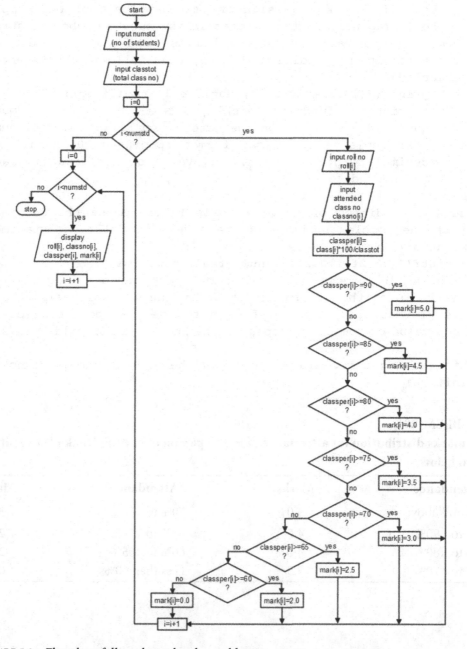

FIGURE 5.3   Flowchart followed to solve the problem.

## Algorithm of the Solution:

Step-1: Start

Step-2: Define struct atten with members roll, classno, classper and mark

Step-3: Read values of numstd and classtot

Step-4: Initialize i←0

Step-5: If i<numstd

    5.1: Read values of stud[i].roll and stud[i].classno

    5.2: stud[i].classper←(stud[i].classno)/classtot)×100

    5.3: If stud[i].classper>=90.0

        5.3.1: stud[i].mark←5.0

        5.3.2: Go to Step-6.11

    5.4: If stud[i].classper>=85.0

        5.4.1: stud[i].mark←4.5

        5.4.2: Go to Step-6.11

    5.5: If stud[i].classper>=80.0

        5.5.1: stud[i].mark←4.0

        5.5.2: Go to Step-6.11

    5.6: If stud[i].classper>=75.0

        5.6.1: stud[i].mark←3.5

        5.6.2: Go to Step-6.11

    5.7: If stud[i].classper>=70.0

        5.7.1: stud[i].mark←3.0

        5.7.2: Go to Step-6.11

    5.8: If stud[i].classper>=65.0

        5.8.1: stud[i].mark←2.5

        5.8.2: Go to Step-6.11

    5.9: If stud[i].classper>=60.0

        5.9.1: stud[i].mark←2.0

        5.9.2: Go to Step-6.11

5.10: stud[i].mark←0.0

5.11: i←i+1

5.12: Go to Step-5

Step-6: Display values of classes and classtot

Step-7: Initialize i←0

Step-8: If i<numstd

8.1: Display values of stud[i].roll, stud[i].classno, stud[i].classper, and stud[i].mark

8.2: i←i+1

8.3: Go to Step-8

Step-9: Stop

Programming Code of the Solution:

```c
#include <stdio.h>
struct atten{
    int roll, classno;
    float classper, mark;
};
int main(){
    struct atten stud[100];
    int numstd, classtot, i;
    printf("Enter the number of students: ");
    scanf("%d", &numstd);
    printf("Enter total number of classes taken: ");
    scanf("%d", &classtot);
    for (i=0; i<numstd; i++){
        printf("\nEnter the roll no. of student #%d: ", i+1);
        scanf("%d", &stud[i].roll);
        printf("Enter number of classes attended: ");
        scanf("%d", &stud[i].classno);
        stud[i].classper=((stud[i].classno)/((float) classtot))*100;

        if (stud[i].classper>=90.0)
            stud[i].mark=5.0;
        else if (stud[i].classper>=85.0)
            stud[i].mark=4.5;
        else if (stud[i].classper>=80.0)
            stud[i].mark=4.0;
        else if (stud[i].classper>=75.0)
            stud[i].mark=3.5;
        else if (stud[i].classper>=70.0)
            stud[i].mark=3.0;
        else if (stud[i].classper>=65.0)
            stud[i].mark=2.5;
        else if (stud[i].classper>=60.0)
            stud[i].mark=2.0;
        else
            stud[i].mark=0.0;
    }
```

```
    printf("\nTotal number of classes: %d\n", classtot);
    printf("Roll No.\tAttended Class\tPercentage\tObtained Marks\n");
    printf("----------------------------------------------------------\n");
    for (i=0; i<numstd; i++)
        printf("%d\t\t%d\t\t%0.2f\t\t%0.1f\n", stud[i].roll,
                stud[i].classno, stud[i].classper, stud[i].mark);
    return 0;
}
```

## Input and Output of the Executed Program:

```
Enter the number of students: 4
Enter total number of classes taken: 30

Enter the roll no. of student #1: 101
Enter number of classes attended: 27

Enter the roll no. of student #2: 102
Enter number of classes attended: 15

Enter the roll no. of student #3: 103
Enter number of classes attended: 21

Enter the roll no. of student #4: 104
Enter number of classes attended: 19

Total number of classes: 30
Roll No.        Attended Class  Percentage        Obtained Marks
-----------------------------------------------------------------
101             27              90.00             5.0
102             15              50.00             0.0
103             21              70.00             3.0
104             19              63.33             2.0
```

## Explanation of the Programming Code:

```
#include <stdio.h>
```
/*header file stdio.h contains prototypes of the library functions printf(), and scanf(); the header file must be included using preprocessor directive #include before the functions are called in the program*/
```
struct atten{
```
/*structured data type atten is created using keyword struct; its members are declared within the curly braces*/
```
    int roll, classno;
```
/*two int type variables are declared, these are the members of the data type struct atten*/
```
    float classper, mark;
```

```
    /*two float type variables are declared as members of the
    structured data type atten*/
};
/*definition of structured data type must end with a semicolon;
no variable of the defined data type struct atten is declared
here*/
int main(){
/*all C program must have a main() function with return type void
or int; here there is no parameter of the main() function and it
returns an integer; opening curly brace specifies start of the
main() function and no statement before that curly brace is executed
by the compiler*/
    struct atten stud[100];
    /*struct atten type array of size 100 is declared; each of the
    array element has two integer type members roll and classno, and
    two float type members classper and mark that can be accessed
    using dot (.) operator*/
    int numstd, classtot, i;
    /*three integer type variables are declared and required memory
    spaces are allocated for these variables to store data*/
    printf("Enter the number of students: ");
    /*output function printf() displays the text in the quotations
    as it is on the screen*/
    scanf("%d", &numstd);
    /*function scanf() reads an integer from input terminal and
    stores the value in the memory spaces allocated for the variable
    numstd*/
    printf("Enter total number of classes taken: ");
    /*output function printf() displays the text in the quotations
    as it is on the screen*/
    scanf("%d", &classtot);
    /*function scanf() reads an integer from input terminal and stores
    it in the memory spaces allocated for the variable classtot*/
    for (i=0; i<numstd; i++){
    /*here i=0 is initialization, i<numstd is condition and i++ is
    increment; initialization is done once at the beginning of the
    loop; then the condition is checked, if it is true statements in
    the body, enclosed by curly braces, are executed and value of i
    is incremented by 1 before the condition is re-checked; these
    steps continue until the condition becomes false in which case
    the program control flow exits the loop*/
        printf("\nEnter the roll no. of student #%d: ", i+1);
        /*output function printf() displays the text in the
        quotations as it is on the screen except for the value
        of i+1 replaces the format specifier %d and a newline
        replaces \n*/
```

```
scanf("%d", &stud[i].roll);
/*function scanf() reads an integer from input terminal and
stores it in the member roll of struct atten type array
element stud[]; in each iteration roll number of individual
student is read*/
printf("Enter number of classes attended: ");
/*output function printf() displays the text in the
quotations as it is on the screen*/
scanf("%d", &stud[i].classno);
/*function scanf() reads an integer from input terminal
and stores it in the member classno of struct atten type
array element stud[]; in each iteration number of classes
attended for individual student is read*/
stud[i].classper=((stud[i].classno)/((float) classtot))*100;
/*this arithmetic operation calculates percentage of classes
attended by a student in each iteration; here classtot is
converted to float so that the division operation gives
decimal result rather than integer*/
if (stud[i].classper>=90.0)
/*if the condition is true, means class percentage of a
particular student is greater than or equal to 90, following
statement is executed*/
    stud[i].mark=5.0;
    /*if class percentage of a student is greater than or
    equal to 90 then his mark is 5.0*/
else if (stud[i].classper>=85.0)
/*if the condition is true, means class percentage of a
particular student is between 85 and 90, following statement
is executed*/
    stud[i].mark=4.5;
    /*value 4.5 is assigned to member mark of a particular
    student*/
else if (stud[i].classper>=80.0)
/*if the condition is true, means class percentage of a
particular student is between 80 and 85, following statement
is executed*/
    stud[i].mark=4.0;
    /*value 4.0 is assigned to member mark of a particular
    student*/
else if (stud[i].classper>=75.0)
/*if the condition is true, means class percentage of a
particular student is between 75 and 80, following statement
is executed*/
    stud[i].mark=3.5;
    /*value 3.5 is assigned to member mark of a particular
    student*/
```

```
else if (stud[i].classper>=70.0)
/*if the condition is true, means class percentage of a
particular student is between 70 and 75, following statement
is executed*/
    stud[i].mark=3.0;
    /*value 3.0 is assigned to member mark of a particular
    student*/
else if (stud[i].classper>=65.0)
/*if the condition is true, means class percentage of a
particular student is between 65 and 70, following statement
is executed*/
    stud[i].mark=2.5;
    /*value 2.5 is assigned to member mark of a particular
    student*/
else if (stud[i].classper>=60.0)
/*if the condition is true, means class percentage of a
particular student is between 60 and 65, following statement
is executed*/
    stud[i].mark=2.0;
    /*value 2.0 is assigned to member mark of a particular
    student*/
else
/*if all the above condition is false, means class percentage
of a particular student is less than 60, following statement
executed*/
    stud[i].mark=0.0;
    /*value 0.0 is assigned to member mark of a particular
    student*/
}
/*this closing curly brace specifies the end of 'for' loop*/
printf("\nTotal number of classes: %d\n", classtot);
/*output function printf() displays the text in the quotations
as it is on the screen except for the value of classtot replaces
the format specifier %d and a newline replaces \n*/
printf("Roll No. \tAttended Class \tPercentage \tObtained"
        " Marks\n");
/*output function printf() displays the text in the quotations
as it is on the screen except for a newline replaces \n and a
tab replaces \t*/
printf("------------------------------------------------------\n");
/*output function printf() displays the text in the quotations
as it is on the screen except for a newline replaces \n*/
for (i=0; i<numstd; i++)
/*here i=0 is initialization, i<numstd is condition and i++ is
increment; initialization is done once at the beginning of the
```

loop; then the condition is checked, if it is true statement in the body is executed and value of i is incremented by 1 before the condition is re-checked; these steps continue until the condition becomes false in which case the program control flow exits the loop*/

```
    printf("%d\t\t%d\t\t%0.2f\t\t%0.1f\n", stud[i].roll,
            stud[i].classno, stud[i].classper, stud[i].mark);
```

/*output function printf() displays the text in the quotations as it is on the screen except for the value of stud[i].roll replaces the 1st format specifier %d, value of stud[i].classno replaces the 2nd %d, value of stud[i]. classper replaces the 3rd format specifier %0.2f with two decimal points precision, value of stud[i].mark replaces the 4th %0.1f with single decimal point precision, a newline replaces \n and a tab replaces \t*/

**return 0;**

/*0 is returned as it is the standard for the successful execution of the program*/

```
}
```
/*the closing curly brace specifies the end of the main() function's body, as well as the program's end; after that curly brace, no statement is executed*/

## PROBLEM-10

**Answer scripts of final examination of the Department of EEE, Dhaka University, have been examined by two examiners independently. The obtained final marks of any course will be average of the two marks. But, if their marks for any particular script differ by 20% or more, then the script is evaluated by another independent third examiner. And the obtained final marks of that course will be average of the two marks of the examiners whose marks are closer. Write a program to read the following data and determine:**

(a) Whether third examination is necessary for a particular answer script.

(b) Obtained final marks (out of 70) by each student of a particular course after third examination if necessary.

| Roll No. | 1st Examiner | 2nd Examiner | Roll No. | 1st Examiner | 2nd Examiner |
|----------|--------------|--------------|----------|--------------|--------------|
| 1001 | 65 | 58 | 1004 | 68 | 48 |
| 1002 | 55 | 54 | 1005 | 50 | 52 |
| 1003 | 40 | 30 | 1006 | 15 | 32 |

Flowchart of the Solution:

Figure 5.4 shows the flowcharts followed to solve this problem.

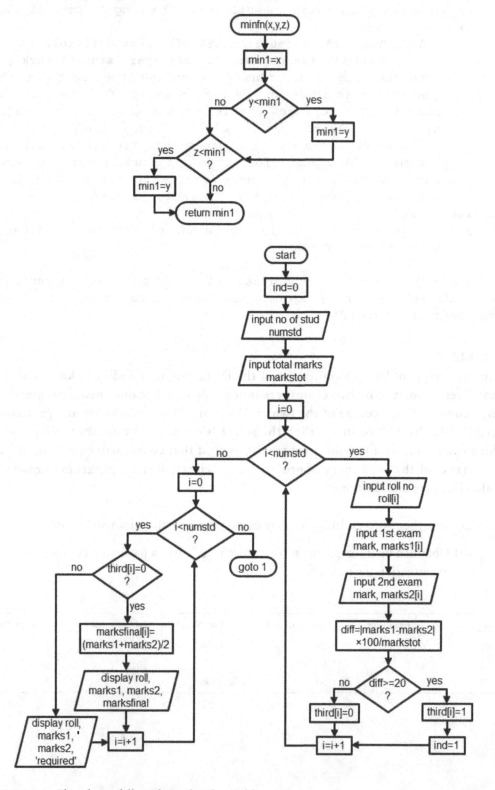

FIGURE 5.4   Flowcharts followed to solve the problem.

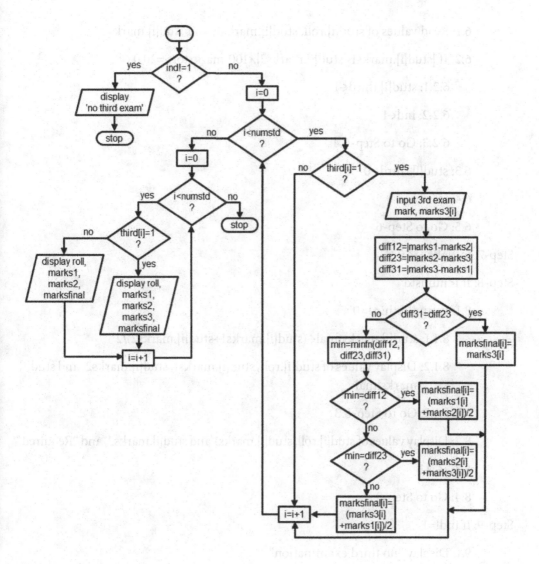

FIGURE 5.4 (Continued)

## Algorithm of the Solution:

Step-1: Start

Step-2: Define struct marks with members roll, marks1, marks2, marks3, third and marksfinal

Step-3: Initialize ind←0

Step-4: Read values of numstd and markstot

Step-5: Initialize i←0

Step-6: If i<numstd

6.1: Read values of stud[i].roll, stud[i].marks1, and stud[i].marks2

6.2: If |stud[i].marks1−stud[i].marks2|×100/markstot>=20.0

6.2.1: stud[i].third←1

6.2.2: ind←1

6.2.3: Go to Step-6.4

6.3: stud[i].third←0

6.4: i←i+1

6.5: Go to Step-6

Step-7: Initialize i←0

Step-8: If i<numstd

8.1: If stud[i].third=0

8.1.1: stud[i].marksfinal←(stud[i].marks1+stud[i].marks2)/2

8.1.2: Display values of stud[i].roll, stud[i].marks1, stud[i].marks2, and stud[i].marksfinal

8.1.3: Go to Step-8.3

8.2: Display values of stud[i].roll, stud[i].marks1 and stud[i].marks2, and "Required"

8.3: i←i+1

8.4: Go to Step-8

Step-9: If ind!=1

9.1: Display "no third examination"

9.2: Go to Step-14

Step-10: Initialize i←0

Step-11: If i<numstd

11.1: If stud[i].third=1

11.1.1: Read value of stud[i].marks3

11.1.2: diff12←|stud[i].marks1−stud[i].marks2|

11.1.3: diff23←|stud[i].marks2−stud[i].marks3|

11.1.4: diff31←|stud[i].marks1−stud[i].marks3|

11.1.5: If diff23=diff31

11.1.5.1: stud[i].marksfinal←stud[i].marks3

11.1.5.2: Go to Step-11.2

11.1.6: min←minfn(diff12, diff23, diff31)

11.1.6.1: If min=diff12

11.1.6.1.1: stud[i].marksfinal←(stud[i].marks1+ stud[i].marks2)/2

11.1.6.1.1: Go to Step-11.2

11.1.6.2: If min=diff23

11.1.6.2.1: stud[i].marksfinal←(stud[i].marks2+ stud[i].marks3)/2

11.1.6.2.2: Go to Step-11.2

11.1.6.3: stud[i].marksfinal←(stud[i].marks3+ stud[i].marks1)/2

11.2: i←i+1

11.3: Go to Step-11

Step-12: Initialize i←0

Step-13: If i<numstd

13.1: If stud[i].third=1

13.1.1: Display values of stud[i].roll, stud[i].marks1, stud[i].marks2, stud[i].marks3, and stud[i].marksfinal

13.1.2: Go to Step-14.3

13.2: Display values of stud[i].roll, stud[i].marks1, stud[i].marks2, and stud[i].marksfinal

13.3: i←i+1

13.4: Go to Step-13

Step-14: Stop

## Algorithm for the function minfn(x, y, z):

Step-1: Declare and initialize min1←x

Step-2: If y<min1

2.1: min1←y

Step-3: If z<min1

3.1: min1←z

Step-4: Return value of min1

Programming Code of the Solution:

```c
#include <stdio.h>
#include <stdlib.h>
#include <math.h>
struct marks{
    int roll;
    int marks1, marks2, marks3;
    int third, marksfinal;
};
int minfn(int x, int y, int z){
    int min1=x;
    if (y<min1)
        min1=y;
    if (z<min1)
        min1=z;
    return min1;
}
int main(){
    struct marks stud[100];
    int numstd, markstot, ind=0, i;
    int diff12, diff23, diff31, min;
    printf("Enter number of students: ");
    scanf("%d", &numstd);
    printf("Enter total marks of the exam: ");
    scanf("%d", &markstot);
    for (i=0; i<numstd; i++){
        printf("\nEnter roll no. of student #%d: ", i+1);
        scanf("%d", &stud[i].roll);
        printf("Enter marks of 1st examiner: ");
        scanf("%d", &stud[i].marks1);
        printf("Enter marks of 2nd examiner: ");
        scanf("%d", &stud[i].marks2);
        if (abs(stud[i].marks1-stud[i].marks2)*100/
            (float) markstot>=20.0){
            stud[i].third=1;
            ind=1;
        }
        else
            stud[i].third=0;
    }
    printf("\nRoll No.\t1st Examiner\t2nd Examiner\t3rd Examiner"
        "\tFinal Marks\n");
    printf("---------------------------------------------------------------\n");
    for (i=0; i<numstd; i++)
        if (stud[i].third==0){
            stud[i].marksfinal=ceil((stud[i].marks1+
                                    (float) stud[i].marks2)/2);
```

```
            printf("%d\t\t%d\t\t%d\t\t%c\t\t%d\n", stud[i].roll,
                    stud[i].marks1, stud[i].marks2, ' ',
                    stud[i].marksfinal);
        }
        else
            printf("%d\t\t%d\t\t%d\t\t%s\n", stud[i].roll,
                    stud[i].marks1, stud[i].marks2, "Required");
if (ind!=1)
    printf("\nThere is no third examination and the above result"
            " is final.\n");
else{
    for (i=0; i<numstd; i++){
        if (stud[i].third==1){
            printf("\nEnter 3rd examiner marks of roll %d: ",
                    stud[i].roll);
            scanf("%d", &stud[i].marks3);
            diff12=abs(stud[i].marks1-stud[i].marks2);
            diff23=abs(stud[i].marks2-stud[i].marks3);
            diff31=abs(stud[i].marks1-stud[i].marks3);
            if (diff23==diff31)
                stud[i].marksfinal=stud[i].marks3;
            else{
                min=minfn(diff12, diff23, diff31);
                if (min==diff12)
                    stud[i].marksfinal=ceil((stud[i].marks1+
                                        (float) stud[i].marks2)/2);
                else if (min==diff23)
                    stud[i].marksfinal=ceil((stud[i].marks2+
                                        (float) stud[i].marks3)/2);
                else
                    stud[i].marksfinal=ceil((stud[i].marks3+
                                        (float) stud[i].marks1)/2);
            }
        }
    }
    printf("\nFinal result after third examination");
    printf("\nRoll No.\t1st Examiner\t2nd Examiner\t3rd Examiner"
            "\tFinal Marks\n");
    printf("------------------------------------------------------------\n");
    for (i=0; i<numstd; i++)
        if (stud[i].third==1)
            printf("%d\t\t%d\t\t%d\t\t%d\t\t%d\n", stud[i].roll,
                    stud[i].marks1, stud[i].marks2, stud[i].marks3,
                    stud[i].marksfinal);
        else
            printf("%d\t\t%d\t\t%d\t\t%c\t\t%d\n", stud[i].roll,
                    stud[i].marks1, stud[i].marks2, ' ',
                    stud[i].marksfinal);
    }
    return 0;
}
```

Input and Output of the Executed Program:

```
Enter number of students: 3
Enter total marks of the exam: 70

Enter roll no. of student #1: 101
Enter marks of 1st examiner: 56
Enter marks of 2nd examiner: 49

Enter roll no. of student #2: 102
Enter marks of 1st examiner: 60
Enter marks of 2nd examiner: 40

Enter roll no. of student #3: 103
Enter marks of 1st examiner: 61
Enter marks of 2nd examiner: 43

Roll No.        1st Examiner    2nd Examiner    3rd Examiner    Final Marks
-----------------------------------------------------------------------
101             56              49                              53
102             60              40              Required
103             61              43              Required

Enter 3rd examiner marks of roll 102: 50

Enter 3rd examiner marks of roll 103: 50

Final result after third examination
Roll No.        1st Examiner    2nd Examiner    3rd Examiner    Final Marks
-----------------------------------------------------------------------
101             56              49                              53
102             60              40              50              50
103             61              43              50              47
```

## Explanation of the Programming Code:

**#include <stdio.h>**
/*header file stdio.h contains prototypes of the library functions printf(), and scanf(); the header file must be included using preprocessor directive #include before the functions are called in the program*/
**#include <stdlib.h>**
/*header file stdlib.h contains prototypes of the library function abs(); the header file must be included using preprocessor directive #include before the function is called in the program*/
**#include <math.h>**
/*header file math.h contains prototypes of the library function ceil(); the header file must be included using preprocessor directive #include before the function is called in the program*/
**struct marks{**

```
/*structured data type marks is defined using keyword struct; its
members are declared within the curly braces*/
    int roll;
    /*integer type variable roll is declared as first member of the
    data type struct marks*/
    int marks1, marks2, marks3;
    /*three integer type variables are declared, these are the
    members of the data type struct marks*/
    int third, marksfinal;
    /*two integer type variables are declared, these are the members
    of the data type struct marks*/
};
/*definition of structured data type must end with a semicolon; no
variable of the defined data type struct marks is declared here*/
int minfn(int x, int y, int z){
/*user-defined function minfn() is defined here; definition starts
with the function header and body of the function; x, y and z are
the virtual parameters which are replaced by the real arguments
passed during function call; this function computes the minimum of
three integers, and returns the value */
    int min1=x;
    /*integer min1 is declared and initialized to x; min1 is
    local to the function minfn(), and is not visible outside the
    function*/
    if (y<min1)
    /*if condition y<min1 is true then the following statement is
    executed*/
        min1=y;
        /*value of y is assigned to min1*/
    if (z<min1)
    /*if condition z<min1 is true then the following statement is
    executed*/
        min1=z;
        /*valur of z is assigne to min1*/
    return min1;
    /*value of min1 is returned to the point where the function was
    called*/
}
/*this closing curly brace specifies the end of definition of
minfn() function*/
int main(){
/*all C program must have a main() function with return type void
or int; here there is no parameter of the main() function and it
returns an integer; opening curly brace specifies start of the
main() function and no statement before that curly brace is executed
by the compiler*/
```

```
struct marks stud[100];
```
/*struct marks type array of size 100 is declared; each of the array element has six integer type members that can be accessed using dot (.) operator*/
```
int numstd, markstot, ind=0, i;
```
/*integer type variables numstd, markstot and i are declared; another integer type variable ind is declared and initialized to 0*/
```
int diff12, diff23, diff31, min;
```
/*four integer type variables are declared and required memory spaces are allocated for these variables to store data*/
```
printf("Enter number of students: ");
```
/*output function printf() displays the text in the quotations as it is on the screen*/
```
scanf("%d", &numstd);
```
/*function scanf() reads an integer from the input terminal and stores it in the memory spaces allocated for the variable numstd*/
```
printf("Enter total marks of the exam: ");
```
/*output function printf() displays the text in the quotations as it is on the screen*/
```
scanf("%d", &markstot);
```
/*function scanf() reads an integer from the input terminal and stores it in the memory spaces allocated for the variable markstot*/
```
for (i=0; i<numstd; i++){
```
/*here i=0 is initialization, i<numstd is condition and i++ is increment; initialization is done once at the beginning of the loop; then the condition is checked, if it is true statements in the body, enclosed by curly braces, are executed and the value of i is incremented by 1 before the condition is re-checked; these steps continue until the condition becomes false in which case the program control flow exits the loop*/
```
    printf("\nEnter roll no. of student #%d: ", i+1);
```
/*output function printf() displays the text in the quotations as it is on the screen except for the value of i+1 replaces the format specifier %d and a newline replaces \n*/
```
    scanf("%d", &stud[i].roll);
```
/*this scanf() function reads an integer from the input terminal and stores it in the member roll of struct marks type array stud[]*/
```
    printf("Enter marks of 1st examiner: ");
```
/*output function printf() displays the text in the quotation as it is on the screen*/
```
    scanf("%d", &stud[i].marks1);
```

/*this scanf() function reads an integer from the input terminal and stores it in the member marks1 of struct marks type array stud[]*/
**printf("Enter marks of 2nd examiner: ");**
/*output function printf() displays the text in the quotations as it is on the screen*/
**scanf("%d", &stud[i].marks2);**
/*this scanf() function reads an integer from the input terminal and stores it in the member marks2 of struct marks type array stud[]*/
**if(abs(stud[i].marks1-stud[i].marks2)*100/(float)**
    **markstot>=20.0){**
/*here type of markstot is converted to float so that the operation gives us decimal result; if the result is greater than or equal to 20 then the condition is true and the following statements are executed; abs() function in the expression gives absolute value of its parameter*/
    **stud[i].third=1;**
    /*member third of a particular student stud[i] is set to 1; the member third is accessed using dot (.) operator*/
    **ind=1;**
    /*value of ind is set to 1; if there is no third examination for any student then above condition never becomes true and value of ind remains 0*/
**}**
/*this closing curly brace specifies the end of 'if'condition*/
**else**
/*if all the above conditions are false, following statement is executed*/
    **stud[i].third=0;**
    /*member third of a particular student stud[i] is set to 0; the member third is accessed using dot (.) operator*/
**}**
**printf("\nRoll No.\t1st Examiner\t2nd Examiner\t3rd Examiner"**
    **"\tFinal Marks\n");**
/*output function printf() displays the text in the quotations as it is on the screen except for a newline replaces \n and a tab replaces \t; here long string was broken into multiple lines using two double quotes ("")*/
**printf("-------------------------------------------------\n");**
/*output function printf() displays the text in the quotation as it is on the screen except newline character \n is replaced by enter*/

```
for (i=0; i<numstd; i++)
```
/*here i=0 is initialization, i<numstd is condition and i++ is increment; initialization is done once at the beginning of the loop; then the condition is checked, if it is true statement in the body is executed and value of i is incremented by 1 before the condition is re-checked; these steps continue until the condition becomes false in which case the program flow exits the loop*/

```
    if (stud[i].third==0){
```
/*if the condition is true, following statements inside the curly braces are executed*/

```
        stud[i].marksfinal=ceil((stud[i].marks1+
                            (float) stud[i].marks2)/2);
```
/*because no third examination is required, final marks of a particular student is average of the marks - marks1 and marks2; ceil() function computes nearest integer greater than its parameter*/

```
        printf("%d\t\t%d\t\t%d\t\t%c\t\t%d\n",stud[i].
            roll, stud[i].marks1, stud[i].marks2, ' ', stud[i].
            marksfinal);
```
/*output function printf() displays the text in the quotations as it is on the screen except for the value of stud[i].roll replaces the 1st format specifier %d, value of stud[i].marks1 replaces the 2nd %d, the value of stud[i].marks2 replaces the 3rd %d, the value of value of stud[i].marksfinal replaces the 4th %d, a newline replaces \n and a tab replaces \t*/

```
    }
```
/*this closing curly brace specifies the end of 'if' condition*/

```
    else
```
/*if condition of above 'if' is false, following statement is executed*/

```
        printf("%d\t\t%d\t\t%d\t\t%s\n", stud[i].roll,
            stud[i].marks1, stud[i].marks2, "Required");
```
/*output function printf() displays the value of stud[i].roll on the screen in place of 1st format specifier %d, value of stud[i].marks1 in place of 2nd %d, value of stud[i].marks2 in place of 3rd %d and Required in place of %s; also, a newline replaces \n and a tab replaces \t*/

```
if (ind!=1)
```
/*if the condition is true, means no third examination of any student is required, following statement is executed*/

```
    printf("\nThere is no third examination and the above"
        "result is final.\n");
```

```
        /*output function printf() displays the text in the
    quotations as it is on the screen except for a newline
    replaces \n; here long string was broken into multiple
    lines using two double quotes ("")*/
else{
/*if condition of above 'if' is false, means third examination
of at least a single student is required, then following for
loop is executed*/
    for (i=0; i<numstd; i++){
    /*here i=0 is initialization, i<numstd is condition and i++
    is increment; initialization is done once at the beginning
    of the loop; then the condition is checked, if it is true
    statement in the body is executed and the value of i is
    incremented by 1 before the condition is re-checked; these
    steps continue until the condition becomes false in which
    case the program flow exits the loop*/
        if (stud[i].third==1){
        /*if the condition is true, following statements inside
        the curly braces are executeds*/
            printf("\nEnter 3rd examiner marks of roll %d: ",
                    stud[i].roll);
            /*output function printf() displays the text in the
            quotations as it is on the screen except for the
            value of stud[i].roll replaces 1st format specifier
            %d and a newline replaces \n*/
            scanf("%d", &stud[i].marks3);
            /*function scanf() reads an integer from input
            terminal and stores it in the member marks3 of
            struct atten type array element stud[]*/
            diff12=abs(stud[i].marks1-stud[i].marks2);
            /*this arithmetic operation calculates the absolute
            value of the differences between 1st and 2nd
            examination marks*/
            diff23=abs(stud[i].marks2-stud[i].marks3);
            /*this arithmetic operation calculates the absolute
            value of the differences between 2nd and 3rd
            examination marks*/
            diff31=abs(stud[i].marks1-stud[i].marks3);
            /*this arithmetic operation calculates the absolute
            value of the differences between 1st and 2nd
            examination marks*/
            if (diff23==diff31)
            /*if this condition is true, means 3drd
            examination marks is exactly in the middle of 1st
            and 2nd examination marks, following statement is
            executed*/
```

```
        stud[i].marksfinal=stud[i].marks3;
        /*this statement sets the marksfinal to 3rd
        examination marks of that student*/
    else{
    /*if condition of above 'if' is false, means 3drd
    examination marks is not in the middle of 1st and
    2nd examination marks, following statements inside
    the curly braces are executed*/
        min=minfn(diff12, diff23, diff31);
        /*minfn() is called with real parameters diff12,
        diff23 and diff31, program control flow shifts
        to the function definition; function minfn()
        does some defined operations and returns an
        integer that is assigned to min*/
        if (min==diff12)
        /*if this condition is true, means 1st and
        2nd examination marks are closest, following
        statement is executed*/
            stud[i].marksfinal=ceil((stud[i].marks1+
            (float) stud[i].marks2)/2);
            /*final marks of a particular student is
            calculated as average of the marks- marks1
            and marks2; ceil() function computes nearest
            integer greater than its parameter*/
    else if (min==diff23)
    /*if condition of above 'if' (min==diff12) is false but
    this condition is true, means 2nd and 3rd examination
    marks are closest, following statement is executed*/
            stud[i].marksfinal=ceil((stud[i].marks2+
            (float) stud[i].marks3)/2);
            /*final marks of a particular student is
            calculated as average of the marks- marks2
            and marks3; ceil() function computes nearest
            integer greater than its parameter*/
    else
    /*if both conditions of 'if' (min==diff12) and
    'else if' (min==diff23) are false, means 3rd
    and 1st examination marks are closest, following
    statement is executed*/
            stud[i].marksfinal=ceil((stud[i].marks3+
            (float) stud[i].marks1)/2);
            /*final marks of a particular student is
            calculated as average of the marks- marks3
            and marks1; ceil() function computes nearest
            integer greater than its parameter*/
}
```

```
                /*this closing curly brace specifies the end of 'else'
                with conditions diff23==diff31*/
        }
        /*this closing curly brace specifies the end of 'if' with
        condition (stud[i].third==1)*/
}
/*this closing curly brace specifies the end of 'for' loop*/
printf("\nFinal result after third examination");
/*output function printf() displays the text in the quotations
as it is on the screen except for a newline replaces \n*/
printf("\nRoll No.\t1st Examiner\t2nd Examiner\t3rd Examiner"
        "\tFinal Marks\n");
/*output function printf() displays the text in the quotations
as it is on the screen except for a newline replaces \n and a
tab replaces \t; here long string was broken into multiple lines
using two double quotes ("")*/
printf("---------------------------------------------------"
"--------------------\n");
/*output function printf() displays the text in the quotations
as it is on the screen except for a newline replaces \n*/
for (i=0; i<numstd; i++)
/*here i=0 is initialization, i<numstd is condition and i++ is
increment; initialization is done once at the beginning of the
loop; then the condition is checked, if it is true statement in
the body is executed and value of i is incremented by 1 before
the condition is re-checked; these steps continue until the
condition becomes false in which case the program flow exits
the loop*/
    if (stud[i].third==1)
    /*if the condition is true, means third examination was
    done for that student, following statement is executed*/
        printf("%d\t\t%d\t\t%d\t\t%d\t\t%d\n",stud[i].roll,
                stud[i].marks1, stud[i].marks2, stud[i].marks3,
                stud[i].marksfinal);
        /*output function printf() displays the text in the
        quotations as it is on the screen except for the value
        of stud[i].roll replaces the 1st format specifier %d,
        value of stud[i].marks1 replaces the 2nd %d, value of
        stud[i].marks3 replaces the 3rd %d, value of stud[i].
        marksfinal replaces the 4th %d, a newline replaces \n
        and a tab replaces \t*/
    else
    /*if condition of above 'if' is false, means no third
    examination is required, following statement is executed*/
        printf("%d\t\t%d\t\t%d\t\t%c\t\t%d\n",stud[i].roll,
                stud[i].marks1, stud[i].marks2, ' ', stud[i].
                marksfinal);
```

```
            /*output function printf() displays the text in the
            quotations as it is on the screen except for the value
            of stud[i].roll replaces 1st format specifier %d, value
            of stud[i].marks1 replaces 2nd %d, value of stud[i].
            marksfinal replaces 3rd %d, a newline replaces \n and
            a tab replaces \t*/
        }
        /*this closing curly brace specifies the end of 'else' with
        condition ind!=1*/
        return 0;
        /*0 is returned as it is the standard for the successful
        execution of the program*/
}
/*the closing curly brace specifies the end of the main() function's
body, as well as the program's end; after that curly brace, no
statement is executed*/
```

## PROBLEM-11

The annual examination results of n students are tabulated as follows:

| Roll No. | EEE-1101 | EEE-1102 | EEE-1103 |
|---|---|---|---|
| 101 | 69 | 56 | 89 |
| 102 | 80 | 65 | 91 |
| 103 | 45 | 36 | 68 |

Write a program to read the data and determine the following:

(a)  Grade obtained by each student in each subject.

| Marks | Letter Grade | Grade Point |
|---|---|---|
| 90% and above | A+ | 4.00 |
| 80% to <90% | A | 3.50 |
| 70% to <60% | B | 3.00 |
| 60% to <70% | C | 2.50 |
| 50% to <60% | D | 2.00 |
| Less than 50% | F | 0.00 |

(b)  Total marks and GPA obtained by each student.

(c)  The position of each student based on GPA (for equal GPA, consider who gets the higher total marks).

(d)  The result should be displayed according to the roll number and merit.

Flowchart of the Solution:

Figure 5.5 shows the flowcharts followed to solve this problem.

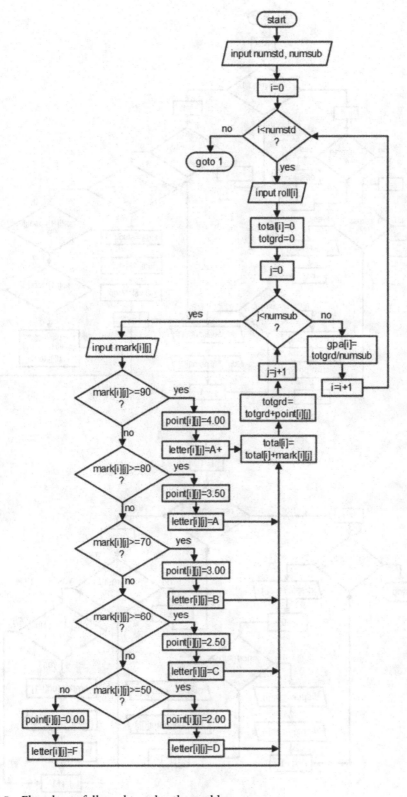

FIGURE 5.5   Flowcharts followed to solve the problem.

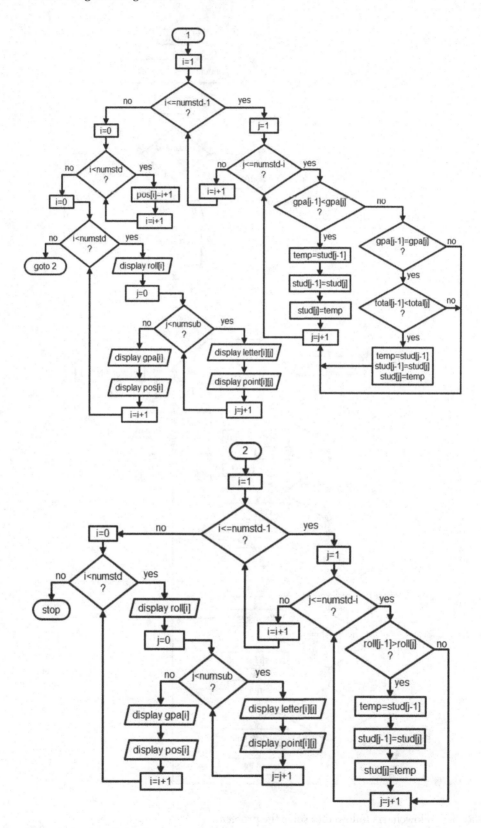

FIGURE 5.5 (Continued)

## Algorithm of the Solution:

Step-1: Start

Step-2: Define struct subject with members mark, point, and letter

Step-3: Define struct exam with members roll, sub[100], total, gpa, and pos

Step-4: Read values of numstd and numsub

Step-5: Initialize i←0

Step-6: If i<numstd

    6.1: Read value of stud[i].roll

    6.2: Initialize stud[i].total←0, totgrd←0 and j←0

    6.3: If j<numsub

        6.3.1: Read value of stud[i].sub[j].mark

        6.3.2: If stud[i].sub[j].mark>=90

            6.3.2.1: stud[i].sub[j].point←4.00

            6.3.2.2: stud[i].sub[j].letter←"A+"

            6.3.2.3: Go to Step-6.3.9

        6.3.3: If stud[i].sub[j].mark>=80

            6.3.3.1: stud[i].sub[j].point←3.50

            6.3.3.2: stud[i].sub[j].letter←"A"

            6.3.3.3: Go to Step-6.3.9

        6.3.4: If stud[i].sub[j].mark>=70

            6.3.4.1: stud[i].sub[j].point←3.00

            6.3.4.2: stud[i].sub[j].letter←"B"

            6.3.4.3: Go to Step-6.3.9

        6.3.5: If stud[i].sub[j].mark>=60

            7.4.5.1: stud[i].sub[j].point←2.50

            7.4.5.2: stud[i].sub[j].letter←"C"

            7.4.5.3: Go to Step-6.3.9

        6.3.6: If stud[i].sub[j].mark>=50

6.3.6.1: stud[i].sub[j].point←2.00

6.3.6.2: stud[i].sub[j].letter←"D"

6.3.6.3: Go to Step-6.3.9

6.3.7: stud[i].sub[j].point←0.00

6.3.8: stud[i].sub[j].letter←"F"

6.3.9: stud[i].total← stud[i].total+stud[i].sub[j].mark

6.3.10:     totgrd←totgrd+stud[i].sub[j].point

6.3.11: j←j+1

6.3.12: Go to Step-6.3

6.4: stud[i].gpa←totgrd/numsub

6.5: i←i+1

6.6: Go to Step-6

Step-7: Initialize i←1

Step-8: If i<=numstd−1

8.1: Initialize j←1

8.2: If j<=numstd−i

8.2.1: If stud[j−1].gpa<stud[j].gpa

8.2.1.1: temp←stud[j−1]

8.2.1.2: stud[j−1]←stud[j]

8.2.1.3: stud[j]←temp

8.2.1.4: Go to Step-8.2.3

8.2.2: If stud[j−1].gpa=stud[j].gpa

8.2.2.1: If stud[j−1].total<stud[j].total

8.2.2.1.1: temp←stud[j−1]

8.2.2.1.2: stud[j−1]←stud[j]

8.2.2.1.3: stud[j]←temp

8.2.3: j←j+1

8.2.4: Go to Step-8.2

8.3: i←i+1

8.4: Go to Step-8

Step-9: Initialize i←0

Step-10: If i<numstd

    10.1: stud[i].pos←i+1

    10.2: i←i+1

    10.3: Go to Step-10

Step-11: Initialize i←0

Step-12: If i<numstd

    12.1: Display value of stud[i].roll

    12.2: Initialize j←0

    12.3: If j<numsub

        12.3.1: Display values of stud[i].sub[j].letter, stud[i].sub[j].point, stud[i].gpa and stud[i].pos

        12.3.2: j←j+1

        12.3.3: Go to Step-12.3

    12.4: i←i+1

    12.5: Go to Step-12

Step-13: Initialize i←1

Step-14: If i<=numstd−1

    14.1: Initialize j←1

    14.2: If j<=numstd−i

        14.2.1: If stud[j−1].roll>stud[j].roll

            14.2.1.1: temp←stud[j−1]

            14.2.1.2: stud[j−1]←stud[j]

            14.2.1.3: stud[j]←temp

        14.2.2: j←j+1

        14.2.3: Go to Step-14.2

    14.3: i←i+1

    14.4: Go to Step-14

Step-15: Initialize i←0

Step-16: If i<numstd

    16.1: Display value of stud[i].roll

    16.2: Initialize j←0

    16.3: If j<numsub

        16.3.1: Display values of stud[i].sub[j].letter, stud[i].sub[j].point, stud[i].gpa and stud[i].pos

        16.3.2: j←j+1

        16.3.3: Go to Step-16.3

    16.4: i←i+1

    16.5: Go to Step-16

Step-17: Stop

<u>Programming Code of the Solution:</u>

```c
#include <stdio.h>
struct subject{
    int mark;
    float point;
    char *letter;
};
struct exam{
    int roll, total, pos;
    struct subject sub[10];
    float gpa;
};
int main(){
    struct exam stud[100], temp;
    int numstd, numsub, i, j;
    float totgrd;
    printf("Enter the number of students: ");
    scanf("%d", &numstd);
    printf("How many subjects: ");
    scanf("%d", &numsub);
    for (i=0; i<numstd; i++){
        printf("Enter the roll no. of student #%d: ", i+1);
        scanf("%d", &stud[i].roll);
        stud[i].total=0;
        totgrd=0;
```

```c
    for (j=0; j<numsub; j++){
        printf("Mark obtained in EEE-110%d: ", j+1);
        scanf("%d", &stud[i].sub[j].mark);
        if (stud[i].sub[j].mark>=90){
            stud[i].sub[j].point=4.00;
            stud[i].sub[j].letter="A+";
        }
        else if (stud[i].sub[j].mark>=80){
            stud[i].sub[j].point=3.50;
            stud[i].sub[j].letter="A";
        }
        else if (stud[i].sub[j].mark>=70){
            stud[i].sub[j].point=3.00;
            stud[i].sub[j].letter="B";
        }
        else if (stud[i].sub[j].mark>=60){
            stud[i].sub[j].point=2.50;
            stud[i].sub[j].letter="C";
        }
        else if (stud[i].sub[j].mark>=50){
            stud[i].sub[j].point=2.00;
            stud[i].sub[j].letter="D";
        }
        else{
            stud[i].sub[j].point=0.00;
            stud[i].sub[j].letter="F";
        }
        stud[i].total+=stud[i].sub[j].mark;
        totgrd+=stud[i].sub[j].point;
    }
    stud[i].gpa=totgrd/numsub;
}
for (i=1; i<=numstd-1; i++)
    for (j=1; j<=numstd-i; j++)
        if (stud[j-1].gpa<stud[j].gpa){
            temp=stud[j-1];
            stud[j-1]=stud[j];
            stud[j]=temp;
        }
        else if (stud[j-1].gpa==stud[j].gpa)
            if (stud[j-1].total<stud[j].total){
                temp=stud[j-1];
                stud[j-1]=stud[j];
                stud[j]=temp;
            }
for (i=0; i<numstd; i++)
    stud[i].pos=i+1;
printf("\nResult according to merit position:\n");
```

```
    for (i=0; i<numstd; i++){
        printf("Roll No.: %d\n", stud[i].roll);
        for (j=0; j<numsub; j++)
            printf("EEE-110%d: %s (%0.2f)\n", j+1,
                    stud[i].sub[j].letter, stud[i].sub[j].point);
        printf("GPA: %0.2f\nMerit Position: %d\n\n",
                stud[i].gpa, stud[i].pos);
    }
    for (i=1; i<=numstd-1; i++)
        for (j=1; j<=numstd-i; j++)
            if (stud[j-1].roll>stud[j].roll){
                temp=stud[j-1];
                stud[j-1]=stud[j];
                stud[j]=temp;
            }
    printf("\nResult according to roll no.:\n");
    for (i=0; i<numstd; i++){
        printf("Roll No.: %d\n", stud[i].roll);
        for (j=0; j<numsub; j++)
            printf("EEE-110%d: %s (%0.2f)\n", j+1,
                    stud[i].sub[j].letter, stud[i].sub[j].point);
        printf("GPA: %0.2f\nMerit Position: %d\n\n",
                stud[i].gpa, stud[i].pos);
    }
    return 0;
}
```

#### Input and Output of the Executed Program:

```
Enter the number of students: 3
How many subjects: 3
Enter the roll no. of student #1: 101
Mark obtained in EEE-1101: 69
Mark obtained in EEE-1102: 56
Mark obtained in EEE-1103: 89
Enter the roll no. of student #2: 102
Mark obtained in EEE-1101: 80
Mark obtained in EEE-1102: 65
Mark obtained in EEE-1103: 91
Enter the roll no. of student #3: 103
Mark obtained in EEE-1101: 45
Mark obtained in EEE-1102: 36
Mark obtained in EEE-1103: 68
```

```
Result according to merit position:
Roll No.: 102
EEE-1101: A (3.50)
EEE-1102: C (2.50)
EEE-1103: A+ (4.00)
GPA: 3.33
Merit Position: 1
```

```
Roll No.: 101
EEE-1101: C (2.50)
EEE-1102: D (2.00)
EEE-1103: A (3.50)
GPA: 2.67
Merit Position: 2

Roll No.: 103
EEE-1101: F (0.00)
EEE-1102: F (0.00)
EEE-1103: C (2.50)
GPA: 0.83
Merit Position: 3
```

```
Result according to roll no.:
Roll No.: 101
EEE-1101: C (2.50)
EEE-1102: D (2.00)
EEE-1103: A (3.50)
GPA: 2.67
Merit Position: 2

Roll No.: 102
EEE-1101: A (3.50)
EEE-1102: C (2.50)
EEE-1103: A+ (4.00)
GPA: 3.33
Merit Position: 1

Roll No.: 103
EEE-1101: F (0.00)
EEE-1102: F (0.00)
EEE-1103: C (2.50)
GPA: 0.83
Merit Position: 3
```

**Explanation of the Programming Code:**

```
#include <stdio.h>
/*header file stdio.h contains prototypes of the library functions
printf(), scanf() and gets(); the header file must be included using
preprocessor directive #include before the functions are called in
the program*/
struct subject{
```

```
/*structured data type subject is defined here using keyword struct;
its members are declared within the curly braces*/
    int mark;
    /*integer type variable mark is declared as member of the data
    type struct subject*/
    float point;
    /*float type variable point is declared as member of the data
    type struct subject*/
    char *letter;
    /*character type pointer letter is declared as member of the
    data type struct subject*/
};
/*definition of structured data type must end with a semicolon;
no variable of the defined data type struct subject is declared
here*/
struct exam{
/*structured data type exam is defined here using keyword struct;
its members are declared within the curly braces*/
    int roll, total, pos;
    /*int type variables roll, total and pos are declared as members
    of the structured data type exam, that will be used to store
    roll no, obtained total marks and merit position, respectively
    of a particular student*/
    struct subject sub[10];
    /*structured subject type array sub[] with size 10 is declared
    as member of the structured data type exam, that will be used
    to store information of maximum 10 subjects of a particular
    student*/
    float gpa;
    /*float type variable gpa is declared as member of the structured
    data type exam, that will be used to store gpa calculated for
    a particular student*/
};
/*definition of structured data type must end with a semicolon; no
variable of the defined data type marks is declared here*/
int main(){
/*all C program must have a main() function with return type void
or int; here there is no parameter of the main() function and it
returns an integer; opening curly brace specifies start of the
main() function and no statement before that curly brace is executed
by the compiler*/
    struct exam stud[100], temp;
    /*struct exam type variable temp and an array stud[] of size 100
    are declared; members of the variable and the array elements are
    accessed using dot (.) operator*/
    int numstd, numsub, i, j;
```

```
/*four integer type variables are declared; required memory
spaces are allocated for each of the variables*/
float totgrd;
/*a float type variable is declared; required memory spaces are
allocated for the variable*/
printf("Enter the number of students: ");
/*output function printf() displays the text in the quotations
as it is on the screen*/
scanf("%d", &numstd);
/*scanf() function reads an integer from the input terminal
and stores it in the memory spaces allocated for the variable
numstd*/
printf("How many subjects: ");
/*output function printf() displays the text in the quotations
as it is on the screen*/
scanf("%d", &numsub);
/*scanf() function reads an integer from the input terminal
and stores it in the memory spaces allocated for the variable
numsub*/
for (i=0; i<numstd; i++){
/*here i=0 is initialization, i<numstd is condition and i++ is
increment; initialization is done once at the beginning of the
loop; then the condition is checked, if it is true statements in
the body, enclosed by curly braces, are executed and the value
of i is incremented by 1 before the condition is re-checked;
these steps continue until the condition becomes false in which
case the program flow exits the loop*/
    printf("Enter the roll no. of student #%d: ", i+1);
    /*output function printf() displays the text in the
    quotations as it is on the screen except for the value of
    i+1 replaces the format specifier %d*/
    scanf("%d", &stud[i].roll);
    /*this scanf() function reads an integer from input terminal
    and stores it in roll which is a member of struct subject
    type array stud[]*/
    stud[i].total=0;
    /*member total of struct subject type array stud[] is
    initialized to 0 that is used to store the total marks of
    a particular student; it is initialized to 0, otherwise the
    summation operation may give wrong answer because, when we
    declare a variable a memory space is allocated for that
    variable and the memory space may contain some garbage
    value and it adds in the first summation*/
    totgrd=0;
    /*variable totgrd is initialized to 0 that is used to
    store the total grade of a particular student needed to
```

calculate gpa; it is initialized to 0 to avoid adding up any garbage value in the first summation*/
**for (j=0; j<numsub; j++){**
/*here j=0 is initialization, j<numsub is condition and j++ is increment; initialization is done once at the beginning of the loop; then condition is checked, if it is true statements in the body, enclosed by curly braces, are executed and the value of j is incremented by 1 before the condition is re-checked; these steps continue until the condition becomes false in which case the program flow exits the loop*/

    **printf("Mark obtained in EEE-110%d: ", j+1);**
    /*output function printf() displays the text in the quotations as it is on the screen except for the value of j+1 replaces the format specifier %d*/
    **scanf("%d", &stud[i].sub[j].mark);**
    /*this scanf() function reads an integer from input terminal and stores it in mark which is a member of struct subject type array sub[] which in turn is a member of struct exam type array stud[], hence variable mark is accessed using double dot (.) operators*/
**if (stud[i].sub[j].mark>=90){**
/*if the condition is true, means marks of a particular subject of a particular student is greater than or equal to 90, then following two statements are executed*/

    **stud[i].sub[j].point=4.00;**
    /*point is a member of struct subject type array sub[] which in turn is a member of struct exam type array stud[]; point is accessed using double dot (.) operators and assigned a value 4.00*/
    **stud[i].sub[j].letter="A+";**
    /*character type pointer letter is a member of struct subject type array sub[] which in turn is a member of struct exam type array stud[], hence variable point is accessed using double dot (.) operators and assigned a string A+*/
**}**
/*this closing curly brace specifies end of if (stud[i].sub[j].mark>=90)*/
**else if (stud[i].sub[j].mark>=80){**
/*if the condition is true, means marks of a particular subject of a particular student is between 80 and 90, then following two statements are executed*/

```
stud[i].sub[j].point=3.50;
```
/*point is a member of struct subject type array
sub[] which in turn is a member of struct exam type
array stud[]; point is accessed using double dot
(.) operators and assigned a value 3.50*/
```
stud[i].sub[j].letter="A";
```
/*character type pointer letter is a member of
struct subject type array sub[] which in turn is
a member of struct exam type array stud[], hence
variable point is accessed using double dot (.)
operators and assigned a string A*/
```
}
```
/*this closing curly brace specifies end of else if
(stud[i].sub[j].mark>=80)*/
```
else if (stud[i].sub[j].mark>=70){
```
/*if the condition is true, means marks of a particular
subject of a particular student is between 70 and 80,
then following two statements are executed*/
```
stud[i].sub[j].point=3.00;
```
/*point is a member of struct subject type array
sub[] which in turn is a member of struct exam type
array stud[]; point is accessed using double dot
(.) operators and assigned a value 3.00*/
```
stud[i].sub[j].letter="B";
```
/*character type pointer letter is a member of
struct subject type array sub[] which in turn is
a member of struct exam type array stud[], hence
variable point is accessed using double dot (.)
operators and assigned a string B*/
```
}
```
/*this closing curly brace specifies end of else if
(stud[i].sub[j].mark>=70)*/
```
else if (stud[i].sub[j].mark>=60){
```
/*if the condition is true, means marks of a particular
subject of a particular student is between 60 and 70,
then following two statements are executed*/
```
stud[i].sub[j].point=2.50;
```
/*point is a member of struct subject type array
sub[] which in turn is a member of struct exam type
array stud[]; point is accessed using double dot
(.) operators and assigned a value 2.50*/
```
stud[i].sub[j].letter="C";
```
/*character type pointer letter is a member of
struct subject type array sub[] which in turn is
a member of struct exam type array stud[], hence

variable point is accessed using double dot (.) operators and assigned a string C*/

```
}
```
/*this closing curly brace specifies end of else if (stud[i].sub[j].mark>=60)*/
**else if (stud[i].sub[j].mark>=50){**
/*if the condition is true, means marks of a particular subject of a particular student is between 50 and 60, then following two statements are executed*/
 **stud[i].sub[j].point=2.00;**
 /*point is a member of struct subject type array sub[] which in turn is a member of struct exam type array stud[]; point is accessed using double dot (.) operators and assigned a value 2.00*/
 **stud[i].sub[j].letter="D";**
 /*character type pointer letter is a member of struct subject type array sub[] which in turn is a member of struct exam type array stud[], hence variable point is accessed using double dot (.) operators and assigned a string D*/
```
}
```
/*this closing curly brace specifies end of else if (stud[i].sub[j].mark>=50)*/
**else{**
/*if all the above conditions of 'if' and 'else if' are false, means marks of a particular subject of a particular student is less than 50, then following two statements are executed*/
 **stud[i].sub[j].point=0.00;**
 /*point is a member of struct subject type array sub[] which in turn is a member of struct exam type array stud[]; point is accessed using double dot (.) operators and assigned a value 0.00*/
 **stud[i].sub[j].letter="F";**
 /*character type pointer letter is a member of struct subject type array sub[] which in turn is a member of struct exam type array stud[], hence variable point is accessed using double dot (.) operators and assigned a string F*/
```
}
```
/*this closing curly brace specifies end of above 'else'*/
**stud[i].total+=stud[i].sub[j].mark;**
/*this arithmetic operation computes total marks of a particular student by adding obtained marks of all the subjects; in each iteration of first 'for' loop one

particular student is considered and in each iteration of second 'for' loop individual subject of that particular student is considered*/

**totgrd+=stud[i].sub[j].point;**

/*this arithmetic operation computes total grades of a particular student by adding all grade-points of individual subject; in each iteration of first 'for' loop one particular student is considered and in each iteration of second 'for' loop individual subject of that particular student is considered*/

}

/*this closing curly brace specifies end of for (j=0; j<numsub; j++)*/

**stud[i].gpa=totgrd/numsub;**

/*gpa of each student is calculated from total grade-point totgrd of that particular student; in each iteration of first 'for' loop individual student is considered*/

}

/*this closing curly brace specifies end of for (i=0; i<numstd; i++)*/

**for (i=1; i<=numstd-1; i++)**

/*here i=1 is initialization, i<=numstd-1 is condition and i++ is increment; initialization is done once at the beginning of the loop; then the condition is checked, if it is true statement in the body is executed and the value of i is incremented by 1 before the condition is re-checked; these steps continue until the condition becomes false in which case the program flow exits the loop; this for loop together with the following for loop sort students based on their gpa in ascending order*/

**for (j=1; j<=numstd-i; j++)**

/*here j=1 is initialization, j<numstd-i is condition and j++ is increment; initialization is done once at the beginning of the loop; then the condition is checked, if it is true statement in the body is executed and the value of j is incremented by 1 before the condition is re-checked; these steps continue until the condition becomes false in which case the program flow exits the loop*/

**if (stud[j-1].gpa<stud[j].gpa){**

/*if the condition is true then following statements, enclosed within curly braces, are executed; here gpa of two contiguous students are compared, if the larger gpa stays above the smaller one then they are swapped*/

**temp=stud[j-1];**

/*array element stud[j-1] is stored in variable temp*/

```
                 stud[j-1]=stud[j];
                 /*array element stud[j] is stored in array element
                 stud[j-1]*/
                 stud[j]=temp;
                 /*value of temp is stored in array element stud[j],
                 that is stud[j-1] now becomes stud[j]*/
               }
               /*this closing curly brace specifies the end of 'if'*/
               else if (stud[j-1].gpa==stud[j].gpa)
               /*if above 'if' condition is false then this 'else
               if' condition is checked; if this condition is true,
               means gpa of two contiguous students are equal then
               following 'if' condition is executed to sort students
               according to their obtained total marks in ascending
               order*/
                 if (stud[j-1].total<stud[j].total){
                 /*if this condition is true then following
                 statements, enclosed in the curly braces, are
                 executed; here total of two contiguous students
                 are compared, if the larger total stays above the
                 smaller one then they are swapped*/
                     temp=stud[j-1];
                     /*array element stud[j-1] is stored in
                     variable temp*/
                     stud[j-1]=stud[j];
                     /*array element stud[j] is stored in array
                     element stud[j-1]*/
                     stud[j]=temp;
                     /*value of temp is stored as array element
                     stud[j], that is stud[j-1] now becomes
                     stud[j]*/
                 }
                 /*this closing curly brace specifies the end of
                 'if' with condition*/
  for (i=0; i<numstd; i++)
  /*this for loop is used to set position of individual student
  according to sorted gpa; here i=0 is initialization, i<numstd
  is condition and i++ is increment; initialization is done once
  at the beginning of the loop; then the condition is checked, if
  it is true statement in the body is executed and the value of i
  is incremented by 1 before the condition is re-checked; these
  steps continue until the condition becomes false in which case
  the program flow exits the loop*/
      stud[i].pos=i+1;
      /*member pos of struct exam type array stud[] is set to i+1;
      at 1st iteration position of 1st student is set to stud[0].
```

pos=1, at 2nd iteration position of 2nd student is set to stud[1].pos=2, and so on*/

**printf("\nResult according to merit position:\n");**

/*output function printf() displays the text in the double quotations as it is on the screen except for a newline replaces \n*/

**for (i=0; i<numstd; i++){**

/*this for loop is used to display information of individual student according to sorted gpa; here i=0 is initialization, i<numstd is condition and i++ is increment; initialization is done once at the beginning of the loop; then the condition is checked, if it is true statements in the body are executed and the value of i is incremented by 1 before the condition is re-checked; these steps continue until the condition becomes false in which case the program flow exits the loop*/

    **printf("Roll No.: %d\n", stud[i].roll);**

/*output function printf() displays the text in the quotations as it is on the screen except for the value of stud[i].roll replaces the format specifier %d and a newline replaces \n*/

    **for (j=0; j<numsub; j++)**

/*this for loop is used to display information of all subjects of individual student according to sorted gpa; here j=0 is initialization, j<numsub is condition and j++ is increment; initialization is done once at the beginning of the loop; then the condition is checked, if it is true statements in the body is executed and the value of i is incremented by 1 before the condition is re-checked; these steps continue until the condition becomes false in which case the program flow exits the loop*/

        **printf("EEE-110%d: %s (%0.2f)\n", j+1, stud[i].sub[j].letter, stud[i].sub[j].point);**

/*output function printf() displays the text in the quotations as it is on the screen except for the value of j+1 replaces format specifier %d, string value of stud[i].sub[j].letter replaces %s, value of stud[i].sub[j].point replaces %0.2f with two decimal points precision and a newline replaces \n*/

    **printf("GPA: %0.2f\nMerit Position: %d\n\n", stud[i].gpa, stud[i].pos);**

/*output function printf() displays the text in the quotations as it is on the screen except for the value of stud[i].pos replaces format specifier %d, value of stud[i].gpa replaces %0.2f with two decimal points precision and a newline replaces \n*/

}

```
/*this closing curly brace specifies the end of for (i=0;
i<numstd; i++) loop*/
for (i=1; i<=numstd-1; i++)
/*here i=1 is initialization, i<=numstd-1 is condition and i++
is increment; initialization is done once at the beginning of
the loop; then condition is checked, if it is true statement
in the body is executed and value of i is incremented by 1
before the condition is re-checked; these steps continue until
the condition becomes false in which case the program flow
exits the loop; this for loop together with the following for
loop sort students according to their roll no in ascending
order*/
      for (j=1; j<=numstd-i; j++)
      /*here j=1 is initialization, j<numstd-i is condition
      and j++ is increment; initialization is done once at the
      beginning of the loop; then the condition is checked, if it
      is true statement in the body is executed and the value of
      j is incremented by 1 before the condition is re-checked;
      these steps continue until the condition becomes false in
      which case the program flow exits the loop*/
          if (stud[j-1].roll>stud[j].roll){
          /*if this condition is true then following statements,
          enclosed in the curly braces, are executed; here
          roll of two contiguous students are compared, if the
          larger roll stays above the smaller one then they are
          swapped*/
                temp=stud[j-1];
                /*array element stud[j-1] is stored in variable
                temp*/
                stud[j-1]=stud[j];
                /*array element stud[j] is stored in array element
                stud[j-1]*/
                stud[j]=temp;
                /*value of temp is stored in array element stud[j],
                that is stud[j-1] now becomes stud[j]*/
          }
          /*this closing curly brace specifies the end of 'if'
          condition*/
printf("\nResult according to roll no.:\n");
/*output function printf() displays the text in the double
quotations as it is on the screen except for a newline replaces
\n*/
for (i=0; i<numstd; i++){
/*this for loop is used to display information of individual
student according to sorted roll; here i=0 is initialization,
i<numstd is condition and i++ is increment; initialization is
```

done once at the beginning of the loop; then the condition is checked, if it is true statements in the body are executed and the value of i is incremented by 1 before the condition is re-checked; these steps continue until the condition becomes false in which case the program flow exits the loop*/

    **printf("Roll No.: %d\n", stud[i].roll);**

/*output function printf() displays the text in the quotations as it is on the screen except for the value of stud[i].roll replaces the format specifier %d and a newline replaces \n*/

    **for (j=0; j<numsub; j++)**

/*this for loop is used to display information of all subjects of individual student according to sorted gpa; here j=0 is initialization, j<numsub is condition and j++ is increment; initialization is done once at the beginning of the loop; then the condition is checked, if it is true statements in the body are executed and the value of i is incremented by 1 before the condition is re-checked; these steps continue until the condition becomes false in which case the program flow exits the loop*/

    **printf("EEE-110%d: %s (%0.2f)\n", j+1, stud[i].sub[j].**
             **letter, stud[i].sub[j].point);**

/*output function printf() displays the text in the quotations as it is on the screen except for the value of j+1 replaces the format specifier %d, string value of stud[i].sub[j].letter replaces %s, value of stud[i].sub[j].point replaces %0.2f with two decimal points precision and a newline replaces \n*/

**printf("GPA: %0.2f\nMerit Position: %d\n\n", stud[i].gpa,**
      **stud[i].pos);**

/*output function printf() displays the text in the quotations as it is on the screen except for the value of stud[i].pos replaces the format specifier %d, value of stud[i].gpa replaces the %0.2f with two decimal points precision and a newline replaces \n*/

}

/*this closing curly brace specifies the end of for (i=0; i<numstd; i++) loop*/

**return 0;**

/*0 is returned as it is the standard for the successful execution of the program*/

}

/*the closing curly brace specifies the end of the main() function's body, as well as the program's end; after that curly brace, no statement is executed*/

## PROBLEM-12

**Write a program to create a linear linked list interactively and delete a specified node from the list. The program will display all the items before and after deletion.**

Flowchart of the Solution:

Figure 5.6 shows the flowcharts followed to solve this problem.

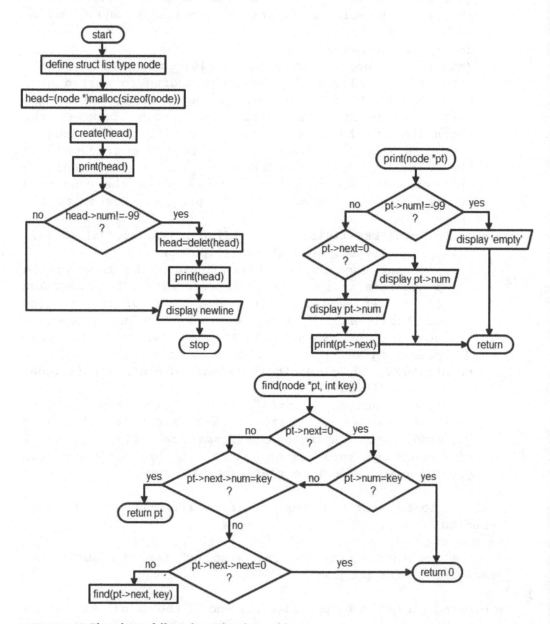

FIGURE 5.6   Flowcharts followed to solve the problem.

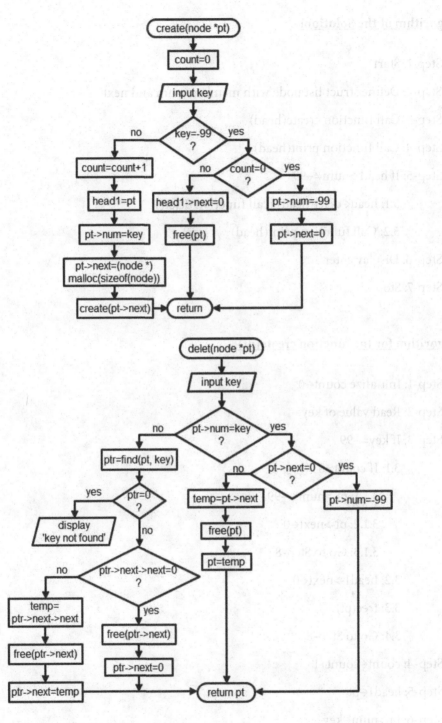

FIGURE 5.6    (Continued)

**Algorithm of the Solution:**

Step-1: Start

Step-2: Define struct list node with members num and next

Step-3: Call function create(head)

Step-4: Call function print(head)

Step-5: If head->num≠−99

      5.1: head←delet(head) [call function delet()]

      5.2: Call function print(head)

Step-6: Display enter

Step-7: Stop


**Algorithm for the function create(pt):**

Step-1: Initialize count←0

Step-2: Read value of key

Step-3: If key=−99

      3.1: If count=0

          3.1.1: pt->num←−99

          3.1.2: pt->next←0

          3.1.3: Go to Step-8

      3.2: head1->next←0

      3.3: free(pt)

      3.4: Go to Step-8

Step-4: count←count+1

Step-5: head1←pt

Step-6: pt->num←key

Step-7: Call function create(pt->next)

Step-8: Return.

## Algorithm for the function print(pt):

Step-1: If pt->num=-99

    1.1: Display 'empty list'

    1.2: Go to Step-4

Step-2: If pt->next=0

    2.1: Display value of pt->num

    2.2: Go to Step-4

Step-3: Display value of pt->num

Step-4: Return.

## Algorithm for the function find(pt, key):

Step-1: If pt->next=0

    1.1: If pt->num≠key

        1.1.1: Go to Step-3.1

Step-2: If pt->next->num=key

    2.1: Return value of pt

Step-3: If pt->next->next=0

    3.1: Return 0

Step-4: Call function find(pt->next, key)

## Algorithm for the function delet(pt):

Step-1: Read value of key

Step-2: If pt->num=key

    2.1: If pt->next=0

        2.1.1: pt->num←-99

        2.1.2: Go to Step-9

    2.2: temp←pt->next

    2.3: free(pt)

    2.4: pt←temp

2.5: Go to Step-9

Step-3: ptr←find(pt, key) [call function find()]

Step-4: If ptr=0

4.1: Display 'key not found'

4.1: Go to Step-9

Step-5: If ptr->next->next=0

5.1: free(ptr->next)

5.2: ptr->next←0

5.3: Go to Step-9

Step-6: temp←ptr->next->next

Step-7: free(ptr->next)

Step-8: ptr->next→temp

Step-9: Return value of pt

<u>Programming Code of the Solution:</u>

```c
#include <stdio.h>
#include <stdlib.h>
typedef struct list{
    int num;
    struct list *next;
} node;
void create(node *pt);
void print(node *pt);
node *find(node *pt, int key);
node *delet(node *pt);
int main(){
    node *head;
    head=(node *)malloc(sizeof(node));
    create(head);
    printf("List of items before deletion:\n");
    print(head);
    if (head->num!=-99){
        head=delet(head);
        printf("List of items after deletion:\n");
        print(head);
    }
    printf("\n");
    return 0;
}
```

```
void create(node *pt){
    int key;
    static int count=0;
    static node *head1;
    printf("Input a number (-99 to end): ");
    scanf("%d", &key);
    if (key==-99){
        if (count==0){
            pt->num=-99;
            pt->next=0;
        }
        else{
            head1->next=0;
            free(pt);
        }
    }
    else{
        count++;
        head1=pt;
        pt->num=key;
        pt->next=(node *)malloc(sizeof(node));
        create(pt->next);
    }
}
void print(node *pt){
    if (pt->num==-99)
        printf("The list is empty.");
    else if (pt->next==0)
        printf("%d, ", pt->num);
    else{
        printf("%d, ", pt->num);
        print(pt->next);
    }
}
node *find(node *pt, int key){
    if (pt->next==0 && pt->num!=key)
        return 0;
    else if (pt->next->num==key)
        return pt;
    else if (pt->next->next==0)
        return 0;
    else
        find(pt->next, key);
}
```

```
node *delet(node *pt){
    int key;
    node *ptr, *temp;
    printf("\nWhat is the item to be deleted? ");
    scanf("%d", &key);
    if (pt->num==key){
        if (pt->next==0)
            pt->num=-99;
        else{
            temp=pt->next;
            free(pt);
            pt=temp;
        }
    }
    else{
        ptr=find(pt, key);
        if (ptr==0)
            printf("Key not found.\n");
        else if (ptr->next->next==0){
            free(ptr->next);
            ptr->next=0;
        }
        else{
            temp=ptr->next->next;
            free(ptr->next);
            ptr->next=temp;
        }
    }
    return pt;
}
```

<u>Input and Output of the Executed Program:</u>

```
Input a number (-99 to end): 23
Input a number (-99 to end): 27
Input a number (-99 to end): 31
Input a number (-99 to end): 35
Input a number (-99 to end): 39
Input a number (-99 to end): -99
List of items before deletion:
23, 27, 31, 35, 39,
What is the item to be deleted? 31
List of items after deletion:
23, 27, 35, 39,
```

## Explanation of the Programming Code:

```
#include <stdio.h>
```
/*header file stdio.h contains prototypes of the library functions printf(), scanf() and sizeof(); the header file must be included using preprocessor directive #include before the functions are called in the program*/
```
#include <stdlib.h>
```
/*header file stdio.h contains prototypes of the library functions free(), and malloc(); the header file must be included using preprocessor directive #include before the functions are called in the program*/
```
typedef struct list{
```
/*new data type struct list is created using keyword struct; members of struct list are declared in the curly braces*/
```
    int num;
```
/*integer type variable num is declared, this is a member of the data type struct list*/
```
    struct list *next;
```
/*struct list type pointer next is declared as second member of the data type struct list; next contains address of another struct list*/
```
} node;
```
/*keyword typedef gives struct list a new name node and after this definition identifier node can be used as an abbreviation of the data type struct list; definition of the structured data type must end with a semicolon; no variable of the defined data type struct list is declared here*/
```
void create(node *pt);
```
/*this is the prototype (or declaration) of the user-defined function create() that must end with a semicolon; create() takes node type pointer as parameter, performs some predefined operations, and returns nothing*/
```
void print(node *pt);
```
/*this is the prototype (or declaration) of the user-defined function print() that must end with a semicolon; print() takes node type pointer as parameter, performs some predefined operations, and returns nothing*/
```
node *find(node *pt, int key);
```
/*this is the prototype (or declaration) of the user-defined function find() that must end with a semicolon; find() takes a node type pointer and an integer as parameters, performs some predefined operations, and returns a node type pointer*/
```
node *delet(node *pt);
```
/*this is the prototype (or declaration) of the user-defined function delet() that must end with a semicolon; delet() takes

a node type pointer as parameter, performs some predefined operations, and returns a node type pointer*/

**int main(){**

/*all C program must have a main() function with return type void or int; here there is no parameter of the main() function and it returns an integer; opening curly brace specifies start of the main() function and no statement before that curly brace is executed by the compiler*/

   **node *head;**

   /*node type pointer head is declared; head is the address of a struct list type variable that has two members- num to store an integer and next to store address of another node type variable*/

   **head=(node *)malloc(sizeof(node));**

   /*sizeof() function computes the size of node type data, needed to store an integer and address of another node; required memory spaces are dynamically allocated by malloc(); address of the memory space is assigned to node type pointer variable head*/

   **create(head);**

   /*user-defined function create() is called with real parameter head that refers to the 1st node of the linked list; program control flow shifts to the definition of the function*/

   **printf("List of items before deletion:\n");**

   /*printf() function displays the text in the quotations as it is on the screen except for a newline replaces \n*/

   **print(head);**

   /*user-defined function print() is called with real parameter head that refers to the first node of the linked list; program control flow shifts to the definition of the function*/

   **if (head->num!=-99){**

   /*member of structured data type variable is accessed using pointer operator; pointer head refers to the first node of the linked list; if value of member num of first node head is any integer other than -99, then the linked list is not empty, and following statements, enclosed in the curly braces, are executed*/

      **head=delet(head);**

      /*user-defined function delet() is called with real parameter head that refers to the first node of the linked list; program control flow shifts to the definition of the function that does some pre-defined operation and returns a node type pointer that is assigned to head*/

      **printf("List of items after deletion:\n");**

      /*printf() function displays the text in the double quotations as it is on the screen except for a newline replaces \n*/

```
        print(head);
        /*user-defined function print() is called with real
        parameter head that refers to the first node of the linked
        list; program control flow shifts to the definition of the
        function*/
    }
    /*this closing curly brace specifies the end of 'if'*/
    printf("\n");
    /*this printf() displays a newline on the screen*/
    return 0;
    /*0 is returned as it is the standard for the successful
    execution of the program*/
}
/*the closing curly brace specifies the end of the main() function's
body, as well as the program's end; after that curly brace, no
statement is executed*/
void create(node *pt){
/*definition of create() function starts here with function header
and body; function header is same as function prototype without
semicolon; body of the function is enclosed in curly braces; real
argument that is passed during the function call replaces virtual
parameter pt*/
    int key;
    /*an integer type variable key is declared; required memory
    space is allocated for the variable; this variable is local
    to the function create() and is not visible outside that
    function*/
    static int count=0;
    /*an integer type variable count is declared and initialized to
    0; the variable is declared as static, means the value of count
    is preserved between the function calls and until the end of
    the program execution*/
    static node *head1;
    /*a node type pointer head1 is declared; the pointer is declared
    as static, means this pointer is alive until the end of the
    program execution; this is done so that address of a created
    node is preserved between function calls*/
    printf("Input a number (-99 to end): ");
    /*printf() function displays the text in the double quotations
    as it is on the screen*/
    scanf("%d", &key);
    /*scanf() function reads an integer from input terminal and
    stores the value in the memory spaces allocated for the key*/
    if (key==-99){
    /*if key is -99, we do not want to add anymore node in the
    linked list, and the statements in the body of 'if', enclosed
    by curly braces, are executed*/
```

```
if (count==0){
/*if count equals 0, the linked list is empty, and
following statements, enclosed in the curly braces, are
executed*/
        pt->num=-99;
        /*value of the member num of first node of the linked
        list is set to -99*/
        pt->next=0;
        /*next pointer of the first node is set to 0; there is
        no more node after that in the linked list*/
}
/*this is the end of 'if' with condition (count==0)*/
else{
/*if key=-99 but count≠0, the linked list is not empty and
we do not want to add anymore node to the linked list, and
following statements, enclosed in the curly braces, are
executed*/
        head1->next=0;
        /*next pointer of the last node is set to 0, here is no
        more node after that in the linked list*/
        free(pt);
        /*memory space allocated for node pt is freed*/
}
/*this is the end of above 'else' with condition (count==0)*/
}
/*this is the end of 'if' with condition (key==-99)*/
else{
/*if key≠-99, we want to add more node in the linked list
and following statements, enclosed by curly braces, are
executed*/
    count++;
    /*value of 'count' is incremented by 1 to count the number
    of node added in the linked list*/
    head1=pt;
    /*node pointer pt, passed as argument in the function call,
    is assigned to head1; that is, head1 always refer to the
    last node of the linked list*/
    pt->num=key;
    /*value of key, entered by user, is assigned to member num
    of the last node pt*/
    pt->next=(node *)malloc(sizeof(node));
    /*a new node is created whose address is assigned to the
    member next of last node pt of the linked list, hence next
    of pt points to another node; sizeof() function calculates
    the size of node type data, needed to store an integer
    and address of another node; required memory spaces are
    dynamically allocated by malloc()*/
```

```
    create(pt->next);
    /*user-defined function create() is called again to define
    the newly created node; program control flow shifts to
    definition of the function create()*/
}
    /*this is the end of else with condition (key==-99)*/
}
/*this closing curly brace specifies the end of definition of
create() function; program control flow returns to the point where
the function was called*/
void print(node *pt){
/*definition of print() function starts here with function header
and body; function header is same as function prototype without
semicolon; body of the function is enclosed in curly braces; real
argument that is passed during the function call replaces virtual
parameter pt*/
    if (pt->num==-99)
    /*if value of the member num of first node pt is -99, the linked
    list is empty, and following statement is executed*/
        printf("The list is empty.");
        /*printf() function displays the text in the quotations as
        it is on the screen*/
    else if (pt->next==0)
    /*if pt->num≠-99, linked list is not empty, and we check if pt
    is the last node; if pt is the last node of the linked list
    then condition of 'else if' is true and following statement is
    executed*/
        printf("%d, ", pt->num);
        /*printf() function displays the value of num of last node
        pt on the screen in place of format specifier %d*/
    else{
    /*if pt->num≠-99, linked list is not empty, and pt->next≠0, pt is
    not the last node, in that case, following statements are executed*/
        printf("%d, ", pt->num);
        /*printf() function displays the value of num of current
        node pt on the screen in place of format specifier %d*/
        print(pt->next);
        /*user-defined function print() is called with real
        parameter pt->next that refers to the next node of the
        linked list; program control flow shifts to the definition
        of the function*/
    }
    /*this closing curly brace specifies the end of else*/
}
/*this closing curly brace specifies the end of the definition of
print() function; program control flow returns to the point where
the function was called*/
```

```
node *find(node *pt, int key){
```
/\*definition of the user-defined function find() begins with the function header and body of the function; function header is exactly same as the function prototype except for no semicolon is used, and body of the function is enclosed in curly braces; here pt and key are the virtual parameters which are replaced by real arguments passed during function call\*/

    ```if (pt->next==0 && pt->num!=key)```
    /\*if pt is the last node and value of num is not the key, the item is not found in the linked list, and the following statement is executed\*/

        **return 0;**
        /\*this statement returns 0 to the point where the function was called\*/

    **else if (pt->next->num==key)**
    /\*if pt is not the last node or key is not found in the current node, then we check the value of num of the next node; if the value of num of the next node of pt equals key following statement is executed\*/

        **return pt;**
        /\*if the key is found in the next node of pt, then this statement returns the pointer of node pt to the point where the function was called\*/

    **else if (pt->next->next==0)**
    /\*if pt is not the last node or key is not found in the current node or the next node, and next node is the last node following statement is executed\*/

        **return 0;**
        /\*this statement returns 0 to the point where the function was called\*/

    **else**
    /\*if current node pt or next node of pt is not the last node and key is not found in that node, then the following statement is executed\*/

        **find(pt->next, key);**
        /\*if the key is not available in the current or next node, we call function find() again to search the next nodes for the key; program control flow shifts to the definition of the function\*/

```
}
```
/\*this closing curly brace specifies the end of definition of find() function\*/

```
node *delet(node *pt){
```
/\*definition of user-defined function delet() begins with the function header and body of the function; function header is exactly same as the function prototype except for no semicolon is used and body of the function is enclosed in curly braces; here pt is the
```

virtual parameter which is replaced by real argument passed during function call*/

```
int key;
```
/*an integer type variable key is declared that is local to the function delet() and is not visible outside that function*/

```
node *ptr, *temp;
```
/*two node type pointers ptr and temp are declared; these pointers are local to the function delet() and are not visible outside that function*/

```
printf("\nWhat is the item to be deleted? ");
```
/*printf() function displays the text in the quotations as it is on the screen except for a newline replaces \n*/

```
scanf("%d", &key);
```
/*scanf() function reads an integer from input terminal and stores the value in the memory spaces allocated for the key*/

```
if (pt->num==key){
```
/*if key is found in the first node pt, then the condition of 'if' is true and following 'if else', enclosed in the curly braces, are executed*/

```
    if (pt->next==0)
```
/*if key is found in the first node pt and eventually it is the last node also then condition of this 'if' is true and following statement is executed*/

```
        pt->num=-99;
```
/*value of num of the first and last node is set to -99 that deletes the only node of the linked list and convert it to an empty list*/

```
    else{
```
/*if key is found in the first node pt but it is not the last node then to delete that first node pt, following statements in the body of 'else' (enclosed by curly braces) are executed*/

```
        temp=pt->next;
```
/*next node of pt is stored in the node type pointer temp*/

```
        free(pt);
```
/*calling library function free() with parameter pt, that deletes the first node pt*/

```
        pt=temp;
```
/*second node of the linked list that was saved in pointer temp is now assigned to pt that makes it the first node of the list*/

```
    }
```
/*this is the end of 'else'*/

```
}
```
/*this is the end of 'if' with condition (pt->num==key)*/

```
else{
/*if key is not found in the first node then following
statements in the body of 'else', enclosed in curly braces, are
executed*/
    ptr=find(pt, key);
    /*user-defined function find() is called with argument pt
    and key; program control flow shifts to the definition of
    the function; find() searches the linked list for key, if
    key is not found it returns 0 that is assigned to ptr; if
    key is found in the next node of pt then pointer pt is
    returned that is assigned to ptr*/
    if (ptr==0)
    /*if key is not found in the linked list then above condition
    is true and following statement is executed*/
        printf("Key not found.\n");
        /*printf() function displays the text in the quotations
        as it is on the screen except for a newline replaces
        \n*/
    else if (ptr->next->next==0){
    /*if key is found in the last node then above condition of
    'else if' is true and following statements, enclosed in the
    curly braces, are executed to delete the last node*/
        free(ptr->next);
        /*library function free() is called to free next node
        of ptr, which is the last node of the linked list where
        the key was found*/
        ptr->next=0;
        /*make the current node ptr as the last node by setting
        its 'next' value to 0*/
    }
    /*this is the end of 'else if' with condition (ptr->next-
    >next==0)*/
    else{
    /*if key is found in the next node of ptr, but the node is not
    the last one of the linked list then following statements,
    enclosed in curly braces, are executed to delete the next
    node of ptr; this operation is more understandable if we
    consider ptr as the 3rd node, ptr->next refers to 4th node
    and ptr->next->next refers to 5th node; here we need to
    delete the 4th node*/
        temp=ptr->next->next;
        /*next node of the node ptr->next (5th node) is saved
        to node type pointer temp; temp now refers to the 5th
        node of the linked list*/
        free(ptr->next);
        /*library function free() is called to free next node
        of ptr, which is the 4th node of the linked list where
        the key was found*/
```

```
        ptr->next=temp;
        /*5th node is linked with the 3rd node; previously next
        of the 3rd node (ptr->next) holds the address of the
        4th node and now ptr->next holds the address of the 5th
        node*/
      }
      /*this is the end of 'else' with condition (ptr==0)*/
    }
    /*this is the end of 'else' with condition (pt->num==key)*/
    return pt;
    /*pointer of the first node pt of the linked list is returned
    to the point where the function was called*/
}
/*this closing curly brace specifies the end of the definition of
delet() function*/
```

## PROBLEM-13
**Write a program to create a linear linked list interactively and insert a given item before and after a specified node of the list. The program will display all the items before and after insertion.**

Flowchart of the Solution:

Figure 5.7 shows the flowcharts followed to solve this problem.

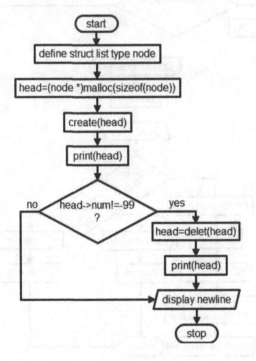

FIGURE 5.7  Flowcharts followed to solve the problem.

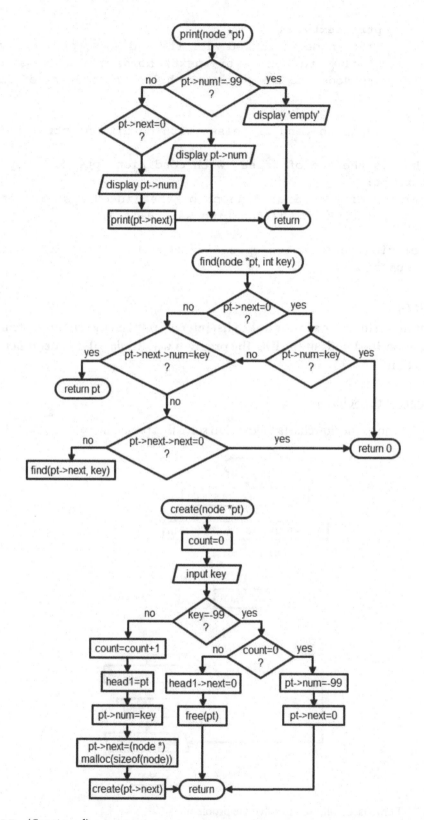

FIGURE 5.7 (Continued)

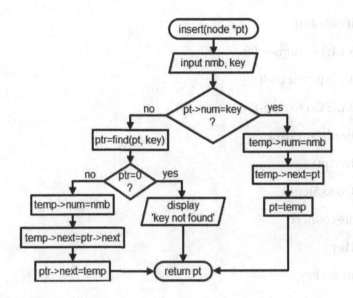

FIGURE 5.7   (Continued)

## Algorithm of the Solution:

Step-1: Start

Step-2: Define struct list node with members num and next

Step-3: Call function create(head)

Step-4: Call function print(head)

Step-5: If head->num≠−99

      5.1: head←insert(head) [call function insert()]

      5.2: Call function print(head)

Step-6: Display enter

Step-7: Stop

## Algorithm for the function create(pt):

Step-1: Initialize count←0

Step-2: Read value of key

Step-3: If key=−99

        3.1: If count=0

            3.1.1: pt->num←−99

            3.1.2: pt->next←0

            3.1.3: Go to Step-8

        3.2: head1->next←0

        3.3: free(pt)

        3.4: Go to Step-8

Step-4: count←count+1

Step-5: head1←pt

Step-6: pt->num←key

Step-7: Call function create(pt->next)

Step-8: Return.

## Algorithm for the function print(pt):

Step-1: If pt->num=−99

        1.1: Display 'empty list'

        1.2: Go to Step-4

Step-2: If pt->next=0

        2.1: Display value of pt->num

        2.2: Go to Step-4

Step-3: Display value of pt->num

Step-4: Return.

## Algorithm for the function find(pt, key):

Step-1: If pt->next=0

        1.1: If pt->num≠key

            1.1.1: Go to Step-3.1

Step-2: If pt->next->num=key

        2.1: Return value of pt

Step-3: If pt->next->next=0

      3.1: Return 0

Step-4: Call function find(pt->next, key)

## Algorithm for the function insert(pt):

Step-1: Read value of nmb and key

Step-2: If pt->num=key

      2.1: temp->num←nmb

      2.2: temp->next←pt

      2.3: pt←temp

      2.4: Go to Step-8

Step-3: ptr←find(pt, key) [call function find()]

Step-4: If ptr=0

      4.1: Display 'key not found'

      4.1: Go to Step-8

Step-5: temp->num←nmb

Step-6: temp->next←ptr->next

Step-7: ptr->next←temp

Step-8: Return value of pt

Programming Code of the Solution:

```c
#include <stdio.h>
#include <stdlib.h>
typedef struct list{
    int num;
    struct list *next;} node;
void create(node *pt);
void print(node *pt);
node *find(node *pt, int key);
node *insert(node *pt);
int main(){
    node *head;
    head=(node *)malloc(sizeof(node));
    create(head);
```

```
        head=(node *)malloc(sizeof(node));
        create(head);
        printf("List of items before insertion:\n");
        print(head);
        if (head->num!=-99){
            head=insert(head);
            printf("List of items after insertion:\n");
            print(head);
        }
        printf("\n");
        return 0;
}
void create(node *pt){
    int key;
    static int count=0;
    static node *head1;
    printf("Input a number (-99 at end): ");
    scanf("%d", &key);
    if (key==-99){
        if (count==0){
            pt->num=-99;
            pt->next=0;
        }

        else{
            head1->next=0;
            free(pt);
        }
    }
    else{
        count++;
        head1=pt;
        pt->num=key;
        pt->next=(node *)malloc(sizeof(node));
        create(pt->next);
    }
}
void print(node *pt){
    if (pt->num==-99)
        printf("The list is empty.");
    else if (pt->next==0)
        printf("%d, ", pt->num);
```

```c
void print(node *pt){
    if (pt->num==-99)
        printf("The list is empty.");
    else if (pt->next==0)
        printf("%d, ", pt->num);
    else{
        printf("%d, ", pt->num);
        print(pt->next);
    }
}
node *find(node *pt, int key){
    if (pt->next==0 && pt->num!=key)
        return 0;
    else if (pt->next->num==key)
        return pt;
    else if (pt->next->next==0)
        return 0;
    else
        find(pt->next, key);
}
node *insert(node *pt){
    int key, nmb;
    node *ptr, *temp;
    printf("\nWhat is the item to be inserted? ");
    scanf("%d", &nmb);
    printf("What is the item before which the item to be inserted? ");
    scanf("%d", &key);
    if (pt->num==key){
        temp=(node *)malloc(sizeof(node));
        temp->num=nmb;
        temp->next=pt;
        pt=temp;
    }
    else{
        ptr=find(pt, key);
        if (ptr==0)
            printf("Key not found. Item cannot be inserted.\n");
        else{
            temp=(node *)malloc(sizeof(node));
            temp->num=nmb;
            temp->next=ptr->next;
            ptr->next=temp;
        }
    }
    return pt;
}
```

Input and Output of the Executed Program:

```
Input a number (-99 at end): 12
Input a number (-99 at end): 23
Input a number (-99 at end): 34
Input a number (-99 at end): 45
Input a number (-99 at end): 56
Input a number (-99 at end): 67
Input a number (-99 at end): 78
Input a number (-99 at end): 89
Input a number (-99 at end): -99
List of items before insertion:
12, 23, 34, 45, 56, 67, 78, 89,
What is the item to be inserted? 40
What is the item before which the item to be inserted? 45
List of items after insertion:
12, 23, 34, 40, 45, 56, 67, 78, 89,
```

## Explanation of the Programming Code:

**#include <stdio.h>**
/*header file stdio.h contains prototypes of the library functions printf(), scanf(), and sizeof(); the header file must be included using preprocessor directive #include before the functions are called in the program*/
**#include <stdlib.h>**
/*header file stdlib.h contains prototypes of the library functions free(), and malloc(); the header file must be included using preprocessor directive #include before the functions are called in the program*/
**typedef struct list{**
/*new data type struct list is created using keyword struct; members of struct list are declared in the curly braces*/
    **int num;**
    /*integer type variable num is declared, this is a member of the data type struct list*/
    **struct list *next;**
    /*struct list type pointer next is declared as second member of the data type struct list; next contains address of another struct list*/
**} node;**
/*keyword typedef gives struct list a new name node and after this definition identifier node can be used as an abbreviation of the data type struct list; definition of the structured data type must end with a semicolon; no variable of the defined data type struct list is declared here*/
**void create(node *pt);**

```
/*this is the prototype (or declaration) of the user-defined function
create() that must end with a semicolon; create() takes node type
pointer as a parameter, performs some predefined operations, and
returns nothing*/
void print(node *pt);
/*this is the prototype (or declaration) of the user-defined function
print() that must end with a semicolon; print() takes node type
pointer as a parameter, performs some predefined operations, and
returns nothing*/
node *find(node *pt, int key);
/*this is the prototype (or declaration) of the user-defined
function find() that must end with a semicolon; find() takes a node
type pointer and an integer as parameters, performs some predefined
operations, and returns a node type pointer*/
node *insert(node *pt);
/*this is the prototype (or declaration) of the user-defined function
delet() that must end with a semicolon; delet() takes a node type
pointer as a parameter, performs some predefined operations, and
returns a node type pointer*/
int main(){
/*all C programs must have a main() function with return type void
or int; here, there is no parameter of the main() function, and it
returns an integer; opening curly brace specifies the start of the
main() function and no statement before that curly brace is executed
by the compiler*/
    node *head;
    /*node type pointer head is declared; head is the address of a
    struct list type variable that has two members- num to store
    an integer and next to store address of another node type
    variable*/
    head=(node *)malloc(sizeof(node));
    /*sizeof() function computes the size of node type data, needed
    to store an integer and address of another node; required
    memory spaces are dynamically allocated by malloc(); address
    of the memory space is assigned to node type pointer variable
    head*/
    create(head);
    /*user-defined function create() is called with real parameter
    head that refers to the 1st node of the linked list; program
    control flow shifts to the definition of the function*/
    printf("List of items before deletion:\n");
    /*printf() function displays the text in the quotations as it
    is on the screen except for a newline replaces \n*/
    print(head);
    /*user-defined function print() is called with real parameter
    head that refers to the first node of the linked list; program
    control flow shifts to the definition of the function*/
```

```
if (head->num!=-99){
```
/*member of structured data type variable is accessed using pointer operator; pointer head refers to the first node of the linked list; if value of member num of first node head is any integer other than -99, then the linked list is not empty, and following statements, enclosed in the curly braces, are executed*/

```
    head=insert(head);
```
/*user-defined function insert() is called with real parameter head that refers to the first node of the linked list; program control flow shifts to the definition of the function that does some pre-defined operation and returns a node type pointer that is assigned to head*/

```
    printf("List of items after deletion:\n");
```
/*printf() function displays the text in the double quotations as it is on the screen except for a newline replaces \n*/

```
    print(head);
```
/*user-defined function print() is called with real parameter head that refers to the first node of the linked list; program control flow shifts to the definition of the function*/

```
}
```
/*this closing curly brace specifies the end of 'if'*/

```
printf("\n");
```
/*this printf() displays a newline on the screen*/

```
return 0;
```
/*0 is returned as it is the standard for the successful execution of the program*/

```
}
```
/*the closing curly brace specifies the end of the main() function's body, as well as the program's end; after that curly brace, no statement is executed*/

```
void create(node *pt){
```
/*definition of create() function starts here with function header and body; function header is same as function prototype without semicolon; body of the function is enclosed in curly braces; real argument that is passed during the function call replaces virtual parameter pt*/

```
    int key;
```
/*an integer type variable key is declared; required memory space is allocated for the variable; this variable is local to the function create() and is not visible outside that function*/

```
    static int count=0;
```
/*an integer type variable count is declared and initialized to 0; the variable is declared as static, means the value of

count is preserved between the function calls and until the end of the program execution*/

**static node *head1;**

/*a node type pointer head1 is declared; the pointer is declared as static, means this pointer is alive until the end of the program execution; this is done so that address of a created node is preserved between function calls*/

**printf("Input a number (-99 to end): ");**

/*printf() function displays the text in the double quotations as it is on the screen*/

**scanf("%d", &key);**

/*scanf() function reads an integer from input terminal and stores the value in the memory spaces allocated for the key*/

**if (key==-99){**

/*if key is -99, we do not want to add anymore node in the linked list, and the statements in the body of 'if', enclosed by curly braces, are executed*/

    **if (count==0){**

    /*if count equals 0, the linked list is empty, and following statements, enclosed in the curly braces, are executed*/

        **pt->num=-99;**

        /*value of the member num of first node of the linked list is set to -99*/

        **pt->next=0;**

        /*next pointer of the first node is set to 0; there is no more node after that in the linked list*/

    **}**

    /*this is the end of 'if' with condition (count==0)*/

    **else{**

    /*if key=-99 but count≠0, the linked list is not empty and we do not want to add anymore node to the linked list, and following statements, enclosed in the curly braces, are executed*/

        **head1->next=0;**

        /*next pointer of the last node is set to 0, here is no more node after that in the linked list*/

        **free(pt);**

        /*memory space allocated for node pt is freed*/

    **}**

    /*this is the end of above 'else' with condition (count==0)*/

**}**

/*this is the end of 'if' with condition (key==-99)*/

**else{**

/*if key≠-99, we want to add more node in the linked list and following statements, enclosed by curly braces, are executed*/

```
        count++;
        /*value of 'count' is incremented by 1 to count the number
        of node added in the linked list*/
        head1=pt;
        /*node pointer pt, passed as argument in the function call,
        is assigned to head1; that is, head1 always refer to the
        last node of the linked list*/
        pt->num=key;
        /*value of key, entered by user, is assigned to member num
        of the last node pt*/
        pt->next=(node *)malloc(sizeof(node));
        /*a new node is created whose address is assigned to the
        member next of last node pt of the linked list, hence next
        of pt points to another node; sizeof() function calculates
        the size of node type data, needed to store an integer
        and address of another node; required memory spaces are
        dynamically allocated by malloc()*/
        create(pt->next);
        /*user-defined function create() is called again to define
        the newly created node; program control flow shifts to
        definition of the function create()*/
    }
    /*this is the end of else with condition (key==-99)*/
}
```
/*this closing curly brace specifies the end of definition of
create() function; program control flow returns to the point where
the function was called*/
```
void print(node *pt){
```
/*definition of print() function starts here with function header
and body; function header is same as function prototype without
semicolon; body of the function is enclosed in curly braces; real
argument that is passed during the function call replaces virtual
parameter pt*/
```
    if (pt->num==-99)
```
    /*if value of the member num of first node pt is -99, the linked
    list is empty, and following statement is executed*/
```
        printf("The list is empty.");
```
        /*printf() function displays the text in the quotations as
        it is on the screen*/
```
    else if (pt->next==0)
```
    /*if pt->num≠-99, linked list is not empty, and we check if pt
    is the last node; if pt is the last node of the linked list
    then condition of 'else if' is true and following statement is
    executed*/
```
        printf("%d, ", pt->num);
```
        /*printf() function displays the value of num of last node
        pt on the screen in place of format specifier %d*/

```
    else{
    /*if pt->num≠-99, linked list is not empty, and pt->next≠0, pt
    is not the last node, in that case, following statements are
    executed*/
        printf("%d, ", pt->num);
        /*printf() function displays the value of num of current
        node pt on the screen in place of format specifier %d*/
        print(pt->next);
        /*user-defined function print() is called with real
        parameter pt->next that refers to the next node of the
        linked list; program control flow shifts to the definition
        of the function*/
    }
    /*this closing curly brace specifies the end of else*/
}
/*this closing curly brace specifies the end of the definition of
print() function; program control flow returns to the point where
the function was called*/
node *find(node *pt, int key){
/*definition of the user-defined function find() begins with the
function header and body of the function; function header is exactly
same as the function prototype except for no semicolon is used,
and body of the function is enclosed in curly braces; here pt and
key are the virtual parameters which are replaced by real arguments
passed during function call*/
    if (pt->next==0 && pt->num!=key)
    /*if pt is the last node and value of num is not the key,
    the item is not found in the linked list, and the following
    statement is executed*/
        return 0;
        /*this statement returns 0 to the point where the function
        was called*/
    else if (pt->next->num==key)
    /*if pt is not the last node or key is not found in the current
    node, then we check the value of num of the next node; if
    the value of num of the next node of pt equals key following
    statement is executed*/
        return pt;
        /*if the key is found in the next node of pt, then this
        statement returns the pointer of node pt to the point where
        the function was called*/
    else if (pt->next->next==0)
    /*if pt is not the last node or key is not found in the current
    node or the next node, and next node is the last node following
    statement is executed*/
        return 0;
```

```
       /*this statement returns 0 to the point where the function
       was called*/
   else
   /*if current node pt or next node of pt is not the last node
   and key is not found in that node, then the following statement
   is executed*/
       find(pt->next, key);
       /*if the key is not available in the current or next node,
       we call function find() again to search the next nodes for
       the key; program control flow shifts to the definition of
       the function*/
}
/*this closing curly brace specifies the end of definition of find()
function*/
node *insert(node *pt){
/*definition of user-defined function insert() starts here with the
function header and body of the function; function header is exactly
same as the function prototype except for no semicolon is used and
body of the function is enclosed in the curly braces; here pt is the
virtual parameter which is replaced by real argument passed during
function call*/
   int key, nmb;
   /*two integer type variables are declared that are local
   to the function insert() and are not visible outside that
   function*/
   node *ptr, *temp;
   /*two node type pointers are declared; these pointers are local
   to the function insert() and are not visible outside that
   function*/
   printf("\nWhat is the item to be inserted? ");
   /*printf() function displays the text in the quotations as it
   is on the screen except for a newline replaces \n*/
   scanf("%d", &nmb);
   /*scanf() function reads an integer from input terminal and
   stores it in the memory spaces allocated for the nmb*/
   printf("What is the item before which the item to be"
          " inserted? ");
   /*printf() function displays the text in the quotations as it
   is on the screen*/
   scanf("%d", &key);
   /*function scanf() reads an integer from input terminal and
   stores it in the memory spaces allocated for the key*/
   if (pt->num==key){
   /*if key is found in the first node pt, then the condition of
   'if' is true and following statements, enclosed in the curly
   braces, are executed that inserts a new node before pt and makes
   it the first node*/
```

```
temp=(node *)malloc(sizeof(node));
```
/*a new node temp is created; sizeof() function calculates
the size of node type data, needed to store an integer and
address of another node, and required memory spaces are
dynamically allocated by malloc(); address of the memory
space is assigned to node type pointer temp*/
```
temp->num=nmb;
```
/*value of nmb is stored in num of the node temp*/
```
temp->next=pt;
```
/*newly created node temp is linked with the first node pt,
member next of node temp now refers to the first node pt of
the linked list*/
```
pt=temp;
```
/*newly created node temp is now assigned to pt that makes
pt the first node of the linked list*/
```
}
```
/*this is the end of 'if' with condition (pt->num==key)*/
```
else{
```
/*if key is not found in the first node, following statements
in the body of 'else', enclosed in the curly braces, are
executed*/
```
    ptr=find(pt, key);
```
/*user-defined function find() is called with argument pt
and key; program control flow shifts to the definition of
the function; find() searches the linked list for key, if
key is not found it returns 0 which is assigned to ptr;
if key is found in the next node of pt then pointer pt is
returned which is assigned to ptr*/
```
    if (ptr==0)
```
/*if key is not found in the linked list, above condition
is true and following statement is executed*/
```
        printf("Key not found. Item cannot be inserted.\n");
```
/*printf() function displays the text in the quotations
as it is on the screen except for a newline replaces
\n*/
```
    else{
```
/*if key is found in the next node of ptr, then following
statements are executed to insert the new node after ptr;
this operation is more understandable if we consider ptr as
the 3rd node and ptr->next refers to 4th node; here we need
to insert the new node before the 4th node*/
```
        temp=(node *)malloc(sizeof(node));
```
/*a new node temp is created; sizeof() function computes
the size of node type data, needed to store an integer
and address of another node, and required memory spaces
are dynamically allocated by malloc(); address of the
memory space is assigned to node type pointer temp*/

```
                    temp->num=nmb;
                    /*value of nmb is assigned to num of the node temp*/
                    temp->next=ptr->next;
                    /*newly created node temp is linked with the 4th node,
                    member next of node temp now refers to the 4th node
                    (next node of ptr)*/
                    ptr->next=temp;
                    /*newly created node temp is now assigned to member
                    next of ptr (next of 3rd node) that makes temp the 4th
                    node and old 4th node the 5th node of the linked list*/
            }
            /*this is the end of 'else' with condition (ptr==0)*/
        }
        /*this is the end of 'else' with condition (pt->num==key)*/
        return pt;
        /*pointer of the first node pt of the linked list is returned
        to the point where the function was called*/
}
/*this closing curly brace specifies the end of the definition of
delet() function*/
```

## EXERCISES

MCQ with Answers

1) What is the size of a C structure?

   A) C structure is always 128 bytes

   B) The size of the C structure is the total bytes of all elements of a structure

   C) The size of the C structure is the size of the largest element

   D) None of the above

2) Choose a correct statement about C structure.

   A) Structure elements can be initialized at the time of declaration

   B) Structure members cannot be initialized at the time of declaration

   C) Only integer members of a structure can be initialized at the time of declaration

   D) None of the above

3) Choose a correct statement about C structure elements.

   A) Structure elements are stored on random free memory locations

   B) Structure elements are stored in register memory locations

C) Structure elements are stored in contiguous memory locations

D) None of the above

4) In a nested structure definition, with division.district.station statement, member district is actually present in the structure

A) division

B) district

C) station

D) All of the above

5) What is actually passed if you pass a structure variable to a function?

A) Copy of structure variable

B) Reference of a structure variable

C) Starting address of structure variable

D) Ending address of structure variable

6) What are the types of data allowed inside a structure?

A) int, float, double, long double

B) char, enum, union

C) pointers and same structure type members

D) All of the above

7) Can we declare a function inside a structure of a C program?

A) Yes

B) No

C) Depends on compiler

D) Yes, but run-time error

8) What is the important difference between structure and union?

A) There is no difference

B) Union takes less memory

C) Union is faster

D) Structure is faster

9) Which of the following operation is illegal in structures?

    A) Typecasting of structure

    B) Pointer to a variable of the same structure

    C) Dynamic allocation of memory for the structure

    D) All of the above

10) Presence of code like "div.dis.pol = 10" indicate

    A) Syntax error

    B) Structure

    C) Double data type

    D) An ordinary variable name

11) Which of the following is themselves a collection of different data types?

    A) string

    B) structure

    C) char

    D) All of the above

12) A user-defined data type can be derived by

    A) struct

    B) enum

    C) typedef

    D) All of the above

13) Which operator connects the structure name to its member name?

    A) –

    B) .

    C) <–

    D) Both <– and .

14) Which of the following cannot be a structure member?

    A) Another structure

    B) Function

C) Array

D) None of the above

15) Which of the following structure declaration will throw an error?

A) struct temp{}s;

B) struct temp{}; struct temp s;

C) struct temp s; struct temp{};

D) None of the above

16) Number of bytes in memory taken by the below structure is as follows:

struct test{int n; char c;};

A) Multiple of integer size

B) Integer size + character size

C) Depends on the platform

D) Multiple of word size

17) What is the similarity between a structure, union, and enumeration?

A) All of them let us define new values

B) All of them let us define new data types

C) All of them let us define new pointers

D) All of them let us define new structures

18) Size of a union is determined by the size of

A) First member in the union

B) Last member in the union

C) Biggest member in the union

D) Sum of the sizes of all members

19) Members of a union are accessed as

A) union-name.member

B) union-pointer->member

C) Both union-name.member & union-pointer->member

D) None of the above

20) Which of the following user-defined data type shares its memory with each other?

   A) structure

   B) union

   C) class

   D) array

21) Which of the following share a similarity in syntax?

   (1) union, (2) structure, (3) arrays, and (4) pointers

   A) 3 and 4

   B) 1 and 2

   C) 1 and 3

   D) 1, 3 and 4

[Ans. B, B, C, A, A, D, B, B, A, B, B, D, B, B, D, C, B, C, C, B, B]

## Questions with Short Answers

1) Define structure.

   Ans. The structure is a user-defined datatype in the C programming language that combines different data types. Structure aids in the creation of a more meaningful complex data type. It is comparable to an array; however, an array only retains the same data type. Structure, on the other hand, may store different data types, making it more practical.

2) Can the structure variable be initialized as soon as it is declared?

   Ans. Structure variables can be initialized when they are declared. This procedure is similar to that for initializing arrays. The structure declaration is followed by an equal sign and a list of initialization values with respect to the order of structure elements only, separated by commas and enclosed in braces. For example, look at the following statements for initializing the values of the members of the complex structure variable.

```
struct num{
        int real;
        int imag;
} complex = {10, 15};
```

3) Can the members of a structure be initialized as soon as it is declared?

   Ans. We cannot initialize structure members with its declaration; consider the given code that is incorrect, and the compiler generates an error.

```
struct num{
        int real=10;
        int imag=15;
};
```

The reason for the error is simple; when a datatype is declared, no memory is allocated for it. Memory is allocated only when variables are created.

4) Is there a way to compare two structure variables?

Ans. In c, it is not permitted to check or compare structure variables directly with logical operators. We need to compare element by element of the structure variables.

5) What is a stack? What is the method to save data in a stack?

Ans. A stack is a linear data structure. The First In Last Out (FILO) technique is used to store data in the stack data structure type. At any given time, just the top of the stack is accessible. A PUSH is a storage mechanism, whereas a POP is a retrieval mechanism.

6) Describe dynamic data structure in C programming language?

Ans. Dynamic data structures are those that expand and contract as needed. Dynamic data structures allocate memory blocks from the heap as required and use pointers to connect those blocks into some data structure. When a data structure no longer requires a memory block, it returns it to the heap for reuse. This recycling makes very efficient use of memory.

7) What is a nested structure?

Ans. In C, a nested structure is a structure within a structure. As we define structure members inside a structure, one structure can be declared inside another structure. For example, the college structure is declared inside the student structure in the following structure declarations:

```
struct college{
        int colid;
        char colname[50];
};
struct student{
        int stid;
        char stname[20];
        float cgpa;
        struct college;
} stdata;
```

8) What is a self-referential structure?

Ans. A self-referential structure is one whose members can point to the same type of structure variable. They can point to the same type of structure as their member with one or more pointers. In dynamic data structures such as trees, linked lists, and so on, the self-referential structure is widely used. A linked list of the same struct type will be used to point to the next node of a node. In the example below, the pointer next refers to a structure of type node. As a result, the structure node is a self-referential structure with the referencing pointer next.

```
struct node{
        int data;
        struct node *next;
};
```

9) What are enumerations?

Ans. An enumeration (enum) is a special data type that represents a group of constants. It is used to assign names to the integral constants, making a program easy to read and maintain. The enum keyword is used to create an enum. The constants declared inside are separated by commas. Enumerated types enable programmers to use more meaningful words as variable values. By default, the first item in the list is assigned the value 0, the second item is assigned the value 1, and so on. In the following example, red=0, green=1, and blue=2.

```
enum color{
    red;
    green;
    blue;
};
```

Assigning custom values to enum elements is also allowed in C. In the example below- red=12, green=13, and blue=15.

```
enum color{
    red=12;
    green;
    blue=15;
};
```

10) What are linked lists?

Ans. A linked list is a dynamic data structure in which each element (called a node) consists of two items: data and a reference (or pointer) to another node. A linked list is a collection of nodes, each of which is linked to another via a pointer. After array, the linked list is the most often used data structure. Using linked lists to store data is an efficient way to use memory.

11) What is FIFO?

Ans. A data structure known as a queue exists in C programming. The FIFO format is used to store and access data in this structure. First In, First Out is abbreviated as FIFO. It is a data structure processing approach in which the oldest element is processed first and the newest element is processed last.

12) What are binary trees?

Ans.

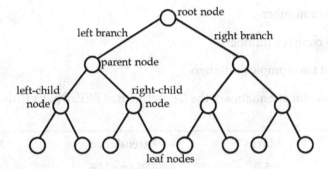

Binary trees are an extension of the concept of linked lists. A binary tree is a nonlinear data structure of the tree type with a maximum of two children for each parent. Along with the data element, every node in a binary tree has a left and right reference. The root node is the node at the very top of a tree's hierarchy. The parent nodes are the nodes that include additional subnodes. The left child and right child are the two child nodes of a parent node.

13) What is a heap? What are the advantages and disadvantages of a heap?

Ans. A heap is a customized tree-based data structure that is essentially an almost complete tree that satisfies the heap property: in a max-heap, the key of parent node P is larger than or equal to the key of child node C for any given node C. The key of P in a min-heap is less than or equal to the key of C.

It takes longer to store data on the heap than it does on the stack. The main benefit of employing the heap, though, is its adaptability. This is because the memory in this structure can be allocated and removed in any sequence. If an algorithm is well-designed and implemented, it can compensate for the slowness in a heap.

Problems to Practice

1) Write a program to read and display information of a student using structure.

2) Write a program to read and display information of n number of students using structure and dynamic memory allocation.

3) Write a program to add two complex numbers using structure.

4) Write a program to create and display a singly linked list of n nodes.

5) Write a program to create and display a doubly linked list of n nodes.

6) Write a program to create and display a circular linked list of n nodes.

7) Write a program to display the truth table of three input EX-OR gate.

8) Write a program that uses functions to perform the following operations:

(a) Reading a complex number

(b) Writing a complex number

(c) Addition of two complex numbers

(d) Multiplication of two complex numbers

9) The marks distribution for attendance of the Department of EEE, Dhaka University, is given below:

| Attendance | Marks | Attendance | Marks |
|---|---|---|---|
| 90% and above | 5.0 | 70% to <75% | 3.0 |
| 80% to <90% | 4.5 | 65% to <70% | 2.5 |
| 70% to <80% | 4.0 | 60% to <65% | 2.0 |
| 60% to <70% | 3.5 | Less than 60% | 0.0 |

There were 30 classes of EEE-1102 in the current session. Calculate the obtained attendance marks of the following n students:

| Class Roll | No. of Classes | Class Roll | No. of Classes |
|---|---|---|---|
| 101 | 27 | 106 | 28 |
| 102 | 15 | 107 | 12 |
| 103 | 21 | 108 | 27 |
| 104 | 19 | 109 | 9 |
| 105 | 12 | 110 | 28 |

10) Answer scripts of final examination of the Department of EEE, Dhaka University, have been examined by two examiners independently. The obtained final marks of any course will be average of the two marks. But, if their marks for any particular script differ by 20% or more, then the script is evaluated by another independent third examiner. And the obtained final marks of that course will be average of the two marks of the examiners whose marks are closer. Write a program to read the following data and determine:

(a) Whether third examination is necessary for a particular answer script.

(b) Obtained final marks (out of 70) by each student of a particular course after third examination if necessary.

| Roll No. | 1st Examiner | 2nd Examiner | Roll No. | 1st Examiner | 2nd Examiner |
|---|---|---|---|---|---|
| 1001 | 65 | 58 | 1004 | 68 | 48 |
| 1002 | 55 | 54 | 1005 | 50 | 52 |
| 1003 | 40 | 30 | 1006 | 15 | 32 |

11) The annual examination results of n students are tabulated as follows:

| Roll No. | EEE-1101 | EEE-1102 | EEE-1103 |
|----------|----------|----------|----------|
| 101 | 69 | 56 | 89 |
| 102 | 80 | 65 | 91 |
| 103 | 45 | 36 | 68 |

Write a program to read the data and determine the following:

(a)  Grade obtained by each student in each subject.

| Marks | Letter Grade | Grade Point |
|-------|-------------|-------------|
| 90% and above | A+ | 4.00 |
| 80% to <90% | A | 3.50 |
| 70% to <60% | B | 3.00 |
| 60% to <70% | C | 2.50 |
| 50% to <60% | D | 2.00 |
| Less than 50% | F | 0.00 |

(b)  Total marks and GPA obtained by each student.

(c)  The position of each student based on GPA (for equal GPA, consider who gets the higher total marks).

(d)  The result should be displayed according to the roll number and merit.

12) Write a program to create a linear linked list interactively and delete a specified node from the list. The program will display all the items before and after deletion.

13) Write a program to create a linear linked list interactively and insert a given item before and after a specified node of the list. The program will display all the items before and after insertion.

14) Write a program to add two distances (in an inch-feet system) using structure.

15) Write a program to compute the difference between two time periods.

16) Write a program to read and display a student's information (roll no., name, and cgpa) using structure.

17) Write a program to create a singly linked list of n nodes and display it in reverse order.

18) Write a program to insert a new node at the beginning of a singly linked list.

19) Write a program to insert a new node at the end of a singly linked list.

20) Write a program to delete the first node of a singly linked list.

21) Write a program to delete the last node of a singly linked list.

22) Write a program to search an existing element in a singly linked list.

23) Write a program to create and display a doubly linked list of n nodes.

24) Write a program to insert a new node at the beginning of a doubly linked list.

25) Write a program to insert a new node at the end of a doubly linked list.

26) Write a program to delete the first node of a doubly linked list.

27) Write a program to delete the last node of a doubly linked list.

28) Write a program to search an existing element in a doubly linked list.

29) Write a program to insert a new node at any position in a doubly linked list.

30) Write a program to delete a node from any position of a doubly linked list.

31) Write a program to create and display a circular linked list of n nodes.

32) Write a program to create a circular linked list of n nodes and display it in reverse order.

33) Write a program to insert a new node at the end of a circular linked list.

34) Write a program to delete the first node of a circular linked list.

35) Write a program to delete the last node of a circular linked list.

36) Write a program to search an existing element in a circular linked list.

37) Write a program to insert a new node at any position in a circular linked list.

38) Write a program to delete a node from any position of a circular linked list.

# File Management

$\mathbf{A}$ FILE IS A MEMORY space where some data is stored. C provides various functions to deal with the file. This chapter provides mechanisms/operations how to manipulate files, known as the file management.

## 6.1  FILE TYPES

Files are needed in C for the following three main reasons:

(1) To preserve data after termination of the program

(2) To input a large amount of data through access of the file that may store the data

(3) To move data from one computer to another.

Two types of files are allowed to use in C program:

(1) Text file: any text editor or .txt file. All the contents are in plain text and can be easily edited or deleted.

(2) Binary file: any .bin file. All the contents are in binary form (0's and 1's) and cannot be easily edited and hence provide better security.

## 6.2  FILE OPERATIONS

Some major operations on file in C are as follows:

(1) *Opening a file:* fopen() is used to open a file. When fopen() opens a file successfully, it will return the address of the first character of the file; otherwise, it returns NULL. Syntax is as follows:

FILE *ptr_name fopen("file_name", "mode");

FILE is a structured data type defined in stdio.h header file and used to refer different file operation.

DOI: 10.1201/9781003302629-6

ptr_name is any pointer name of your choice.

file_name is the name of the file that you want to open with full address path.

mode determines the various operations allowed to perform on the file.

Various file opening modes are as follows:

r, rb – read only mode, return the address of the first character.

w, wb – write only mode, return the address of the first character.

a, ab – use to append content at the end of the file, return the address of the last character.

r+, rb+ or w+, wb+ – read, write, or modify the content, return the address of the first character.

a+, ab+ – read or append content, but modification is not allowed.

Example:

```
FILE *fpr;
fpr = fopen("c:\\myfiles\\newfile.txt", "r");
```

We should always check whether the file was opened successfully before using the file or any file operation is performed. The following code will do the job:

```
if (fpr==NULL){
    printf("Error in opening file…");
    exit();      //program will be prematurely terminated
}
```

(2) *Reading a file:* A file first needs to open in reading mode. After that fgetc() function reads the characters sequentially one after another until EOF (end of file) is reached. Example:

```
char ch = fgetc(fpr);       //at the end ch = EOF
fscanf(fpr, "%c", &ch);
```

To read a string from the file, fgets() function is used. Example:

fgets(str, 10, fpr);

str is the array of char where the string will be stored after the read and 10 is the number of characters to be read.

(3) *Writing to a file:* A file first needs to open in writing or append mode. After that fprintf() or fputc() function is used to write data to the file. Example:

```
FILE *fpw = fopen("c:\\myfiles\\newfile.txt", "w");
scanf("%c", ch);
fprintf(fpw, %c, ch);
fputc(ch, fpw);
```

fputs() function is used to write a string to the file. Example: fputs(str, fpw);

(4) *Closing a file:* fclose() function is used to close an opened file. Syntax: fclose(fpw);

Calling fclose() function ensures file descriptor is properly disposed of and output buffer flushed so that data written to the file will be saved in the file. If anyone failed to do so, operating system properly closes the file before termination of the program.

To read or write in a binary, we need to change the file name and mode of operation as shown below:

```
FILE *fbpr, *fbpw;
fbpr = fopen("c:\\myfiles\\binary.exe", "rb");
fread(&ch, sizeof(char), 1, fbpr);   //1 is the number of character to read

fbpw = fopen("c:\\myfiles\\binary.exe", "wb");
fwrite(&ch, sizeof(char), 1, fbpw); //character ch will be written to file
```

## 6.3 PREPROCESSORS

Preprocessor allows defining macros and transforms the source code before compilation. The directives instruct the preprocessor to do something. Some common uses of preprocessing directives are as follows:

(1) Including header file: #include <stdio.h>, this will replace the contents of the header file stdio.h while transformation.

(2) Macros using #define: #define PI 3.14, this will replace 3.14 in place of PI during transformation.

(3) Function like macros: #define CIRCLE(rad) 3.14*rad*rad, this will replace 3.14*arg* arg every time the program encounters CIRCLE(arg).

## 6.4 CONDITIONAL COMPILATION

Conditional directives are used to instruct the preprocessor to include a block of data or statements depending on some certain conditions. Through conditional directives, same source file can be used for two different programs. Few important conditional directives are as follows:

```
1) #ifdef MAC
          //block of codes
          //these codes will be included in the program if
          //MAC is defined
   #endif
```

```
2) #if expression
        //block of codes
        //these codes will be included if the value of
        //expression is non-zero
   #endif
3) #if expression
        //block of codes
        //these codes will be included if the value of
        //expression is non-zero
   #else
        //block of codes
        //these codes will be included if the value of
        //expression is zero
   #endif
4) #if expression
        //block of codes
        //these codes will be included if the value of
        //expression is non-zero
   #elif expression1
        //block of codes
        //codes will be included if the value of the
        //expression1 is non-zero
   #elif expression2
        //block of codes
        //codes will be included if the value of the
        //expression2 is non-zero
   #else
        //block of codes
        //codes will be included if values of all the
        //above expressions are zero
   #endif
```

## 6.5 EXAMPLES

**PROBLEM-01**

**Write a program to read name and marks of a student and store them in a file.**

Programming Code of the Solution:

```
#include <stdio.h>
#include <stdlib.h>
int main(){
    char name[50];
    float mark;
    FILE *fptr;
    fptr = fopen("C:\\Intel\\student.txt", "w");
```

```
    if (fptr == NULL) {
        printf("Error in opening the file, exiting...");
        exit(1);
    }
    printf("Enter name of the student: ");
    gets(name);
    printf("Enter marks of the student: ");
    scanf("%f", &mark);
    fprintf(fptr, "\nName: %s\nMarks: %0.2f\n", name, mark);
    fclose(fptr);
    return 0;
}
```

<u>Input and Output of the Executed Program:</u>

```
Enter name of the student: Atiq
Enter marks of the student: 78
```

<u>Explanationof the Programming Code:</u>

**#include <stdio.h>**
/*stdio.h header file contains the prototypes of the library functions printf(), scanf(), gets(), fopen(), fprintf() and fclose(), hence needs to be included using #include preprocessor directive*/
**#include <stdlib.h>**
/*stdlib.h header file contains the prototype of the library function exit(), hence needs to be included using #include preprocessor directive*/
**int main(){**
/*C program starts from main() function which will return an integer and there is no argument for the function; the opening curly brace indicates the start of the body of the main() function and the program execution starts from the first statement just after this brace*/
  **char name[50];**
  /*char type array is declared which can take only characters. Size of the array is 50, means it can take up to 50 characters. Each array elements can be accessed using indexes starting from 0 to 49, that is- name[0], name[1], . . ., name[49]*/
  **float mark;**
  /*float type variable is declared which can take and store any decimal value*/
  **FILE *fptr;**
  /*FILE is a structured data type defined in stdio.h header file. Here a FILE type pointer is declared to refer any file*/

```
fptr = fopen("C:\\Intel\\student.txt", "w");
```
/*fopen() function opens a text file named student.txt in the
address C:\\Intel\\ with write mode, indicated by "w", and
returns a FILE type pointer*/
```
if (fptr == NULL){
```
/*after opening a file in C, we must always check whether
the file opens successfully. To do that we check the pointer
returned by fopen() function. If it is NULL then file could not
open. Hence, here if the file failed to open the condition is
true and following two statements will be executed*/
```
    printf("Error in opening the file, exiting . . .");
```
/*output function printf() will display the message inside
the double quotation as it is on the screen*/
```
    exit(1);
```
/*exit(1) function causes abnormal termination of the
program. All buffers, temporary files, streams are deleted
or cleared before the termination*/
```
}
```
/*this closing curly brace indicates the end of the if body*/
```
printf("Enter name of the student:");
```
/*output function printf() will display the message inside the
double quotation as it is on the screen*/
```
gets(name);
```
/*gets() is an input function that can take any string or
array of characters, including space, tab, etc., end with NULL
character \0 and store the string to its parameter name*/
```
printf("Enter marks of the student:");
```
/*output function printf() will display the message inside the
double quotation as it is on the screen*/
```
scanf("%f", &mark);
```
/*scanf() function takes a decimal value from the standard
input terminal and store the float value to the variable
mark*/
```
fprintf(fptr, "\nName: %s\nMarks: %0.2f\n", name, mark);
```
/*fprintf() function will write information inside the double
quotation as it is in the file referred by the pointer fptr.
Here enter is written in place of new line character, string
name in place of %s format specifier and decimal value mark in
place of %0.2f format specifier with 2 point precision*/
```
fclose(fptr);
```
/*once a file is open in C, it is a good practice to close the
file before end of the program to properly flush the output
buffer. This is done here by the fclose() function which close
the file referred by its argument fptr*/
```
return 0;
```
/*0 is returned as it is the standard for the successful
execution of the program*/
```
}
```

/*the closing curly brace indicates the end of the body of main()
function and the end of the program. No statement will execute after
that curly brace*/

## PROBLEM-02
**Write a program to open the file created in the last problem, read name and marks
of a student, and append them in the file.**

Programming Code of the Solution:

```
#include <stdio.h>
#include <stdlib.h>
int main(){
    char name[50];
    float mark;
    FILE *fptr;
    fptr = fopen("C:\\Intel\\student.txt", "a");
    if (fptr == NULL){
        printf("Error in opening the file, exiting...");
        exit(1);
    }
    printf("Enter name of the student: ");
    gets(name);
    printf("Enter marks of the student: ");
    scanf("%f", &mark);
    fprintf(fptr, "\nName: %s\nMarks: %0.2f\n", name, mark);
    fclose(fptr);
    return 0;
}
```

Input and Output of the Executed Program:

```
Enter name of the student: Ahad
Enter marks of the student: 87.5
```

Explanation of the Programming Code:

```
#include <stdio.h>
```
/*stdio.h header file contains the prototypes of the library functions
printf(), scanf(), gets(), fopen(), fprintf() and fclose(), hence
needs to be included using #include preprocessor directive*/
```
#include <stdlib.h>
```
/*stdlib.h header file contains the prototype of the library function
exit(), hence needs to be included using #include preprocessor
directive*/
```
int main(){
```
/*C program starts from main() function which will return an
integer and there is no argument for the function; the opening
curly brace indicates the start of the body of the main() function

and the program execution starts from the first statement just after this brace*/

**char name[50];**
/*char type array is declared which can take only characters. Size of the array is 50, means it can take up to 50 characters. Each array elements can be accessed using indexes starting from 0 to 49, that is- str[0], str[1], . . ., str[49]*/
**float mark;**
/*float type variable is declared which can take and store any decimal value*/
**FILE *fptr;**
/*FILE is a structured data type defined in stdio.h header file. Here a FILE type pointer is declared to refer any file*/
**fptr = fopen("C:\\Intel\\student.txt", "a");**
/*fopen() function opens a text file named student.txt in the address C:\\Intel\\ with append mode, indicated by "a", and returns a FILE type pointer. Anything written into the file will be appended after the previous information*/
**if (fptr == NULL){**
/*after opening a file in C, we must always check whether the file opens successfully. To do that we check the pointer returned by fopen() function. If it is NULL then file could not open. Hence, here if the file failed to open the condition is true and following two statements will be executed */
    **printf("Error in opening the file, exiting . . .");**
    /*output function printf() will display the message inside the double quotation as it is on the screen*/
    **exit(1);**
    /*exit(1) function causes abnormal termination of the program. All buffers, temporary files, streams are deleted or cleared before the termination*/
**}**
/*this closing curly brace indicates the end of the if body*/
**printf("Enter name of the student:");**
/*output function printf() will display the message inside the double quotation as it is on the screen*/
**gets(name);**
/*gets() is an input function that can take any string or array of characters, including space, tab, etc., end with NULL character \0 and store the string to its parameter name*/
**printf("Enter marks of the student:");**
/*output function printf() will display the message inside the double quotation as it is on the screen*/
**scanf("%f", &mark);**
/*scanf() function takes a decimal value from the standard input terminal and store the float value to the variable

mark*/

```
fprintf(fptr, "\nName: %s\nMarks: %0.2f\n", name, mark);
```
/*fprintf() function will write information inside the double
quotation as it is in the file referred by the pointer fptr.
Here enter is written in place of new line character, string
name in place of %s format specifier and decimal value mark in
place of %0.2f format specifier with 2 point precision. As fptr
referred to a file opened as mode "a", these information will
be written after the existing information in the file*/

```
fclose(fptr);
```
/*once a file is open in C, it is a good practice to close the
file before end of the program to properly flush the output
buffer. This is done here by the fclose() function which close
the file referred by its argument fptr*/

```
return 0;
```
/*0 is returned as it is the standard for the successful
execution of the program*/

}
/*the closing curly brace indicates the end of the body of main()
function and the end of the program. No statement will execute after
that curly brace*/

## PROBLEM-03

Write a program to open the file created in the last problem, read information from the file, and display them on the screen.

Programming Code of the Solution:

```c
#include <stdio.h>
#include <stdlib.h>
int main(){
    char ch;
    FILE *fptr;
    fptr = fopen("C:\\Intel\\student.txt", "r");
    if (fptr == NULL){
        printf("Error in opening the file, exiting...");
        exit(1);
    }
    printf("Contents of the file are:\n");
    ch = fgetc(fptr);
    while (ch != EOF){
        printf("%c", ch);
        ch = fgetc(fptr);
    }
    fclose(fptr);
    return 0;
}
```

Input and Output of the Executed Program:

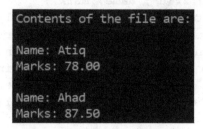

```
Contents of the file are:

Name: Atiq
Marks: 78.00

Name: Ahad
Marks: 87.50
```

## Explanationof the Programming Code:

**#include <stdio.h>**
/*stdio.h header file contains the prototypes of the library functions printf(), fgetc(), fopen() and fclose(), hence needs to be included using #include preprocessor directive*/
**#include <stdlib.h>**
/*stdlib.h header file contains the prototype of the library function exit(), hence needs to be included using #include preprocessor directive*/
**int main(){**
/*C program starts from main() function which will return an integer and there is no argument for the function; the opening curly brace indicates the start of the body of the main() function and the program execution starts from the first statement just after this brace*/
    **char ch;**
    /*char type variable is declared which can take and store only character*/
    **FILE *fptr;**
    /*FILE is a structured data type defined in stdio.h header file. Here a FILE type pointer is declared to refer any file*/
    **fptr = fopen("C:\\Intel\\student.txt", "r");**
    /*fopen() function opens a text file named student.txt in the address C:\\Intel\\ with read mode, indicated by "r", and returns a FILE type pointer*/
    **if (fptr == NULL){**
    /*after opening a file in C, we must always check whether the file opens successfully. To do that we check the pointer returned by fopen() function. If it is NULL then file could not open. Hence, here if the file failed to open the condition is true and following two statements will be executed*/
        **printf("Error in opening the file, exiting . . .");**
        /*output function printf() will display the message inside the double quotation as it is on the screen*/
        **exit(1);**

```
        /*exit(1)  function  causes  abnormal  termination  of  the
        program. All buffers, temporary files, streams are deleted
        or cleared before the termination*/
    }
    /*this closing curly brace indicates the end of the if body*/
    printf("Contents of the file are:\n");
    /*output function printf() will display the message inside the
    double quotation as it is on the screen*/
    ch = fgetc(fptr);
    /*fgetc() function reads a character from the file referred by
    the pointer fptr. At start, it reads the 1st character and the
    pointer automatically points to the next character. Here ch=1st
    character, pointer points to the 2nd character*/
    while (ch!= EOF){
    /*ch is compared with EOF, means whether we reach the end-of-
    file or not. If not, then statements inside the body of the
    while loop will execute*/
        printf("%c", ch);
        /*output function printf() will display the character
        corresponding to ch in place of format specifier %c on
        screen*/
        ch = fgetc(fptr);
        /*now fgetc() function reads 2nd character in the file in the
        1st iteration and pointer points to the 3rd character. This
        ch=2nd character is compared with EOF and if we don't reach
        at the end-of-the file, printf() function prints ch=2nd
        character and fgetc() function reads the 3rd character.
        This continues till we reach the EOF in which case the
        condition becomes false and the program steps out of the
        while loop*/
    }
    /*this closing curly brace indicates the end of the while
    loop*/
    fclose(fptr);
    /*once a file is open in C, it is a good practice to close the
    file before end of the program to properly flush the output
    buffer. This is done here by the fclose() function which close
    the file referred by its argument fptr*/
    return 0;
    /*0 is returned as it is the standard for the successful
    execution of the program*/
}
/*the closing curly brace indicates the end of the body of main()
function and the end of the program. No statement will execute after
that curly brace*/
```

## PROBLEM-04
The annual examination results of n students are tabulated as follows:

| Roll No. | EEE-1101 | EEE-1102 | EEE-1103 |
|----------|----------|----------|----------|
| 101 | 69 | 56 | 89 |
| 102 | 80 | 65 | 91 |
| 103 | 45 | 36 | 68 |

Write a program to read the data and determine the following:

(a) Grade obtained by each student in each subject.

| Marks | Letter Grade | Grade Point |
|-------|--------------|-------------|
| 90% and above | A+ | 4.00 |
| 80% to <90% | A | 3.50 |
| 70% to <60% | B | 3.00 |
| 60% to <70% | C | 2.50 |
| 50% to <60% | D | 2.00 |
| Less than 50% | F | 0.00 |

(b) Total marks and GPA obtained by each student.

(c) The position of each student based on GPA (for equal GPA, consider who gets the higher total marks).

(d) The result should be displayed according to the roll number and merit.

(e) Save the results in a text file and retrieve and print the results from the text file.

Flow Chart of the Solution:

Figure 6.1 shows the flowcharts followed to solve this problem.

Algorithm of the Solution:

Step-1: Start

Step-2: Define struct subject with members mark, point, and letter

Step-3: Define struct exam with members roll, sub[100], total, gpa, and pos

Step-4: Read values of numstd and numsub

Step-5: Initialize i←0

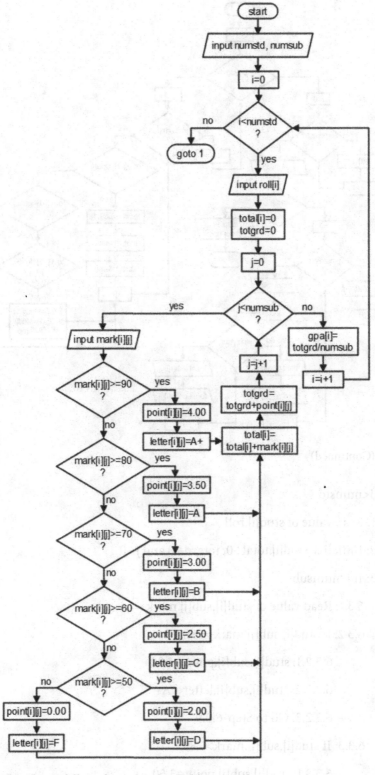

FIGURE 6.1   Flowcharts followed to solve the problem.

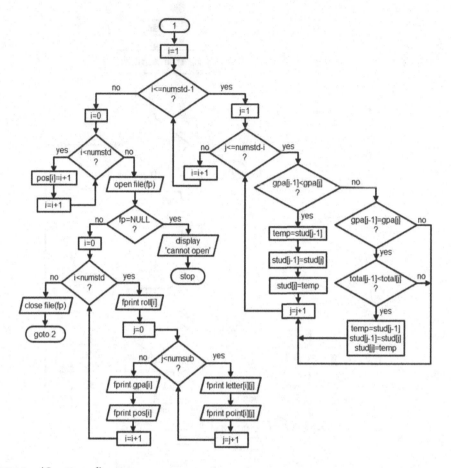

FIGURE 6.1 (Continued)

Step-6: If i<numstd

      6.1: Read value of stud[i].roll

      6.2: Initialize stud[i].total←0, totgrd←0 and j←0

      6.3: If j<numsub

            6.3.1: Read value of stud[i].sub[j].mark

            6.3.2: If stud[i].sub[j].mark>=90

                  6.3.2.1: stud[i].sub[j].point←4.00

                  6.3.2.2: stud[i].sub[j].letter←"A+"

                  6.3.2.3: Go to Step-6.3.9

            6.3.3: If stud[i].sub[j].mark>=80

                  6.3.3.1: stud[i].sub[j].point←3.50

                  6.3.3.2: stud[i].sub[j].letter←"A"

                  6.3.3.3: Go to Step-6.3.9

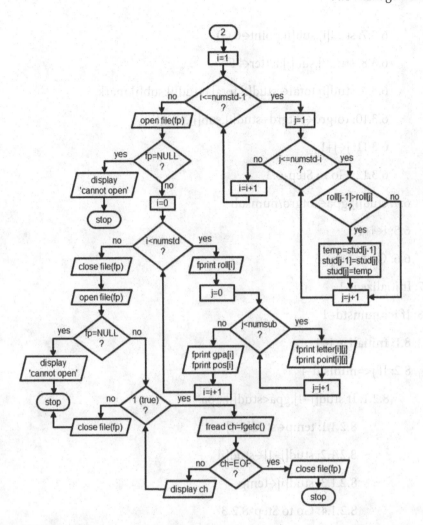

FIGURE 6.1 (Continued)

6.3.4: If stud[i].sub[j].mark>=70

    6.3.4.1: stud[i].sub[j].point←3.00

    6.3.4.2: stud[i].sub[j].letter←"B"

    6.3.4.3: Go to Step-6.3.9

6.3.5: If stud[i].sub[j].mark>=60

    6.3.5.1: stud[i].sub[j].point←2.50

    6.3.5.2: stud[i].sub[j].letter←"C"

    6.3.5.3: Go to Step-6.3.9

6.3.6: If stud[i].sub[j].mark>=50

    6.3.6.1: stud[i].sub[j].point←2.00

    6.3.6.2: stud[i].sub[j].letter←"D"

    6.3.6.3: Go to Step-6.3.9

6.3.7: stud[i].sub[j].point←0.00

6.3.8: stud[i].sub[j].letter←"F"

6.3.9: stud[i].total← stud[i].total+stud[i].sub[j].mark

6.3.10: totgrd←totgrd+stud[i].sub[j].point

6.3.11: j←j+1

6.3.12: Go to Step-6.3

6.4: stud[i].gpa←totgrd/numsub

6.5: i←i+1

6.6: Go to Step-6

Step-7: Initialize i←1

Step-8: If i<=numstd−1

8.1: Initialize j←1

8.2: If j<=numstd−i

8.2.1: If stud[j−1].gpa<stud[j].gpa

8.2.1.1: temp←stud[j−1]

8.2.1.2: stud[j−1]←stud[j]

8.2.1.3: stud[j]←temp

8.2.1.4: Go to Step-8.2.3

8.2.2: If stud[j−1].gpa=stud[j].gpa

8.2.2.1: If stud[j−1].total<stud[j].total

8.2.2.1.1: temp←stud[j−1]

8.2.2.1.2: stud[j−1]←stud[j]

8.2.2.1.3: stud[j]←temp

8.2.3: j←j+1

8.2.4: Go to Step-8.2

8.3: i←i+1

8.4: Go to Step-8

Step-9: Initialize i←0

Step-10: If i<numstd

    10.1: stud[i].pos←i+1

    10.2: i←i+1

    10.3: Go to Step-10

Step-11: fp←fopen()

Step-12: If fp=NULL

    12.1: Display 'Cannot open'

    12.2: Go to Step-24

Step-13: Initialize i←0

Step-14: If i<numstd

    14.1: Save to file stud[i].roll

    14.2: Initialize j←0

    14.3: If j<numsub

        14.3.1: Save values of stud[i].sub[j].letter, stud[i].sub[j].point, stud[i].gpa and stud[i].pos to fp

        14.3.2: j←j+1

        14.3.3: Go to Step-14.3

    14.4: i←i+1

    14.5: Go to Step-14

Step-15: Initialize i←1

Step-16: If i<=numstd−1

    16.1: Initialize j←1

    16.2: If j<=numstd−i

        16.2.1: If stud[j−1].roll>stud[j].roll

            16.2.1.1: temp←stud[j−1]

            16.2.1.2: stud[j−1]←stud[j]

            16.2.1.3: stud[j]←temp

        16.2.2: j←j+1

        16.2.3: Go to Step-16.2

16.3: i←i+1

16.4: Go to Step-16

Step-17: fp←fopen()

Step-18: If fp=NULL

18.1: Display 'Cannot open'

18.2: Go to Step-24

Step-19: Initialize i←0

Step-20: If i<numstd

20.1: Save value of stud[i].roll to fp

20.2: Initialize j←0

20.3: If j<numsub

20.3.1: Save values of stud[i].sub[j].letter, stud[i].sub[j].point, stud[i].gpa, and stud[i].pos to fp

20.3.2: j←j+1

20.3.3: Go to Step-20.3

20.4: i←i+1

20.5: Go to Step-20

Step-21: fp←fopen()

Step-22: If fp=NULL

22.1: Display 'Cannot open'

22.2: Go to Step-25

Step-23: If 1 or true

23.1: ch←fgetc(fp)

23.2: If ch=EOF

23.2.1: Go to Step-24

23.3: Display value of ch

23.4: Go to Step-23

Step-24: Stop

<u>Programming Code of the Solution:</u>

```c
#include <stdio.h>
#include <stdlib.h>
struct subject{
    int mark;
    float point;
    char *letter;
};
struct exam{
    int roll, total, pos;
    struct subject sub[10];
    float gpa;
};
int main(){
    FILE *fp;
    struct exam stud[100], temp;
    int numstd, numsub, i, j;
    float totgrd;
    char ch;
    printf("Enter the number of students: ");
    scanf("%d", &numstd);
    printf("How many subjects: ");
    scanf("%d", &numsub);
    for (i=0; i<numstd; i++){
        printf("Enter the roll no. of student #%d: ", i+1);
        scanf("%d", &stud[i].roll);
        stud[i].total=0;
        totgrd=0;
        for (j=0; j<numsub; j++){
            printf("Mark obtained in EEE-110%d: ", j+1);
            scanf("%d", &stud[i].sub[j].mark);
            if (stud[i].sub[j].mark>=90){
                stud[i].sub[j].point=4.00;
                stud[i].sub[j].letter="A+";
            }
            else if (stud[i].sub[j].mark>=80){
                stud[i].sub[j].point=3.50;
                stud[i].sub[j].letter="A";
            }
            else if (stud[i].sub[j].mark>=70){
                stud[i].sub[j].point=3.00;
                stud[i].sub[j].letter="B";
            }
```

```
        else if (stud[i].sub[j].mark>=60){
            stud[i].sub[j].point=2.50;
            stud[i].sub[j].letter="C";
        }
        else if (stud[i].sub[j].mark>=50){
            stud[i].sub[j].point=2.00;
            stud[i].sub[j].letter="D";
        }
        else{
            stud[i].sub[j].point=0.00;
            stud[i].sub[j].letter="F";
        }
        stud[i].total+=stud[i].sub[j].mark;
        totgrd+=stud[i].sub[j].point;
    }
    stud[i].gpa=totgrd/numsub;
}

for (i=1; i<=numstd-1; i++)
    for (j=1; j<=numstd-i; j++)
        if (stud[j-1].gpa<stud[j].gpa){
            temp=stud[j-1];
            stud[j-1]=stud[j];
            stud[j]=temp;
        }
        else if (stud[j-1].gpa==stud[j].gpa)
            if (stud[j-1].total<stud[j].total){
                temp=stud[j-1];
                stud[j-1]=stud[j];
                stud[j]=temp;
            }
for (i=0; i<numstd; i++)
    stud[i].pos=i+1;
```

```
fp=fopen("c:\\myfiles\\Results.txt", "w");
if (fp==NULL){
    puts("Cannot open source file!\n");
    exit(1);
}
fprintf(fp, "\nResult according to merit position...\n");
for (i=0; i<numstd; i++){
    fprintf(fp, "Roll No.: %d\n", stud[i].roll);
    for (j=0; j<numsub; j++)
        fprintf(fp, "EEE-110%d: %s (%0.2f)\n", j+1,
                stud[i].sub[j].letter, stud[i].sub[j].point);
    fprintf(fp, "GPA: %0.2f\nMerit Position: %d\n\n",
            stud[i].gpa, stud[i].pos);
}
fclose(fp);
for (i=1; i<=numstd-1; i++)
    for (j=1; j<=numstd-i; j++)
        if (stud[j-1].roll>stud[j].roll){
            temp=stud[j-1];
            stud[j-1]=stud[j];
            stud[j]=temp;
        }
fp=fopen("c:\\myfiles\\Results.txt", "a");
if (fp==NULL){
    puts("Cannot open target file!\n");
    exit(1);
}
fprintf(fp, "\nResult according to roll no....\n");
for (i=0; i<numstd; i++){
    fprintf(fp, "Roll No.: %d\n", stud[i].roll);
    for (j=0; j<numsub; j++)
        fprintf(fp, "EEE-110%d: %s (%0.2f)\n", j+1,
                stud[i].sub[j].letter, stud[i].sub[j].point);
    fprintf(fp, "GPA: %0.2f\nMerit Position: %d\n\n",
            stud[i].gpa, stud[i].pos);
}
```

Input and Output of the Executed Program:

```
Enter the number of students: 3
How many subjects: 3
Enter the roll no. of student #1: 101
Mark obtained in EEE-1101: 69
Mark obtained in EEE-1102: 56
Mark obtained in EEE-1103: 89
Enter the roll no. of student #2: 102
Mark obtained in EEE-1101: 80
Mark obtained in EEE-1102: 65
Mark obtained in EEE-1103: 91
Enter the roll no. of student #3: 103
Mark obtained in EEE-1101: 45
Mark obtained in EEE-1102: 36
Mark obtained in EEE-1103: 68
```

```
Result according to merit position...
Roll No.: 102
EEE-1101: A (3.50)
EEE-1102: C (2.50)
EEE-1103: A+ (4.00)
GPA: 3.33
Merit Position: 1

Roll No.: 101
EEE-1101: C (2.50)
EEE-1102: D (2.00)
EEE-1103: A (3.50)
GPA: 2.67
Merit Position: 2
```

```
Result according to roll no....
Roll No.: 101
EEE-1101: C (2.50)
EEE-1102: D (2.00)
EEE-1103: A (3.50)
GPA: 2.67
Merit Position: 2

Roll No.: 102
EEE-1101: A (3.50)
EEE-1102: C (2.50)
EEE-1103: A+ (4.00)
GPA: 3.33
Merit Position: 1
```

```
Roll No.: 103
EEE-1101: F (0.00)
EEE-1102: F (0.00)
EEE-1103: C (2.50)
GPA: 0.83
Merit Position: 3
```

## Explanation of the Programming Code:

```
#include <stdio.h>
```
/*header file stdio.h contains prototypes of the library functions like printf(), scanf(), fopen(), fclose(), fprint() etc., hence needs to be included using preprocessor directive #include before they can be used in the program*/

```
#include <stdlib.h>
/*header file stdlib.h contains prototypes of the library function
exit(), hence needs to be included using preprocessor directive
#include before they can be used in the program*/
struct subject{
/*structured data type subject is defined here using keyword struct;
its members are declared within the curly braces*/
    int mark;
    /*int type variable mark is declared as member of the structured
    data type subject, that will be used to store the obtained mark
    in a particular subject*/
    float point;
    /*float type variable point is declared as member of the
    structured data type subject, that will be used to store the
    obtained grade-point in a particular subject*/
    char *letter;
    /*char type pointer letter is declared as member of the
    structured data type subject, that will be used to store the
    obtained letter-grade in a particular subject*/
};
/*definition of structured data type must end with a semicolon; no
variable of the defined data type marks is declared here*/
struct exam{
/*structured data type exam is defined here using keyword struct;
its members are declared within the curly braces*/
    int roll, total, pos;
    /*int type variables roll, total and pos are declared as members
    of the structured data type exam, that will be used to store
    roll no, obtained total marks and merit position, respectively
    of a particular student*/
    struct subject sub[10];
    /*structured subject type array sub[] with size 10 is declared
    as member of the structured data type exam, that will be used to
    store information of maximum 10 subjects of a particular student*/
    float gpa;
    /*float type variable gpa is declared as member of the structured
    data type exam, that will be used to store gpa calculated for
    a particular student*/
};
/*definition of structured data type must end with a semicolon; no
variable of the defined data type marks is declared here*/
int main(){
/*here main() function returns an integer and parameters/arguments
of the main() function also remain void; execution of the program
starts with main() function; no statement before opening curly
brace of the main() function will be executed by the compiler*/
```

```
FILE *fp;
```
/*FILE is a structured data type defined in stdio.h header file.
Here a FILE type pointer fp is declared to refer any file*/
```
struct exam stud[100], temp;
```
/*structured exam type variable temp and an array stud[] with
size 100 are declared here; members of each of the array element
can be accessed through dot (.) operator*/
```
int numstd, numsub, i, j;
```
/*integer type variables numstd, numsub, i and j are declared;
required memory spaces have been allocated for each of the
variables*/
```
float totgrd;
```
/*float type variable totgrd is declared that can store any
decimal value*/
```
char ch;
```
/*char type variable is declared which can take and store only
character*/
```
printf("Enter the number of students: ");
```
/*output function printf() displays the message in the quotation
as it is on screen*/
```
scanf("%d", &numstd);
```
/*number of student will be input using this input function
scanf() which will take decimal value from input terminal and
keep the value in the memory spaces allocated for the variable
numstd*/
```
printf("How many subjects: ");
```
/*output function printf() displays the message in the quotation
as it is on screen*/
```
scanf("%d", &numsub);
```
/*number of subject will be input using this input function
scanf() which will take decimal value from input terminal and
keep the value in the memory spaces allocated for the variable
numsub*/
```
for (i=0; i<numstd; i++){
```
/*here i=0 is initialization, i<numstd is condition and i++ is
increment; this for loop works as follows- initialization is
done only once at the start; then condition is checked, if it is
true statements in the body, enclosed by curly braces, execute
and value of i is incremented by 1; now the condition is checked
again and if it is true the body executes again; these steps
continue till the condition becomes false; this for loop is
used here to input necessary information of all numstd students
and calculate marks, gpa and letter-grade; in each iteration
individual student is considered*/
```
    printf("Enter the roll no. of student #%d: ", i+1);
```
/*output function printf() displays the message in the
quotation as it is on screen except format specifier %d is
replaced by the value of i+1*/

```
scanf("%d", &stud[i].roll);
```
/*this scanf() function takes a decimal value from input terminal and save the value in roll which is a member of struct subject type array stud[]*/
```
stud[i].total=0;
```
/*member total of structured subject type array stud[] is initialized to 0 that will be used to store the total marks of a particular student; it is initialized to 0, otherwise the summation operation may give wrong answer because, when we declare a variable a memory space is allocated for that variable and the memory space may contain some garbage value; when we sequentially add the data with the total and result will be accumulated in the total variable, the garbage value may add up in the first summation*/
```
totgrd=0;
```
/*variable totgrd is initialized to 0 that will be used to store the total grade of a particular student needed to calculate gpa; it is initialized to 0 to avoid add up any garbage value in the first summation and get any wrong answer*/
```
for (j=0; j<numsub; j++){
```
/*here j=0 is initialization, j<numsub is condition and j++ is increment; this for loop works as follows- initialization is done only once at the start; then condition is checked, if it is true statements in the body, enclosed by curly braces, execute and value of j is incremented by 1; now the condition is checked again and if it is true the body executes again; these steps continue till the condition becomes false; this for loop is used here to input necessary information of all numsub subjects and calculate marks, gpa and letter-grade; in each iteration individual subject is considered*/
```
    printf("Mark obtained in EEE-110%d: ", j+1);
```
/*output function printf() displays the message in the quotation as it is on screen except format specifier %d is replaced by the value of j+1*/
```
    scanf("%d", &stud[i].sub[j].mark);
```
/*this scanf() function takes a decimal value from input terminal and save the value in mark which is a member of struct subject type array sub[] which is in turn is a member of structured exam type array stud[], hence variable mark is accessed through double dot (.) operators*/
```
    if (stud[i].sub[j].mark>=90){
```
/*if the condition is true, means marks of a particular subject of a particular student is greater than or equal to 90, then following two statements execute; multiple statements in the body of 'if' is enclosed with curly braces*/

```
        stud[i].sub[j].point=4.00;
        /*point is a member of struct subject type array
        sub[] which is in turn is a member of structured
        exam type array stud[], hence variable point is
        accessed through chain of dot (.) operators and
        assigned a value 4.00*/
        stud[i].sub[j].letter="A+";
        /*character type pointer letter is a member of
        struct subject type array sub[] which is in turn
        is a member of structured exam type array stud[],
        hence variable point is accessed through chain of
        dot (.) operators and assigned a string A+*/
}
/*this closing curly brace indicates end of if (stud[i].
sub[j].mark>=90)*/
else if (stud[i].sub[j].mark>=80){
/*if the condition is true, means marks of a particular
subject of a particular student is greater than or equal to
80 but less than 90, then following two statements execute;
condition of 90 has already been checked in the previous
'if' condition and condition of 80 is only checked if the
above 'if' condition of 90 is false; multiple statements
in the body of 'if' is enclosed with curly braces*/
        stud[i].sub[j].point=3.50;
        /*point is a member of struct subject type array sub[]
        which is in turn is a member of structured exam type
        array stud[], hence variable point is accessed through
        chain of dot (.) operators and assigned a value 3.50*/
        stud[i].sub[j].letter="A";
        /*character type pointer letter is a member of
        struct subject type array sub[] which is in turn
        is a member of structured exam type array stud[],
        hence variable point is accessed through chain of
        dot (.) operators and assigned a string A*/
}
/*this closing curly brace indicates end of else if
(stud[i].sub[j].mark>=80)*/
else if (stud[i].sub[j].mark>=70){
/*if the condition is true, means marks of a particular
subject of a particular student is greater than or equal
to 70 but less than 80, then following two statements
execute; condition of 90 and 80 have already been
checked in the previous 'if' and 'else if' conditions
and condition of 70 is only checked if the both of
the above 'if' and 'else if' conditions of 90 and 80
are false; multiple statements in the body of 'if' is
enclosed with curly braces*/
```

```
        stud[i].sub[j].point=3.00;
        /*point is a member of struct subject type array
        sub[] which is in turn is a member of structured
        exam type array stud[], hence variable point is
        accessed through chain of dot (.) operators and
        assigned a value 3.00*/
        stud[i].sub[j].letter="B";
        /*character type pointer letter is a member of
        struct subject type array sub[] which is in turn
        is a member of structured exam type array stud[],
        hence variable point is accessed through chain of
        dot (.) operators and assigned a string B*/
}
/*this closing curly brace indicates end of else if
(stud[i].sub[j].mark>=70)*/
else if (stud[i].sub[j].mark>=60){
/*if the condition is true, means marks of a particular
subject of a particular student is greater than or equal
to 60 but less than 70, then following two statements
execute; this condition of 60 is checked only if all the
above 'if' and 'else if' conditions are false*/
        stud[i].sub[j].point=2.50;
        /*point is a member of struct subject type array
        sub[] which is in turn is a member of structured
        exam type array stud[], hence variable point is
        accessed through chain of dot (.) operators and
        assigned a value 2.50*/
        stud[i].sub[j].letter="C";
        /*character type pointer letter is a member of
        struct subject type array sub[] which is in turn
        is a member of structured exam type array stud[],
        hence variable point is accessed through chain of
        dot (.) operators and assigned a string C*/
}
/*this closing curly brace indicates end of else if
(stud[i].sub[j].mark>=60)*/
else if (stud[i].sub[j].mark>=50){
/*if the condition is true, means marks of a particular
subject of a particular student is greater than or equal
to 50 but less than 60, then following two statements
execute; this condition of 50 is checked only if all the
above 'if' and 'else if' conditions are false*/
        stud[i].sub[j].point=2.00;
        /*point is a member of struct subject type array
        sub[] which is in turn is a member of structured
        exam type array stud[], hence variable point is
        accessed through chain of dot (.) operators and
```

```
                    assigned a value 2.00*/
                    stud[i].sub[j].letter="D";
                    /*character type pointer letter is a member of
                    struct subject type array sub[] which is in turn
                    is a member of structured exam type array stud[],
                    hence variable point is accessed through chain of
                    dot (.) operators and assigned a string D*/
            }
            /*this closing curly brace indicates end of else if
            (stud[i].sub[j].mark>=50)*/
            else{
            /*if all the above conditions of 'if' and 'else if'
            are false, means marks of a particular subject of a
            particular student is less than 50, then following two
            statements execute*/
                    stud[i].sub[j].point=0.00;
                    /*point is a member of struct subject type array
                    sub[] which is in turn is a member of structured
                    exam type array stud[], hence variable point is
                    accessed through chain of dot (.) operators and
                    assigned a value 0.00*/
                    stud[i].sub[j].letter="F";
                    /*character type pointer letter is a member of
                    struct subject type array sub[] which is in turn
                    is a member of structured exam type array stud[],
                    hence variable point is accessed through chain of
                    dot (.) operators and assigned a string F*/
            }
            /*this closing curly brace indicates end of above
            'else'*/
            stud[i].total+=stud[i].sub[j].mark;
            /*this arithmetic operation calculates total marks
            of a particular student by adding obtained marks of
            all the subjects; in each iteration of first 'for'
            loop one particular student is considered and in each
            iteration of second 'for' loop individual subject of
            that particular student is considered*/
            totgrd+=stud[i].sub[j].point;
            /*this arithmetic operation calculates total grades of
            a particular student by adding all grade-points of
            individual subject; in each iteration of first 'for'
            loop one particular student is considered and in each
            iteration of second 'for' loop individual subject of
            that particular student is considered*/
    }
    /*this closing curly brace indicates end of for (j=0;
    j<numsub; j++)*/
```

```
        stud[i].gpa=totgrd/numsub;
        /*gpa of each student is calculated from total grade-point
        totgrd of that particular student; in each iteration of
        first 'for' loop individual student is considered*/
}
/*this closing curly brace indicates end of for (i=0; i<numstd;
i++)*/
for (i=1; i<=numstd-1; i++)
/* this for loop is used to repeat the following 'for' loop as
long as the condition satisfies; here i=1 is initialization,
i<=numstd-1 is condition and i++ is increment; this for loop
works as follows- initialization is done only once at the start;
then condition is checked, if it is true statement in the body
executes and value of i is incremented by 1; now the condition
is checked again and if it is true the body executes again;
these steps continue till the condition becomes false; this for
loop together with the following for loop are used here to sort
students based on their earned gpa in ascending order*/
        for (j=1; j<=numstd-i; j++)
        /*this for loop is used to compare gpa of each student
        and swap if necessary to place one student in its right
        position in each iteration; hence after each iteration,
        number of gpa of students to be compared is decreased
        by 1, as the student which is already placed in right
        position in previous iteration does not need to be compared
        again in the subsequent iteration; here j=1 is initialization,
        j<numstd-i is condition and j++ is increment; this for loop
        works as follows- initialization is done only once at the
        start; then condition is checked, if it is true statement in
        the body executes and value of j is incremented by 1; now the
        condition is checked again and if it is true the body executes
        again; these steps continue till the condition becomes false*/
            if (stud[j-1].gpa<stud[j].gpa){
            /*body of above 'for' loop contains only this 'if'
            condition; if the condition of 'if' is true then following
            three statements will execute; as there are multiple
            statements in the body of 'if' they are enclosed with
            curly braces; here gpa of two contiguous students are
            compared, if the larger gpa stays above the smaller one
            then they are swapped to always keep the student with
            smaller gpa above the larger one*/
                temp=stud[j-1];
                /*array element stud[j-1] is stored in variable temp*/
                stud[j-1]=stud[j];
                /*array element stud[j] is stored as array
                element stud[j-1], that is and stud[j] now becomes
                stud[j-1]*/
```

```
            stud[j]=temp;
            /*value of temp is stored as array element stud[j],
            that is stud[j-1] now becomes stud[j]*/
        }
        /*this closing curly brace indicates the end of 'if'*/
        else if (stud[j-1].gpa==stud[j].gpa)
        /*if above 'if' condition is false then this 'else if'
        condition is checked; if this condition is true, means
        gpa of two contiguous students are equal then following
        'if' condition executes to sort students according to
        their obtained total marks in ascending order*/
            if (stud[j-1].total<stud[j].total){
            /*if this condition is true then following three
            statements will execute; means- here total of two
            contiguous students are compared, if the larger
            total stays above the smaller one then they are
            swapped to always keep the student with smaller
            total above the larger one*/
                temp=stud[j-1];
                /*array element stud[j-1] is stored in variable
                temp*/
                stud[j-1]=stud[j];
                /*array element stud[j] is stored as array
                element stud[j-1], that is and stud[j] now
                becomes stud[j-1]*/
                stud[j]=temp;
                /*value of temp is stored as array element
                stud[j], that is stud[j-1] now becomes
                stud[j]*/
            }
            /*this closing curly brace indicates the end of
            'if' with condition*/
for (i=0; i<numstd; i++)
/*this for loop is used to set position of each student
according to sorted gpa; here i=0 is initialization, i<numstd is
condition and i++ is increment; this for loop works as follows-
initialization is done only once at the start; then condition is
checked, if it is true statement in the body executes and value
of i is incremented by 1; now the condition is checked again
and if it is true the body executes again; these steps continue
till the condition becomes false*/
    stud[i].pos=i+1;
    /*member pos of structured exam type array stud[] is set to
    i+1; at 1st iteration position of first student is set to
    stud[0].pos=1, at 2nd iteration position of second student
    is set to stud[1].pos=2, and so on*/
```

```
fp=fopen("c:\\myfiles\\Results.txt", "w");
```
/*fopen() function opens a text file named Results.txt in the address C:\\myfiles\\ with write mode, indicated by "w", and returns a FILE type pointer*/
```
if (fp==NULL){
```
/*after opening a file in C, we must always check whether the file opens successfully; to do that we check the pointer returned by fopen() function; if it is NULL then file could not open; hence, here if the file failed to open the condition is true and following two statements will be executed*/

```
    puts("Cannot open source file!\n");
```
    /*output function puts() will display the string message inside the double quotation as it is on screen except newline character \n is replaced by enter*/

```
    exit(1);
```
    /*exit(1) function causes abnormal termination of the program; all buffers, temporary files, streams are deleted or cleared before the termination*/

```
}
```
/*this closing curly brace indicates the end of the 'if' body*/
```
fprintf(fp, "\nResult according to merit position . . . \n");
```
/*fprintf() function writes information inside the double quotation as it is in the file referred by the pointer fp; here enter is written in place of new line character*/
```
for (i=0; i<numstd; i++){
```
/*this for loop is used to display information of each student according to sorted gpa; in each iteration individual student is considered; here i=0 is initialization, i<numstd is condition and i++ is increment; this for loop works as follows- initialization is done only once at the start; then condition is checked, if it is true statements in the body execute and value of i is incremented by 1; now the condition is checked again and if it is true the body executes again; these steps continue till the condition becomes false*/

```
    fprintf(fp, "Roll No.: %d\n", stud[i].roll);
```
    /*fprintf() function will write information inside the double quotation as it is in the file referred by the pointer fp; here enter is written in place of new line character, value of stud[i].roll in place of %d format specifier*/
```
    for (j=0; j<numsub; j++)
```
    /*this for loop is used to display information of all subjects of each student according to sorted gpa; in each iteration individual subject of a particular student is considered; here j=0 is initialization, j<numsub is condition and j++ is increment; this for loop works as follows- initialization is done only once at the start; then condition is checked,

if it is true statements in the body execute and value of i is incremented by 1; now the condition is checked again and if it is true the body executes again; these steps continue till the condition becomes false*/

```
fprintf(fp, "EEE-110%d: %s (%0.2f)\n", j+1, stud[i].
        sub[j].letter, stud[i].sub[j].point);
```
/*fprintf() function writes information in the quotation as it is in the file referred by the pointer fp; here format specifier %d is replaced by the value of j+1, %s by string value of stud[i].sub[j].letter, %0.2f by stud[i].sub[j].point with 2 decimal point precision and newline character \n by enter*/

```
fprintf(fp, "GPA: %0.2f\nMerit Position: %d\n\n", stud[i].
        gpa, stud[i].pos);
```
/*fprintf() function writes information in the quotation as it is in the file referred by the pointer fp; here format specifier %d is replaced by the value of stud[i].pos, %0.2f by stud[i].gpa with 2 decimal point precision and newline character \n by enter*/

```
}
```
/*this closing curly brace indicates the end of for (i=0; i<numstd; i++) loop*/
```
fclose(fp);
```
/*once a file is open in C, it is a good practice to close the file before end of the program or reuse the file to properly flush the output buffer; this is done here by the fclose() function which close the file referred by its argument fp*/
```
for (i=1; i<=numstd-1; i++)
```
/* this for loop is used to repeat the following 'for' loop as long as the condition satisfies; here i=1 is initialization, i<=numstd-1 is condition and i++ is increment; this for loop works as follows- initialization is done only once at the start; then condition is checked, if it is true statement in the body executes and value of i is incremented by 1; now the condition is checked again and if it is true the body executes again; these steps continue till the condition becomes false; this for loop together with the following for loop are used here to sort students according to their roll no in ascending order*/

```
for (j=1; j<=numstd-i; j++)
```
/*this for loop is used to compare roll of each student and swap if necessary to place one student in its right position in each iteration; hence after each iteration, number of roll of students to be compared is decreased by 1, as the student which is already placed in right position in previous iteration does not need to be compared again in the subsequent iteration; here j=1 is initialization, j<numstd-i is condition and j++ is increment; this for loop works as

follows- initialization is done only once at the start; then condition is checked, if it is true statement in the body executes and value of j is incremented by 1; now the condition is checked again and if it is true the body executes again; these steps continue till the condition becomes false*/

```
    if (stud[j-1].roll>stud[j].roll){
```
/*if this condition is true then following three statements in the body of if, enclosed by curly braces, will execute; means- here roll of two contiguous students are compared, if the larger roll stays above the smaller one then they are swapped to always keep the student with smaller roll above the larger one*/

```
    temp=stud[j-1];
```
/*array element stud[j-1] is stored in variable temp*/

```
    stud[j-1]=stud[j];
```
/*array element stud[j] is stored as array element stud[j-1], that is and stud[j] now becomes stud[j-1]*/

```
    stud[j]=temp;
```
/*value of temp is stored as array element stud[j], that is stud[j-1] now becomes stud[j]*/

```
    }
```
/*this closing curly brace indicates the end of 'if' condition*/

```
fp=fopen("c:\\myfiles\\Results.txt", "a");
```
/*fopen() function opens the same text file, in which some information was saved, named Results.txt in the address C:\\myfiles\\ with append mode, indicated by "a", and returns a FILE type pointer*/

```
if (fp==NULL){
```
/*after opening a file in C, we must always check whether the file opens successfully; to do that we check the pointer returned by fopen() function; if it is NULL then file could not open; hence, here if the file failed to open the condition is true and following two statements will be executed*/

```
    puts("Cannot open target file!\n");
```
/*output function puts() will display the string message inside the double quotation as it is on screen except newline character \n is replaced by enter*/

```
    exit(1);
```
/*exit(1) function causes abnormal termination of the program; all buffers, temporary files, streams are deleted or cleared before the termination*/

```
}
```
/*this closing curly brace indicates the end of the 'if' body*/

```
fprintf(fp, "\nResult according to roll no . . . . \n");
```
/*fprintf() function will write information inside the double quotation as it is in the file referred by the pointer fp; here enter is written in place of new line character \n*/

```
for (i=0; i<numstd; i++){
```
/*this for loop is used to display information of each student according to sorted roll; in each iteration individual student is considered; here i=0 is initialization, i<numstd is condition and i++ is increment; this for loop works as follows- initialization is done only once at the start; then condition is checked, if it is true statements in the body execute and value of i is incremented by 1; now the condition is checked again and if it is true the body executes again; these steps continue till the condition becomes false*/
```
    fprintf(fp, "Roll No.: %d\n", stud[i].roll);
```
/*fprintf() function will write information inside the double quotation as it is in the file referred by the pointer fp; here enter is written in place of newline character, value of stud[i].roll in place of %d format specifier*/
```
    for (j=0; j<numsub; j++)
```
/*this for loop is used to display information of all subjects of each student according to sorted gpa; in each iteration individual subject of a particular student is considered; here j=0 is initialization, j<numsub is condition and j++ is increment; this for loop works as follows- initialization is done only once at the start; then condition is checked, if it is true statements in the body execute and value of i is incremented by 1; now the condition is checked again and if it is true the body executes again; these steps continue till the condition becomes false*/
```
        fprintf(fp, "EEE-110%d: %s (%0.2f)\n", j+1, stud[i].
               sub[j].letter, stud[i].sub[j].point);
```
/*fprintf() function writes information in the quotation as it is in the file referred by the pointer fp; here format specifier %d is replaced by the value of j+1, %s by string value of stud[i].sub[j].letter, %0.2f by stud[i].sub[j].point with 2 decimal point precision and newline character \n by enter*/
```
    fprintf(fp, "GPA: %0.2f\nMerit Position: %d\n\n", stud[i].
           gpa, stud[i].pos);
```
/*fprintf() function writes information in the quotation as it is in the file referred by the pointer fp; here format specifier %d is replaced by the value of stud[i].pos, %0.2f by stud[i].gpa with 2 decimal point precision and newline character \n by enter*/
```
}
```
/*this closing curly brace indicates the end of for (i=0; i<numstd; i++) loop*/
```
fclose(fp);
```
/*once a file is open in C, it is a good practice to close the file before end of the program or reuse the file to properly flush the output buffer; this is done here by the fclose() function which close the file referred by its argument fp*/

```
fp=fopen("c:\\myfiles\\Results.txt", "r");
```
/*fopen() function opens a text file, same file used before to write information of the students, named Result.txt in the address C:\\my files\\ with read mode, indicated by "r", and returns a FILE type pointer*/
```
if (fp==NULL){
```
/*after opening a file in C, we must always check whether the file opens successfully; to do that we check the pointer returned by fopen() function; if it is NULL then file could not open; hence, here if the file failed to open the condition is true and following two statements execute*/
```
    puts("Cannot open target file!\n");
```
  /*output function puts() will display the string message inside the double quotation as it is on screen except newline character \n is replaced by enter*/
```
    exit(1);
```
  /*exit(1) function causes abnormal termination of the program; all buffers, temporary files, streams are deleted or cleared before the termination*/
```
}
```
/*this closing curly brace indicates the end of the 'if' body*/
```
printf("\n");
```
/*output function printf() displays enter due to newline character \n*/
```
while (1){
```
/*as the 1 means true, the condition of 'while' is always true and following statements in the body of while, enclosed by curly braces, execute in any case; in each iteration character is read sequentially from the file and displayed on screen*/
```
    ch=fgetc(fp);
```
  /*fgetc() function reads a character from the file referred by the pointer fp; at 1st iteration, it reads the 1st character (ch=1st character) and the pointer automatically points to the 2nd character; at 2nd iteration, it reads the 2nd character (ch=2nd character) and the pointer automatically points to the 3rd character; and so on*/
```
    if (ch==EOF)
```
  /*ch is compared with EOF, means whether we reach the end-of-file or not; if yes, then the program steps out of the while loop*/
```
        break;
```
   /*program control immediately comes out of the while loop skipping following statement*/
```
    printf("%c", ch);
```
  /*output function printf() displays character ch due to format specifier %c*/
```
}
```
/*this closing curly brace indicates the end of while loop*/

```
fclose(fp);
/*once a file is open in C, it is a good practice to close the
file before end of the program or reuse the file to properly
flush the output buffer; this is done here by the fclose()
function which close the file referred by its argument fp*/
return 0;
/*0 is returned as it is the standard for the successful
execution of the program*/
}
/*the closing curly brace indicates the end of the body of main()
function and the end of the program; no statement will execute after
that curly brace*/
```

## EXERCISES

MCQ with Answers

1) What is the keyword used to declare a C file pointer?

   A) file

   B) FILE

   C) FILEFP

   D) filefp

2) What is a C FILE data type?

   A) FILE is like a structure only

   B) FILE is like a union only

   C) FILE is like a user-defined int data type

   D) None of the above

3) Where is a file temporarily stored before read or write operation in C language?

   A) Notepad

   B) RAM

   C) Hard disk

   D) Buffer

4) What is the syntax for writing a file in C using binary mode?

   A) fp=fopen("abc.txt", "wr");

   B) fp=fopen("abc.txt", "wb");

   C) fp=fopen("abc.txt", "wbin");

   D) fp=fopen("abc.txt", "b");

5) What are the C functions used to read or write a file in text mode?

   A) fprintf(), fscanf()

   B) fread(), fwrite()

   C) fprint(), fscan()

   D) read(), write()

6) What are the C functions used to read or write a file in binary mode?

   A) fprintf(), fscanf()

   B) fread(), fwrite()

   C) readf(), writef()

   D) printf(), scanf()

7) What is the C function used to move current pointer to the beginning of file?
   FILE *fp;

   A) rev(fp)

   B) rewind(fp)

   C) rew(fp)

   D) wind(fp)

8) Choose a correct syntax for FSCANF and FPRINTF in C language?

   A) fprintf("format specifier",variables, fp);

      fscanf("format specifier",variables, fp);

   B) fprintf(fp,count, "format specifier",variables);

      fscanf(fp,count,"format specifier",variables);

   C) fprintf(fp, "format specifier",variables);

      fscanf(fp, "format specifier",variables);

   D) None of the above

9) What is the use of rewind() function in C?

   A) Set the position to the starting point

   B) Gives current position in the file

   C) Set the position to the desired point

   D) None of the above

[Ans. B, A, D, B, A, B, B, C, A]

## Questions with Short Answers

1) What is the difference between text files and binary files?

   Ans. Text files contain data that humans can easily comprehend. It consists of letters, numbers, and other symbols and characters. Binary files, on the other hand, contain 1's and 0's that only computers can understand.

2) What is a sequential access file?

   Ans. It is possible to designate a file into several forms while writing programs that store and retrieve data. Data is kept in sequential order in a sequential access file: one data is added after the other to the file. To get to a certain data in the sequential access file, data must be read one by one until the proper one is found.

3) What is the advantage of a random access file?

   Ans. If a file has a vast quantity of data, random access allows looking through it more quickly. If it had been a sequential access file, we would have had to go through each record one by one until we got to the desired information. A random access file allows jumping right to the data's target address.

4) How do you search data in a data file using a random access method?

   Ans. To search data on a file using a random access method, we need to use the fseek() function. Syntax of fseek() function is:

   int fseek(FILE *pointer, long int offset, int position)

   pointer: pointer to a FILE object that identifies the stream.

   offset: number of bytes to offset from position

   position: position from where the offset is added.

   Returns zero if successful, or else it returns a nonzero value.

5) What do the characters "r" and "w" mean when writing programs in C?

   Ans. "r" means read and opens a file to retrieve data. "w" means write, and opens a file to write data in the file. Previous data that was stored on that file will be erased.

6) Describe the file opening mode "w+".

   Ans. "w+" mode opens a file both to read and to write data. If a file does not exist, it creates a one; otherwise, it is overwritten if a file does exist.

7) What is the difference between fopen modes "r+", and "w+"?

   Ans. The difference in the fopen modes r+ and w+ in C:

   "r+": opens a text file both for reading and for writing; neither delete the content if it exists nor create a new file if it doesn't exist.

"w+": opens a text file both for reading and for writing; first truncating the file to zero length if it exists or creating the file if it does not exist.

8) Is FILE a built-in data type?

Ans. No, it is a structure defined in stdio.h.

9) How can we determine whether a file is successfully open or not using fopen() function?

Ans. After opening the file using the fopen() function and assigning the "file" to a variable, we must check the return value. An error has occurred if the variable == NULL; otherwise, the file was successfully open.

## Problems to Practice

1) Write a program to read name and marks of a student and store them in a file.

2) Write a program to open the file created in the last problem, read name and marks of a student and append them in the file.

3) Write a program to open the file created in the last problem, read information from the file, and display them on the screen.

4) Write a program to calculate the area and circumference of a circle.

5) The annual examination results of n students are tabulated as follows:

| Roll No. | EEE-1101 | EEE-1102 | EEE-1103 |
| --- | --- | --- | --- |
| 101 | 69 | 56 | 89 |
| 102 | 80 | 65 | 91 |
| 103 | 45 | 36 | 68 |

Write a program to read the data and determine the following:

(a) Grade obtained by each student in each subject:

| Marks | Letter Grade | Grade Point |
| --- | --- | --- |
| 90% and above | A+ | 4.00 |
| 80% to <90% | A | 3.50 |
| 70% to <60% | B | 3.00 |
| 60% to <70% | C | 2.50 |
| 50% to <60% | D | 2.00 |
| Less than 50% | F | 0.00 |

(b) Total marks and GPA obtained by each student.

(c) The position of each student based on GPA (for equal GPA, consider who gets the higher total marks).

(d) The result should be displayed according to the roll number and merit.

(e) Save the results in a text file and retrieve and print the results from the text file.

6) Write a program to write and read multiple lines in a text file.

7) Write a program to count the number of lines, words, and characters in a text file.

8) Write a program to delete and replace a specific line in a text file.

9) Write a program to copy a file and write it in a new file.

10) Write a program to merge two files and write it in a new file.

11) Write a program to read a string from a file and display it to the user.

# C Graphics

G RAPHICS IS A POWERFUL feature and makes computer applications attractive. This chapter describes the fundamentals of graphics programming in C and for those who do not have any prior knowledge of graphics programming. Graphics programming in C is used to draw geometrical objects, draw curves using mathematical functions, color an object or pattern, and create simple animations such as bouncing balls and driving cars.

## 7.1 INTRODUCTION

C applications usually run in a console window known as CUI (character user interface). C library contains header file graphics.h containing many predefined functions to implement GUI (graphical user interface) in C applications. To implement GUI programming, we need to convert the output screen from CUI (character data) mode to GUI (pixel) mode.

## 7.2 FUNCTION

All the related functions to implement the graphics programming are available in the header file graphics.h. Open graphics.h header file to see all the functions available in the header file. Some of the important functions used are as follows:

| | |
|---|---|
| *initgraph()* | used to convert CUI mode into GUI mode (initialize graphics mode). It takes three arguments: graphics driver, graphics mode, and path. |
| *closegraph()* | used to deallocate all memory allocated by graphics system and shut down the graphics system. |
| *outtextxy()* | displays a message in (x, y) coordinate. It takes three arguments: x and y arguments, and a message as string or char type pointer. |
| *getmaxx()* | returns the maximum x coordinate for current graphics mode and driver. |
| *getmaxy()* | returns the maximum y coordinate for current graphics mode and driver. |

DOI: 10.1201/9781003302629-7

*setcolor()*     sets drawing color. It takes an integer argument whose value (0 to 15) determines a particular color. Or name of the color (BLACK, CYAN, RED, WHITE etc.) can be passed as string argument.

*setbkcolor()*   sets the background color. It takes an integer argument whose value (0 to 15) determines a particular color. Or name of the color (BLACK, CYAN, RED, WHITE etc.) can be passed as string argument.

*settextstyle()* sets the current text characteristics (font, direction, and size). It takes three arguments: first argument sets the font depending on integer constant (0, 1, 2, 3, or 4), second argument sets the font's direction (HORIZ_DIR=0 for horizontal from left to right and VERT_DIR=1 for vertical from bottom to top), and the third argument sets the font's size which gradually increases depending on the integer value you have passed from 1 to 10.

*kbhit()*        checks for recent keystrokes. It returns a nonzero integer if a keystroke is available.

*setfillstyle()* sets the current fill pattern and fill color. First parameter represents the pattern and the second one the color. The allowed patterns are EMPTY_ FILL=0, SOLID_FILL=1, LINE_FILL=2, ..., USER_FILL=12 and the colors are BLACK=0, BLUE=1, ..., WHITE=15.

*floodfill()*    fills an enclosed area at location (x, y) coordinate. The current fill pattern and fill color are used to fill the area. Border color of the enclosed area is passed as third argument of the function.

*delay()*        delay() function is built upon another C library function clock(). This is used to suspend execution of a program for a particular time. The time to be delayed is passed as argument in some integer milliseconds.

*cleardevice()*  clears the screen in graphics mode, like clrscr() function does in CUI mode, and sets the current position to (0, 0). To clear the screen, it just fills the screen with current background color.

*DETECT*         a macro that automatically detect the suitable graphics driver.

## 7.3 COLOR TABLE

In graphics, each color is assigned an integer number. Total number of available colors is 16. While the default drawing color is WHITE, the default background color is BLACK. The following table shows the supported colors and associated integer values:

| Color | Integer Value |
|-------|---------------|
| BLACK | 0 |
| BLUE | 1 |
| GREEN | 2 |

| Color | Integer Value |
|-------|---------------|
| CYAN | 3 |
| RED | 4 |
| MAGENTA | 5 |
| BROWN | 6 |
| LIGHTGRAY | 7 |
| DARKGRAY | 8 |
| LIGHTBLUE | 9 |
| LIGHTGREEN | 10 |
| LIGHTCYAN | 11 |
| LIGHTRED | 12 |
| LIGHTMAGENTA | 13 |
| YELLOW | 14 |
| WHITE | 15 |

## 7.4 FONTS OF TEXT

In graphics, different font is assigned a different number. Total number of available fonts is 11. The following table shows the fonts value with their integer values.

| Font | Integer Value |
|------|---------------|
| DEFAULT_FONT | 0 |
| TRIPLEX_FONT | 1 |
| SMALL_FONT | 2 |
| SANS_SERIF_FONT | 3 |
| GOTHIC_FONT | 4 |
| SCRIPT_FONT | 5 |
| SIMPLEX_FONT | 6 |
| TRIPLEX_SCR_FONT | 7 |
| COMPLEX_FONT | 8 |
| EUROPEAN_FONT | 9 |
| BOLD_FONT | 10 |

## 7.5 FILL PATTERNS

In graphics, different integer values represent different patterns that are used to fill enclosed areas. Following table shows all the available 13 fill patterns and their corresponding integer values.

| Pattern | Integer value |
|---------|---------------|
| EMPTY_FILL | 0 |
| SOLID_FILL | 1 |
| LINE_FILL | 2 |
| LTSLASH_FILL | 3 |

| Pattern | Integer value |
|---|---|
| SLASH_FILL | 4 |
| BKSLASH_FILL | 5 |
| LTBKSLASH_FILL | 6 |
| HATCH_FILL | 7 |
| XHATCH_FILL | 8 |
| INTERLEAVE_FILL | 9 |
| WIDE_DOT_FILL | 10 |
| CLOSE_DOT_FILL | 11 |
| USER_FILL | 12 |

## 7.6 INCLUDING GRAPHICS.H IN CODEBLOCKS

Follow the below steps to compile and execute the graphics code on Code::Blocks success-fully. We assume here that you have installed and using 32-bit CodeBlocks with mingw package.

Step-1: Download WinBGIm from http://winbgim.codecutter.org/ and extract the downloaded file. There will be three files: graphics.h, winbgim.h, and libbgi.a.

Step-2: Open graphics.h file with Notepad++. Go to line number 302, and replace that line with int left=0, int top=0, int right=INT_MAX, int bottom=INT_MAX, and save the file.

Step-3: Copy and paste graphics.h and winbgim.h files into include folder of compiler directory [This PC > WINDOWS10 (C:) > Program Files (x86) > CodeBlocks > MinGW > include].

Step-4: Copy and paste libbgi.a into lib folder of compiler directory [This PC > WINDOWS10 (C:) > Program Files (x86) > CodeBlocks > MinGW > lib].

Step-5: Open CodeBlocks. Go to Settings→Compiler . . . →Linker settings. Click the Add button under the "Link libraries" part; browse and select the libbgi.a file copied to the lib folder, and click OK.

In the "Other linker options" part, paste the command -lbgi -lgdi32 -lcomdlg32 -luuid -loleaut32 -lole32 and click OK.

Step-6: Save the source code with file extension .cpp (not .c) and then build and run the program.

## 7.7 EXAMPLES

**PROBLEM-01**
**Write a program to draw a bar of size 100 × 300 and a circle with a radius of 50.**

Programming Code of the Solution:

```
#include <graphics.h>
#include <conio.h>
int main(){
    int gd=DETECT, gm;
    initgraph(&gd, &gm, (char *)"");
    bar(100, 100, 200, 400);
    circle(400, 250, 50);
    getch();
    closegraph();
    return 0;
}
```

Input and Output of the Executed Program:

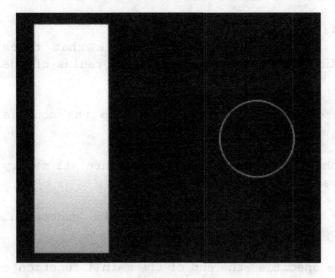

Explanation of the Programming Code:

#include <graphics.h>
/*header file graphics.h contains prototypes of the library functions
initgraph(), bar(), circle(), and closegraph(); the header file
must be included using preprocessor directive #include before the
functions are called in the program*/
#include <conio.h>
/*header file conio.h contains the prototype of the libray function
getch(), hence needs to be included before the function is used in
the program*/
int main(){
/*all C program must have a main() function with return type void
or int; here there is no parameter of the main() function and
it returns an integer; opening curly brace specifies start of

the main() function and no statement before that curly brace is executed by the compiler*/

```
    int gd=DETECT, gm;
    /*two integer type variables gd, and gm are declared. Variable
    gd is initialized to DETECT which is a macro that automatically
    detect graphics driver suitable for hardware*/
    initgraph(&gd, &gm, (char *)"");
    /*library function initgraph() is called here to initialize the
    graphics mode. Graphics mode gm represents screen resolution
    and will be selected implicitly depending on the graphics
    driver gd; as the mentioning path in the third argument is not
    mandatory we write it as empty string*/
    bar(100, 100, 200, 400);
    /*bar() function is called to draw a bar diagram that takes
    (100, 100) as top-left coordinate and (200, 400) as bottom-
    right coordinate*/
    circle(400, 250, 50);
    /*function circle() is called to draw a circle that takes
    (400, 250) as coordinate of the center and 50 as radius of the
    circle*/
    getch();
    /*input function getch() is called here to keep the console
    state visible until we enter any character*/
    closegraph();
    /*function closegraph() is called here to deallocate all memory
    and shut down the graphics system*/
    return 0;
    /*0 is returned as it is the standard for the successful
    execution of the program*/
}
/*the closing curly brace specifies the end of the main() function's
body, as well as the program's end; after that curly brace, no
statement is executed*/
```

Comments:

To run the above program in Turbo C, we need to define the initgraph() function in the program as follows:

```
    initgraph(&gd, &gm, "C:\\TC\\BGI");
```

That is, instead of writing an empty string in the third argument, we need to write the full path address of the BGI folder in TC with double backslash. This modification is needed for all the other graphics program to run in Turbo C.

## PROBLEM-02

**Write a program that prints a message in different colors.**

## Programming Code of the Solution:

```c
#include <graphics.h>
#include <conio.h>
int main(){
    int gd=DETECT, gm;
    int i, x=100, y=50;
    initgraph(&gd, &gm, (char *)"");
    for (i=1; i<16; i=i+2){
        setcolor(i);
        outtextxy(x, y, "Welcome to Learn Programming with C...");
        y = y+30;
    }
    getch();
    closegraph();
    return 0;
}
```

## Input and Output of the Executed Program:

## Explanation of the Programming Code:

**#include <graphics.h>**
/*header file graphics.h contains prototypes of the library functions initgraph(), setcolor(), outtextxy(), and closegraph(); the header file must be included using preprocessor directive #include before the functions are called in the program*/
**#include <conio.h>**
/*header file conio.h contains the prototype of the libray function getch(), hence needs to be included before the function is used in the program*/
**int main(){**
/*all C program must have a main() function with return type void or int; here there is no parameter of the main() function and

it returns an integer; opening curly brace specifies start of the main() function and no statement before that curly brace is executed by the compiler*/

**int gd=DETECT, gm;**

/*two integer type variables gd, and gm are declared. Variable gd is initialized to DETECT which is a macro that automatically detect graphics driver suitable for hardware*/

**int i, x=100, y=50;**

/*three integer type variables i, x and y are declared; compiler assigns required spaces in memory for these three variables; x is initialized to 100 and y to 50 that will be used to select coordinates on the screen*/

**initgraph(&gd, &gm, (char *)"");**

/*library function initgraph() is called here to initialize the graphics mode. Graphics mode gm represents screen resolution and will be selected implicitly depending on the graphics driver gd; as the mentioning path in the third argument is not mandatory we write it as empty string*/

**for (i=1; i<16; i=i+2){**

/*i=1 is initialization, i<16 is condition and i=i+2 is increment; initialization is done once at the beginning of the loop; next the condition is checked, and if it is true, the statements in the body are executed; the value of i is incremented by 2 before the condition is re-checked; this process continues until the condition becomes false at which point the program flow exits the loop*/

    **setcolor(i);**

    /*this function sets the drawing color; as integer 0 represents BLACK color and cannot be seen on black background, we starts from 1 that represents BLUE color; after that as i changes in each iteration, it sets different drawing color*/

    **outtextxy(x, y, "Welcome to Learn Programming with C. . .");**

    /*this function displays the message enclosed by double quotations in the (x, y) coordinate*/

    **y = y+30;**

    /*we have kept the value of x unchanged and increased the y value by 30 in each iteration so that the message is displayed in different coordinate*/

**}**

/*this closing curly brace specifies the end the the for loop*/

**getch();**

/*input function getch() is called here to keep the console state visible until we enter any character*/

**closegraph();**

/*function closegraph() is called here to deallocate all memory and shut down the graphics system*/

```
    return 0;
    /*0 is returned as it is the standard for the successful
    execution of the program*/
}
```
/*the closing curly brace specifies the end of the main() function's
body, as well as the program's end; after that curly brace, no
statement is executed*/

## PROBLEM-03
Write a program that displays different messages in different colors and different
directions on different backgrounds.

Programming Code of the Solution:

```c
#include <graphics.h>
#include <conio.h>
int main(){
    int gd=DETECT, gm;
    initgraph(&gd, &gm, (char *)"");
    setbkcolor(WHITE);
    setcolor(GREEN);
    settextstyle(0, HORIZ_DIR, 2);
    outtextxy(20, 100, "Welcome to Learn Programming with C...");
    outtextxy(20, 150, "Press any key to continue...");
    getch();
    cleardevice();
    setbkcolor(RED);
    setcolor(BLUE);
    settextstyle(1, VERT_DIR, 3);
    outtextxy(50, 50, "Very effective book to learn C...");
    outtextxy(150, 50, "Press any key to close...");
    getch();
    closegraph();
    return 0;
}
```

Input and Output of the Executed Program:

Welcome to Learn Programming with C...

Press any key to continue...

Very effective book to learn C...

Press any key to close...

### Explanation of the Programming Code:

```
#include <graphics.h>
```
/*header file graphics.h contains prototypes of the library functions initgraph(), setbkcolor(), setcolor(), settextsyle(), outtextxy(), cleardevice() and closegraph(); the header file must be included using preprocessor directive #include before the functions are called in the program*/
```
#include <conio.h>
```
/*header file conio.h contains the prototype of the libray function getch(), hence needs to be included before the function is used in the program*/
```
int main(){
```
/*all C program must have a main() function with return type void or int; here there is no parameter of the main() function and it returns an integer; opening curly brace specifies start of the main() function and no statement before that curly brace is executed by the compiler*/
```
    int gd=DETECT, gm;
```
/*two integer type variables gd, and gm are declared. Variable gd is initialized to DETECT which is a macro that automatically detect graphics driver suitable for hardware*/
```
    initgraph(&gd, &gm, (char *)"");
```
/*library function initgraph() is called here to initialize the graphics mode. Graphics mode gm represents screen resolution and will be selected implicitly depending on the graphics driver gd; as the mentioning path in the third argument is not mandatory we write it as empty string*/
```
    setbkcolor(WHITE);
```
/*sets the background color to white; the default color is black*/
```
    setcolor(GREEN);
```
/* sets the drawing color to green*/
```
    settextstyle(0, HORIZ_DIR, 2);
```
/*sets the current text characteristics; first argument sets the font to DEFAULT_FONT=0, second argument sets the font's direction to horizontal and the third argument sets the size of the font to 2*/
```
    outtextxy(20, 100, "Welcome to Learn Programming with C . . . ");
```
/*this displays the message enclosed by double quotations in the coordinate (20, 100) in the horizontal direction*/
```
    outtextxy(20, 150, "Press any key to continue . . . ");
```
/*this displays the message enclosed by double quotations in the coordinate (20, 150) in the horizontal direction*/
```
    getch();
```
/*input function getch() is called here to keep the console state visible until we enter any character; as soon as we enter any key, program flow goes to the next instruction immediately*/

```
cleardevice();
/*this function erases the previous two messages shown and
clears the screen*/
setbkcolor(RED);
/*sets the background color to red from white that was previously
set*/
setcolor(BLUE);
/* sets the drawing color to blue from the green that was
previously set*/
settextstyle(1, VERT_DIR, 3);
/*sets the current text characteristics; first argument sets
the font to TRIPLEX_FONT=1, second argument sets the font's
direction to vertical and the third argument sets the size of
the font to 3*/
outtextxy(50, 50, "Very effective book to learn C . . . ");
/*this displays the message enclosed by double quotations in
the coordinate (50, 50) in the vertical direction; (50, 50) is
the top coordinate*/
outtextxy(150, 50, "Press any key to close . . . ");
/*this displays the message enclosed by double quotations in
the coordinate (150, 50) in the vertical direction; (150, 50)
is the top coordinate*/
getch();
/*input function getch() is called here to keep the console
state visible until we enter any character*/
closegraph();
/*function closegraph() is called here to deallocate all memory
and shut down the graphics system*/
return 0;
/*0 is returned as it is the standard for the successful
execution of the program*/
}
/*the closing curly brace specifies the end of the main() function's
body, as well as the program's end; after that curly brace, no
statement is executed*/
```

## PROBLEM-04

Write a program that draws 16 circles of same size at different coordinates where each circle intersects all its neighbor circles.

Programming Code of the Solution:

```
#include <graphics.h>
#include <conio.h>
int main(){
```

```
      int gd=DETECT, gm;
      int x, y;
      initgraph(&gd, &gm, (char *)"");
      setbkcolor(WHITE);
      setcolor(RED);
      for (y=100; y<=400; y+=100)
          for (x=100; x<=400; x+=100)
              circle(x, y, 50);
      getch();
      closegraph();
      return 0;
}
```

Input and Output of the Executed Program:

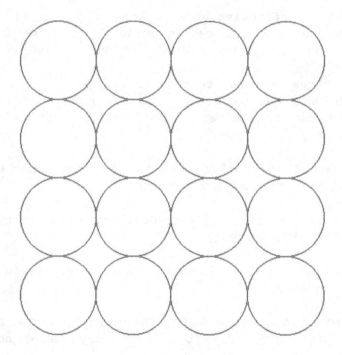

## Explanation of the Programming Code:

**#include <graphics.h>**
/*header file graphics.h contains prototypes of the library functions initgraph(), setbkcolor(), setcolor(), circle(), and closegraph(); the header file must be included using preprocessor directive #include before the functions are called in the program*/

**#include <conio.h>**
/*header file conio.h contains the prototype of the libray function getch(), hence needs to be included before the function is used in the program*/

```
int main(){
```
/*all C program must have a main() function with return type void
or int; here there is no parameter of the main() function and it
returns an integer; opening curly brace specifies start of the
main() function and no statement before that curly brace is executed
by the compiler*/

    **int gd=DETECT, gm;**

    /*two integer type variables gd, and gm are declared. Variable
gd is initialized to DETECT which is a macro that automatically
detect graphics driver suitable for hardware*/

    **int x, y;**

    /*two integer type variables x and y are declared; compiler
assigns required spaces in memory for these two variables*/

    **initgraph(&gd, &gm, (char *)"");**

    /*library function initgraph() is called here to initialize the
graphics mode. Graphics mode gm represents screen resolution
and will be selected implicitly depending on the graphics
driver gd; as the mentioning path in the third argument is not
mandatory we write it as empty string*/

    **setbkcolor(WHITE);**

    /*sets the background color to white; the default color is
black*/

    **setcolor(RED);**

    /* sets the drawing color to red*/

    **for (y=100; y<=400; y+=100)**

    /*y=100 is initialization, y<=400 is condition and y+=100
=> y=y+100 is increment; initialization is done once at the
beginning of the loop; next the condition is checked, and if it
is true, the statement in the body is executed; the value of y
is incremented by 100 before the condition is re-checked; this
process continues until the condition becomes false at which
point the program flow exits the loop*/

        **for (x=100; x<=400; x+=100)**

        /*x=100 is initialization, x<=400 is condition and x+=100
=> x=x+100 is increment; initialization is done once at
the beginning of the loop; next the condition is checked,
and if it is true, the statement in the body is executed;
the value of x is incremented by 100 before the condition
is re-checked; this process continues until the condition
becomes false at which point the program flow exits the
loop*/

            **circle(x, y, 50);**

            /*this function draws a circle of radius 50 cm whose
center is at (x, y) coordinate; we want to draw 4x4=16
circles that touches each others' neighbor circles;
that's why the distance between two centers is 100
and the radius of each circle is 50; for the first 4

circles the y coordinate remains fixed at 100 and the x coordinates change by 100 in each iteration of the 2^nd 'for' loop; in the 2^nd iteration of the 1^st 'for' loop the y coordinate changed to 200 to draw another 4 circles in the 2^nd row and keeping the y value fixed at 200 we again change the x coordinates by 100 in each iteration of the 2^nd 'for' loop*/

```
getch();
/*input function getch() is called here to keep the console
state visible until we enter any character*/
closegraph();
/*function closegraph() is called here to deallocate all memory
and shut down the graphics system*/
return 0;
/*0 is returned as it is the standard for the successful
execution of the program*/
}
```
/*the closing curly brace specifies the end of the main() function's body, as well as the program's end; after that curly brace, no statement is executed*/

## PROBLEM-05
**Write a program that draws dynamic rainbow with beautiful colors.**

<u>Programming Code of the Solution:</u>

```c
#include <graphics.h>
#include <conio.h>
#include <dos.h>
int main(){
    int gd=DETECT, gm;
    int x, y, i;
    initgraph(&gd, &gm, (char *)"");
    x=getmaxx()/2;
    y=getmaxy()/2;
    for (i=40; i<200; i++){
        delay(100);
        setcolor(i/10);
        arc(x, y, 0, 180, i-10);
    }
    getch();
    closegraph();
    return 0;
}
```

Input and Output of the Executed Program:

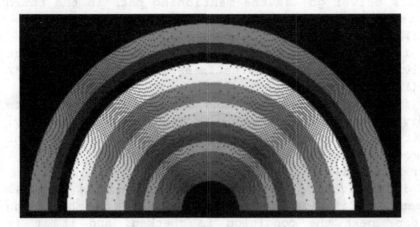

**Explanation of the Programming Code:**

`#include <graphics.h>`
/*header file graphics.h contains prototypes of the library functions initgraph(), getmaxx(), getmaxy(), setcolor(), arc(), and closegraph(); the header file must be included using preprocessor directive #include before the functions are called in the program*/
`#include <conio.h>`
/*header file conio.h contains the prototype of the libray function getch(), hence needs to be included before the function is used in the program*/
`#include <dos.h>`
/*header file dos.h contains the prototype of the libray function delay() and hence, needs to be included before using the function in the program*/
`int main(){`
/*all C program must have a main() function with return type void or int; here there is no parameter of the main() function and it returns an integer; opening curly brace specifies start of the main() function and no statement before that curly brace is executed by the compiler*/
　　`int gd=DETECT, gm;`
　　/*two integer type variables gd, and gm are declared. Variable gd is initialized to DETECT which is a macro that automatically detect graphics driver suitable for hardware*/
　　`int x, y, i;`
　　/*three integer type variables i, x and y are declared; compiler assigns required spaces in memory for these three variables*/
　　`initgraph(&gd, &gm, (char *)"");`
　　/*library function initgraph() is called here to initialize the graphics mode. Graphics mode gm represents screen

resolution and will be selected implicitly depending on the graphics driver gd; as the mentioning path in the third argument is not mandatory we write it as empty string*/

```
x=getmaxx()/2;
```

/*library function getmaxx() returns the maximum x coordinate that is divided by 2 and the value is assigned to variable x*/

```
y=getmaxy()/2;
```

/*library function getmaxy() returns the maximum y coordinate that is divided by 2 and the value is assigned to variable y; thus we get the (x, y) coordinate at the center of the current graphics mode and driver*/

```
for (i=40; i<200; i++){
```

/*i=40 is initialization, i<200 is condition and i++ => i=i+1 is increment; initialization is done once at the beginning of the loop; next the condition is checked, and if it is true, the statements in the body are executed; the value of i is incremented by 1 before the condition is re-checked; this process continues until the condition becomes false at which point the program flow exits the loop*/

```
    delay(100);
```

/*this halts the execution of the next instruction for 100 milliseconds*/

```
    setcolor(i/10);
```

/*this function sets the drawing color; at the 1st 10 iterations of the loop, it sets the color to RED=4; at the 2nd 10 iterations of the loop, it sets the color to MAGENTA=5; and so on*/

```
    arc(x, y, 0, 180, i-10);
```

/*it draws an arc with center at (x, y), 0 is the starting point of the angle, 180 is the ending point of the angle, and i-10 is the radius of the arc; at the 1st 10 iterations of the loop, it draws 10 red color arcs whose radius changes in each iteration from 30 to 39; at the 2nd 10 iterations, it draws 10 magenta color arcs whose radius changes in each iteration from 40 to 49; and so on*/

```
}
```

/*this closing curly brace specifies the end of the for loop*/

```
getch();
```

/*input function getch() is called here to keep the console state visible until we enter any character*/

```
closegraph();
```

/*function closegraph() is called here to deallocate all memory and shut down the graphics system*/

```
return 0;
```

/*0 is returned as it is the standard for the successful execution of the program*/

```
}
```

/*the closing curly brace specifies the end of the main() function's body, as well as the program's end; after that curly brace, no statement is executed*/

## PROBLEM-06
**Write a program that draws a simple house and shows it on the screen.**

Programming Code of the Solution:

```c
#include <graphics.h>
#include <conio.h>
int main(){
    int gd=DETECT, gm;
    initgraph(&gd, &gm, (char *)"");
    line(100, 100, 150, 50);
    line(150, 50, 200, 100);
    line(150, 50, 350, 50);
    line(350, 50, 400, 100);
    rectangle(100, 100, 200, 200);
    rectangle(200, 100, 400, 200);
    rectangle(130, 130, 170, 200);
    rectangle(250, 120, 350, 180);
    setfillstyle(2, 3);
    floodfill(131, 131, WHITE);
    floodfill(201, 101, WHITE);
    setfillstyle(11, 7);
    floodfill(101, 101, WHITE);
    floodfill(150, 52, WHITE);
    floodfill(163, 55, WHITE);
    floodfill(251, 121, WHITE);
    getch();
    closegraph();
    return 0;
}
```

Input and Output of the Executed Program:

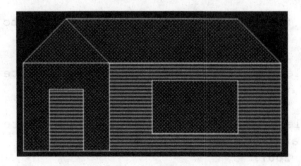

## Explanation of the Programming Code:

```
#include <graphics.h>
```
/*header file graphics.h contains prototypes of the library functions initgraph(), line(), rectangle(), setfillstyle(), floodfill() and closegraph(); the header file must be included using preprocessor directive #include before the functions are called in the program*/

```
#include <conio.h>
```
/*header file conio.h contains the prototype of the libray function getch(), hence needs to be included before the function is used in the program*/

```
int main(){
```
/*all C program must have a main() function with return type void or int; here there is no parameter of the main() function and it returns an integer; opening curly brace specifies start of the main() function and no statement before that curly brace is executed by the compiler*/

```
    int gd=DETECT, gm;
```
/*two integer type variables gd, and gm are declared. Variable gd is initialized to DETECT which is a macro that automatically detect graphics driver suitable for hardware*/

```
    initgraph(&gd, &gm, (char *)"");
```
/*library function initgraph() is called here to initialize the graphics mode. Graphics mode gm represents screen resolution and will be selected implicitly depending on the graphics driver gd; as the mentioning path in the third argument is not mandatory we write it as empty string*/

```
    line(100, 100, 150, 50);
```
/*draws a straight line from a point (100, 100) coordinate to point (150, 50) coordinate*/

```
    line(150, 50, 200, 100);
```
/*draws a straight line from a point (150, 50) coordinate to point (200, 100) coordinate*/

```
    line(150, 50, 350, 50);
```
/*draws a straight line from a point (150, 50) coordinate to point (350, 50) coordinate*/

```
    line(350, 50, 400, 100);
```
/*draws a straight line from a point (350, 50) coordinate to point (400, 100) coordinate*/

```
    rectangle(100, 100, 200, 200);
```
/*draws a rectangle with left-top corner at (100, 100) coordinate and right-bottom corner at (200, 200)*/

```
    rectangle(200, 100, 400, 200);
```
/*draws a rectangle with left-top corner at (200, 100) coordinate and right-bottom corner at (400, 200)*/

```
    rectangle(130, 130, 170, 200);
```
/*draws a rectangle with left-top corner at (130, 130) coordinate and right-bottom corner at (170, 200)*/

```
    rectangle(250, 120, 350, 180);
```

```
/*draws a rectangle with left-top corner at (250, 120) coordinate
and right-bottom corner at (350, 180)*/
setfillstyle(2, 3);
/*sets the current fill pattern to LINE_FILL and fill color to
CYAN*/
floodfill(131, 131, WHITE);
/*filsl the enclosed area at location (131, 131) with current
fill pattern and fill color set in the previous instruction,
and with border color white*/
floodfill(201, 101, WHITE);
/*fills the enclosed area at location (201, 101) with current
fill pattern and fill color set in the previous instruction,
and with border color white*/
setfillstyle(11, 7);
/*sets the current fill pattern to CLOSE_DOT_FILL and fill
color to LIGHTGRAY*/
floodfill(101, 101, WHITE);
/*fills the enclosed area at location (101, 101) with current
fill pattern and fill color set in the previous instruction,
and with border color white*/
floodfill(150, 52, WHITE);
/*fills the enclosed area at location (150, 52) with current
fill pattern and fill color set in the previous instruction,
and with border color white*/
floodfill(163, 55, WHITE);
/*fills the enclosed area at location (163, 55) with current
fill pattern and fill color set in the previous instruction,
and with border color white*/
floodfill(251, 121, WHITE);
/*fills the enclosed area at location (251, 121) with current
fill pattern and fill color set in the previous instruction,
and with border color white*/
getch();
/*input function getch() is called here to keep the console
state visible until we enter any character*/
closegraph();
/*function closegraph() is called here to deallocate all memory
and shut down the graphics system*/
return 0;
/*0 is returned as it is the standard for the successful
execution of the program*/
}
/*the closing curly brace specifies the end of the main() function's
body, as well as the program's end; after that curly brace, no
statement is executed*/
```

## PROBLEM-07
**Write a program to make a dynamic digital clock.**

Programming Code of the Solution:

```c
#include <stdlib.h>
#include <graphics.h>
#include <conio.h>
#include <dos.h>
struct time tm;
void display(int x, int y, int num);
int main(){
    int gd=DETECT, gm;
    int hr, min, sec;
    initgraph(&gd, &gm, (char *)"");
    setcolor(RED);
    while (!kbhit()){
        gettime(&tm);
        hr = tm.ti_hour;
        min = tm.ti_min;
        sec = tm.ti_sec;
        display(100, 100, hr);
        display(200, 100, min);
        display(300, 100, sec);
        sound(400);
        delay(30);
        nosound();
        delay(970);
        cleardevice();
    }
    getch();
    closegraph();
    return 0;
}
void display(int x, int y, int num){
    char str[3];
    itoa(num, str, 10);
    settextstyle(4, HORIZ_DIR, 7);
    outtextxy(180, 100, ":");
    outtextxy(280, 100, ":");
    outtextxy(x, y, str);
    rectangle(90, 90, 380, 200);
    rectangle(70, 70, 400, 220);
}
```

Input and Output of the Executed Program:

## Explanation of the Programming Code:

**#include <stdlib.h>**
/*header file stdlib.h contains the prototype of the libray function itoa(), hence needs to be included before the function is used in the program*/

**#include <graphics.h>**
/*header file graphics.h contains prototypes of the library functions initgraph(), setcolor(), cleardevice(), settextstyle(), outtextxy(), rectangle(), and closegraph(); the header file must be included using preprocessor directive #include before the functions are called in the program*/

**#include <conio.h>**
/*header file conio.h contains the prototypes of the libray functions getch() and kbhit(), hence needs to be included before these functions are used in the program*/

**#include <dos.h>**
/*header file dos.h contains the prototypes of the libray functions gettime(), sound(), nosound() and delay(); hence, needs to be included before using these functions in the program*/

**struct time tm;**
/*struct time type variable tm is declared; the structure contains local calendar date and time broken down into its components; the members that represents the current time in hour, minute and seconds can be accessed using dot (.) operator*/

**void display(int x, int y, int num);**
/*this is the prototype (or declaration) of the user-defined function display() that must end with a semicolon; display() takes three integer values as parameters, executes some predefined instructions, and returns nothing*/

**int main(){**
/*all C program must have a main() function with return type void or int; here there is no parameter of the main() function and it returns an integer; opening curly brace specifies start of the main() function and no statement before that curly brace is executed by the compiler*/

```
int gd=DETECT, gm;
```
/*two integer type variables gd, and gm are declared. Variable
gd is initialized to DETECT which is a macro that automatically
detect graphics driver suitable for hardware*/
```
int hr, min, sec;
```
/*three integer type variables hr, min and sec are declared;
compiler assigns required spaces in memory for these three
variables*/
```
initgraph(&gd, &gm, (char *)"");
```
/*library function initgraph() is called here to initialize the
graphics mode. Graphics mode gm represents screen resolution
and will be selected implicitly depending on the graphics
driver gd; as the mentioning path in the third argument is not
mandatory we write it as empty string*/
```
setcolor(RED);
```
/*this function sets the drawing color RED*/
```
while (!kbhit()){
```
/*body of the while loop contains the following statements,
enclosed by curly braces, which are executed until the condition
becomes false; when any key is pressed, kbhit() returns nonzero
value and due to ! (NOT) sign the value becomes false (or zero)
at which point the program flow exits the loop*/
```
    gettime(&tm);
```
/*this function gets the current time in hour, minutes,
seconds etc. and passed it to the time object tm*/
```
    hr = tm.ti_hour;
```
/*hour of the current time passed by gettime() function
to tm is accessed using the dot operator and assigned to
variable hr*/
```
    min = tm.ti_min;
```
/*minute of the current time passed by gettime() function
to tm is accessed using the dot operator and assigned to
variable min*/
```
    sec = tm.ti_sec;
```
/*second of the current time passed by gettime() function
to tm is accessed using the dot operator and assigned to
variable sec*/
```
    display(100, 100, hr);
```
/*user-defined function display() is called with three
integer values 100, 100 and hr are passed as arguments;
program control goes to the definition of the function
that displays value of hr at coordinate (100, 100) and
the program control returns to the immedicate next
instruction*/
```
    display(200, 100, min);
```
/*user-defined function display() is called with three

integer values 200, 100 and min are passed as arguments; program control goes to the definition of the function that displays value of min at coordinate (200, 100) and the program control returns to the immedicate next instruction*/

**display(300, 100, sec);**

/*user-defined function display() is called with three integer values 300, 100 and sec are passed as arguments; program control goes to the definition of the function that displays value of hr at coordinate (300, 100) and the program control returns to the immedicate next instruction*/

**sound(400);**

/*this function is called to produce the system sound of frequency 400 Hz*/

**delay(30);**

/*this function is called to halt the execution of the next instruction for 30 ms so that the program can continue the system sound of 400 Hz for 30 ms*/

**nosound();**

/*/this function is called to stop the system sound*/

**delay(970);**

/*this function is called to halt the execution of the next instruction for 970 ms so that there remains no system sound for 970 ms*/

**cleardevice();**

/*this clears the screen and fill it with current background color; if we don't clear the screen after showing the current time for one second, then the next time will simply overrite on previous time; as it continues, it will be difficult to undstand the current time at all*/

}

/*this closing curly brace specifies the end of while loop*/

**getch();**

/*input function getch() is called here to keep the console state visible until we enter any character*/

**closegraph();**

/*function closegraph() is called here to deallocate all memory and shut down the graphics system*/

**return 0;**

/*0 is returned as it is the standard for the successful execution of the program*/

}

/*the closing curly brace specifies the end of the main() function's body, as well as the program's end; after that curly brace, no statement is executed*/

```
void display(int x, int y, int num){
```
/*this is the header for the user-defined function display(), which must be identical to the function prototype except for no semicolon is used; the function is defined within the curly braces*/

```
    char str[3];
```
/*a character type array str[] of size 3 is declared; required contiguous memory spaces are allocated for the array*/

```
    itoa(num, str, 10);
```
/*itoa() converts decimal data num to its equivalent string str; here 10 means decimal; this conversion is done as outtextxy() function only displays string*/

```
    settextstyle(4, HORIZ_DIR, 7);
```
/*sets the current text characteristics; first argument sets the font to GOTHIC_FONT=4, second argument sets the font's direction to horizontal and the third argument sets the size of the font to 7*/

```
    outtextxy(180, 100, ":");
```
/*this displays the message enclosed by double quotations in the coordinate (180, 100) in the horizontal direction*/

```
    outtextxy(280, 100, ":");
```
/*this displays the message enclosed by double quotations in the coordinate (280, 100) in the horizontal direction*/

```
    outtextxy(x, y, str);
```
/*this displays the message str in the coordinate (x, y) in the horizontal direction*/

```
    rectangle(90, 90, 380, 200);
```
/*draws a rectangle with left-top corner at (90, 90) coordinate and right-bottom corner at (380, 200)*/

```
    rectangle(70, 70, 400, 220);
```
/*draws a rectangle with left-top corner at (70, 70) coordinate and right-bottom corner at (400, 220)*/

```
}
```
/*the closing curly brace specifies the end of the main() function's body, as well as the program's end; after that curly brace, no statement is executed*/

## PROBLEM-08
**Write a program that displays an animated smiley on the screen.**

Programming Code of the Solution:

```
#include <graphics.h>
#include <conio.h>
#include <dos.h>
int main(){
```

```
int gd=DETECT, gm;
int i=1, midx, midy;
initgraph(&gd, &gm, (char *)"");
midx = getmaxx()/2;
midy = getmaxy()/2;
while (!kbhit()){
    if (i%2==0)
        i=0;
    else
        i=25;
    setcolor(6);
    setfillstyle(SOLID_FILL, YELLOW);
    fillellipse(midx, midy, 200, 200);
    arc(midx, midy+50, 180, 360, 100);
    setfillstyle(SOLID_FILL, BROWN);
    fillellipse(midx+70, midy-70, 20, i);
    fillellipse(midx-70, midy-70, 20, i);
    i++;
    delay(1000);
    cleardevice();
}
getch();
closegraph();
return 0;
}
```

## Input and Output of the Executed Program:

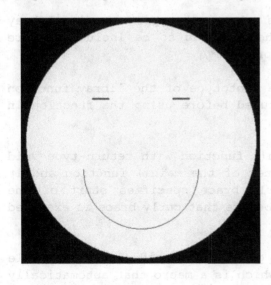

## Explanation of the Programming Code:

**#include <graphics.h>**
/*header file graphics.h contains prototypes of the library functions initgraph(), getmaxx(), getmaxy(), setcolor(), setfillstyle(), fillellipse(), arc(), cleardevice() and closegraph(); the header file must be included using preprocessor directive #include before the functions are called in the program*/
**#include <conio.h>**
/*header file conio.h contains the prototypes of the libray functions getch() and kbhit(), hence needs to be included before these functions are used in the program*/
**#include <dos.h>**
/*header file dos.h contains the prototype of the libray function delay(); hence, needs to be included before using the function in the program*/
**int main(){**
/*all C program must have a main() function with return type void or int; here there is no parameter of the main() function and it returns an integer; opening curly brace specifies start of the main() function and no statement before that curly brace is executed by the compiler*/
    **int gd=DETECT, gm;**
    /*two integer type variables gd, and gm are declared. Variable gd is initialized to DETECT which is a macro that automatically detect graphics driver suitable for hardware*/

```
int i=1, midx, midy;
```
/*three integer type variables i, midx and midy are declared;
compiler assigns required spaces in memory for these three
variables; variable i is also initialized to 1*/
```
initgraph(&gd, &gm, (char *)"");
```
/*library function initgraph() is called here to initialize the
graphics mode. Graphics mode gm represents screen resolution
and will be selected implicitly depending on the graphics
driver gd; as the mentioning path in the third argument is not
mandatory we write it as empty string*/
```
midx = getmaxx()/2;
```
/*library function getmaxx() returns the maximum x coordinate
that is divided by 2 and the value is assigned to variable
midx*/
```
midy = getmaxy()/2;
```
/*library function getmaxy() returns the maximum y coordinate
that is divided by 2 and the value is assigned to variable midy;
thus we get the (midx, midy) coordinate at the center of the
current graphics mode and driver*/
```
while (!kbhit()){
```
/*body of the while loop contains the following statements,
enclosed by curly braces, which are executed until the
condition becomes false; when any key is pressed, kbhit()
returns nonzero value and due to! (NOT) sign the value becomes
false (or zero) at which point the program flow exits the
loop*/
```
    if (i%2==0)
```
/*if i is divisible by 2, then the condition is true and
following statement is executed*/
```
        i=0;
```
/*0 is assigned to variable i*/
```
    else
```
/*statement in the body of else is executed if the condition
of 'if' is false, that is, i is not divisible by 2*/
```
        i=25;
```
/*25 is assigned to variable i; 25 is assigned to i in
the 1st iteration, 0 in the 2nd iteration, again 25 in
the 3rd iteration, and so on; this is done to create
blinking eyes*/
```
    setcolor(6);
```
/* sets the drawing color to BROWN=6*/
```
    setfillstyle(SOLID_FILL, YELLOW);
```
/*sets the current fill pattern to SOLID_FILL and fill
color to YELLOW*/
```
    fillellipse(midx, midy, 200, 200);
```
/*this draws (with brown color) and fills (with yellow

color) an ellipse with center at (midx, midy) and 200 (3ʳᵈ argument) as x-radius, and 200 (4ᵗʰ argument) as y-radius; this is done to create the body of the smiley*/
**arc(midx, midy+50, 180, 360, 100);**
/*it draws an arc with center at (midx, midy+50), 180 is the starting point of the angle, 360 is the ending point of the angle, and 100 is the radius of the arc; this is done to create the smile of the similey*/
**setfillstyle(SOLID_FILL, BROWN);**
/*sets the current fill pattern to SOLID_FILL and fill color to BROWN*/
**fillellipse(midx+70, midy-70, 20, i);**
/*this draws (with brown color) and fills (with brown color) an ellipse with center at (midx+70, midy-70) and 20 as x-radius, and i as y-radius; this is done to create the left-eye of the smiley*/
**fillellipse(midx-70, midy-70, 20, i);**
/*this draws (with brown color) and fills (with brown color) an ellipse with center at (midx+70, midy-70) and 20 as x-radius, and i as y-radius; this is done to create the right-eye of the smiley*/
**i++;**
/*value of i is increamented by 1 at each iteration so that in the 1ˢᵗ iteration, i=0 and we get closed eye; in the 2ⁿᵈ iteration, i=25 and we get opened eye; thus we get blinking eyes of the smiley*/
**delay(1000);**
/*this function is called to halt the execution of the next instruction for 1000 ms so that the smiley with closed eye remains on the screen for 1000 ms, and the smiley with opened eye remains on the screen for the next 1000 ms */
**cleardevice();**
/*this clears the screen and fill it with current background color; if we don't clear the screen after showing each status of the smiley for one second, then the next status will simply overrite on previous status and we cannot clearly see different status of the smiley*/
**}**
/*this closing curly brace specifies the end of while loop*/
**getch();**
/*input function getch() is called here to keep the console state visible until we enter any character*/
**closegraph();**

```
/*function closegraph() is called here to deallocate all memory
and shut down the graphics system*/
return 0;
/*0 is returned as it is the standard for the successful
execution of the program*/
}
```
/*the closing curly brace specifies the end of the main() function's
body, as well as the program's end; after that curly brace, no
statement is executed*/


## PROBLEM-09
**Write a program that shows a man walking in the rain.**


<u>Programming Code of the Solution:</u>

```c
#include <stdlib.h>
#include <graphics.h>
#include <conio.h>
#include <dos.h>
int main(){
    int gd=DETECT, gm;
    int i, j, x, y;
    initgraph(&gd, &gm, (char *)"");
    for (i=0; i<700; i++){
        circle(20+i, 200, 10);
        line(20+i, 210, 20+i, 250);
        line(20+i, 220, 10+i, 250);
        line(20+i, 210, 30+i, 250);
        line(20+i, 250, 30+i, 300);
        line(20+i, 250, 10+i, 300);
        line(0, 300, 700, 300);
        x = getmaxx();
        y = getmaxy();
        for (j=0; j<100; j++)
            outtextxy(rand()%x, rand()%y, "!");
        delay(5);
        cleardevice();
    }
    getch();
    closegraph();
    return 0;
}
```

Input and Output of the Executed Program:

## Explanation of the Programming Code:

**#include <stdlib.h>**
/*header file stdlib.h contains the prototype of the libray function rand(), hence needs to be included before the function is used in the program*/
**#include <graphics.h>**
/*header file graphics.h contains prototypes of the library functions initgraph(), circle(), line(), getmaxx(), getmaxy(), outtextxy(), cleardevice(), and closegraph(); the header file must be included using preprocessor directive #include before the functions are called in the program*/
**#include <conio.h>**
/*header file conio.h contains the prototype of the libray function getch(), hence needs to be included before the function is used in the program*/
**#include <dos.h>**
/*header file dos.h contains the prototype of the libray function delay(); hence, needs to be included before using the function in the program*/
**int main(){**
/*all C program must have a main() function with return type void or int; here there is no parameter of the main() function and it returns an integer; opening curly brace specifies start of the main() function and no statement before that curly brace is executed by the compiler*/

```
int gd=DETECT, gm;
```
/*two integer type variables gd, and gm are declared. Variable gd is initialized to DETECT which is a macro that automatically detect graphics driver suitable for hardware*/
```
int i, j, x, y;
```
/*four integer type variables i, j, x, and y are declared; compiler assigns required spaces in memory for these four variables*/
```
initgraph(&gd, &gm, (char *)"");
```
/*library function initgraph() is called here to initialize the graphics mode. Graphics mode gm represents screen resolution and will be selected implicitly depending on the graphics driver gd; as the mentioning path in the third argument is not mandatory we write it as empty string*/
```
for (i=0; i<700; i++){
```
/*i=0 is initialization, i<700 is condition and i++ => i=i+1 is increment; initialization is done once at the beginning of the loop; next the condition is checked, and if it is true, the statements in the body are executed; the value of i is incremented by 1 before the condition is re-checked; this process continues until the condition becomes false at which point the program flow exits the loop*/
```
    circle(20+i, 200, 10);
```
/*function circle() is called to draw a circle that takes (20+i, 200) as coordinate of the center and 10 as radius of the circle; this is used to create the moving head; at each iteration of the loop, value of i is changed and hence, the position of head as well*/
```
line(20+i, 210, 20+i, 250);
```
/*draws a straight line from a point (20+i, 210) coordinate to point (20+i, 250) coordinate; this is used to create the moving body; at each iteration of the loop, value of i is changed and hence, the position of body as well*/
```
line(20+i, 220, 10+i, 250);
```
/*draws a straight line from a point (20+i, 220) coordinate to point (10+i, 250) coordinate*/
```
line(20+i, 210, 30+i, 250);
```
/*draws a straight line from a point (20+i, 210) coordinate to point (30+i, 250) coordinate; this, together with the previous instruction, is used to create the moving arms; at each iteration of the loop, value of i is changed and hence, the position of arms as well*/
```
line(20+i, 250, 30+i, 300);
```
/*draws a straight line from a point (20+i, 250) coordinate to point (30+i, 300) coordinate*/
```
line(20+i, 250, 10+i, 300);
```

/\*draws a straight line from a point (20+i, 250) coordinate to point (10+i, 300) coordinate; this, together with the previous instruction, is used to create the moving legs; at each iteration of the loop, value of i is changed and hence, the position of legs as well\*/

**line(0, 300, 700, 300);**

/\*draws a straight line from a point (0, 300) coordinate to point (700, 300) coordinate; this draws the 1-D surface on which the man moves\*/

**x = getmaxx();**

/\*library function getmaxx() returns the maximum x coordinate that is assigned to variable x\*/

**y = getmaxy();**

/\*library function getmaxy() returns the maximum y coordinate that is assigned to variable y\*/

**for (j=0; j<100; j++)**

/\*j=0 is initialization, i<100 is condition and j++ => j=j+1 is increment; initialization is done once at the beginning of the loop; next the condition is checked, and if it is true, the statement in the body is executed; the value of j is incremented by 1 before the condition is re-checked; this process continues until the condition becomes false at which point the program flow exits the loop\*/

**outtextxy(rand()%x, rand()%y, "!");**

/\*function rand() generates a random number and the modulus operation in the 1st argument gives any number between 0~x (x=maximum x coordinate) that is used as x coordinate; similarly, 2nd argument gives us any number between 0~y as y coordinate; function outtextxy() now displays the message enclosed by double quotations in the (r, y) coordinate; this is done to create dynamic rain drops\*/

**delay(5);**

/\*this halts the execution of the next instruction for 5 milliseconds\*/

**cleardevice();**

/\*this clears the screen and sets the current postion to (0, 0); if we don't clear the screen after showing a particular position of the man for 5 milliseconds, then in the next iteration of the outer for loop, the man will be shown in two different locations- current and previous; and so on\*/

**}**

/\*this closing curly brace specifies the end of outer for (i=0; i<700; i++) loop\*/

**getch();**

```
/*input function getch() is called here to keep the console
state visible until we enter any character*/
closegraph();
/*function closegraph() is called here to deallocate all memory
and shut down the graphics system*/
return 0;
/*0 is returned as it is the standard for the successful
execution of the program*/
}
```
/*the closing curly brace specifies the end of the main() function's
body, as well as the program's end; after that curly brace, no
statement is executed*/

## PROBLEM-10
**Write a program that displays a moving car on the screen.**

Programming Code of the Solution:

```
#include <graphics.h>
#include <conio.h>
#include <dos.h>
int main(){
    int gd=DETECT, gm;
    int i, x, y;
    initgraph(&gd, &gm, (char *)"");
    x = getmaxx()/2;
    y = getmaxy()/2;
    x -= 300;
    for (i=0; i<600; i=i+5){
        cleardevice();
        line(x-70+i, y, x+70+i, y);
        line(x-69+i, y-3, x+69+i, y-3);
        arc(x-105+i, y, 0, 180, 35);
        circle(x-105+i, y, 25);
        arc(x+105+i, y, 0, 180, 35);
        circle(x+105+i, y, 25);
        line(x+140+i, y, x+190+i, y);
        line(x+140+i, y-3, x+190+i, y-3);
        line(x-190+i, y, x-140+i, y);
        line(x-190+i, y-3, x-140+i, y-3);
        ellipse(x+105+i, y, 0, 90, 85, 50);
        ellipse(x-105+i, y, 90, 180, 85, 50);
        ellipse(x+i, y-50, 0, 180, 105, 35);
```

```
        ellipse(x+i, y-50, 349, 192, 95, 30);
        line(x-92+i, y-44, x+92+i, y-44);
        line(x-92+i, y-41, x+92+i, y-41);
        line(x+i, y-44, x+i, y-80);
        line(x+i, y-40, x+i, y-5);
        delay(50);
    }
    getch();
    closegraph();
    return 0;
}
```

Input and Output of the Executed Program:

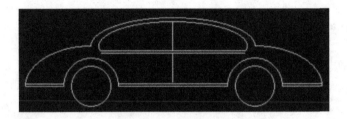

## Explanation of the Programming Code:

**#include <graphics.h>**
/*header file graphics.h contains prototypes of the library functions initgraph(), getmaxx(), getmaxy(), line(), arc(), circle(), ellipse(), cleardevice() and closegraph(); the header file must be included using preprocessor directive #include before the functions are called in the program*/
**#include <conio.h>**
/*header file conio.h contains the prototype of the libray function getch(), hence needs to be included before the function is used in the program*/
**#include <dos.h>**
/*header file dos.h contains the prototype of the libray function delay(); hence, needs to be included before using the function in the program*/
**int main(){**
/*all C program must have a main() function with return type void or int; here there is no parameter of the main() function and it returns an integer; opening curly brace specifies start of the main() function and no statement before that curly brace is executed by the compiler*/
    **int gd=DETECT, gm;**
    /*two integer type variables gd, and gm are declared. Variable gd is initialized to DETECT which is a macro that automatically detect graphics driver suitable for hardware*/

```
int i, x, y;
```
/*three integer type variables i, x and y are declared;
compiler assigns required spaces in memory for these three
variables*/
```
initgraph(&gd, &gm, (char *)"");
```
/*library function initgraph() is called here to initialize the
graphics mode. Graphics mode gm represents screen resolution
and will be selected implicitly depending on the graphics
driver gd; as the mentioning path in the third argument is not
mandatory we write it as empty string*/
```
x = getmaxx()/2;
```
/*library function getmaxx() returns the maximum x coordinate
that is divided by 2 and the value is assigned to variable
x*/
```
y = getmaxy()/2;
```
/*library function getmaxy() returns the maximum y coordinate
that is divided by 2 and the value is assigned to variable y;
thus we get the (x, y) coordinate at the center of the current
graphics mode and driver*/
```
x -= 300;
```
/*x=x-300, that is, the value of x is decreamented by 300*/
```
for (i=0; i<600; i=i+5){
```
/*i=0 is initialization, i<600 is condition and i=i+5 is
increment; initialization is done once at the beginning of the
loop; next the condition is checked, and if it is true, the
statements in the body are executed; the value of i is incremented
by 5 before the condition is re-checked; this process continues
until the condition becomes false at which point the program
flow exits the loop*/
```
    cleardevice();
```
/*this clears the screen and sets the current postion
to (0, 0); if we don't clear the screen after showing a
particular position of the car for 50 milliseconds, then in
the next iteration of the for loop, the car will be shown
in two different locations- current and previous; and so
on*/
```
    line(x-70+i, y, x+70+i, y);
```
/*draws a straight line from a point (x-70+i, y) coordinate
to point (x+70+i, y) coordinate*/
```
    line(x-69+i, y-3, x+69+i, y-3);
```
/*draws a straight line from a point (x-69+i, y-3) coordinate
to point (x+69+i, y-3) coordinate*/
```
    arc(x-105+i, y, 0, 180, 35);
```
/*it draws an arc with center at (x-105+i, y), 0 is the
starting point of the angle, 180 is the ending point of the
angle, and 35 is the radius of the arc*/
```
    circle(x-105+i, y, 25);
```
/*function circle() is called to draw a circle that takes

(x–105+i, y) as coordinate of the center and 25 as radius
of the circle; this circle() and previous arc() functions
are used to create the moving back-wheel of the car*/
**arc(x+105+i, y, 0, 180, 35);**
/*it draws an arc with center at (x+105+i, y), 0 is the
starting point of the angle, 180 is the ending point of the
angle, and 35 is the radius of the arc*/
**circle(x+105+i, y, 25);**
/*function circle() is called to draw a circle that takes
(x+105+i, y) as coordinate of the center and 25 as radius of
the circle; this circle() and previous arc() functions are
used to create the moving front-wheel of the car */
**line(x+140+i, y, x+190+i, y);**
/*draws a straight line from a point (x+140+i, y) coordinate
to point (x+190+i, y) coordinate*/
**line(x+140+i, y–3, x+190+i, y–3);**
/*draws a straight line from a point (x+140+i, y–3)
coordinate to point (x+190+i, y–3) coordinate*/
**line(x–190+i, y, x–140+i, y);**
/*draws a straight line from a point (x–190+i, y) coordinate
to point (x–140+i, y) coordinate*/
**line(x–190+i, y–3, x–140+i, y–3);**
/*draws a straight line from a point (x–190+i, y–3)
coordinate to point (x–140+i, y–3) coordinate*/
**ellipse(x+105+i, y, 0, 90, 85, 50);**
/*draws an ellipse with (x+105+i, y) as the location of the
ellipse, 0 as the starting point of the angle, 90 as the
ending point of the angle, 85 as the x-radius and 50 as the
y-radius*/
**ellipse(x–105+i, y, 90, 180, 85, 50);**
/*draws an ellipse with (x–105+i, y) as the location of the
ellipse, 90 as the starting point of the angle, 180 as the
ending point of the angle, 85 as the x-radius and 50 as the
y-radius*/
**ellipse(x+i, y–50, 0, 180, 105, 35);**
/*draws an ellipse with (x+i, y–50) as the location of the
ellipse, 0 as the starting point of the angle, 180 as the
ending point of the angle, 105 as the x-radius and 35 as
the y-radius*/
**ellipse(x+i, y–50, 349, 192, 95, 30);**
/*draws an ellipse with (x+i, y–50) as the location of the
ellipse, 349 as the starting point of the angle, 192 as the
ending point of the angle, 95 as the x-radius and 30 as the
y-radius*/
**line(x–92+i, y–44, x+92+i, y–44);**
/*draws a straight line from a point (x–92+i, y–44)
coordinate to point (x+92+i, y–44) coordinate*/

```
line(x-92+i, y-41, x+92+i, y-41);
/*draws a straight line from a point (x-92+i, y-41)
coordinate to point (x+92+i, y-41) coordinate*/
line(x+i, y-44, x+i, y-80);
/*draws a straight line from a point (x+i, y-44) coordinate
to point (x+i, y-80) coordinate*/
line(x+i, y-40, x+i, y-5);
/*draws a straight line from a point (x+i, y-40) coordinate
to point (x+i, y-5) coordinate; this, together with the
previous instructions in the for loop, creates body of the
car that moves in the forward x-direction as the value of
i changes in each iteration of the loop*/
delay(50);
/*this function is called to halt the execution of the
next instruction for 50 ms so that the car remains in a
particular position on the screen for 50 ms before it
moves to the next position in the next iteration of the
loop*/
}
/*this closing curly brace specifies the end of the for
loop*/
getch();
/*input function getch() is called here to keep the console
state visible until we enter any character*/
closegraph();
/*function closegraph() is called here to deallocate all memory
and shut down the graphics system*/
return 0;
/*0 is returned as it is the standard for the successful
execution of the program*/
}
/*the closing curly brace specifies the end of the main() function's
body, as well as the program's end; after that curly brace, no
statement is executed*/
```

Problems to Practice

1) Write a program to draw a bar of size 100 × 300 and a circle with a radius of 50.

2) Write a program that prints a message in different colors.

3) Write a program that displays different messages in different colors and different directions on different backgrounds.

4) Write a program that draws 16 circles of same size at different coordinates where each circle intersects all its neighbor circles.

5) Write a program that draws rainbow with beautiful colors.

6) Write a program that draws a simple house and shows it on the screen.

7) Write a program to make a dynamic digital clock.

8) Write a program that displays an animated smiley on the screen.

9) Write a program that shows a man walking in the rain.

10) Write a program that displays a moving car on the screen.

11) Write a program that shows a man walking in the rain with an umbrella.

12) Write a program that creates a car and traffic light signal.

13) Write a program that shows a moving car with a flag in front.

14) Write a program to make a flying plane in C graphics.

15) Write a program to draw six concentric circles with different radius and colors.

16) Write a program that shows many circles with different colors and animation.

# C Cross-platform

T HE LANGUAGE C IS cross-platform because it can work across multiple types of platforms or operating environments. We do not run C codes directly on machines; first, the source code is compiled to a platform-specific assembly. Therefore, we can use the same C source code to compile with different compilers to create the specific assembly needed. This chapter describes how the C source codes can be compiled and run on different platforms and operating systems.

## 8.1 CREATING OWN LIBRARY

There are some inbuilt functions in C known as standard library functions. Prototypes and data definition of the functions are available in corresponding header files. We need to include the header files in our C programs before using these standard functions. Similarly, we can define our own functions and create our own library so that we can reuse the codes or functions we have defined. Two types of libraries in C are static library (*.a) and dynamic library (*.dll)

### 8.1.1 Creating Static Library

Static library is a collection of object files (*.o) that contains definition of C functions. Creating a static library is nothing but simply generating an archive (*.a) of one or more object files. The object files of a static library are linked to the main program module during linking stage of compilation. After successful linking, the compiler generates a single executable file (.exe) that contains both main program module and the libraries. The following flow diagram explains how a C static library is generated from three different C source files.

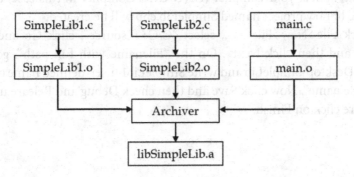

DOI: 10.1201/9781003302629-8

Steps to follow to create a user-defined C static library libSimpleLib.a are as follows.

Step-1: Open CodeBlocks C compiler. Now, click File→New→Project . . ., select "Static library", and click on Go.

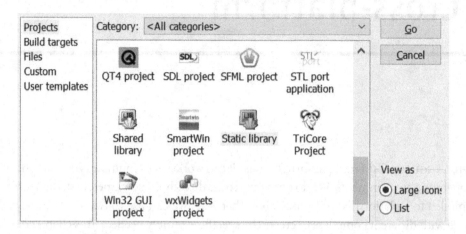

Now click on Next> and write SimpleLib on "Project title": and select a folder where to create the project (may be in C:\Users\SazzadImran\Desktop\ for example).

Now click Next>, select your compiler (GNU GCC Compiler in this case) and then click Finish. A static library project named SimpleLib.cbp will be created.

Step-2: Click File→New→File . . ., select "C/C++ source", click Go and then Next>. Now select C and then click Next>. On the "Filename with full path": go to C:\Users\ SazzadImran\Desktop\SimpleLib and write SimpleLib1 (user-defined name of the C source file) on the "File name". Now click Save and then check Debug and Release under 'In build target(s):' before click on Finish.

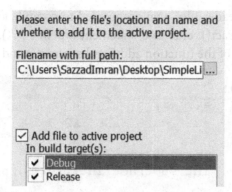

Step-3: On the SimpleLib1.c define any function. We define a function named add(), as an example, that takes two integers as argument and return sum of the values. Include the user-defined header file, where the prototype of the function will be available, using double quotation in the definition of the function.

```
SimpleLib1.c ×
1    #include "Simplelib2.h"
2    int add(int a, int b){
3        int sum1;
4        sum1 = a+b;
5        return sum1;
6    }
```

Define another function subtract() in another source file named SimpleLib3.c in a similar way as we have defined function add() in SimpleLib1.c.

```
SimpleLib3.c ×
1    #include "SimpleLib2.h"
2    int subtract(int a, int b){
3        int sub1;
4        sub1 = a-b;
5        return sub1;
6    }
```

Step-4: Click File→New→File . . ., select "C/C++ header", click Go and then Next>. On the "Filename with full path:" go to C:\Users\SazzadImran\Desktop\SimpleLib and write SimpleLib2 as user-defined name of the C header file (may also be same as the source file) on the "File name" and then click Save. Now check Debug and Release under "In build target(s):" and then click on Finish.

Include all standard header files, that are needed to compile and run the user-defined functions add() and subtract(), after 2nd statement (#define . . .). After including header files, write the prototypes of the function add() and subtract() and then save the file.

```
SimpleLib2.h ×
1    #ifndef SIMPLELIB2_H_INCLUDED
2    #define SIMPLELIB2_H_INCLUDED
3
4    int add(int, int);
5    int subtract(int, int);
6
7    #endif // SIMPLELIB2_H_INCLUDED
```

Step-5: Open main.c source file, write the following codes in the file, and click Save. You may rename the main.c source file as example1.c to write the following codes.

```
main.c ×
1    #include <stdio.h>
2    #include "SimpleLib2.h"
3    int main(){
4        int sum, sub;
5        sum = add(7, 15);
6        sub = subtract(7, 15);
7        printf("Summation: %d\n", sum);
8        printf("subtraction: %d\n", sub);
9        return 0;
10   }
```

Step-6: Now click Build→Build. All object files with .o extension are created in our target folder obj\Debug, and a static library named libSimpleLib with .a extension is created in our target folder bin\Debug.

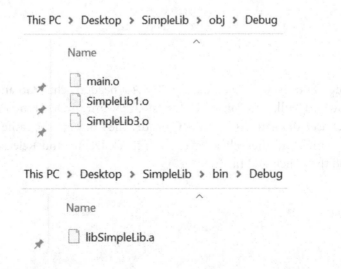

This PC > Desktop > SimpleLib > obj > Debug

Name

☐ main.o
☐ SimpleLib1.o
☐ SimpleLib3.o

This PC > Desktop > SimpleLib > bin > Debug

Name

☐ libSimpleLib.a

Step-7: To run the program, click Project→Properties...→"Build targets", select "Console application" under Type: drop-down menu and check "Pause when execution ends". Now, click OK and then "Build and run". After successful compilation, an executable file SimpleLib.exe is created in our target folder bin\Debug and the output of the program will look as follows:

```
Summation: 22
Subtraction: -8
```

## 8.1.2 Creating Dynamic Library

Like static library, C dynamic library is also a collection of object files (*.o) that contains the definition of C functions. But unlike C static library, object files of the dynamic library are loaded into main program module at run time (not during compilation). So rather than generating a single stand-alone executable file containing both the main program module and libraries, here the exe file contains only references to the functions and data defined in C dynamic libraries. Hence, both libraries and exe file are required to execute the program.

Steps to follow to create a user-defined C dynamic link library SimpleLib.dll are as follows:

Step-1: Open CodeBlocks C compiler. Now, click File→New→Project..., select "Dynamic Link Library" and click on Go.

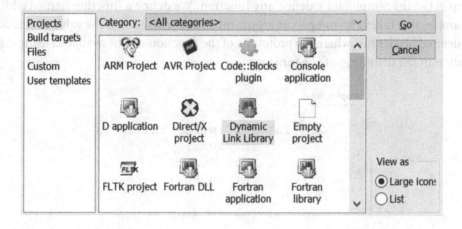

Now click on Next> and write SimpleLib on "Project title:" and select a folder where to create the project (may be in C:\Users\SazzadImran\Desktop\ for example).

Please select the folder where you want the new project to be created as well as its title.

Project title:
SimpleLib

Folder to create project in:
C:\Users\SazzadImran\Desktop\

Project filename:
SimpleLib.cbp

Resulting filename:
C:\Users\SazzadImran\Desktop\SimpleLib\SimpleLib.cb

Now click Next>, select your compiler (GNU GCC Compiler in this case) and then click Finish. A dynamic library project named SimpleLib.cbp will be created.

Step-2: Click File→New→File . . ., select "C/C++ source", click Go and then Next>. Now select C and then click Next>. On the "Filename with full path:" go to C:\Users\ SazzadImran\Desktop\SimpleLib and write SimpleLib1 (user-defined name of the C source file) on the 'File name'. Now click Save and then check Debug and Release under 'In build target(s):' before click on Finish.

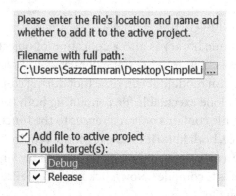

Step-3: On the SimpleLib1.c define any function. We define a function named add(), as an example, that takes two integers as argument and returns sum of the values. Include the user-defined header file, where the prototype of the function will be available, using double quotation in the definition of the function.

**SimpleLib1.c** ×

```
1    #include "Simplelib2.h"
2    int add(int a, int b){
3        int sum1;
4        sum1 = a+b;
5        return sum1;
6    }
```

Define another function subtract() in another source file named SimpleLib3.c in a similar way as we have defined function add() in SimpleLib1.c.

**SimpleLib3.c** ×

```
1    #include "SimpleLib2.h"
2    int subtract(int a, int b){
3        int sub1;
4        sub1 = a-b;
5        return sub1;
6    }
```

Step-4: Click File→New→File . . ., select "C/C++ header", click Go and then Next>. On the 'Filename with full path:' go to C:\Users\SazzadImran\Desktop\ SimpleLib and write SimpleLib2 as user-defined name of the C header file (may also be same as the source file) on the 'File name' and then click Save. Now check Debug and Release under 'In build target(s):' and then click on Finish.

Include all standard header files that are needed to compile and run the user-defined functions add() and subtract(), after 2nd statement (#define . . .). After including header files, write the prototypes of the function add() and subtract() and then save the file.

```
SimpleLib2.h ×
1    #ifndef SIMPLELIB2_H_INCLUDED
2    #define SIMPLELIB2_H_INCLUDED
3
4    int add(int, int);
5    int subtract(int, int);
6
7    #endif // SIMPLELIB2_H_INCLUDED
```

Step-5: Open another source file named example1.c, write the following codes in the file and click Save.

```
example1.c ×
1    #include <stdio.h>
2    #include "SimpleLib2.h"
3    int main(){
4        int sum, sub;
5        sum = add(7, 15);
6        sub = subtract(7, 15);
7        printf("Summation: %d\n", sum);
8        printf("subtraction: %d\n", sub);
9        return 0;
10   }
```

Step-6: Delete main.cpp and main.h files from the project. Now click Build→Build. All object files with .o extension are created in our target folder obj\Debug, and a dynamic link library named SimpleLib with .dll extension is created in our target folder bin\Debug.

This PC › Desktop › SimpleLib › obj › Debug

Name

* example1.o
* SimpleLib1.o
* SimpleLib3.o

This PC › Desktop › SimpleLib › bin › Debug

Name

* libSimpleLib.a
* libSimpleLib.def
* SimpleLib.dll

Other than .dll file, a module definition file libSimpleLib.def and a static library libSimpleLib.a were also created. The .def file provides information to the linker about exported files, attributes, etc., of the program to be linked, and is necessary while building a dll file.

Step-7: To run the program, click Project→Properties . . . →"Build targets", select "Console application" under Type: drop-down menu and check "Pause when execution ends". Now, click OK and then "Build and run". After successful compilation, an executable file SimpleLib.exe is created in our target folder bin\Debug and the output of the program will look like as follows:

```
Summation: 22
Subtraction: -8
```

## 8.2 TURBO C

Turbo C is a compiler for the C programming language from Borland. It includes a source code editor, a fast compiler, and a linker. Though it is discontinued nowadays, many still use this compiler to edit and run C programs. Therefore, a step-by-step procedure to run C programs using the Turbo C compiler is given below.

Step-1: Download and install Turbo C/C++ for windows. It may be downloaded from https://techdecodetutorials.com/download/.

Step-2: Open the program and click on File -> New, an empty blue window appears. Write your C program codes on the file and click File -> Save as . . ., write a file name of your choice with .cpp extension (Example1.cpp, for example) and then click OK.

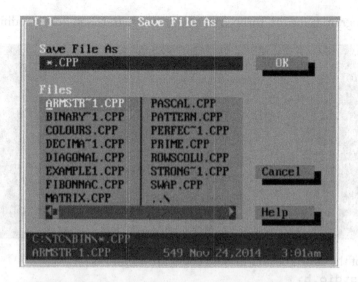

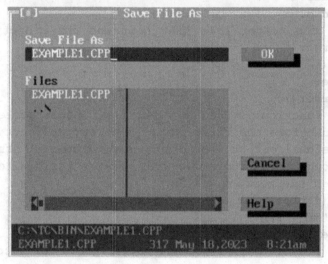

Step-3: Three extra lines need to be added to run a program on the Turbo C platform. For example, our first C program in Chapter 1 was as follows:

```c
#include <stdio.h>
int main(){
    int age;
    printf("Enter your age: ");
    scanf("%d", &age);
    if (age<18)
        printf("Sorry, you are not eligible for vaccination.");
    else
        printf("Congratulation, you are eligible for vaccination.");
    return 0;
}
```

To run this program using the Turbo C compiler, the program should be modified as follows:

```
#include <stdio.h>
#include <conio.h>
int main(){
    int age;
    clrscr();
    printf(                  );
    scanf(    , &age);
    if (age<18)
        printf(                                      );
    else
        printf(                                                    );
    getch();
    return 0;
}
```

Explanation of the added header file and codes are as follows:

```
#include <stdio.h>
#include <conio.h>
/*conio.h is the header file that contains the prototypes of the
functions clrscr() and getch()*/
int main(){
        int age;
        int clrscr();
        /*this function is used to clear the console screen. clrscr()
        is used before the first printf() or output function to clear
        any residual output from previous program run, otherwise when
        we execute this program we will see the residual output first
        and then the current output*/
        printf("Enter your age: ");
        scanf("%d", &age);
        if (age<18)
                printf("Sorry, you are not eligible for vaccination.");
        else
                printf("Congratulation, you are eligible for vaccination.");
        getch();
        /*this is an input function that takes any character from the
        standard input terminal. This input function is used here to
        keep the console screen alive to see the program output. Here
        the console screen wait until we press any key; otherwise,
        the program output is just shown for a second, and the console
        screen is closed immediately*/
        return 0;
}
```

So, as described, we need to add three extra lines in each C program if we want to run the program using the Turbo C compiler:

(1) Call function clrscr() before using any output function.

(2) Call getch() function before last line of the program, that is, "return 0;".

(3) Include header file conio.h that contains prototypes of clrscr() and getch() functions.

Step-4: Press Alt+F9 to compile the program. Correct any error(s) or warning(s) on the codes. Correcting the errors is a must, though it is optional to correct the warnings. Recompile the program until we get 0 error(s) and 0 warning(s).

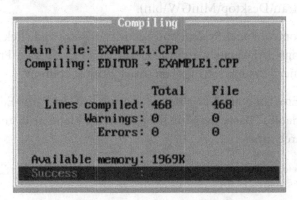

Step-5: Press Ctrl+F9 to execute the program. The output may look like as follows:

```
Enter your age: 21
Congratulation, you are eligible for vaccination.
```

## 8.3 VISUAL STUDIO CODE

Visual studio code, also known as VS code, is a source-code editor developed by Microsoft for Windows, Linux, and macOS. The source-code editor can be used with various programming languages, including Java, JavaScript, Python, and C/C++, and features that differ per language. A notable feature of the visual studio code is its ability to create extensions that support new languages. Step-by-step procedures to run a C program using visual studio code are given below:

Step-1: Download the C compiler "MinGW w64". MinGW stands for Minimalist GNU for Windows. It may be downloaded from the link https://bit.ly/mingw10.

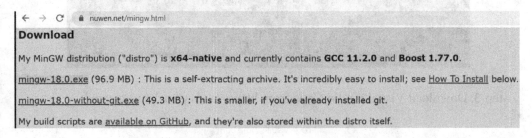

Now extract mingw-18.0 to any destination, for example, on Desktop.

Step-2: Add path in environment variable to access gcc in visual studio code. To do that,

    – copy the path of the bin directory of MinGW (for example, C:\Users\ SazzadImran\Desktop\MinGW\bin).

    – go to Control Panel\System and Security\System and click on "Advanced system settings". Alternately, right-click on This PC, click on Properties, and then on "Advanced system settings" on the rightmost column.

    – click "Environment Variables . . ." and click on Path→Edit→New under the "User variables", paste the MinGW path in the blank field, and then click on OK button three times.

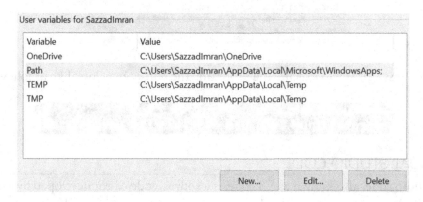

    – go to Command Prompt (press Win+R, write cmd, and press Enter) and write "gcc – version" and press Enter. If it shows the version number on the screen, then the MinGW gcc is successfully installed.

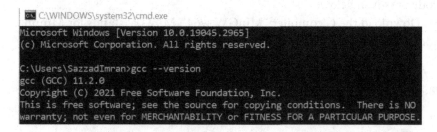

Step-3: Download Visual Studio Code from https://code.visualstudio.com/.

Now install the software. During setup, we must check "Add to PATH" option.

**Select Additional Tasks**
Which additional tasks should be performed?

Select the additional tasks you would like Setup to perform while installing Visual Studio Code, then click Next.

Additional icons:

☐ Create a desktop icon

Other:

☐ Add "Open with Code" action to Windows Explorer file context menu

☐ Add "Open with Code" action to Windows Explorer directory context menu

☑ Register Code as an editor for supported file types

☑ Add to PATH (requires shell restart)

Step-4: Start and configure the visual studio code for running C programs. For that,

    – install the C extension in the visual studio code (needed only for the first time). To do that, press the extension button, type c/c++ in the search bar, and install the first option from Microsoft.

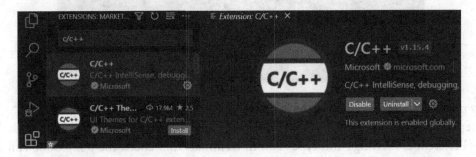

    – again, type code runner in the search bar and install (needed only for the first time) the first option from Jun Han.

Step-5: Click File→New File . . . → "Text File Built-In"→ "Select a Language" and then C (c) to create a new source file in the visual studio code. Now click File→Save and choose C:\Users\SazzadImran\Desktop\MinGW\bin to save your file (in the bin directory of

MinGW) and give a name to your file as you wish (for example, example1) and click on the Save button.

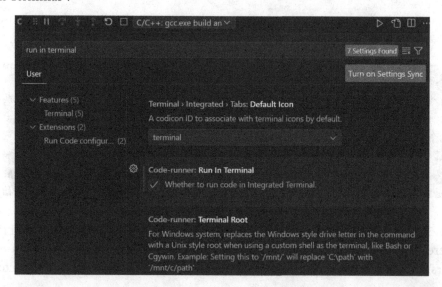

Step-6: Write your C programming codes on the file and save the program.

```c
#include <stdio.h>
int main(){
    int sum, n1, n2;
    printf("Enter two integers: ");
    scanf("%d %d", &n1, &n2);
    sum = n1+n2;
    printf("Summation: %d\n", sum);
    return 0;
}
```

Now press ctrl+alt+n or click on the small play button in the top-right corner.

Step-7: To run a program that includes input from the user, first click on File→Preferences→Settings and type "run in terminal" and check the box "Code runner: Run in Terminal".

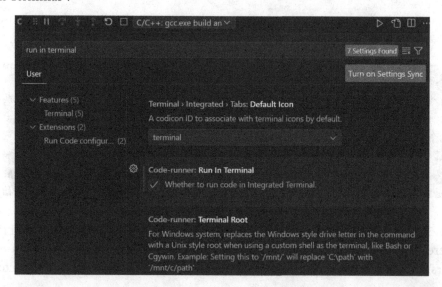

Now cancel the settings and return to the program. Run the code by pressing the run play button. The output will look like as follows:

```
PS C:\Users\SazzadImran\Desktop\MinGW\bin> cd "c:\Users\SazzadImran\Desktop\
MinGW\bin\" ; if ($?) { gcc example1.c -o example1 } ; if ($?) { .\example1
}
Enter two integers: 23 45
Summation: 68
```

If there is an error message showing "#include errors detected. Please update your include-Path" while compiling or running a program even after following all the above steps; in that case, it should be enough to correct the error if we just restart the program "Visual Studio Code".

## 8.4 VISUAL STUDIO

Visual Studio is a powerful integrated development environment (IDE) that supports a full-featured editor, resource managers, debuggers, and compilers for many languages and platforms. It is to mention that the cross-platform Visual Studio Code is an editor while the Visual Studio is an IDE. The following are the steps to run a C program using Visual Studio 2022 or the latest version.

Step-1: Download Visual Studio from
https://visualstudio.microsoft.com/downloads/

To install Visual Studio, click on VisualStudioSetup and then uncheck all the Workloads except "Desktop development with C++". Now click on "Install while downloading".

Step-2: Start the Visual Studio program and click on "Create a new project". Select "Empty Project" and click Next.

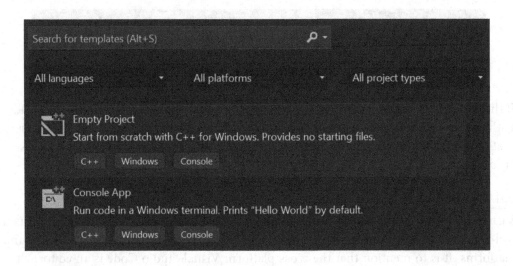

Enter an appropriate project name (Project1, for example), choose a suitable location (for example, C:\Users\SazzadImran\Desktop\), and click "Create". A folder of the project name will be added to the location.

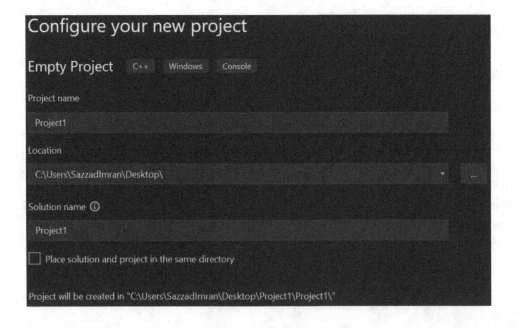

Step-3: In the "Solution Explorer" window, right-click on "Source Files", and choose "Add" and "New Item". Now give a file name of your choice with .c extension (for example, example1.c) and click Add. A blank file will be created in the project.

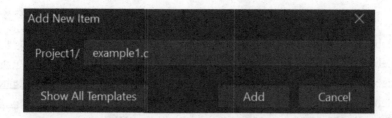

Step-4: Write your C programming codes in the editor window and save the file.

```
example1.c  ⊅  ✕
⊞ Project1                              ▾     (Global Scope)
1      #include <stdio.h>
2    ⊟int main() {
3          int sum, n1, n2;
4          printf("Enter two integers: ");
5          scanf_s("%d %d", &n1, &n2);
6          sum = n1 + n2;
7          printf("Summation: %d\n", sum);
8          return 0;
9      }
```

We may need to use more secure version scanf_s() instead of scanf() as input function. Because the Visual Studio considers scanf() as an unsafe function and returns error code C4996 while compiling the program. The format and structure of both scanf_s() and scanf() functions are identical.

Step-5: Now click Build→"Build Solution" to create the executable file. If there is any syntax error in the program, the error messages will be displayed in the output window. Make necessary corrections in the source code, save it again, and then click Build→"Build Solution". Continue correcting the source codes until there is no more error.

Step-6: Now press ctrl+F5 to run and execute the program. The output will show in the output window accordingly.

```
 ⌨ Microsoft Visual Studio Debug Console
Enter two integers: 23 87
Summation: 110
```

## 8.5 COMMAND LINE

If you want to run a C program on your computer, you need to install the C toolset. We will use MinGW to compile and execute C programs. The following is the step-by-step procedure to create and run a C program using the command line.

Step-1: Properly install CodeBlocks IDE along with MinGW from www.codeblocks.org/downloads/binaries/.

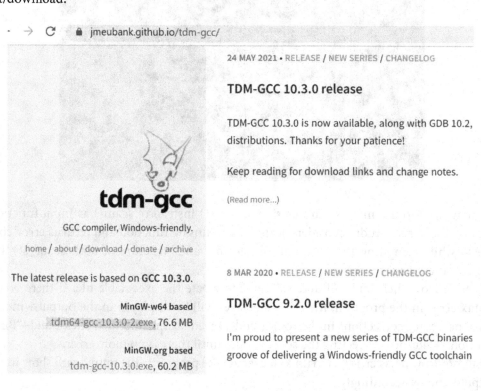

Or, download and install the GCC compiler for the system from http://tdm-gcc.tdragon. net/download.

Step-2: Properly set the Path environment variable to access the program from any other location. To do that,

– copy the path of the bin directory of MinGW or TDM-GCC-64 (for example, C:\Program Files (x86)\CodeBlocks\MinGW\bin or, C:\TDM-GCC-64\bin).

– go to Control Panel\System and Security\System and click on "Advanced system settings". Alternately, right-click on This PC, click on Properties, and then on "Advanced system settings" on the rightmost column.

– click "Environment Variables . . . " and click on Path→Edit→New under the "System variables" and paste the bin path in the blank field, and then click on OK button three times.

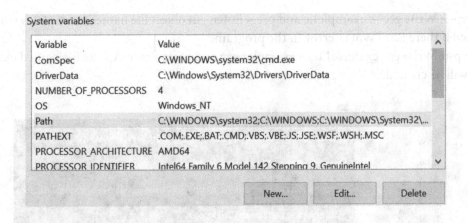

– go to Command Prompt (press Win+R, write cmd, and press Enter), write "gcc – version" and press Enter. If it shows the version number on the screen, then the GCC is successfully installed.

**Step-3:** Write C programming codes using any text editor, for example, Notepad, and save the file in any location (for example, in Desktop) with a suitable name with extension .c (for example, example1.c).

```
example1 - Notepad

File  Edit  Format  View  Help
#include <stdio.h>
int main(){
    int sum, n1, n2;
    printf("Enter two integers: ");
    scanf("%d %d", &n1, &n2);
    sum = n1+n2;
    printf("Summation: %d\n", sum);
    return 0;
}
```

**Step-4:** Open the command prompt in the location where you have saved your file example1.c. To do that, go to the location, and in the address bar, write cmd and press Enter. Or, we can do that using the cd command.

Step-5: Write gcc -c example1.c and press Enter. An object file named example1.o will be created if there is no syntax error in the program.

Step-6: Write gcc example1.o -o example1.exe and press Enter. An exe file named example1 will be created.

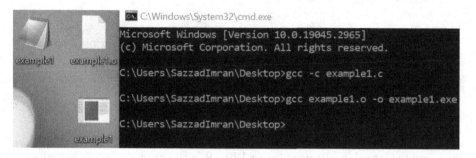

Step-7: We can create exe file with a single command also. Just write gcc example1.c and press Enter. An executable file will be generated as a.exe. If we want to give a name of our choice to the executable file, then write gcc -o example1 example1.c and press Enter.

Step-8: To run the program, write a or example1 and press Enter. The output will be shown on the command prompt accordingly.

```
C:\Users\SazzadImran\Desktop>example1
Enter two integers: 23 67
Summation: 90
```

## 8.6 COMMAND LINE ARGUMENTS

The most important function in any C program is the main() function, usually defined without arguments. But we can pass some values from the command line to the C program during run time through arguments in the main() function. To pass command line arguments, we need to follow two steps:

(1) main() function is defined with two arguments as follows:

```
int main(int argc, char *argv[]){
     . . . }
```

- first one (argc = ARGument Count) is the number of arguments that must be a positive integer, and

- second (argv = ARGument Vector) is the list of command-line arguments. Here, argv[0] is the program name, and then argv[1], argv[2], . . ., argv[argc-1] is the arguments that will be written in the command line shell of the operating systems.

2) Command line arguments are given after the program name in the command line shell.

Example:

```c
#include <stdio.h>
int main(int argc, char *argv[]){
    int cnt;
    printf("Name of the program: %s", argv[0]);
    if (argc==1)
        printf("\nNo command-line argument is passed.");
    else{
        printf("\nNumber of command line arguments: %d", argc);
        for (cnt=0; cnt<argc; cnt++)
            printf("\nArgument #%d: %s", cnt+1, argv[cnt]);
    }
    return 0;
}
```

Save the above program on desktop as example1.c and compile the program. Now open the command prompt (Win+cmd and press Enter) and type cd desktop, and press Enter to change the path to where we save the program. Now write the commands to run the program. The following four scenarios may arise:

(1) Without argument:

```
Command Prompt

Microsoft Windows [Version 10.0.19044.2846]
(c) Microsoft Corporation. All rights reserved.

C:\Users\SazzadImran>cd desktop

C:\Users\SazzadImran\Desktop>example1
Name of the program: example1
No command-line argument is passed.
C:\Users\SazzadImran\Desktop>
```

(2) Single argument:

```
C:\Users\SazzadImran\Desktop>example1 first
Name of the program: example1
Number of command line arguments: 2
Argument #1: example1
Argument #2: first
```

(3) Three arguments:

```
C:\Users\SazzadImran\Desktop>example1 first second third
Name of the program: example1
Number of command line arguments: 4
Argument #1: example1
Argument #2: first
Argument #3: second
Argument #4: third
```

(4) Single arguments in quotes separated by space:

```
C:\Users\SazzadImran\Desktop>example1 "first second third"
Name of the program: example1
Number of command line arguments: 2
Argument #1: example1
Argument #2: first second third
```

If we want to pass two integers through the command line and add or multiply the two integers, we need to convert the string values to integers using atoi() function in the main() program. We can only pass string values to the main() function through command-line arguments, not integers or other data types. Given below is such an example.

```c
#include <stdio.h>
#include <stdlib.h>
/*header file stdlib.h includes the prototype of the function atoi()*/
int main(int argc, char *argv[]){
    int cnt, x, sum=0;
    if (argc<3)
        printf("\nNot enough command line arguments is passed.");
    else{
        printf("\nNumber of command line arguments: %d", argc);
        for (cnt=1; cnt<argc; cnt++){
            x = atoi(argv[cnt]);
            /*function atoi() converts string value of the argument
            to its equivalent integer value*/
            sum = sum + x;
        }
        printf("\nSum of arguments: %d", sum);
    }
    return 0;
}
```

Save the program as add.c and compile the program. Then, in the command prompt if we write "add 10 20 and press Enter", the output will be as follows:

```
C:\Users\SazzadImran\Desktop>add 10 20

Number of command line arguments: 3
Sum of arguments: 30
```

## 8.7 LINUX

Linux is an open-source operating system that is freely available to everyone. Hence, it has become a developer's programming paradise. There are many versions available for Linux OS. Here, we will explain how to write, compile, and run C programs in WSL Linux Ubuntu.

Step-1: Open the Linux command-line tool, the Terminal. Login as root using the following command and entering your password:

$ sudo su

Step-2: Connect to the internet and enter the following command as root in the Linux terminal to update the resources of the linux system:

# apt-get update

🔥 root@HP-ZBOOK: /home/sazzad

```
sazzad@HP-ZBOOK:~$ sudo su
[sudo] password for sazzad:
root@HP-ZBOOK:/home/sazzad# apt-get update
```

Step-3: Now, enter the following command as root in the Linux terminal and press Enter to install the GCC compiler:

# apt-get install gcc – y

🔥 root@HP-ZBOOK: /home/sazzad

```
root@HP-ZBOOK:/home/sazzad# apt-get install gcc -y
Reading package lists... Done
Building dependency tree... Done
Reading state information... Done
The following additional packages will be installed:
```

Step-4: To create and edit text files right from the Linux terminal, install gedit text editor using the following command as root in the Linux terminal:

# apt-get install gedit -y

🔥 root@HP-ZBOOK: /home/sazzad

```
root@HP-ZBOOK:/home/sazzad# apt-get install gedit -y
Reading package lists... Done
Building dependency tree... Done
Reading state information... Done
The following additional packages will be installed:
```

Step-5: After installing the GCC and gedit packages, write the following command in the Linux terminal as root and press Enter:

# gedit example1.c

```
🐧 root@HP-ZBOOK: /home/sazzad
[sudo] password for sazzad:
root@HP-ZBOOK:/home/sazzad# gedit example1.c
```

This will create and open a file named example1.c, where you can write and save your C programming codes.

```
Open ▼    ⊞                                    example1.c
                                               /home/sazzad
 1 #include <stdio.h>
 2 int main(){
 3      int sum, sub, n1, n2;
 4      printf("Enter two integers: ");
 5      scanf("%d %d", &n1, &n2);
 6      sum = n1+n2;
 7      sub = n1-n2;
 8      printf("Summation: %d\n", sum);
 9      printf("Subtraction: %d\n", sub);
10      return 0;
11 }
```

Step-6: Write the following command in the Linux terminal to compile the program that will make an executable file named example1, if there is no error.

# gcc example1.c -o example1

If we write only # gcc example1.c, then an executable file named a.out will be created.

```
🐧 root@HP-ZBOOK: /home/sazzad
root@HP-ZBOOK:/home/sazzad# gcc example1.c -o example1
root@HP-ZBOOK:/home/sazzad# gcc example1.c
root@HP-ZBOOK:/home/sazzad# ls
a.out   example1   example1.c
root@HP-ZBOOK:/home/sazzad#
```

If the program is not located in the Home folder, we need to specify the appropriate paths in the command. For example, if the file is saved on the Desktop, write # cd Desktop/ in the Terminal and press Enter to change the directory.

Step-5: To run the compiled program, write the following command in the Terminal and press Enter.

# ./example1 or # ./a.out

The output of the program will be shown in the Terminal accordingly:

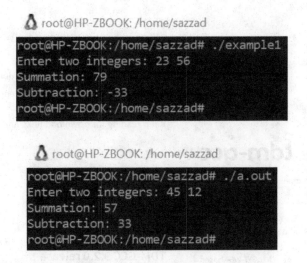

```
root@HP-ZBOOK:/home/sazzad# ./example1
Enter two integers: 23 56
Summation: 79
Subtraction: -33
root@HP-ZBOOK:/home/sazzad#
```

```
root@HP-ZBOOK:/home/sazzad# ./a.out
Enter two integers: 45 12
Summation: 57
Subtraction: 33
root@HP-ZBOOK:/home/sazzad#
```

## 8.8 EMBEDDING C CODE INTO MATLAB®

We can compile and run the C program directly from MATLAB using the MinGW-w64 compiler. Alternatively, we can call external C code to the Simulink model using a C Function block or a C Caller block. C Function block and C Caller block bring C algorithms into Simulink, while S-Function Builder is used to model dynamic systems.

Using MinGW-W64 Compiler

https://stackoverflow.com/questions/27383807/mex-file-compiled-without-errors-but-not-working-in-matlab

The following is the step-by-step procedure to compile and run C programs directly from the MATLAB command window.

Step-1: Go to www.mathworks.com/matlabcentral/fileexchange/52848-matlab-support-for-mingw-w64-c-c-compiler.

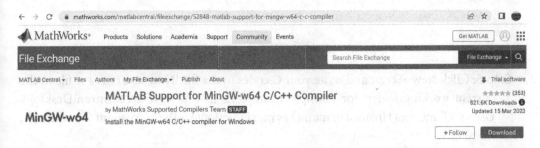

Download "MATLAB Support for MinGW-w64 C/C++ Compiler". Now open MATLAB and browse to this downloaded file using the current folder browser. Double-click on this file to install the MinGW-w64 C/C++ Compiler for MATLAB.

Step-2: Download MinGW-w64 compiler from https://jmeubank.github.io/tdm-gcc/.

Install the tdm-gcc in a location (pathname must not contain any space), for example, C:\TDM-GCC-64.

Step-3: In the MATLAB Command window, run the command:

>setenv('MW_MINGW_64_LOC', 'path')

for example, setenv('MW_MINGW_64_LOC', 'C:\TDM-GCC-64')

Step-4: In the Command window, run the command:

>mex -setup

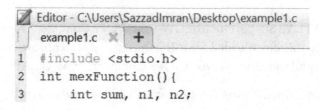

```
Command Window
>> setenv('MW_MINGW_64_LOC', 'C:\TDM-GCC-64')
>> mex -setup
MEX configured to use 'MinGW64 Compiler (C)' for C language compilation.
```

Step-5: Click New→Script and write your C codes in the file. Now save it as a .c file in the current working folder (for example, example1.c in C:\Users\SazzadImran\Desktop). Use mexFunction() instead of main() as mexFunction() is the entry point for a mex file.

```
Editor - C:\Users\SazzadImran\Desktop\example1.c
example1.c  ×  +
1   #include <stdio.h>
2   int mexFunction(){
3       int sum, n1, n2;
```

```
4      printf("Enter two integers: ");
5      scanf("%d %d", &n1, &n2);
6      sum = n1+n2;
7      printf("Summation: %d\n", sum);
8      return 0;
9    }
```

Step-6: In the Command window of the MATLAB program, run the command mex example1.c

and press Enter. A MATLAB executable file example1.mexw64 will be created in the current folder.

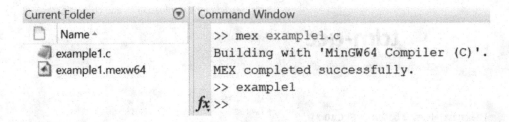

*Note:* When we run the mex file example1 in the MATLAB command prompt, it will show nothing. This is due to the fact that the functions printf(), scanf(), etc., only works in native C. For example, printf() function only displays any string or message on standard output and does not display that on MATLAB command window. To create mex files that work on MATLAB command prompt just like a native C program, we need to use different mex functions. However, this is a separate topic and out of scope for discussion in this book.

Generating mex file (Matlab EXecutable file) of C program is necessary to call external C code into different Matlab Simulink model.

## Using S-Function Builder

The following is the step-by-step procedure to call external C code into the Simulink model using the MATLAB S-Function block.

Step-1: Go to www.mathworks.com/matlabcentral/fileexchange/52848-matlab-support-for-mingw-w64-c-c-compiler.

Download "MATLAB Support for MinGW-w64 C/C++ Compiler". Now open MATLAB and browse this downloaded file using the current folder browser. Double-click on this file to install the MinGW-w64 C/C++ Compiler for MATLAB.

Step-2: Download MinGW-w64 compiler from https://jmeubank.github.io/tdm-gcc/.

Install the tdm-gcc in a location (pathname must not contain any space), for example, C:\TDM-GCC-64.

Step-3: In the MATLAB Command window, run the command

setenv('MW_MINGW_64_LOC', 'path')

for example, setenv('MW_MINGW_64_LOC', 'C:\TDM-GCC-64')

Step-4: In the Command window, run the command

mex -setup

```
Command Window
>> setenv('MW_MINGW_64_LOC', 'C:\TDM-GCC-64')
>> mex -setup
MEX configured to use 'MinGW64 Compiler (C)' for C language compilation.
```

Step-5: Create a header file SimpleLib2.h containing prototype of the user-defined function prototype add() in the current working directory (for example, in C:\Users\

SazzadImran\Desktop\MatlabSfunction). It may include other header files needed to compile the user-defined function.

```
Editor - C:\Users\SazzadImran\Desktop\MatlabSfunction\SimpleLib2.h
SimpleLib2.h ✕ +
1  #ifndef SIMPLELIB2_H_INCLUDED
2  #define SIMPLELIB2_H_INCLUDED
3
4  double add(double, double);
5
6  #endif // SIMPLELIB2_H_INCLUDED
```

Step-6: Create a C source file in the same directory, define its function, and save the file with a .c extension. Use double quotations to include the header file created in Step-5. For example, the SimpleLib1.c file may contain the definition of the function add().

```
Editor - C:\Users\SazzadImran\Desktop\MatlabSfunction\SimpleLib1.c
SimpleLib1.c ✕ +
1  #include "SimpleLib2.h"
2  double add(double a, double b){
3      double sum1;
4      sum1 = a+b;
5      return sum1;
6  }
```

Step-7: In the Command window of the MATLAB program, run the following commands:

(i) Initialize the structure of the S-function:

def = legacy_code('initialize') and press Enter

(ii) Give a name of your choice to the S function:

def.SFunctionName = 'MySFunction' and press Enter

iii) For the output function specification, use only y and u as parameters:

def.OutputFcnSpec = 'double y1 = add(double u1, double u2)' and press Enter

iv) Add header and source files:

def.HeaderFiles = {'SimpleLib2.h'} and press Enter

def.SourceFiles = {'SimpleLib1.c'} and press Enter

```
Command Window
  def =

    struct with fields:

                    SFunctionName: 'MySFunction'
      InitializeConditionsFcnSpec: ''
                    OutputFcnSpec: 'double y1 = add(double u1, double u2)'
                     StartFcnSpec: ''
                 TerminateFcnSpec: ''
                      HeaderFiles: {'SimpleLib2.h'}
                      SourceFiles: {'SimpleLib1.c'}
                     HostLibFiles: {}
                   TargetLibFiles: {}
                         IncPaths: {}
                         SrcPaths: {}
                         LibPaths: {}
                       SampleTime: 'inherited'
                          Options: [1×1 struct]
```

v) legacy_code('sfcn_cmex_generate', def) and press Enter

A file named MySFunction.c will be generated.

vi) legacy_code('compile', def) and press Enter

MATLAB executable file MySFunction.mexw64 will be generated.

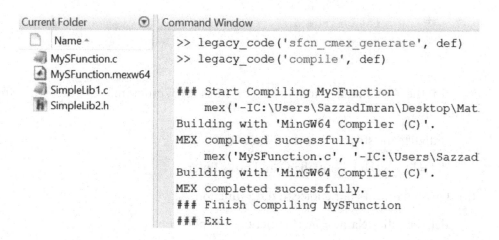

Step-8: Create a new Simulink model and save it as MyModel.mdl. To do that, click New→Simulink Model and then click "Blank Model". Now click File→Save As . . ., write MyModel in the "File name:" box, select Simulink Models (*.mdl)' in "Save as type:" box and click on Save.

| File name: | MyModel |
|---|---|
| Save as type: | Simulink Models (*.mdl) |

Step-9: Add a MATLAB S-Function block from Library Browser→Simulink→ User-Defined Functions library to the model. Double-click on the S-Function block to open S-Function Block Parameters. In the S-function name box, write MySFunction and click OK.

Step-10: Connect two Constant blocks to the input ports and a Display block to the output port of the MATLAB Function Block. For Constant blocks, click View→ Library Browser→Simulink→Sources and drag two Constant blocks to MyModel. For Display block, click View→Library Browser→Simulink→Sinks and drag Display block to MyModel.

Step-11: Input 3 and 4.5 in the two input Constant blocks. Now, save the model and run the simulation; 7.5 appears in the Display output block.

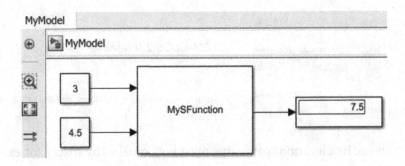

## Using C Function Block

Follow the following steps to call external C code into the Simulink model using the C Function block.

Step-1: Go to www.mathworks.com/matlabcentral/fileexchange/52848-matlab-support-for-mingw-w64-c-c-compiler.

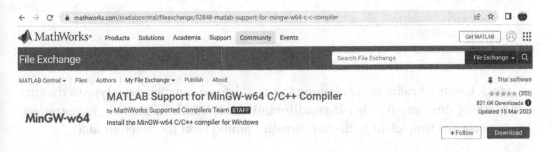

Download "MATLAB Support for MinGW-w64 C/C++ Compiler". Now open MATLAB and browse to this downloaded file using the current folder browser. Double-click on this file to install the MinGW-w64 C/C++ Compiler for Matlab.

Step-2: Download MinGW-w64 compiler from https://jmeubank.github.io/tdm-gcc/.

Install the tdm-gcc in a location (pathname must not contain any space), for example, C:\ TDM-GCC-64.

Step-3: In the MATLAB Command window, run the command
setenv('MW_MINGW_64_LOC', 'path')
for example, setenv('MW_MINGW_64_LOC', 'C:\TDM-GCC-64')
Step-4: In the Command window, run the command
mex -setup

```
Command Window
>> setenv('MW_MINGW_64_LOC', 'C:\TDM-GCC-64')
>> mex -setup
MEX configured to use 'MinGW64 Compiler (C)' for C language compilation.
```

Step-5: Create a header file containing the user-defined function prototype in the current working directory (C:\Users\SazzadImran\Desktop\MatlabCfunction, for example). For example, the SimpleLib2.h file may contain a prototype of the function add().

```
Editor - C:\Users\SazzadImran\Desktop\MatlabCfunction\SimpleLib2.h
 SimpleLib2.h  ×  +
1  #ifndef SIMPLELIB2_H_INCLUDED
2  #define SIMPLELIB2_H_INCLUDED
3
4  double add(double, double);
5
6  #endif // SIMPLELIB2_H_INCLUDED
```

Step-6: Create a C source file in the same directory, define its function, and save the file with a .c extension. Use double quotations to include the header file created in Step-5. For example, the SimpleLib1.c file may contain the definition of the function add().

```
Editor - C:\Users\SazzadImran\Desktop\MatlabCfunction\SimpleLib1.c
  SimpleLib1.c  ×  +
1  #include "SimpleLib2.h"
2  double add(double a, double b){
3      double sum1;
4      sum1 = a+b;
5      return sum1;
6  }
```

Step-7: Create a new Simulink model and save it as MyModel.mdl. To do that, click Home→New→Simulink Model and then click "Blank Model". Now click File→Save As . . ., write MyModel in the "File name:" box, select Simulink Models (*.mdl)' in "Save as type:" box and click on Save.

|  |  |
|---|---|
| File name: | MyModel |
| Save as type: | Simulink Models (*.mdl) |

Step-8: Add a MATLAB Function block to the model. To do that, click View→ Library Browser→Simulink→User-Defined Functions and then drag MATLAB Function block to MyModel. Double-click on the Function block to open MATLAB Function Block Editor and enter Matlab code that uses the coder.ceval Matlab function to call the C function add().

```
Editor - Block: MyModel/MATLAB Function
  MATLAB Function  ×  +
  function y = callingAdd(u1, u2)
      y = 0.0;
      y = coder.ceval("add", u1, u2);
```

Step-9: Connect two Constant blocks to the input ports and a Display block to the output port of the MATLAB Function Block. For Constant blocks, click View→ Library Browser→Simulink→Sources and drag two Constant blocks to MyModel. For Display block, click View→Library Browser→Simulink→Sinks and drag Display block to MyModel.

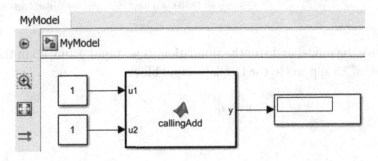

Step-10: Open the Model Configuration Parameters window, and navigate the Simulation Target pane.

(i) Click "Header file" in the "Insert custom C code in generated:" tab and enter #include "SimpleLib2.h".

(ii) Click "Source file" in the "Additional build information:" tab and enter SimpleLib1.c. Now click Apply and then OK.

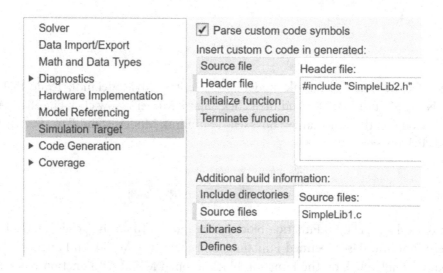

(iii) If the C source file and the header file are outside the MATLAB current folder where the MyModel.mdl was saved, click Set Path₃Add Folder . . . select the folder where C source and header files were saved, and then click "Select Folder"₃Save₃Close.

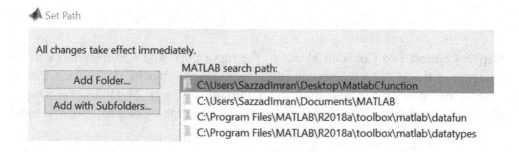

Step-11: Save the model and run the simulation. If we input 3 and 4.5 in the two input Constant blocks, 7.5 appears in the Display output block.

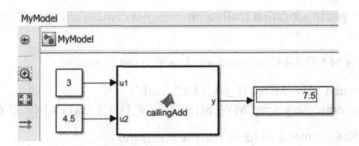

## Using C Caller Block

First of all, it is to mention that the C Caller block is only available in MATLAB R2018b and later versions. Follow the following steps to call external C code into the Simulink model using the C Caller block.

Step-1: Go to www.mathworks.com/matlabcentral/fileexchange/52848-matlab-support-for-mingw-w64-c-c-compiler.

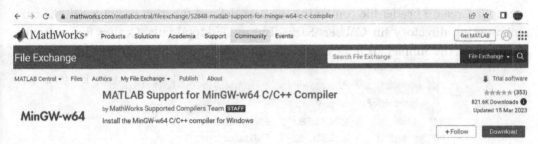

Download "MATLAB Support for MinGW-w64 C/C++ Compiler". Now open MATLAB and browse to this downloaded file using the current folder browser. Double-click on this file to install the MinGW-w64 C/C++ Compiler for Matlab.

Step-2: Download MinGW-w64 compiler from https://jmeubank.github.io/tdm-gcc/.

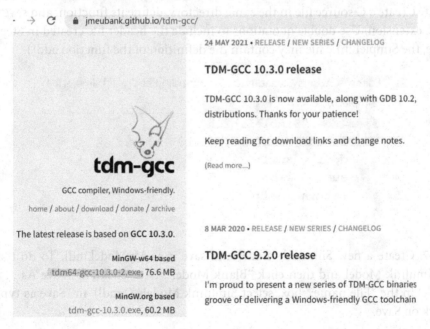

Install the tdm-gcc in a location (pathname must not contain any space), for example, C:\ TDM-GCC-64.

Step-3: In the MATLAB Command window, run the command

> setenv('MW_MINGW_64_LOC', 'path')
> for example, setenv('MW_MINGW_64_LOC', 'C:\TDM-GCC-64')

Step-4: In the Command window, run the command

> mex -setup

```
Command Window
>> setenv('MW_MINGW_64_LOC', 'C:\TDM-GCC-64')
>> mex -setup
MEX configured to use 'MinGW64 Compiler (C)' for C language compilation.
```

Step-5: Create a header file containing the user-defined function prototype in the current working directory (in C:\Users\SazzadImran\Desktop\MatlabCcaller for example). For example, the SimpleLib2.h file may contain a prototype of the function add().

```
Editor - C:\Users\SazzadImran\Desktop\MatlabCcaller\SimpleLib2.h
SimpleLib2.h    +
1   #ifndef SIMPLELIB2_H_INCLUDED
2   #define SIMPLELIB2_H_INCLUDED
3
4   double add(double, double);
5
6   #endif // SIMPLELIB2_H_INCLUDED
```

Step-6: Create a C source file in the same directory, define its function, and save the file with a .c extension. Use double quotations to include the header file created in Step-2. For example, the SimpleLib1.c file may contain the definition of the function add().

```
Editor - C:\Users\SazzadImran\Desktop\MatlabCcaller\SimpleLib1.c
SimpleLib1.c    +
1   #include "SimpleLib2.h"
2   double add(double a, double b) {
3       double sum1;
4       sum1 = a+b;
5       return sum1;
6   }
```

Step-7: Create a new Simulink model and save it as MyModel.mdl. To do that click New→Simulink Model and then click "Blank Model". Now click File→Save As . . ., write MyModel in the "File name:" box, select Simulink Models (*.mdl)' in "Save as type:" box and click on Save.

| File name: | MyModel |
|---|---|
| Save as type: | Simulink Models (*.mdl) |

Step-8: Open the Model Configuration Parameters window, and navigate to the Simulation Target pane.

(i) Click the Header file under "Insert custom C code in generated:" bar and enter the name of the header file with #include "SimpleLib2.h".

(ii) If the model and the header files are stored in different folders, click "Include directories" under "Additional build information" and list the path of the header files in the text box.

(iii) Click Source files under "Additional build information:" and enter SimpleLib1.c. If the model and the source file are in different folders, enter the source file's path address before the source file name and click OK.

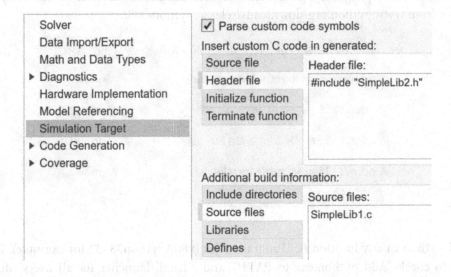

Step-9: Add a MATLAB C Caller block from Library Browser→Simulink→ User-Defined Functions library to the model. Double click on the C Caller block to open the Block Parameters dialog box. Click on the Refresh button to import the source code. Select your C function in the "Function name:" box (for example, add) and click OK.

Step-10: Connect two Constant blocks to the input ports and a Display block to the output port of the MATLAB Caller Block. For Constant blocks click View→ Library Browser→Simulink→Sources and drag two Constant blocks to MyModel. For Display block click View→Library Browser→Simulink→Sinks and drag Display block to MyModel.

Step-12: Save the model and run the simulation. If we input 3 and 4.5 in the two input Constant blocks, 7.5 appears in the Display output block.

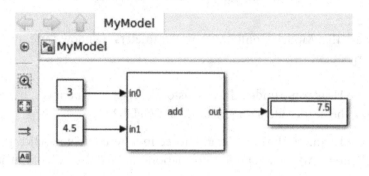

## 8.9 INTEGRATING C CODE INTO PYTHON

Python is an interpreted, object-oriented, high-level programming language that provides increased productivity compared to other languages. A step-by-step procedure to run C code from a Python program is given below. At first, download the latest version of Python installer from www.python.org/downloads/release/python-383/.

| ← → C  🔒 python.org/downloads/release/python-383/ | |
|---|---|
| Windows x86-64 executable installer | Windows |
| Windows x86-64 web-based installer | Windows |
| Windows x86 embeddable zip file | Windows |
| Windows x86 executable installer | Windows |
| Windows x86 web-based installer | Windows |

Install Python in any location (C:\Program Files (x86)\Python38–32 for example). Don't forget to check "Add python.exe to PATH" and "Install launcher for all users" during installation of the Python program. We choose 32-bit version as we have GCC from 32-bit-MinGW to create *.so shared object file.

Now, download and install any C compiler (for example, CodeBlocks with 32-bit MinGW from www.codeblocks.org/downloads/binaries/) on your PC.

← → C 🔺 Not secure | codeblocks.org/downloads/binaries/

| codeblocks-20.03-32bit-setup.exe | FossHUB or Sourceforge.net |
| codeblocks-20.03-32bit-setup-nonadmin.exe | FossHUB or Sourceforge.net |
| codeblocks-20.03-32bit-nosetup.zip | FossHUB or Sourceforge.net |
| codeblocks-20.03mingw-32bit-setup.exe | FossHUB or Sourceforge.net |
| codeblocks-20.03mingw-32bit-nosetup.zip | FossHUB or Sourceforge.net |

Step-1: Open CodeBlocks C compiler. Now, click File→New→ "Empty file". An empty text file will open. Now, click "File→Save file as . . . ", write SimpleLib in the "File name:" box, select a folder of your choice (for example, C:\Users\SazzadImran\Desktop\ CfromPython), and click Save.

Step-2: Define one or more of your C functions in the file except main(). For example, we have defined functions add() and subtract(), and save the file.

```
SimpleLib.c ×
 1    int add(int a, int b){
 2        int sum1;
 3        sum1 = a+b;
 4        return sum1;
 5    }
 6
 7    int subtract(int a, int b){
 8        int sub1;
 9        sub1 = a-b;
10        return sub1;
11    }
```

Step-3: Open Command Prompt as administrator and using cd command go to the folder where *.c file is saved (in this case, C:\Users\SazzadImran\Desktop\ CfromPython). Now, write the following command and press Enter.

gcc -o SimpleLib.so – shared -fPIC SimpleLib.c

```
Administrator: Command Prompt
Microsoft Windows [Version 10.0.19045.2965]
(c) Microsoft Corporation. All rights reserved.

C:\WINDOWS\system32>cd\

C:\>cd Users\SazzadImran\Desktop\CfromPython

C:\Users\SazzadImran\Desktop\CfromPython>gcc -o SimpleLib.so --shared -fPIC SimpleLib.c
```

A shared object file SimpleLib.so is created in the destination folder. We can give any name of our choice to the shared object file (*.so). It does not necessarily be the same as that of the *.c file.

Step-4: Click on Windows, write IDLE, and click on IDLE (Python 3.8 32-bit) to open Python shell. Click File→New File and save it with any name (for example, example1) as Python files in any location (may be in the same folder where we saved *.so file, C:\Users\ SazzadImran\Desktop\CfromPython).

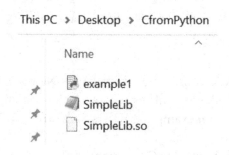

This PC > Desktop > CfromPython

Name

example1

SimpleLib

SimpleLib.so

Step-4: Now write your Python codes in example1.py file. In the coding, we must do the following to use any function defined in the *.c file:

(i) Import Python Ctypes objects using the following code:

from ctypes import *

(ii) Define path of the shared object file SimpleLib.so relative to the path of example1. py and store it to a variable. Use forward slash in place of back slash while writing the path address.

lib_path = './SimpleLib.so'

If .so and .py files are in different location, simply write full address path of the .so file.

(iii) Pass the variable lib_path to function CDLL() to define a Python object where all functions and variables from the .c file are stored.

c_fun = CDLL(lib_path)

(iv) Call any function defined in the SimpleLib.c using . (dot) operator.

result = c_fun.add(25, 19)

(v) Write any other necessary Python codes in the example1.py file, save the file.

example1.py - C:\Users\SazzadImran\Desktop\CfromPython\example1.py (3.8.3)

File Edit Format Run Options Window Help

```
from ctypes import *
lib_path = './SimpleLib.so'
c_fun = CDLL(lib_path)

print("Enter two integers:")
num1, num2 = int(input()), int(input())
res1 = c_fun.add(num1, num2)
res2 = c_fun.subtract(num1, num2)
```

```
print("Summation:", res1)
print("Subtraction:", res2)
```

(vi) Now click Run, "Run Module" to run the program. The output will be as follows"

```
>>>
========= RESTART: C:\Users\SazzadImran\Desktop\CfromPython\example1.py ==
Enter two integers:
34
67
Summation: 101
Subtraction: -33
>>>
```

We can also do the same task using dynamic link library (*.dll) created in Section 8.1.2 in folder C:\Users\SazzadImran\Desktop\SimpleLib\ bin\Debug.

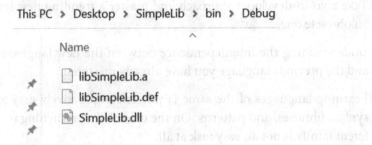

This PC > Desktop > SimpleLib > bin > Debug

Name

☐ libSimpleLib.a
☐ libSimpleLib.def
▣ SimpleLib.dll

To call C functions using DLL file, write full path of the location of SimpleLib.dll as it is in separate location from that of example1.py. Also, we can use WinDLL() function to define the Python object. The Python file will look like as follows

example1.py - C:\Users\SazzadImran\Desktop\CfromPython\example1.py (3.8.3)

File  Edit  Format  Run  Options  Window  Help

```
from ctypes import *
lib_path = 'C:/Users/SazzadImran/Desktop/SimpleLib/bin/Debug/SimpleLib.dll'
c_fun = WinDLL(lib_path)

print("Enter two integers:")
num1, num2 = int(input()), int(input())
res1 = c_fun.add(num1, num2)
res2 = c_fun.subtract(num1, num2)

print("Summation:", res1)
print("Subtraction:", res2)
```

Now if we run the module, we will get the same output.

## 8.10 SWITCHING FROM ONE LANGUAGE TO ANOTHER

In addition to any programming tool, an experienced programmer should be able to expand their knowledge and skills to any programming language. Programming languages evolve regularly, and today, it is not enough to know only one language. Knowing multiple languages gives anyone a competitive edge over others in the job market. This section highlights some benefits and tips on effective switching from one language to another.

Many programmers might think that mastering one language is enough. But, in reality, many coders practice switching programming languages to improve their professional skills and get their desired job. If we know the reason behind our switching language, we can switch and learn the right language for us.

When choosing a language to learn, always pay attention to the following six points:

(1) Try to understand its relevance and flexibility.

(2) Analyze the market trends, demands, and potential vacancies to get your desired job.

(3) What is your end goal, that is, your purpose of learning? Two main reasons may be new project requirements or expanding portfolio.

(4) Take a go-to-developer approach and master a trending new language rather than an obsolete one.

(5) Understanding the interdependence between the new language you want to learn and the previous language you have already mastered.

(6) Learning languages of the same family is comparatively easy as they have related syntax, libraries, and patterns. On the other hand, switching to a language of a different family is not an easy task at all.

Most experts argue that first you need to master a fundamental language. After that, you can quickly learn another language of your needs. Take into account the following simple tips to master another language of your choice:

(1) You must be patient and consistent.

(2) Be focused and motivated, knowing why you want to learn a particular language and where you can apply it.

(3) Do not switch before you are entirely comfortable with the new language. Switching while still learning a language may slow down the learning process.

(4) Start with books for beginners and then toward more advanced texts. Take help from available video tutorials and other free resources.

(5) Practice a lot. Write strings of codes and simple to complex programs.

(6) Find someone who masters the language and is willing to review your codes. He may also guide you toward the right path.

(7) Try to convert programs from one language to another. Transferring codebase from an existing project is a challenging and time-consuming but helpful process for experimenting with new concepts and paradigms.

To be an expert developer, you need to learn new programming languages mastering their principles and algorithms. There are no alternatives other than improving your programming skills based on recent market trends to be competitive in the job market.

## 8.11 TRANSITION TO C++ OR C# FROM C

C++ is an intermediate language that adds object-oriented programming capabilities to C. C++ is used to develop operating systems, PC software, and high-profile servers. C#, on the other hand, is a high-level, component-oriented language that was built as an extension of the C programming language. C# is used in enterprise applications and client and server development in the Microsoft .NET framework. Though complicated, C# is less error-prone and easier to learn of the three.

It is easy to migrate from C to C++, as C is often considered a subset of C++. A first step may be to program in the C subset of C++ and find a better experience than C, as C++ provides extra type-checking and more notational support. C++ exclusively supports new and delete operators, classes, templates, operator and function overloading, strict type casts conversions, and typedef to create unique types. Hence, C++ is known as "a better C".

The following three phases may be deployed sequentially, separately, or in parallel for the transition to C++ from C.

(1) Write new codes in C++ and link these with existing C codes.

(2) Develop codes in C and then modify them so that the codes are compatible with C++ compiler.

(3) Start using C++ language features to improve programming style without initially using OOP features.

C programmers need to throw away and forget some of the C concepts they are familiar with and get used to C++ or OOP features. Some of such C concepts are as follows:

(1) Think of everything as objects. Create a class and create as many functions as you need inside it.

(2) Instead of defining lots of global functions, make them member functions of a class.

(3) Group similar functions of different types in a template.

(4) There is no need to use a prefix in the identifiers to avoid name conflicts, as they can be put in a namespace.

(5) We may use references and derived classes instead of so many pointers and type casts.

C and C# are two completely different programming languages. There are more differences than similarities between these two languages. C# adds garbage collection, bound checking, uninitialized variable checking, and type checking capabilities. Having a background in C may help learn C# as many of the syntaxes are similar, but anyone can learn C# quickly without knowing anything about C.

# C Projects

IMPLEMENTING DIFFERENT TYPES OF projects enhances C programming skills. Developing problem-solving abilities and sharpening essential programming skills allow programmers to navigate innovation. The following are some C language projects and ideas that you can try to implement to improve your programming skills.

## PROJECT-1

Create a **student management system** that can store all information of all students, teachers, and staff of your department in the form of structures. The following information needs to be stored for each student:

Name, Semester, Class Roll, Exam Roll, Course Name and Grade Point Earned in the Current Semester, GPA Earned in Previous Semesters, CGPA.

Employ files as a database to conduct file handling activities such as add, search, change, and remove entries.

## PROJECT-2

Create a simple **address book** that automatically generates an external file to permanently store the user's data. The user's data will be Name, Phone Number, E-mail ID, and Address. Keep the option to add, search, edit, and delete data from the record.

## PROJECT-3

Create a simple **online mini voting system** that securely enables organizations to conduct votes and elections. In the voting system, users can enter their preferences, total votes, and leading candidates can be calculated. The voting system can identify a legitimate voter, and one voter can vote only once.

## PROJECT-4

Create a **Tic-Tac-Toe game** in the C programming language using 2D arrays. It is a two-person game where each player alternately marks squares in a 3×3 grid with X or O. The winner is the player who successfully places his three markers in a horizontal, vertical, or diagonal row.

DOI: 10.1201/9781003302629-9

## PROJECT-5

Create a simple **library management system** that manages and preserves book data. The book data will be Name, Authors, Publisher, and Year. Both students and library administrators can use the system to keep track of all the books available in the library. The library administrators can search, add, delete, or issue books and the students can only search and make a request to issue books. As one particular student can keep three books at a time for a maximum of one month, the system will check that before issuing any book to a student.

## PROJECT-6

Create a simple **bus reservation system** that can book bus tickets in advance. The user can check the bus schedule, book tickets, cancel a reservation, and check the bus status. When purchasing tickets, the user must enter the bus number, seat number, the number of tickets, and passengers' names.

## PROJECT-7

Create a simple **bank management system** that can create a new account and remove an existing account. It can also update the information of an existing account (name, contact number, and address) and check the details of an existing account (name, account number, total debit, credit and current balance). The system can view the existing customers' lists and manage each account's transactions (debit and credit).

## PROJECT-8

Create an **employee management system** that can store all information of all staff of an organization in the form of structures. Name, Designation, Contact Number, Job Responsibility, and Monthly Salary need to be stored for each staff. Employ files as a database to conduct file-handling activities such as add, search, modify, and remove entries.

## PROJECT-9

Create a **student attendance management system** that will take and store the daily attendance of each student in a particular subject. The system will show Name, Class Roll, Total Class Taken, Total Class Attended, Percentage and Marks for Attendance for each student. Employ files as a database to conduct file-handling activities such as add, search, modify, and remove entries.

## PROJECT-10

Create a simple **quiz game** that will ask a number of questions to the user. If the user can give a correct answer, a cash prize will be awarded for each correct answer, and a fine will be imposed for each wrong answer. Questions may be asked randomly from science, movies, sports, geography, etc. We can divide the game into two rounds. The contestant will move to the "advanced round" only if he can get qualified in the preliminary round. The questions will be more challenging in the "advanced round", and prize money and fine will be higher.

## PROJECT-10

Create a simple **snake game** in which the snake's food is provided in different coordinates of the screen to eat. When the snake eats the food, its length is automatically increased by one element, and the score is increased by 10 points.

## PROJECT-11

Create a simple **cricket score display system** that will display the following information on the screen:

For batsman- Name, Runs, Balls, 4s, 6s, Out/Not-Out, Strike-rate etc.

For bowler- Name, Over, Wide, No-ball, Wickets etc.

Date and Time of the game, Toss, Name of the teams, Target, Current and required run rate, Remaining wickets etc.

## PROJECT-12

Create a simple **cash-flow manager** that allows users to keep track of their daily cash inflow and outflow. It will show total income, categorize expenses, and balance each month. It also has the provision to store data in a file for each month and display the yearly data.

## PROJECT-13

Create a simple **ATM machine management system** that allows users to withdraw cash after entering the PIN and amount to be withdrawn. After successful withdrawal, the amount will be debited from their bank account. The user can also check his current balance using the system.

## PROJECT-14

Create a simple **matrix calculator** that allows users to add, subtract, or multiply two matrices. It can also perform division and transpose operations. First, it checks the matrices' size and then performs the operation only if the size is allowed.

## PROJECT-15

Create a **modern periodic table** that accurately stores the name, symbol, atomic number, atomic weight, and other properties of the chemical elements. Users can search by name or any properties of the elements.

## PROJECT-16

Design a **CE amplifier with voltage divider bias** of a given gain. The C project will calculate and provide values of all the elements (resistors, capacitors, voltage source, etc.) needed to get the output gain.

## PROJECT-17

Develop a **vaccine registration portal** that verifies users through NID or BRN numbers and checks their age and status. The portal gives a date, time, and place to receive a particular vaccine based on the information. The portal also shows the list of people with their NID or BRN numbers who have already received vaccines.

## PROJECT-18

Develop a **password management system** used by the cyber cafes and computer centers to keep a record of the clients. Clients first need to sign-up to use a computer there. The signed-up users need to log in with their valid credentials (user name and password) to use a computer. The system also maintains a database that stores all the users' data (name, contact number, user name, password, date and time of use) and shows a particular user's information on demand.

## PROJECT-19

Create a **monthly calendar** with days and dates. It shows the list of holidays and the schedule of events of a particular user. Users can edit, add, or delete their events as well. The calendar also gives reminders 24 hours and 10 minutes before the occurrence of each event.

## PROJECT-20

Create a **medical store management system** that shows the list of all available medicines in the store. Unit price, packet price, and name of the pharmaceutical company for each drug are also available. Users can search for any medication by name or by indication.

## PROJECT-21

Develop a **hospital management system** that adds new patient's records (name, age, sex, disease description, and referred room number) and searches, edits, or deletes patient's records. Users can list patient's records by names (alphabetic order), emergency patients, OPD patients, or dates.

## PROJECT-22

Develop a **telephone billing system** that shows the current month's telephone billing records (customer name, phone number, and amount to be paid). The system can add new records and search, modify, and delete old records.

# Index

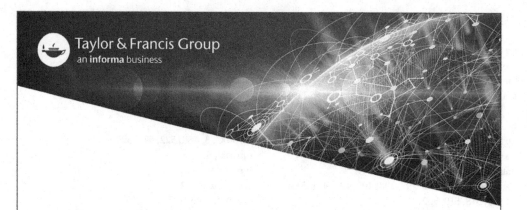

Printed in the United States
by Baker & Taylor Publisher Services